Black Internationalist Feminism

Black Internationalist Feminism

Women Writers of the Black Left, 1945–1995

CHERYL HIGASHIDA

UNIVERSITY OF ILLINOIS PRESS
Urbana, Chicago, and Springfield

Manufactured in the United States of America

∞ This book is printed on acid-free paper.

Cataloging-in-Publication Data
available from the Library of Congress
ISBN 978-0-252-03650-7 (cloth : alk.)
ISBN 978-0-252-09354-8 (ebook)

In memory of Henry Kunio Higashida,
Alice Sayoko Higashida,
Jeannie Higashida,
and Vincent Maurice Woodard

Contents

Acknowledgments ix

Introduction. Black Internationalist Feminism: A Definition 1

1. The Negro Question, the Woman Question, and the "Vital Link": Histories and Institutions 31
2. Lorraine Hansberry's Existentialist Routes to Black Internationalist Feminism 57
3. Rosalind on the Black Star Line: Alice Childress, Black Minstrelsy, and Garveyite Drag 82
4. Rosa Guy, Haiti, and the Hemispheric Woman 112
5. Audre Lorde Revisited: Nationalism and Second-Wave Black Feminism 134
6. Reading Maya Angelou, Reading Black Internationalist Feminism Today 158

Notes 177

Bibliography 223

Index 243

Acknowledgments

I can only begin to indicate the many ways that colleagues, mentors, friends, and family helped bring this book to fruition.

At Cornell, Biodun Jeyifo, Hortense Spillers, Sunn Shelley Wong, and Barry Maxwell were rigorous and caring advisors who nurtured my interest in radical writers. Gary Okihiro and Eric Cheyfitz imparted invaluable advice. The Graduate Student Radical Caucus and our *Report on the State of the English Department* brought left critique to life for me. I especially thank Priya Gopal, Sue Kim, and Ed White.

This project developed at the University of Colorado at Boulder amid wonderful colleagues. John-Michael Rivera has been a sharp critic, savvy mentor, and true friend through it all. I am grateful for the support given in myriad forms by John Stevenson, Katherine Eggert, Jeffrey Robinson, William Kuskin, David Glimp, Marcia Douglas, Jane Garrity, Karen Jacobs, Sidney Goldfarb, Scarlet Bowen, Adam Bradley, Steve Lamos, Ruth Widmann, Laura Winkiel, Elisabeth Sheffield, Jeffrey DeShell, Jenny Dorn, John Escobedo, Arturo Aldama, and Emma Pérez. Even when my paperwork intimidated me, order and happiness prevailed thanks to Mary Lowe and Jeanine Reinke. Christie Yoshinaga-Itano was a tremendous advocate for faculty of color at Boulder. Shannon Rathod's stellar research assistance and the students in my "African American Fictions of Travel" seminars pushed my readings in new directions. Long talks with the brilliant, beautiful, and greatly missed Vincent Woodard were crucial to my understanding of Lorraine Hansberry, Audre Lorde, and Black feminist critique.

Bill Maxwell, Jim Smethurst, Judy Smith, Michelle Stephens, Anna Brickhouse, Adam Bradley, Karen Jacobs, Ed White, Dan Won-gu Kim, Vincent Woodard, and John-Michael Rivera took the time to read and comment incisively on portions of the manuscript. This book and my sanity have benefited enormously from working with Alex Lubin, Bill Mullen, Fred Ho, Aaron Lecklider, Gary Holcolmb, Malini Johar Schueller, Chris Vials, Michiko Hase, Adélékè Adéẹ̀kọ́, and Frederick Aldama. I learned much from enjoyable conversations with Michael Anderson, Barbara Foley, Tracy Heather Strain, Alan Wald, Mary Helen Washington, Rebeccah Welch, and Eric White. Rachel Peterson generously shared research with me. I relished the opportunity to present work from this book at stimulating conferences organized by Ivy Wilson at Northwestern, Eric Cheyfitz and Shirley Samuels at Cornell, and the American Studies Association.

At the Schomburg Center for Research in Black Culture, Steven Fullwood and Diana Lachatanere were immensely knowledgeable and helpful. I am grateful to Joi Gresham and Matthew Lyons, trustees of the Lorraine Hansberry Properties Trust, for permission to quote from Hansberry's manuscripts and papers and to the estate of Alice Childress for allowing me to quote from Childress's papers. I also thank the Special Collections and Archives Department of the John Hope and Aurelia Elizabeth Franklin Library at Fisk University for permission to use Ann Allen Shockley's interview of Alice Childress. The University of Colorado at Boulder generously supported research for this project with a Junior Faculty Development Award, a Kayden Research Grant, and a Council on Research and Creative Work Grant-in-Aid.

I wish to thank Joan Catapano and Daniel Nasset at the University of Illinois Press for their expertise, enthusiasm, and professionalism. This book is much the better for the work of my excellent copyeditor Kate Babbitt and the two anonymous readers who provided thoughtful and detailed feedback. All errors in the book, of course, are mine.

The Labor/Community Strategy Center of Los Angeles has been a major source of inspiration with its multiracial, anti-imperialist organizing. Eric Mann and Lian Hurst Mann are great leaders, thinkers, and friends.

Some very special people never failed to lift my spirits while keeping me grounded: my brothers Steve and Randy Higashida and my girlfriends Julie Ha, Stephanie Bernardo, Grace Jiménez, Melissa Birnbaum, Johnna Christian, and Sylvia Tamashiro. Mia Kim, Tom Feder, and Aiden Kim Feder made their love palpable across distance and time. Jeannie Higashida, the best of big sisters, remains in my heart always. My parents Henry and Alice Higashida left a legacy of love and perseverance that I see every day in Nat and Sen. Juggling work with these energetic little boys would have been impossible without the innumerable stroller rides, meals, UNO games, and bedtime stories provided by Nat and Sen's truly extraordinary grandparents, Jee-Il and Young-Ja Kim.

Dan Won-gu Kim, an incredible scholar, editor, organizer, and parent, made this book possible with his perceptive criticism and wise counsel. I thank him for devoting countless hours to reading my drafts and debating the national question with me and ultimately for reminding me that there should be no struggle without love, no love without struggle.

INTRODUCTION

Black Internationalist Feminism

A Definition

In 1971, an unlikely trip took place. An African American delegation to the Soviet Union followed in the steps of Harry Haywood, Claude McKay, Maude White Katz, W. E. B. Du Bois, Langston Hughes, Louise Thompson Patterson, Dorothy West, Paul Robeson, Claudia Jones, and numerous other Black radicals who, since the Bolshevik Revolution, had journeyed to see firsthand the country that claimed to have abolished racial oppression along with economic exploitation. The 1971 tour was organized by George B. Murphy Jr., the Left editor and journalist who was a leading figure at the *Afro-American* newspaper chain run by his family. Murphy explained in an article for the pro-Soviet *New World Review* that the delegates' motives for going lay in their belonging to "some 25 million Black people who for nearly 400 years have suffered oppression, racism, and genocide." Seeing themselves as part of an internal colony or nation with a nation, the Black delegates compared their condition with what had been that of the "formerly enslaved nationalities" of the Central Asian Soviet republics before Soviet policy left them "in full charge of their destiny."[1] The delegates tasted the possibility for their own political and cultural autonomy as they marveled at the (selective) presentation of life in Uzbekistan and Tajikistan. And they believed that their freedom dreams would be realized through international solidarity with the USSR, African independence movements, and Southeast Asian resistance to U.S. imperialist aggression. Following Lenin on the revolutionary nature of anticolonial movements, they advocated nationalist internationalism: self-determination for all oppressed nations in order to bring about worldwide socialism.[2]

I call attention to the improbable, anachronistic nature of this trip because by most accounts the Black Communist Left was rendered irrelevant or nonexistent long before 1971.[3] Seemingly rejected or altogether ignored by the civil rights establishment and then by the Black Power and Black Arts movements, Black Leftists—with the exception of Angela Davis—were skeletons in the closet. Even the delegation's view that African Americans, as a nation oppressed by U.S. imperialism, shared the anticolonial struggles of countries such as Angola, South Africa, and Vietnam, reflected the contours of the Black Belt Nation Thesis, a political line that the Communist Party itself had declared dead more than once.[4]

However, I propose reading this event not as a mere oddity or an aberration but as an indication that the Black delegates' nationalist internationalism and the political formation to which it can be traced, the post–World War II Harlem-based Black Left, continued to shape African American culture and thought throughout the second half of the twentieth century. The delegates represented key organizations of the postwar Black Left, some of which were still in existence. Murphy had been general manager of Paul Robeson's 1950s internationalist newspaper, *Freedom,* for which delegate Alice Childress wrote a column. While rabid anticommunism had led to *Freedom*'s folding, its spirit lived on through its successor, *Freedomways,* "a beacon of left-wing Black intellectualism, artistry, social criticism, and political debate" from 1961 to 1985.[5] As *Freedomways*' director of special events, delegate Norma Rogers explained to the Soviets that the journal was responsible for "opening doors for Black artists and writers, while interpreting the meaning and scope of the Black Freedom movement in the United States."[6] The Harlem Writers Guild, represented by Childress, was another postwar Black Left institution that in the 1970s was still supporting African American authors through workshops, conferences, and promotional events.

Of greatest importance to this book, the presence of Rogers and especially Childress points to the feminist critique that was engendered by the postwar Black Left and that was alive and evolving in the latter half of the twentieth century.[7] What I call Black internationalist feminism challenged heteronormative and masculinist articulations of nationalism while maintaining the importance, even centrality, of national liberation movements for achieving Black women's social, political, and economic rights.[8] As a corollary of the Communist Party's Black Belt Nation Thesis, which prioritized African American struggles for equality, justice, and self-determination, women of the Black Left asserted that Black women had special problems that could not be deferred or subsumed within the rubrics of working-class or Black oppression and that in fact were integral to the universal struggle for human rights and economic freedom. This feminism was internationalist in two different but related senses. First, it held that self-determination for oppressed nations would bring about socialism for the working classes of all nations. Second, it linked the struggles of African Americans in the United States to struggles for national self-determination in the Caribbean, the Americas, Africa, Asia, and Australia. Women of the Black Left understood that essential to the liberation of African Americans, the Third World, and the worldwide proletariat was the fight against heteropatriarchy, which exacerbated oppression within as well as between nations.

Alice Childress's observations on the Soviet Union's significance to Black America serve as an example of Black internationalist feminist critique. Unlike George Murphy, who remarked on the relevance of Soviet national policy to African Americans and Central Asian women but said nothing about Black women, Childress presented a materialist feminist analysis centered on Central Asian *and* Black women. Childress explored the meaning of national liberation through the eyes of an Uzbek woman: "We, as Moslems, have come a long way from past years when we had to cover our faces with a veil and had no privileges, from the many years ago when women were sold as a commodity. . . . Now we have equal rights and many other special rights needed for women. We have special care for our children." The liberation achieved by the women of the Soviet republics, Childress implied, provided a model for fighting the oppression of the women "of Harlem, all the Harlems, places where Black children receive little or no care. Socialism is acutely needed in the Black community. This kind of child care, provided by the government, frees the mother. . . . The woman is then able to get out and take part in bettering her society and the world; she is able to add to her education and her income."[9] To be sure, Childress idealized the conditions of the Central Asian Soviet republics and their implications for African Americans—a tendency shared by many on the Left. Yet Black, feminist, and/or radical scholarship is ill served by leaving our assessment of Childress's remarks at that.

Consider instead that Childress's challenge to Murphy's erasure of Black women's concerns stems from a rich body of Black feminist thought and politics that can be studied productively through the lens of literature. As Kevin Gaines observes in his essay on postwar Black feminism, "African American women writers . . . were at the forefront of bringing to light the struggles and perspectives of black women against their marginalization and silencing."[10] Making use of a decades-long tradition of Communist and

Communist-affiliated cultural work and institution building, women writers of the Black Left worked within and against established forms in order to represent the ways that the everyday lives of Black women, lesbians, and gay men were linked with and transformative of internationalist projects. Lorraine Hansberry's appropriation of nonrealist and absurdist techniques to heighten her social realism; Alice Childress's chronotopes of the ship and the minstrel show in her feminist bildungsroman; Rosa Guy's revision of masculinist tropes of Black revolution within the potboiler romance; and the shift in Audre Lorde's poetics of difference in response to nationalist struggles demonstrate the vibrant literary experimentalism resulting from Black women writers' Leftist commitments. Setting the stage for contemporary cultural developments, Black internationalist feminists of the postwar Left contributed to and engaged critically with the renaissance of African American women's fiction beginning in the 1970s.

Examining the work of women writers of the Black Left from 1945 to 1995, this book reconceptualizes the relationships between Left, civil rights, Black Power and second-wave Black women's movements. Drawing on Black Power Studies and scholarship on the Left, *Black Internationalist Feminism* considers the persistence beyond the 1930s of African American popular front cultural politics that illuminate the civil rights movement's militancy and global concerns.[11] These lines of inquiry are extended by investigating the development in the decades following World War II of Black internationalist feminism, which has been doubly marginalized by discussions of race radicalism and of feminisms of color. My starting point is 1945 not only because of the end of World War II but also because in that year the prominent Black Communist Claudia Jones wrote a discussion article that reinvigorated both the Black Belt Nation Thesis and Left feminism. The intertwining of international alliances for national liberation and literary explorations of transgressive sexualities and genders provides the narrative arc of this study.

Reconstructing this narrative entails rethinking the opposition between nationalism and Black feminism, along with the broader postnationalist paradigm that this binary supports. What I call the postnationalist position assumes that all nationalisms enforce a homogeneous citizenry bound by heteropatriarchal norms and/or a timeless, self-generating culture contained within national boundaries. From this perspective, second-wave Black feminism of the late 1960s and 1970s represents a break from nationalism with its entrenched patriarchy, homophobia, and sameness. While I do not entirely dispute this claim, it does not represent the last word on contemporary Black feminism. Lorraine Hansberry's anticolonial play *Les Blancs* examines the historical necessity of Black national liberation through a critique of heteropatriarchy. Audre Lorde's later feminism shifted considerably in response to diverse struggles for national sovereignty, including Grenada's New Jewel Movement, indigenous land rights movements in New Zealand and Australia, and the anti-apartheid struggle. Alice Childress and Rosa Guy, who revisit Black Left anticolonialism in novels published in 1979 and 1995, reveal along with Lorde that revolutionary nationalism shaped Black feminist and queer politics well into the late twentieth century and that radical Black women re-theorized revolutionary nationalism through feminist and queer of color critique. For these reasons, my book sets out to delink *post*nationalist analysis from *trans*national approaches in order to account for Black internationalist feminist literary art and praxes that were indelibly marked by the age of nationalist revolt.

▫ ▫ ▫

Black women leftists have increasingly if unevenly received historicized, theoretically nuanced critical attention in the last two decades.[12] Still, there is great need to examine the work and legacy of Black women writers on the Left, who have been the subject of essays and book chapters but not book-length studies. This is somewhat surprising, given the flourishing of Black and radical cultural studies.[13] However, racism, patriarchy, and homophobia have combined potently with anticommunism to marginalize and silence radical Black women within communities, social movements, academia, and U.S. society at large.

Paradoxically, there is also a sense that Black women's radicalism has received its scholarly due, insofar as it culminates in Black and Third World feminism of the 1960s and 1970s. In *Soul Power: Culture, Radicalism, and the Making of a U.S. Third World Left,* Cynthia Young acknowledges that womanism, Alice Walker's conceptualization of an autonomous Black feminism rooted in Black women's histories, cultures, epistemologies, and relationships with each other, "emerged as a central legacy of U.S. Third World Leftists" and that "analysis of the specific forms of discrimination facing women of color and a rigorous antihomophobic stance remain hallmarks of this rich feminist tradition." Nonetheless, this tradition is not studied in Young's book "due in part to the fact that numerous scholars have analyzed the textual contributions of Third World feminism."[14] Young is right about the wealth of critical discussion of Third World, including Black, feminisms.[15] However, with only a few notable exceptions, scholarship on U.S. Black feminism frames it in response to the patriarchy of the civil rights and Black Power movements and the racism of the second wave of the white women's movement.[16] There is little consideration of the Black feminism developed by women affiliated with the post–World War II Black Left, who in the process of analyzing the forms of oppression specific to women of color, re-theorized nationalist internationalism itself.[17]

Redressing this erasure of Black internationalist feminism and its sources in postwar radicalism has major implications for American, Ethnic, Women's, and LGBT Studies. Understanding the internationalist, anticolonial antecedents of Black feminism is integral to and transformative of the ongoing efforts within these fields to contest the historical amnesia about U.S. imperialism and racism and the radical movements that have challenged them. This forgetting perpetuates and is perpetuated by beliefs about American exceptionalism; the notion that U.S. social, political, and economic formations disavow and break with "European" feudalism, class conflict, and imperialism; and the idea that the United States is leading the world to democracy and freedom. Such beliefs isolate the United States from hemispheric and global histories and processes.[18] Nation-based frameworks based on beliefs about U.S. exceptionalism narrow the scope and substance of Black freedom struggles by disconnecting them from radical, often international or transnational movements. The civil rights movement in particular becomes narrowly defined by the exceptionalist underpinnings of U.S. liberal anticommunism, which excludes socialist and anti-imperialist politics, privileging instead "a patriotic, straightforward civil rights or integrationist spirit that evolves or devolves, depending on the writer's perspective, into calls for Black Power, increased militancy, and Black nationalism."[19] This approach confines civil rights struggle to a domestic context; unhelpfully situates Old Left, civil rights, Black Power, and New Left movements in discrete periods or decades; and assigns them mutually exclusive, oversimplified politics of integrationism versus separatism, reformism versus militarism, and nationalism versus feminism.[20]

The Black Left as a whole challenges these limiting paradigms. Not only does its political roots and activism span the Old and New Lefts, civil rights, and Black Power (as I show in chapter 1), but its views of emancipation defy the aforementioned binaries. For these radicals, national liberation movements in Africa, Asia, and the Caribbean portended social transformation within the United States. Much of their writing expresses the sentiment of Black Left novelist John O. Killens that

> we Black folk *are* Americans, and many of us believe our solution lies in and with America. We have been sowers here for centuries and we are determined to be reapers. But just as many of us believe the ultimate solution for the Negro

> is in America, we are even more firmly convinced that the ultimate salvation of America is in the Negro.[21]

Or as Lorraine Hansberry wrote,

> I am the first to say that ours is a complex and difficult country and some of our complexities are indeed grotesque. We who are Negro Americans can offer that last remark with unwavering insistence. It is, on the other hand, also a great nation with certain beautiful and indestructible traditions and potentials which can be seized by all of us who possess imagination and love of man.[22]

The project of reclaiming America did not entail reprising the "singular identifications . . . of U.S. nationalist subject formation based on homogeneity, equivalence, and identification."[23] Nor were demands for civil rights centered exclusively or uncritically on recognition by or assimilation into the liberal-democratic U.S. nation-state. As novelist Julian Mayfield, Killens's and Hansberry's comrade on the postwar Black Left, put it, the Black writer "owe[d] it to the future of his art to analyze the contents of the American mainstream to determine the full significance of his commitment to it." By exposing the racial violence, subordination, segregation, and exploitation that constituted American society, Black radicals aspired to engender truly universal rights to life, liberty, and the pursuit of happiness. Such U.S. nation-based politics were not necessarily incommensurate with Black nationalism; Mayfield in fact objected to the notion that Black and white Americans "are forever bound together and must, perforce, pursue a common destiny."[24] Nor was this project at odds with internationalist and transnational alliances that strained against liberal notions of race, rights, and citizenship. Enacting forms of what Malini Johan Schueller calls "Post-Colonial citizenship," African American radicals such as Robert F. Williams linked their struggles for U.S. democracy to global struggles for emancipation and self-determination and conceived civil rights in terms of human rights.[25]

Black women writers of the postwar anticolonial Left also make it necessary to rethink the opposition between nationalism and Black feminism and its postnationalist presuppositions. For those who understand Black nationalism to be fundamentally monadic and patriarchal because it views gender and sexual liberation as irrelevant, secondary, and/or inimical, Black feminism is opposed to Black nationalism.[26] Nationalism, in this light, centers on building and preserving Black male domination. Trenchantly critiquing such shortsighted racial politics, feminist and queer of color cultural critics have argued that the Black and Third World feminisms that emerged in the United States in the mid-1960s and 1970s "allowed passage away from national liberation and into a completely different understanding of alliances across difference."[27] Instead of singularly privileging a Black male (and usually working-class) revolutionary identity, feminists and queers of color promote multiply situated, coalitional subjects who adopt historically contingent strategies of resistance. Consequently, postmodern theorists have characterized Black and women of color feminists as, in Chela Sandoval's words, "'*feministas de la planeta tierra*'—those who break apart *national* borders," women who create "revolutionary, mobile, and global coalitions of citizen-activists."[28]

This feminist and queer of color politics dovetails with what I call the postnationalist position that all nationalisms and nation-states, even anticolonial ones, possess Enlightenment roots and investments in heteropatriarchy, homogeneity, and racial essentialism. Hence nationalism no longer constitutes (if it ever did) a liberatory praxis especially for Third World women.[29] As Inderpal Grewal and Caren Kaplan write, "When modernity takes shape as feminism . . . it collaborates with nationalism. In its nationalist guise, it cannot be oppositional. The need to free feminism from nationalist discourses is clear."[30] Postnationalist critics have indeed made it abundantly clear that it is not only colonial regimes but "postcolonial," or nominally independent, nation-states and oppositional national liberation movements that marginalize women and other "deviants." An oft-remarked-upon tendency in postnationalist analysis is to homogenize all nationalisms, both revolutionary and reactionary, by finding them totalizing and repressive without distinguishing between, for example, the ideologies of liberal democratic U.S. nationalism and oppositional race-based nationalisms or between colonial and anticolonial nation-states.[31] Postnationalist critics view the era of national liberation and the revolutionary hopes it sparked with skepticism and suspicion or simply overlook them altogether.[32] Utopic possibilities are relocated in transnational or regional movements, sites, and practices that bypass national agendas. The failures of revolutionary nationalisms and nation-states appear to be beyond question in their perpetuation of male-dominated, heteronormative ideologies; their inability to establish transparent, democratic governments; and their economic dependence on transnational corporations, former colonial masters, and neoliberal policy.

Yet as Neil Lazarus points out, even the most crushing of these failures, of which there have been many, cannot eradicate the historical fact of anticolonial independence and its impact on hundreds of millions throughout the world. Moreover, Lazarus writes, "the concrete *achievements* of this struggle [for national liberation] are still intact and continue to provide a vital resource for present-day social and cultural practice."[33] Whether by reminding us that the rights of small nations and struggles for sovereignty continue to matter or that rich traditions of resistance to U.S. neoimperialism and alternative formulations of transnational citizenship point beyond the impasses of the war on terror or that woman of color and/or lesbian feminisms have been forged out of battles for self-determination, political movements centrally concerned with national liberation, such as the postwar Black Left and the Black Power movement to which it helped give rise, are major landmarks on the terrain of progressive politics and culture.

This is not to say that the triumphs of Third Worldist national liberation movements negate their often-virulent heteropatriarchy, but that their limitations with respect to gender and sexuality do not primarily define their (ir)relevance to contemporary social movements, especially when considering African American women writers on the postwar Black Left. Their work challenges the narrative of decline of anticolonial nationalism as a historical force, which Aijaz Ahmad dates to the mid-1970s.[34] As Timothy Brennan observes, this periodization

> does not fit details like the rise of the New People's Army of the Philippines, the right-wing clerical antiimperialism of the Iranian revolution, the victory of the New Jewel movement in Granada [*sic*], and the battle of Quito Carnavale in Angola between the Cuban and South African armies that led directly to the Namibian accords—all of them post-1975, and all of them (again) with resonant activist effects in the metropolis, particularly in the form of the American antiapartheid movement as well as Jesse Jackson's foreign-policy statements in the 1984 presidential elections.[35]

Audre Lorde, who was inspired by Grenada's New Jewel Movement to make national liberation central to her feminism; Lorraine Hansberry, whose Fanonian analysis in her posthumously completed play *Les Blancs* (1970), remained relevant to the unfolding Angolan revolution; and Alice Childress and Rosa Guy, who revisited the histories and politics of the anticolonial Black Left in novels published in 1979 and 1995, demonstrate that revolutionary nationalism continued to shape Black feminist and queer politics well into the late twentieth century—and that radical Black women writers reshaped revolutionary nationalism. When we dismiss intellectual and political formations that hold national liberation to be indispensable to emancipatory politics, we silence a rich strand of Black feminism and deny the very heterogeneity it strives to foster.

□ □ □

In the interest of recovering this heterogeneity within the second-wave Black women's movement, let us consider some notable examples of its nationalist internationalism before turning to its roots in the postwar anticolonial Left's earlier analyses of gender and sexuality. Among the activists appearing in this section, Audre Lorde, Toni Cade Bambara, and Jean Carey Bond created links between the postwar Black Left and second-wave Black feminism. But regardless of political affiliation, all of the women discussed below exemplify a feminist tradition of exploring Black women's histories and experiences in terms of both their centrality and their irreducibility to leftist nationalism.

While the Combahee River Collective's (CRC) formulation of intersectionality is a cornerstone of contemporary Black feminism for good reason, its critique of Black nationalism is not wholly representative.[36] In "Revolution: It's Not Neat or Pretty or Quick," which was published with the CRC's statement in *This Bridge Called My Back: Writings by Radical Women of Color* (1981), Black lesbian poet and self-identified revolutionary feminist Pat Parker amplifies the CRC's call for multifaceted, coalitional struggle based on intersectional analysis of oppression. But whereas the CRC explicitly addresses nationalism only with regard to U.S.-based Black Power sexism, Parker supports anti-imperialist national liberation throughout the world while extensively critiquing the heteropatriarchy of radical movements:

> At the same time that we must understand and support the men and women of national liberation struggles—the left must give up its undying loyalty to the nuclear family. . . . The nuclear family is the basic unit of capitalism and in order for us to move to revolution it has to be destroyed. And I mean destroyed. The male left has duped too many women with cries of genocide into believing it is revolutionary to be bound to babies. As to the question of abortion, I am appalled at the presumption of men. The question is whether or not we have control of our bodies which in turn means control of our community and its growth.[37]

Along with transgressing androcentric boundaries of revolutionary nationalist struggle to advance reproductive rights and the transformation of the private sphere, Parker argues that feminists must be concerned with issues concerning Third World people: "If the passage of the ERA means that I am going to become an equal participant in the exploitation of the world; that I am going to bear arms against other Third World people who are fighting to reclaim what is rightfully theirs—then I say Fuck the ERA."[38] Parker's intersectional thought defines feminist praxis in terms of revolutionary nationalist goals and theorizes revolutionary nationalism through feminist of color critique.

U.S.-based Black nationalism, which Parker did not explicitly address, is central to Frances Beal's critique of Black Power sexism, "Double Jeopardy: To Be Black and Female" (1970). But unlike Michele Wallace's (in)famous denunciation of Black Power nearly a decade later in *Black Macho and the Myth of the Superwoman* (1978), Beal presents a critical yet sympathetic materialist analysis of nationalism that reprises the feminism of the African American popular front and the postwar anticolonial Left.[39] Black people, Beal argues, have been conditioned by the advertising media to accept white bourgeois gender roles. Black men and women need to stop scapegoating each other and instead come to terms with "the true nature of the forces working upon them," that is, "the system of capitalism (and its afterbirth—racism)." Beal goes so far as to emphasize that "Black women are not resentful of the rise to power of Black men. We welcome it. We see in it the eventual liberation of all Black people from this corrupt system of capitalism." That said, she warns that "it is fallacious reasoning that in order for the Black man to be strong, the Black woman has to be weak." All forms of male chauvinism have to be wiped out in order for African Americans to achieve freedom by "building a strong nation, capable of throwing of the yoke of nationalist oppression." Beal importantly does not negate or jettison nationalist politics and theory in critiquing their patriarchal articulations. She conceptualizes African Americans—whom she refers to as an "enslaved nation" and a "colonized population"—in terms of national oppression, which buttresses her internationalist commitment to "the liberation of our people and other oppressed peoples around the world."

Because Beal's materialist feminism is articulated through nationalist internationalism, she asserts that "the main emphasis of Black women must be to combat the capitalist, racist exploitation of Black people. While it is true that male chauvinism has become institutionalized in American society, one must always look for the main enemy—the fundamental cause of the female condition."[40] This claim echoes that of Black Communist and feminist Claudia Jones, who insisted that "the Negro question in the United States is *prior* to, and not equal to, the woman question."[41] At the same time, Beal makes it clear that women's liberation is not guaranteed by socialist revolution or Black liberation, nor is the struggle for women's rights to be deferred. Like Jones, Beal puts Black women at the center of revolutionary struggle:

> This racist, chauvinistic, and manipulative use of Black workers and women, especially Black women, has been a severe cancer on the American labor scene. It therefore becomes essential for those who understand the workings

> of capitalism and imperialism to realize that the exploitation of Black people and women works to everyone's disadvantage and that the liberation of these two groups is a stepping-stone to the liberation of all oppressed people in this country and around the world.[42]

Drawing on Department of Labor statistics for 1967, Beal examines Black women workers' exploitation in ways that are tragically similar to the situation Jones had described nearly two decades earlier. Furthermore, Beal extends the analysis of Black women's special problems to address their "*right and responsibility to determine when it is in the interest of the struggle to have children or not to have them.*" Eliminating forced sterilization and ensuring access to safe birth control methods and legal abortions are crucial in order to "free Black women for full participation in the revolution, and thereafter, in the building of the new society."[43] Beal thus rearticulates revolutionary nationalism to meet the needs of Black working women and all women of color.

Beal put her feminist and internationalist analysis into practice through founding the Third World Women's Alliance (TWWA), which "formally established solidarity with Asian, Chicana, Native American, and Puerto Rican women based on anti-imperialist ideology."[44] The alliance's roots lay in the formation in 1968 of the Black Women's Liberation Caucus of the Student Nonviolent Coordinating Committee (SNCC) and then the autonomous Black Women's Alliance (BWA). The TWWA's formation was spurred when several Puerto Rican women asked to join the BWA since there was no analogous organization within the Puerto Rican community. Including Puertorriqueñas brought anti-imperialism and national liberation to the fore of TWWA's intersectional feminism, as Beal's assessment of this decision underscores:

> When we looked at the Puerto Rican sisters, we saw that they were trying to deal with both their national oppression of living within the United States and a kind of racial and class thing that was separate from just being a part of America as a whole, and then how does your gender fit in when you have this other overriding oppression. Then Black women were essentially trying to deal with the same thing: how do you deal with the question of race and class and gender, in terms of what kinds of inter[sections].[45]

National oppression was central to the intersectional thought of the group that sociologist Benita Roth refers to as "the first self-consciously feminist Black women's social movement organization of the second wave."[46]

The theoretical and political implications of recovering the intersections of Black feminism and nationalism are further clarified by the career of Audre

Lorde. Lorde is one of the most frequently cited contemporary Black feminists, and her work has become foundational within postmodern, often postnationalist studies of race, gender, and sexuality. This critical attention, I argue, selectively focuses on Lorde's earlier writings while ignoring later prose and poetry that make national liberation central to theorizing intersectionality and difference. Specifically, the U.S. invasion in 1983 of Grenada, the birthplace of Lorde's parents, marks a turning point in Lorde's thought and activism, within which struggles for national liberation become increasingly pressing. After the invasion, Lorde discussed nationalist struggles not primarily in terms of sexist, U.S.-based Black identity politics but in terms of Third World liberation movements that extend to African Americans as an internal colony. Lorde shows these movements to be essential to fostering heterogeneity. "Difference" is not attained through cultural hybridity or transnational mobility but through opposing the "racism, destruction, and a borrowed sameness" of settler nationalisms in Australia, South Africa, and the United States.[47] Concepts of coalition and the multiplicity and interconnectedness of struggles also take on new meanings: whereas Lorde formerly refrained from hierarchizing struggles in order to break with homogenizing and monadic identity politics, later essays such as "Turning the Beat Around" prioritize anticolonial nationalism for lesbians and gays of color, who in turn redefine the content and outcome of nationalist struggle. Lorde's nationalist internationalism, fostered by the Committee for the Negro in the Arts and the Harlem Writers Guild, testifies to the historical, institutional, interpersonal, and theoretical ties between the second-wave Black women's movement and the postwar Black Left.[48]

These ties invigorate Toni Cade Bambara's groundbreaking anthology, *The Black Woman* (1970), perhaps the richest text bridging the younger generation of Black feminists with Black women writers of the old and postwar lefts.[49] Of the earlier generation, the anthology's contributors include longtime Communist Maude White Katz, who had attended the Sixth Comintern Congress that issued the Black Belt Nation Thesis; revolutionary theorist and organizer Grace Lee Boggs, who had been a core member of the Trotskyist Johnson-Forest tendency established by C. L. R. James and Raya Dunayevskaya; performer and anticolonial activist Abbey Lincoln; *Freedomways* editor and cultural critic Jean Carey Bond; and novelist Paule Marshall. Alice Childress was a supporter of Bambara's anthology, to which she contributed a story (which for unclear reasons was not included).[50] The younger Black women writers featured in the anthology include Audre Lorde, Frances Beal (whose "Double Jeopardy: To Be Black and Female" appeared both in *The Black Woman* and in Robin Morgan's interracial collection of feminist writings, *Sisterhood is Powerful* [1970]), Nikki Giovanni, Alice Walker, and Sherley Williams.

Second-wave Black feminism both inspired and angered the editors and writers of the Black Left journal *Freedomways* as they undertook to analyze women's issues. Managing editor Esther Cooper Jackson had been a leader of early Black feminist activism and the civil rights struggle during and after World War II. Under her stewardship, *Freedomways* published and reviewed the work of Black women of the Old and New Lefts, women of the Black Arts Movement, and writers who sparked the renaissance of African American women's fiction beginning in the 1970s. Thus, the stage was set in the second half of the 1970s for *Freedomways* to address Black women's concerns with greater depth and frequency, thereby bringing the Black internationalist feminism of the postwar anticolonial Left to bear on what were often heated debates over second-wave Black feminism.

A catalyst for the journal's increased coverage of Black women's issues was International Women's Year in 1975. The editorial for the first issue of 1975 amounted to the journal's programmatic position on Black women. Titled "Black Women: Internationalizing the Struggle," the editorial contended that "what will take the struggle for Black liberation to a higher level from this point, is the identification of Black women as a major force and component part of the struggle to advance the cause of liberation for *all* races and nationalities of peoples in this country." Because Black women were super-exploited, "advancing the special demands for [their] rights" would "raise the level of democracy for all."[51] The editors essentially took up the thesis of leading Black Communist Claudia Jones that to the extent that "the cause of the Negro woman worker is promoted, she will be enabled to take her rightful place in the Negro proletarian leadership of the national liberation movement, and by her active participation contribute to the entire American working class, whose historic mission is the achievement of a Socialist America." Beyond extending solidarity to "our Black, Puerto Rican, Chicana, Native American sisters, and our white working-class sisters here in the United States," the editors hailed "our heroic sisters of Africa and Latin America, of Asia and especially Vietnam" in the name of internationalizing Black women's "special struggle" for economic, political, and social equality. This effort required the right theory to guide it; namely, historical materialism or "analysis of [Black women's] position within the framework of their historical relationship to the objective social forces and the objective conditions existing today."[52] Such analysis would be forthcoming in each of *Freedomways*' 1975 issues featuring articles honoring International Women's Year, such as a readers' forum, "Two Young Black Women Speak of African Liberation"; Elizabeth Murrell's coverage of the World Congress for International Women's Year in Berlin; and Jean Carey Bond's essay on "The Media Image of Black Women."

In the next few years, Bond would be *Freedomways*' most vocal exponent of the ideas set out by "Black Women: Internationalizing the Struggle," especially in relation to the contemporary Black women's movement and the related renaissance of African American women's literature. A member of the youngest generation of radicals of the postwar Black Left, Bond had joined the African American expatriate community in Ghana in 1965, thereby gaining the ability to introduce young Ghanaian writers to *Freedomways* readers.[53] Bond's anticolonial Left background informed the materialist Black feminism that she outlined in reviews of two landmarks in African American literary feminism, the 1978 Broadway production of Ntozake Shange's play *for colored girls who have considered suicide* and the publication the following year of Michele Wallace's *Black Macho and the Myth of the Superwoman.* Bond deemed Shange's play to be "powerful" but hampered by "a kind of Black female chauvinist manifesto" that she later subjected to detailed critique in her review of *Black Macho.*[54]

Wallace's book, with its denunciation of Black Power sexism, had sparked widespread, acrimonious debate among African Americans.[55] In 1979 both *Freedomways* and *The Black Scholar* published commentary on *Black Macho*; the commentary in *Freedomways* took the form of paired reviews by Bond and Carole E. Gregory. Bond and Gregory analyzed *Black Macho* from a shared socialist perspective, but they diverged sharply in appraising Wallace's feminism. While Gregory lauded Wallace's call for a Black women's movement (albeit with reservations over her lack of historicization and her distorted assessment of Angela Davis), Bond excoriated Wallace's embrace of white feminism and its "near deification of sexual combat through the persistent oversimplification of complicated phenomena." This type of feminism, according to Bond, narrowly focused on sexual conflict to the exclusion of its origins in "the warfare of the marketplace," which "increasingly filters into the social order" and ravages the private sphere. While aspects of Bond's criticism appear to rehearse the hostility to feminism a number of Black nationalists and Marxists later displayed, Bond's critique is ultimately of a different species altogether. In contrast to those seeking to preserve male privilege, Bond did not dismiss feminism—even "white bourgeois" feminism—out of hand. She asserted instead that "undeniably, Black women should zero in on the range of problems that confront them in society," including sexism. In this respect, she acknowledged that Wallace's critique of "Black macho" held "some grains of truth." Consequently, Bond called for an intersectional, materialist feminism that would provide "definitive analysis of how the forces of sexism and racism interact in our economic structure to the disadvantage of Black women and men, as well as of other people of color." She concluded by rhetorically asking, "What could be more logical than for such an analysis to come forth from the ranks of Black American women?"[56]

But unlike Wallace's thought, Bond's vision for Marxist, intersectional Black feminism would recuperate Black nationalism. Bond wrote that it was shortsighted and politically disastrous to forsake nationalism to embark on the separatist path of "Black female chauvinism" (to recall the label Bond affixed to Shange's drama). In fact, Wallace's dismissal of Black Power parroted the white-dominated mass media's ahistorical reduction of the movement to a "display of raised fists, guns and other phallic indulgences" propagated by "histrionic celebrities." In doing so, Wallace undermined Black Power's meaningful emancipatory goals as a nationalist internationalist project to "demand a share in the decision-making power of whites in determining the policies of local, state and federal government" and to forge links with "Black Africa's and the rest of the Third World's burgeoning drive for freedom from colonial and neo-colonial domination."[57] Black women needed to support these goals at the same time that they dealt with the specific problems confronting them as Black women, because they were

> members of a caste, the other members of which are equally discriminated against. Clearly, the destinies of Black women are bonded, at the very least for the remainder of this century, to the destinies of their fathers, sons, husbands and lovers. Therefore, the theoretical framework of any movement by Black women to improve their own condition must contain the reality of both the Black female *and* male conditions.[58]

Bond thus reiterated a nationalist internationalist framework for Black feminism in line with that of Claudia Jones and, more recently, Frances Beal and Angela Davis (the latter of whom made similar points to Bond's in her assessment of *Black Macho* at a *Freedomways* forum on "Afro-American Literature of the 70s").[59] Beyond critiquing second-wave Black feminism, Bond's review discloses that the contemporary Black women's movement enriched Black Left analysis of gender: an earlier essay from 1969 co-authored by Bond and Patricia Peery also dealt with gender roles in the Black liberation struggle but strikingly elided the situation of Black women in order to affirm a masculine tradition of race resistance.[60] Bond's significantly greater awareness of and receptiveness to Black feminism in her 1979 review of *Black Macho* speaks to the development of Black women's activism in the ensuing years.

▫ ▫ ▫

The postwar Black Left was a movement of Black radicals allied to varying degrees with the Communist Party USA (CPUSA). They supported or participated in national liberation and working-class movements throughout the world in conjunction with pursuing social, political, and economic rights in the United States.[61] African American popular front coalitional politics carried over into the postwar decades, when Black activists worked within, alongside, and outside of the CPUSA to fight racism and imperialism. Fluid relations among Communists, nationalists, and other leftists and progressives were facilitated by divisions within the Communist Party that grew in the 1950s as a result of McCarthyism, Khrushchev's exposure of Stalinism, the Soviet invasion of Hungary, and the Bandung Conference.[62] Black artists and intellectuals on the Left such as Maya Angelou, Rosa Guy, and John O. Killens were especially open to allying with nationalists, even as many Communist Party cadres and rank-and-file Communists repudiated nationalism in the 1950s and 1960s. Figures who maintained or developed distance from the CPUSA due to their "left nationalism" or Third World Marxism, including Richard Moore, John Henrik Clarke, and Shirley Graham Du Bois, were also central to the Harlem anticolonial Left. The postwar Black Left overlapped considerably, then, with the civil rights and Black Arts/Black Power movements as well as with the Maoist and anti-revisionist (anti-Soviet) Left.[63]

The cross-fertilization of Black nationalist, liberal, and Left activism had been particularly vibrant in Harlem—and in New York City more broadly—since the Bolshevik Revolution. A cosmopolitan locus of nationalist and leftist movements, the New Negro Renaissance, and organizations concerned with civil rights and racial uplift, Harlem brought together constituents of these groups and movements not only to compete with and denounce each other but also to cooperate in ways that belie rancorous histories of Black/Communist conflict and betrayal. In the postwar decades, Harlem continued to be a center of Black struggles that attracted internationally minded progressives.[64] Their activism and art were shaped by the fact that New York City had the "largest single urban concentration of Negroes anywhere in the world" as well as the greatest density of older Marxists and nationalists of any U.S. city.[65] While Harlem's cultural scene was not as vibrant as it had been, important institutions remained (the Schomburg Collection at the 135th Street branch of the New York Public Library, the Apollo Theater, the National Memorial

African Bookstore), while new ones (*Freedom* and *Freedomways*, the Committee for the Negro in the Arts, the Harlem Writers Guild) were created by Black artists and activists who drew on Harlem's rich legacy.

Black anticolonial radicals struggled with Communist hostility toward nationalism, but it was also the case that they expressed and acted on their nationalist internationalism from *within* the CP and its venues, networks, and affiliates. Through organs such as *Political Affairs*, the party's journal of theory; *The Daily Worker*, its newspaper (*The Weekly Worker* after 1958); *Freedom*; and *Masses and Mainstream*, the Left-affiliated periodical of culture and politics, Communists such as Harry Haywood, James S. Allen, Lloyd Brown, and Claudia Jones espoused Black self-determination. Left-wing transnational networks such as the World Youth Conference and the Women's International Democratic Federation gave African Americans the opportunity to meet like-minded activists from the colonies and metropoles engaged in anticolonial struggle. Consequently, it oversimplifies to oppose a monolithically class-centered CPUSA to Black nationalist movements that existed outside the Left. As Julian Mayfield wrote, the struggle for racial autonomy was "an intra-Communist Party struggle which could only have occurred between communists."[66] Furthermore, we cannot assume that hidebound party leaders were uniformly at odds with the rank and file or a body of fellow travelers that more flexibly championed Black liberation. It was as some of the party's leading figures that Haywood, Jones, Brown, and others advanced theory and strategy pertaining to the national question prioritizing African American freedom.

Through the Marxist-Leninist lens of the national question, Black Leftists understood the substantive implementation of civil rights to entail the liberation of African Americans as an oppressed nationality. African Americans, that is, formed a group for whom slavery, segregation, disenfranchisement, racial terror, and other forms of institutionalized, systemic, and de facto racism produced distinct struggles that could not be subsumed under those of the proletariat. This meant that Black liberation could not be achieved "simply" through integrating African Americans into the liberal-democratic, imperialist U.S. nation-state. Instead, Black liberation was predicated on the right of African Americans in the Black Belt region of the South, where they formed a majority, to secede as their own nation under the correct historical conditions. In the post–World War II years this was not "a slogan of immediate action" but a "guiding principle" of "the present practical struggle for full Negro rights, in behalf of which there must be established both the broadest Negro unity and the broadest Negro and white alliance."[67] Black liberation, by this definition, was not separatist (nor narrowly integrationist) but was internationalist in its centrality to and reliance on interracial—and transnational—working-class movements. Hence I use the term *nationalist internationalism* to describe the views of those of the Black anticolonial Left who championed self-determination for all oppressed nations, including African Americans, to bring about worldwide socialism.

The global understanding of race and social justice of these radicals reflects their diasporic backgrounds and itinerant careers. For example, Claudia Jones and Rosa Guy were born in Trinidad; Paule Marshall's parents emigrated from Barbados to New York; Audre Lorde's parents emigrated from Grenada. For Black Leftists, travel was a politically fraught matter that carried the pain of having one's mobility circumscribed and determined by the racist and repressive state through imprisonment, deportation, and the revocation of one's passport—but also the promise of pan-African and Third World solidarities generated through international conferences, trips, and expatriate living. The literature produced by this Black Left postcoloniality reminds us that "the writings and cross-cultural genealogy and experience of many writers represent well the inanity of limiting the understanding of Black women's writing to the United States experience or any one geographical location" and that "to identify Black women's writing primarily with United States writing is to identify with US hegemony."[68]

The Harlem Black Left's internationalism was also enriched by its proximity to the headquarters of the United Nations in midtown Manhattan. The UN's presence "ensured that the leaders of newly independent African [and other Third World] states would visit New York, creating occasions for Black transnational networking and increased African American participation in diplomatic protocol."[69] One of the most significant of these occasions was Fidel Castro's 1960 address to the UN General Assembly. Castro's actions mirrored the readiness of many in Harlem to challenge Jim Crow on a global scale. Not only did he use his UN platform to call for "African American nationhood" and "independence from white cultural and political domination," but he also left his elite Manhattan hotel for Harlem's Hotel Theresa, where he received American guests (Malcolm X, Robert F. Williams) and foreign dignitaries (Khrushchev, Nasser, Nehru).[70] In addition, the diplomatic corps of the embassies of newly liberated African, Asian, and American nations at the UN formed important connections with African Americans (one site affording such intermingling was the Du Bois's Brooklyn home). Rosa Guy's relationship with Congolese UN delegates led to the first major U.S. protest against Patrice Lumumba's assassination, which took place at the UN. Finally, the UN set the stage for a broad spectrum of African Americans to address audiences worldwide with demands to end racial injustice as global attention was increasingly drawn to segregation and racial violence in the United States. From 1946 to 1952, the National Negro Congress, the Civil Rights Congress, and the NAACP separately petitioned the UN concerning the violation of African Americans' human rights.[71]

From within this milieu, the Black Left gave rise to Black internationalist feminism, the theoretical grounds for which can be established through the work of Claudia Jones, the CP's most prominent Black woman in the 1940s through the mid-1950s. Jones's writings powerfully articulate intersectional Black feminist thought and its conjunctions with revolutionary nationalism in the postwar era. Because of her intellect and leadership, her analysis had a substantial impact on party organization and theory and on other Black women radicals. However, I do not mean to suggest that Jones single-handedly laid the foundation for Black Left feminism. She built upon and was in dialogue with the theory and activism of other pioneering Black women radicals such as Louise Thompson Patterson, Shirley Graham Du Bois, Esther Cooper Jackson, Thelma Dale, Vicki Garvin, and the Sojourners for Truth and Justice.[72]

Jones is best known for pushing Black women's special forms of oppression and resistance to the center of Communist praxis with her momentous essay "An End to the Neglect of the Problems of the Negro Woman!" (1949). What has received far less scholarly attention despite its significance to Jones's feminism is her earlier writing on African American nationhood. This consequential work is exemplified by her January 1946 article "On the Right to Self-Determination for the Negro People in the Black Belt." There she argued that the national question was central to supporting and extending the African American and working-class alliance that constituted the primary opposition to "the main danger of fascism to the world," the imperialist forces concentrated in the United States. Jones reiterated the CP's Black Belt Nation Thesis, drawing on Stalin's definition of nationhood—"a historically evolved, stable community of language, territory, economic life and psychological make-up manifested in a community of culture"[73]—to show that African Americans in the Black Belt constituted a nation "oppressed by American imperialism, in the ultimate sense as India is oppressed by British nationalism and Indonesia by Dutch imperialism." As Jones explained, the Black Belt encompassed those southern states where African Americans had become a majority with the growth of the plantation economy and sharecropping peonage. This "majority by force" remained in place, while African Americans in the North formed a national minority. Jones contended that "every aspect of Negro oppression in our country stems from the existence of an *oppressed nation* so defined." This understanding of the Negro question as a national question laid the basis for Black and white working-class unity, for Marxist-Leninism held that the freedom of the working classes of an oppressor nation like the United States was contingent on the freedom of oppressed nations, including the Negro people. While acknowledging that socialism would ultimately dissolve nation-states, Jones pointed out that national liberation could not be postponed, obscured, or skipped within the historical process of imperialist conflict. This tenet distinguished "reactionary Social-Democrats" from Leninists, who "reject, even if it is under the name of 'internationalism,' any denial of the right of national self-determination to the oppressed peoples. For true internationalism—that is, Marxism-Leninism—places the right of self-determination as a basic programmatic point."[74] Even if many African Americans did not use these terms to describe their oppression, this did not mean that self-determination was irrelevant, for only self-determination addressed the substance of Black aspirations to do away with Jim Crow, lynching, disenfranchisement, and sharecropper peonage.

In establishing this claim, Jones importantly clarified that self-determination was neither reducible to separation nor opposed to integration. (Confusion around this had resulted in CPUSA general secretary Earl Browder's effective liquidation of the Black Belt Nation Thesis.)[75] The right to separation was "inherent" in the right to self-determination but became "a practical political matter only when the concrete objective conditions for that choice [were] at hand." If African Americans were not demanding separation from the United States, it was because the historical conditions for that choice did not exist. On the other hand, African Americans were fighting for integration as they had "for over two hundred years," but this was not tantamount to demanding assimilation into the status quo. Instead, truly democratic integration entailed the revolutionary measure of enforcing equal economic, political, and social rights for African Americans in the Black Belt. To this end, "partial demands" for land, enfranchisement, and electoral representation, "linked up with the daily needs and problems of the wide masses of the Negro people and the white workers in the Black Belt," had to be connected with the right of self-determination.[76]

Jones's writing on Black self-determination was as influential and important as her work on Black women. At a time when the Black Belt Nation Thesis had been repealed as part of the CP's wartime accommodation with liberal democratic powers, Jones was in the vanguard demanding the reinstatement of the thesis and clarifying its utmost relevance to socialist struggle.

Moreover, her theorizations of the national question and the woman question must be read in relation to each other: Jones's call for the CP to prioritize Black self-determination arose in the context of the party's reaffirmation of women's struggles, in which Jones played a pivotal role.

In fact, Black national liberation is the crux of her analysis of women's emancipation in "An End to the Neglect of the Problems of the Negro Woman!":

> The Negro question in the United States is *prior* to, and not equal to, the woman question; that only to the extent that we fight all chauvinist expressions and actions as regards the Negro people and fight for the full equality of the Negro people, can women as a whole advance their struggle for equal rights. For the progressive women's movement, the Negro woman, who combines in her status the worker, the Negro, and the woman, is the vital link to this heightened political consciousness. To the extent, further, that the cause of the Negro woman worker is promoted, she will be enabled to take her rightful place in the Negro proletarian leadership of the national liberation movement, and by her active participation contribute to the entire American working class, whose historic mission is the achievement of a Socialist America—the final and full guarantee of woman's emancipation.[77]

Carole Boyce Davies rightly points out that this claim "is not as straightforward as the 'race first' assertion of black (male) nationalism." However, Davies weakens and misinterprets Jones's argument by paraphrasing it as follows: "to the extent to which the race issue is central to any analysis of women's experience, then the black woman has to be the representative 'raced' woman in any of these struggles."[78] Davies replaces "race" for "nation" with serious implications.[79] This move substitutes the primary dialectical contradiction between oppressor and oppressed nations with a nonhierarchical and nondialectical conceptualization of race. Thus, Davies implies that Jones's attention to the intersection of race and gender renders neither primary, in contrast to "black (male)" nationalism's promotion of "race first." This view of intersectionality obscures Jones's contention that the Negro question is "*prior* to, and not equal to, the woman question"; that the Negro question is a *national* question (as in "the Negro proletarian leadership of the national liberation movement"); and that nationalism is not inherently masculinist (Jones asserts Black women's "rightful place" at the head of the fight for self-determination).

Jones's feminism is intersectional, but not in the sense espoused by cultural critics who value nonhierarchical conjunctions of different modes of resistance. In specifically giving precedence to national liberation, Jones demonstrates that it is necessarily transformed by centering Black women's struggles within it instead of focusing exclusively on men. Black women, Jones writes, have "become symbols of many present-day struggles of the Negro people," which has "profound meaning, both for the Negro liberation movement and for the emerging anti-fascist, anti-imperialist coalition."[80] Jones makes this case through her discussion of Rosa Lee Ingram, a Black sharecropper and widowed mother of twelve in Georgia sentenced to death by an all-white jury for defending herself from being raped and killed by a white sharecropper. In publicizing Ingram's case as another instance of white supremacist lynching terror, Jones's male comrades largely ignored the implications of her status as a Black woman.[81] Their inability to see gender in conjunction with race reduced the problems of Black women to those of Black men, who came to define the race. This masculinist approach to Black national oppression reiterated the sexism of Communist anti-lynching campaigns from the 1930s, which urged interracial solidarity specifically between working *men*. Homosocial working-class bonds were solidified by demonizing white women, who were no longer virtuous prizes to be defended by white men against Black men (as pro-lynching white supremacists proposed). Instead, within Communist anti-lynching propaganda, white women were the whores of capitalism to be rejected in favor of a united interracial brotherhood of the proletariat. Sexism thus combined with racism to engender a misogynistic view of white women and to erase Black women's oppression altogether.[82]

Challenging this racialized sexism, Jones explained that Rosa Lee Ingram laid bare the oppression of the Black woman "who combines in her status the worker, the Negro, and the woman." These interlocking oppressions meant that Ingram symbolized more than the necessity of Black self-determination because of her "landless, Jim-Crow, oppressed status." Jones took the further step of showing that the Ingram case "illumines particularly the degradation of *Negro women* today under American bourgeois democracy moving to fascism and war." In exemplifying the particularities of Black women's conditions from within "the most oppressed stratum of the whole population," Ingram revealed the need for a "special approach" to Black women's problems that redefined the struggle for socialism and national liberation: the CP needed to understand and act on the economic, historical, and ideological forces giving rise to Black women's "super-exploitation"; recognize "the special character of the role of Negro women's organizations"; and recruit Black women to and promote them within trade unions, progressive groups, and the party.[83]

Jones's intersectional analysis of race, gender, and class also reflected the internationalism of the Black Belt Nation Thesis that African Americans in the South constituted a nation "oppressed by American imperialism, in the ultimate sense as India is oppressed by British nationalism and Indonesia by Dutch imperialism."[84] These comparisons illustrate how leftists of color identified struggles for economic, social, and political equality in the United States with national liberation movements in Africa, Asia, the Caribbean, and the Americas. Such was the importance of internationalist identifications that Jones concluded "An End to the Neglect of the Problems of the Negro Woman!" by calling attention to Black women's solidarity with the peace movement exemplified by the women in North Africa who "stand against a Third World War, with 81 million women in 57 nations, in the Women's International Democratic Federation."[85] Another article by Jones on International Women's Day lauding the militancy of U.S. working women sought "to arouse their sense of internationalism with millions upon millions of their sisters the world over," such as the women in Africa who "barricaded the roads with their bodies to prevent their men from being carted away as prisoners in a militant strike struggle charged with slogans of anti-colonialism and peace."[86]

While mainstream African American politics had adopted a global perspective on domestic civil rights as a result of World War II, the dawn of independence throughout the Third World, and the end of formal, direct imperialism, things had changed dramatically by the end of the 1940s. U.S. anticommunism successfully co-opted the mainstream civil rights movement, which Black liberals then delinked from decolonization abroad.[87] That anticolonial internationalism survived the peak of Cold War persecution was due in no small part to Black Left feminists such as Jones who clarified the stakes of the national question and its relationship to the woman question. Jones's theory and activism were instrumental in enabling other Black women writers to develop feminist praxis in "the age of nationalist revolt,"[88] which witnessed the Viet Minh victory over France in 1954; the first gathering of non-aligned nations in Bandung, Indonesia, in 1955; the emergence of twenty-one new nation-states from 1955 to 1961; the war of independence waged against France by the Front de Libération Nationale in Algeria; African liberation beginning with Ghana in 1957 and culminating in "The Year of Africa," when fourteen nations in West and Equatorial Africa declared independence in 1960; the Cuban Revolution in 1959; the demonstration at the UN in response to Patrice Lumumba's assassination, sparking the revival of Black nationalism in the United States; and the founding of the Organization of African Unity in 1963.

As Kevin Gaines argues in his pioneering essay on Black Left feminism, the internationalist politics of the postwar Left enabled a "comprehensive, democratic" feminist perspective that "ground[ed] its critique of patriarchy within radical critiques of racism, capitalist exploitation, and empire." Whereas Black feminists of the late 1960s and 1970s had to contend with virulent fusions of patriarchy and Black nationalism, the radical democratic universalism of the 1950s made room for Black women to examine gender (and sexuality) in relation to race, class, and nation. Gaines's insight into the historical and theoretical intersections of internationalism and Black feminism is invaluable, but I want to reassess his claim that "Black feminism initially emerged as an organic part of postwar Black struggles for equality."[89] It is true that African Americans in the post–World War II anticolonial movement did not internalize misogynistic, homophobic ideologies to the extent that the subsequent generation of Black Power radicals did. It is also the case that in the postwar years the CPUSA revived its support for women's equality, engendering a "red feminism" that conceptualized "women's oppression and liberation within a framework that made race and class central."[90] Nonetheless, masculinism, misogyny, and heteronormativity consistently informed internationalist politics and rhetoric. Masculinist messianic rhetoric was deployed to express the connections between Black American and African struggles, as in John Henrik Clarke's 1961 portrait of Lumumba, "the symbol of the Black man's humanity struggling for recognition," "this 'best son of Africa,' this 'Lincoln of the Congo,' this 'Black Messiah.'"[91] Problematic ideologies of gender and sexuality also underpin John O. Killens's global perspective on race relations in his essay collection *Black Man's Burden* (1965). Killens explains that his androcentric title is meant to be inclusive: "when we say manhood, we also mean womanhood, selfhood." This superficial attempt at inclusion reaches its breaking point when Killens makes the following analogy in order to frame civil rights within the context of a "New World a-borning" in Africa and Asia: "To the extent that the Negro does not employ world opinion as a lever, to that same extent will the Establishment understand that the Negro is not really serious about his freedom. He is not yet angry enough. He is like a woman whose husband beats her nightly, but she does not cry out because she doesn't want the neighbors to know. She's afraid of scandalizing the family. She almost deserves to be beaten."[92] We thus cannot make clear-cut associations of masculinism with post-1965 Black Power nationalism or of feminism with the postwar anticolonialism of older radicals. If internationalism enabled Black women writers to assert agency, it is because they contested and redefined its heteropatriarchal formulations to make it more responsive to feminist and queer concerns.

The chapters that follow examine the development of Black internationalist feminism and several of its most intriguing and representative facets. Chapter 1 historicizes Black internationalist feminism beginning with the intertwinings of Black nationalist and Old Left movements in the interwar years. This chapter demonstrates that the activism and analysis of African American women on the Old Left such as Maude White Katz and Louise Thompson Patterson laid grounds for postwar Black feminism. I contextualize the Black materialist feminism of Claudia Jones in the 1940s and explain how it was fostered on the cultural front by journals such as *Freedom* and *Freedomways* and organizations such as the Harlem Writers Guild and the Cultural Association for Women of African Heritage (CAWAH).

The next five chapters look at how prominent women writers of the postwar Black Left articulated and revised Black internationalist feminism. Each chapter focuses on a single author in order to attend to the depth and breadth of their literary and political engagements. This is necessary because of the dearth of criticism on the work of authors such as Alice Childress and Rosa Guy and because the selective scholarly attention given to Lorraine Hansberry, Audre Lorde, and Maya Angelou has not plumbed their feminist radicalism.

For example, Audre Lorde, Michelle Cliff, Jewelle Gomez, and Barbara Smith have recognized Lorraine Hansberry as a foremother of second-wave Black and lesbian feminism, yet we have only begun to examine the contours of her analysis of gender and sexuality in conjunction with her thinking on race and anticolonialism. To this end, chapter 2 examines Hansberry's investments in existentialism in order to show that her play about African revolution, *Les Blancs* (1970), is a culmination of both her Black queer feminism *and* her internationalism. Hansberry framed *Les Blancs* as a response to Jean Genet's internationally acclaimed play *The Blacks,* an absurdist meditation on power and race in the context of African decolonization. Even as Hansberry attacked what she saw as the corrosive effects of *The Blacks'* existentialist despair and negation of revolutionary praxis, she did not dismiss existentialism in toto: Simone de Beauvoir's *The Second Sex* provided theoretical scaffolding for Hansberry's Black internationalist feminism. Reading two of Hansberry's early unpublished plays along with her essay on *The Second Sex,* I argue that Beauvoir helped Hansberry interrogate dominant views of tragic lesbians, critique heteropatriarchal norms, and represent homosexuality as a political choice with implications for revolutionary movements. Hansberry's later work, including and following the play that brought her worldwide attention, *A Raisin in the Sun* (1959), muted the feminism of her earlier work. Yet in crucial ways she remained committed to critiquing the interpenetration of heteropatriarchy, racialized imperialism, and capitalism, as we see in *Les Blancs*—and to this endeavor, Beauvoirean existentialism was integral.

Chapter 3 turns to Hansberry's comrade and sister dramatist, Alice Childress, to consider the legacy of Garveyism for the postwar Black Left. Despite historical animosity between Marcus Garvey and the Old Left, younger anticolonial radicals recognized Garvey as a political forefather. Paule Marshall and Rosa Guy cited his influence as positive, and John Henrik Clarke was instrumental in disseminating and studying his writing. Childress's novel *A Short Walk* (1979), published five years after Clarke's pioneering collection *Marcus Garvey and the Vision of Africa* (1974), contributed to and intervened in the renaissance of Garveyism among Black radicals and nationalists. Childress exposed Garveyism's rigid hierarchies of gender and sexuality through juxtaposing chronotopes of the ship and the traveling minstrel show.[93] Ships have engendered transnational communities of free(r), mobile Black subjects, but these subjects have mainly been sea*men*, and ships have traditionally been male domains. For Childress, Black women's freedom is afforded not only or even primarily by Garvey's Black Star Line fleet of ships but by the minstrel circuit's negotiation of Jim Crow space. Furthermore, through conventions of minstrelsy Childress imagines an alternative space—the drag ball—that unmoors Black/American identities from heteropatriarchal roles. In exploring the radical potential of minstrel drag, Childress drew upon her experience as a Black Left actor and playwright as well as her intimate involvement with the controversy over the televised *Amos 'n' Andy* series, which was widely viewed as modern blackface minstrelsy. The *Amos 'n' Andy* controversy spurred Childress to fight the racism of the mainstream media but also to recover minstrelsy's roots in popular revolt and its ability to destabilize dominant gender and sexual roles. Through minstrel drag, Childress recuperated Garvey's (trans)nationalism for transgender, queer, and feminist politics of liberation.

Chapter 4 examines Rosa Guy's Black feminist and queer engagement with tropes and discourses of twentieth-century radical literature about the Haitian Revolution generated by the first U.S. occupation of Haiti (1918–1934) and interwar anticolonialism. Although Guy is a little-known figure of the post–World War II Black Left, she cofounded two of its influential institutions, the Harlem Writers Guild and the Cultural Association for Women of African Heritage. Over thirty years after the height of this activism, Guy reflected on the limitations of Black nationalism and its Left articulations in her novel *The Sun, The Sea, a Touch of the Wind* (1995). Guy's novel revises Black masculinist messianism by decentering Toussaint L'Ouverture, the heroic leader of the Haitian Revolution, and focusing instead on Charlemagne Masséna Péralte, the "crucified" leader of the insurgency against the first

U.S. occupation of Haiti. In representing the ongoing history of American military intervention in the Caribbean, the novel makes critique of U.S. imperialism central to Black feminism. The need for Guy's Black internationalist feminism is elucidated by comparing her tale of African American female self-empowerment through Caribbean romance to a similarly themed novel published the following year, Terry McMillan's bestseller *How Stella Got Her Groove Back* (1996). I read the phenomenon encompassing McMillan's novel, a movie based on the novel, and McMillan's very public marriage and divorce from Jonathan Plummer, the gay Jamaican man who inspired *Stella,* as a series of texts that yoke American exceptionalism with homophobic discourses of national belonging. In contrast to McMillan's U.S.-centric and heteronormative construction of Black womanhood, Guy creates a queer Black hemispheric woman and her transgendered lover who raise hard questions about the triumphs, failures, and legacies of the civil rights movement, Black Power, and anticolonial nationalism.

Chapter 5 argues that Audre Lorde's essays and poetry from the 1980s develop an overlooked yet significant strand of second-wave Black feminism that reveals continuities with postwar anticolonial internationalism. But if Lorde's corpus theorizes the relevance of national liberation to postmodern feminist and queer of color identity politics, Maya Angelou's own wide-ranging body of work and iconic status impart more equivocally the persistence of Black internationalist feminism. Chapter 6 reads selections from Angelou's autobiographies as indices of the unvanquished albeit fragile late-twentieth-century legacy of the post–World War II anticolonial Black Left. On one hand, Angelou's autobiographies contest the historiographic erasure of African Americans' internationalist identifications in the Bandung era, especially as they were animated by Black women. On the other hand, Angelou contributes to this erasure by emphasizing personal triumph and individual identity formation over sociohistorical narrative. Indeed, Angelou's remarkable popularity and cultural capital come at the expense of the revolutionary politics she shared with comrades who have been exiled, persecuted, or otherwise banished from public memory. But beyond examining Angelou's celebrity as another instance of mainstream cooptation, I consider how her writings and career provide an avenue for reclaiming Black feminism's postwar internationalist routes.

Hansberry, Childress, Guy, Lorde, and Angelou present diverse aesthetic strategies and lines of inquiry that arose from analyses of gender and sexuality that were intimately shaped by the Black Left. My hope is to encourage further work on these and other African American women writers who illuminate the intersections of Black feminist, Marxist, and nationalist thought. Among African American women writers on the postwar Left, Shirley Graham Du Bois and Sarah Elizabeth Wright in particular await greater critical attention.[94]

What do the historical and theoretical paradigms of Black internationalist feminism suggest about ways to approach these writers? Shirley Graham Du Bois's relationship to Black feminism is not easy to ascertain; as Rebeccah Welch writes: "Although Graham Du Bois often personally defied conventional female roles, race politics took precedence over sexual struggle in her life's work." Yet Graham Du Bois belonged to the Civil Rights Congress women's auxiliary and the Sojourners for Truth and Justice, both of which appealed to Graham Du Bois with their "racially and globally minded feminist perspective."[95] Greater light on the gender politics of this signal member of the anticolonial Left would be shed by looking at Graham Du Bois's cultural work, a body of opera, drama, biographies, political analysis, and reportage that spans genres, decades, and continents. Graham Du Bois wrote and directed for the Federal Theater Project; launched and co-edited *Freedomways*; and served as director of Ghana Television. What could be gleaned from looking at Graham Du Bois's critically acclaimed pan-Africanist opera from the Depression era, *Tom-Tom*; her biographies of Frederick Douglass, Paul Robeson, Phillis Wheatley, Pocahontas, and W. E. B. Du Bois; her novel about South Africa, *Zulu Heart*; and her rejected, unpublished novel about Anne Royall, "a feminist heroine of the early history of the United States"?[96] A consideration of the at-times-implicit views of gender and sexuality expressed in Graham Du Bois's writing would flesh out her evolving Third World nationalism and clarify her relationship to Black Left feminists such as Claudia Jones, Esther Cooper Jackson, and Lorraine Hansberry.

In contrast to the prolific Graham Du Bois, Sarah Wright published one volume of poetry (*Give Me a Child*, 1955), one work of young adult nonfiction (*A. Philip Randolph: Integration in the Workplace*, 1990), and a handful of critical essays in addition to her only novel, *This Child's Gonna Live* (1969). This novel has been all but ignored of late, yet it was a critical success in its time, garnering laudatory reviews across the country; it was named an outstanding book of 1969 by the *New York Times Book Review*. Set on the eastern shore of Maryland in 1930, *This Child's Gonna Live* vividly captures the oystering and farming community of Tangierneck through idiomatic and poetic stream-of-consciousness narrative. Inspired by Russian, African, and Haitian writers' efforts to depict the land and peasantry of their respective countries, *This Child's Gonna Live* exemplified Black national culture as it was defined by Leftists such as the African American novelist and editor Lloyd Brown, who viewed folk culture as the authentic expression of the Black nation.[97]

However, Wright's novel did more than simply express the Black nation; it presented a forceful feminist critique of nationalist aspirations for land and community control that were predicated on the sexual oppression of Black women. The hope for "the coming of the Black nations of the world" is indicated at the novel's end when, as Jennifer Campbell observes, the protagonist Mariah "takes her place at her husband's side to reclaim the lost land that is the literal and figurative foundation for all the children of Tangierneck, Maryland."[98] Nonetheless, this redemptive moment is actualized only by challenging the heteropatriarchal familial relations underlying bourgeois nationhood. Mariah's is now "a newly extended family of children orphaned by systemic and violent racism," including Mariah's biracial baby girl conceived with a man who is not her husband.[99] Whereas Mariah had earlier believed that both she and her daughter would be "*no part of the Black nation*" due to their embodiment of racial and sexual transgressions, the ending illustrates that the rejuvenation of the Black family/Black nation depends on moving away from ideologies of racial purity and patrilineal inheritance.[100] Mariah's biracial daughter is the eponymous child who will live to bring about "the coming of the Black nations of the world."

A tremendous contribution to African American literature with epic designs, Wright's novel was to have culminated in a trilogy. Hopefully, a version of the uncompleted second installment will find publication, thereby providing further insight into a writer deeply engaged with rethinking Black national liberation through the experiences of African American working women.[101]

Without a doubt, Black women writers on the postwar anticolonial Left were remarkable for their intellect, artistry, and courage in openly fighting for causes that to this day the mainstream regards with hostility or at best apathy. What earlier histories, organizations, and Black women and men gave rise to the analyses and aesthetics of these writers? In chapter 1, I will present some answers to this question and elaborate on the impact of Black internationalist feminist thought on radical cultural and political work.

1

The Negro Question, the Woman Question, and the "Vital Link"

Histories and Institutions

Feminism, Marxism, and Black nationalism have had contentious relationships with each other, to say the least. How is it, then, that the Communist Party's theory and tactics of African American nationhood gave rise to the Black internationalist feminist tradition that came into its own in the post–World War II era? This chapter investigates the histories of African American involvement with the Communist Left that shaped Black women writers' strategic commitments to national liberation as they strove to represent emancipatory enactments of gender and sexuality. I begin by discussing the intertwining of Black nationalist and Old Left movements in the interwar years, with special attention to the CP's Black Belt Nation Thesis, which produced political solidarities beyond the limited affiliations engendered and policed by U.S. liberal democracy. While putting the Black Belt Nation Thesis into practice entrenched Left masculinism more fully, several leading Black Communists transformed the meaning of self-determination to allow for intersectional analysis of race and gender and to address the "special oppressed status" of Black women. In doing so, African American Left women in particular paved the way for postwar Black feminism, which Claudia Jones definitively theorized. Jones's Marxist analysis of gender must be understood in light of her leadership in reviving the Black Belt Nation Thesis and its internationalist implications. Her Black internationalist feminism carried over into the cultural front, creating spaces within the Left for writing by and about African American women. I conclude by examining the primary institutions through which Black women writers represented nonheteropatriarchal identities and alignments in the process of exploiting the possibilities for African American freedom that national liberation throughout the Third World opened up.

The antagonism between Black nationalism and Communism is better known than their intersections, but the origins of the Black Left undeniably complicate this narrative. As Robin Kelley writes, "African Americans who joined the Party in the 1920s and 1930s were as much the creation of American communism as of black nationalism; as much the product of African American [and Afro-Caribbean] vernacular cultures and radical traditions as of Euro-American radical thought."[1] This is made evident by considering the major source of the first known Black Communists, the African Blood Brotherhood (ABB). This revolutionary Black nationalist order, which was established in 1919 on the heels of the Red Summer's wave of racial terror, advocated armed self-defense and African liberation along with interracial labor/left solidarity.[2] Many ABB members hailed from the West Indies, including Cyril Briggs, Richard Moore, Otto Huiswood, Arthur Hendricks, Claude McKay, and W. A. Domingo, and the colonial and immigrant background of these Black radicals honed their awareness of both national oppression and class exploitation. A turning point in ABB founder Cyril Briggs's politics came with the first congress of the Communist International (Comintern) in 1919, which "topp[ed] Wilson's post-war principle of national self-determination with outright calls for revolution in the colonial world, backed by promises to aid it."[3] When the short-lived ABB folded in the early 1920s, its members turned to the CPUSA, which had been established in 1919, "largely because of the Communist International's commitment to supporting 'racial and national movements against imperialism.'"[4]

While the emergent CPUSA tended to either ignore issues of race or reduce them to economic factors, the Soviet Union—which owed the success of its revolution to minorities within the Russian Empire—perceived African Americans to be strategically important as the largest and most oppressed minority group in the United States. Consequently, the Soviet-dominated Comintern not only pushed the CPUSA to fight for Black rights but also welcomed African Americans to the USSR as visitors, settlers, students to be trained at multinational Soviet schools, and Comintern delegates and speakers. There is good evidence that in the latter positions, Black Americans and Afro-Caribbeans impacted Communist theory on the national question.[5] ABB member and Communist Claude McKay, for example, appears to have influenced the crafting and adoption at the 4th World Congress of the Comintern in 1922 of the "Theses on the Negro Question," which declared that the "Negro problem has become the urgent and decisive question for world revolution" and that "the Negroes' fight against imperialism is not the fight of one nation, but of all the nations of the world."[6]

These theses set the stage for the adoption of the Black Belt Nation Thesis at the 6th World Congress of the Comintern in 1928. According to this resolution, the African American majority in the Black Belt from Virginia through the deep South reaching to eastern Texas comprised a nation within a nation with the right to self-determination; whites could live within the Black republic as minorities with full rights if they submitted to majority rule.[7] African Americans in the North, on the other hand, comprised a national minority with the right to full integration. This resolution was fiercely debated, with Black and white Communists objecting to its segregationism, its incongruence with the experience of southern Blacks who did not see themselves in national terms, and its privileging of agricultural workers at the expense of the urban industrial class. Regardless of perceived and real shortcomings and ambiguities, the Black Belt Nation Thesis, "within the Leninist lexicon of values, endowed the black struggle with unprecedented dignity and importance."[8] The resolution recognized African Americans as a distinct and primary revolutionary force that was integral but not identical to proletarian struggle and that maintaining the solidarity of Black and white workers was essential to Black liberation.

The practical consequence of this line was to prioritize Black struggle, racial equality, integration, and anti-imperialism within Communist work at a time when racial chauvinism and segregation were largely unchallenged. Enacting the resolution's precepts, the CP prioritized the recruitment, training, and promotion of African Americans; prepared white comrades for work among African Americans; refused to tolerate white chauvinism; and put the Negro problem at the forefront of party work. One of the greatest priorities was organizing African Americans in the South, where Communists established the Alabama Sharecroppers' Union, pushed for interracial solidarity among striking textile mill workers, and defended Angelo Herndon, a young Black Communist sentenced to twenty years on a chain gang for organizing an interracial rally for welfare relief. Of especial importance to African Americans was the CP's anti-lynching Scottsboro campaign, which did not substantially increase the party's Black membership but nonetheless raised its profile among African Americans and attracted individuals such as Claudia Jones who would become influential race radicals. In the North, the Left formed the Harlem Unemployed Council, which fought evictions as well as discrimination in employment and relief distribution; organized the anti-lynching League of Struggle for Negro Rights; and launched the Needle Trades Workers Industrial Union.

The possibility of a free African American nation also generated political identifications and solidarities that exposed the limits and exceeded the purview of U.S. liberal democracy. As a result of forced removal, enslavement, disenfranchisement, segregation, and super-exploitation, African Americans had been barred from full economic, political, and social rights within the liberal democratic U.S. nation-state. Oppressed national status illuminated the need for wider affiliations with other oppressed nations and the worldwide proletariat against oppressor nations. The forms of political community authorized by the Black Belt Nation Thesis included but went beyond claiming the full rights of U.S. citizenship.

Black Communists' internationalist identifications were most powerfully manifested in the interwar years in response to Italy's 1935 invasion of Ethiopia (Abyssinia), the only independent Black African nation at the time.[9] African Americans nationwide mobilized funds and manpower in support of Emperor Haile Selassie and the Ethiopian people. Although Black Communists shared the party's critical view of the monarchy, they joined nationalists and other African Americans regardless of political affiliation to defend the imperiled Black nation against imperialist aggression. When efforts to rally around Ethiopia were thwarted by the U.S. government and the CP itself, over eighty African American men and one African American woman—mostly Communists—channeled their energies into defending the Spanish Republic against Franco the following year. Black radicals connected the Spanish Civil War to the fascist invasion of Ethiopia and to their own struggles against racism and exploitation in the United States, an internationalist perspective deepened by coming into contact with soldiers of African descent from throughout the world who were serving in the International Brigades.[10]

While sharpening the fight against racism and imperialism, the Left's program for Black self-determination generally relied upon and exacerbated Communist masculinism at the expense of women's liberation. This version of Communism gendered the revolutionary class as male and subordinated women's concerns to those of the proletariat when they were not ignored altogether.[11] Patriarchy was generally not treated with the seriousness with which racism was attacked, especially insofar as rank-and-file women were affected. In fact, Robin Kelley contends that "the Party's position on black liberation after 1928 . . . not only took precedence over women's struggles, but it essentially precluded a serious theoretical framework that might combine the 'Negro' and 'Woman' questions." The cultural implications of the self-determination argument tightened patriarchy's grip on Black nationalism, which "conjured up masculine historical figures such as Toussaint L'Ouverture, Denmark Vesey, and Nat Turner" and "relied on metaphors from war and emphasized violence as a form of male redemption" while "render[ing] women invisible or ancillary."[12] According to James Smethurst, "The concepts of black folk culture that derived from the Black Belt Thesis gendered the folk, and 'authentic' literary representations and recreations of the folk, as male to an extent never seen before even in black nationalism and modernism before the 1930s."[13] In the mid-1930s, Stalin reversed progressive laws pertaining to gender and sexuality that the Bolsheviks had enacted earlier in the decade, a move that strengthened the mutual reinforcement of nationalism and patriarchy. This intensified the CPUSA's conservative views on women, the family, and homosexuality.[14] In the latter half of the 1930s, the Left's popular front expressions of Black militancy were often informed by its use of "sex roles in the conventional nuclear family [to furnish] a ground on which to base working-class political activism, rather than a target for political critique."[15]

Nonetheless, many Black Communists, women and men, strained against the gendered limitations imposed on Black self-determination, broadening and transforming it to account for the struggles of Black women and to generate intersectional analyses of race and gender. Claude McKay contended in *The Negroes in America* (1923) that "the Negro question is inseparably connected with the question of women's liberation."[16] William Maxwell has pointed out that McKay nonetheless equates womanhood with whiteness and thereby compounds the invisibility of Black women's histories and subjectivities.[17] However, Kate Baldwin's examination of McKay's *Trial by Lynching: Stories about Negro Life in North America* (1925), which was written at the same time as *The Negroes in America*, argues that "McKay was attempting to reclaim the denigrated space of black femininity often occluded in conventional accounts of the lynching scenario and certainly overlooked by Soviet theorization on the women question."[18] Over ten years later, Richard Wright strove for a similar goal with his collection of novellas, *Uncle Tom's Children* (1938). Executing therein his "Blueprint for Negro Writing" (1937)—which Smethurst describes as the "most extended discussion of the literary applications of the Black Belt Thesis, and the burning necessity of such applications, by a leading writer connected to the Communist Left"—Wright depicted nationalism's dialectical transformation through Black female radicalism rooted in motherhood and feminine interracial solidarity.[19]

To an even greater extent and in larger numbers than their male comrades, Black women on the Left established as a corollary to nationalism that they had special problems—subjection to super-exploitation, marginalization in organizational and interpersonal settings, and distortion or outright erasure by progressive as well as mainstream cultural forms—that could not be deferred by or subsumed under masculinist theories of race or class. The activism of two leading African American women of the Old Left, Maude White and Louise Thompson, reveals that Marxist-Leninist internationalism spurred their commitments to addressing these issues, which in turn reformulated androcentric and misogynistic ideologies that occluded Black women's centrality to the program for self-determination. Furthermore, White and Thompson's longevity as radical activists, evidenced by their connections with the postwar anticolonial Left and the beginnings of the second-wave Black women's movement, provide crucial insight into contemporary Black feminism's roots in nationalist internationalism.

While enrolled at Moscow's University of the Toilers of the East (KUTV) along with Ho Chi Minh, Deng Xiaoping, and Jomo Kenyatta, Maude White attended the 6th World Congress of the Comintern as it debated and passed the 1928 resolution on Black self-determination. In addition to monitoring discussions of the Negro question, African American KUTV students demanded and got a Negro section at the school "to allow them to explore the global dimensions of the black struggle by collecting and analyzing information on conditions and prospects for change in the black colonies of Africa as well as in the United States."[20] The nationalist internationalism that White imbibed in the Soviet Union indelibly marked her political consciousness, as "in the ensuing years, she would fight relentlessly against racism wherever it appeared and for the right of African Americans to determine their own path to liberation within the framework of unity with all who were exploited by the dominant system."[21] In conjunction with pursuing autonomous Black struggle in solidarity with proletarian movements, White raised the issue of the special character of the exploitation of Black women workers and prioritized organizing them. This White did soon after returning to the United States, when with the Needle Trades Workers Industrial Union she fought the subcontracting of African American women pressers, who were made to work harder for lower wages than their white peers earned. When party leaders informed White that the union would handle the complaints of Black workers no differently from those of whites, White demanded recognition of Black women's special oppression while pressing for interracial solidarity within the working class. White's militancy in denouncing the racism of the needle trades union resulted in the Yokinen trial, "one of the most spectacular and publicized anti-racist actions to that point in the nation's history."[22]

The political and intellectual leadership of Louise Thompson similarly needs to be understood in the context of Left nationalist internationalism. By the early 1930s, Thompson was a leading radical well versed in Marx, Engels, and Lenin. With sculptor Augusta Savage she formed the Vanguard, "the most successful left-wing salon in 1930s Harlem," which drew other New Negro artists and writers to its social events, political forums, and Marxist discussion groups.[23] She led middle-class whites and Blacks into the South to challenge segregation, and she organized the Harlem branch of the Friends of the Soviet Union. As part of this last group, Thompson led a delegation of African American artists and intellectuals to the USSR to make a film about Black workers in the United States. When the film fell through, Thompson was instrumental in arranging for the delegates to travel to Soviet Central Asia to see firsthand, as she later put it, colored "nations arising out of centuries of illiteracy, poverty and even nomad life."[24]

Thompson's Soviet experience deepened her commitment to Black liberation. She joined the CP in mid-1933 and left her position with the liberal Congregational Educational Society to work for the Scottsboro campaign as assistant national secretary of the left-wing National Committee for the Defense of Political Prisoners. In this capacity, Thompson was involved (as was Maude White) with one of the most important Left campaigns to demonstrate CP commitment to African American struggle—one that theorists of Black nationhood interpreted as validating their position. The anti-lynching Scottsboro campaign (1931–1937) centered on nine young African American men falsely accused of rape; eight were sentenced to death by a series of all-white juries. As Dan T. Carter observes, such legalized lynching was nothing new in the South, but the nature of the trials—the youth and number of the condemned, the summariness with which they had been found guilty, and the extremity of the punishment—catapulted Scottsboro into international attention.[25] For Harry Haywood, who had played a major role in developing the Black Belt Nation Thesis, Scottsboro was

> but a single expression of the whole system of national oppression of the Negro people—a system which in this country of "enlightened" capitalist democracy holds in shameless suppression a nation of 14,000,000 human beings, subjects them to super-exploitation on the plantations and in the factories, [and] through a system of segregation and Jim-Crowism, denies them even the most elementary political rights and relegates them to a position of social pariahs.[26]

As executive secretary of the National Scottsboro Action Committee, Thompson challenged the masculinist terms through which the Left fought this egregious instantiation of national oppression. The sexism of the Communists' "Scottsboro rhetoric," which William Maxwell has illuminated, resulted from their efforts to counter the triangulation of race/gender relations that justified lynching with the formulation that white men were the virile defenders of white feminine virtue against black male rapists.[27] As part of its defense of the Scottsboro boys, the International Labor Defense, the legal arm of the CP, emphasized that the youths' white female accusers were prostitutes in order to discredit their allegations of rape, while calling on Black and white male workers to unite behind the boys. The southern "lynching triangle" was thus countered by a Communist "homosocial triangle trade" whereby Black and white men bonded through negatively libidinizing white women, now portrayed as capitalist whores instead of exemplars of moral and racial purity. In addition to negating white women's radicalism, this rhetoric erased the presence of Black women.

Thompson and other women involved with the Scottsboro campaign contested its masculinist premises of proletarian and race radicalism. While the campaign centered on the eight young men threatened with legal lynching, their mothers were critical to their defense and became Left icons of Black militancy. Although they were frequently represented in traditional maternal roles, their courage and leadership were also played up by the Left press, especially *Working Woman,* the CP's periodical for female industrial, agricultural, and domestic workers.[28] This is evident in Thompson's report on the 1933 march in Washington, D.C., for the Scottsboro boys' release.[29] Thompson drew her readers' attention to the fact that the "vanguard of the marchers" and "living symbol of that increased unity" between the Black and white masses was represented by Scottsboro mother Janie Patterson marching with Ruby Bates, one of the accusers who had recanted her charge of rape. The accompanying photo depicted Thompson herself marching arm in arm with Bates. The text and image in Thompson's story implied that women were redefining the masculinist terms of worker solidarity and Black militancy.

Thompson analyzed Black struggles for social, political, and economic rights in terms of national liberation even as the party downplayed the Black Belt Nation Thesis after the militant Third Period gave way to popular front alliances with bourgeois democratic and imperialist forces in an effort to stem the rising tide of fascism.[30] National liberation informed the Black feminist analysis of party work that Thompson presented to the Central Committee's plenary meeting in 1937. Thompson's speech "Negro Women in Our Party" echoed Maude White's struggle with the Needle Trades Workers' Industrial Union to act on Black women workers' special needs and presaged elements of Claudia Jones's landmark essay, "An End to the Neglect of the Problems of the Negro Woman!" Indeed, Thompson's friendship with White and Jones, and with Esther Cooper Jackson, who prioritized Black women's rights through the Southern Negro Youth Congress, indicates some of the sources and reach of her feminist position. In "Negro Women in Our Party," Thompson reported on a conference where ninety-two official delegates and seventy-five visitors "discussed very frankly and freely all the problems concerning Negro women"—"the first such conference." The event's main outcome, Thompson wrote, was a proposal "that special attention be given to Negro women on the basis of their special problems; that special classes be organized where necessary; that more women be brought into the trade unions, the peace movement, and the Party." Thompson's case for the urgency of this proposal was informed by the Black Belt Nation Thesis: she wrote that without sustained effort to recruit and promote Black women, party "work in the Negro *territories* [was] going to be seriously hampered."[31] Prioritizing autonomous Black struggle enabled Thompson to argue for Black women's special needs and for their ability to lead the fight to address these needs.

Thompson's efforts to advance Black women received institutional support by African American popular front alliances among groups affiliated with the National Negro Congress (NNC) and the Southern Negro Youth Congress (SNYC).[32] Drawing large numbers of Black women into coalitional work, these organizations were ahead of both white-led Left and mainstream Black organizations in assigning leadership positions to Black women, prioritizing their issues, and analyzing the intersections of gender, race, and class.[33] At the NNC's first national meeting in 1936, among the resolutions passed was one "against the special discriminations and exploitation suffered by Negro women."[34] Mary Inman, the CP's leading feminist of the 1930s, was influenced by the NNC's platform and noted the organization's understanding of Black women to be "thrice exploited, as women, as workers, and as Negroes" in her widely read book *In Woman's Defense* (1936).[35] Analysis of this triple exploitation was cogently developed by NNC treasurer Marion Cuthbert in her booklet *Democracy and the Negro* (1936):

> While the fight of Black men for work can be told as part of the story of the gains and retreats of labor as a whole, the story of the Negro woman worker needs to be told as a separate chapter in a dark history. Belonging to the most exploited group in the country, she adds to the exploitation based upon color the exploitation based on sex. Forced to work outside of her home in greater

numbers than any other group in our country, she finds herself at the mercy of the poorest, most labor demanding and dirtiest of industries. Her treatment at the hands of white women who employ her in their homes is often nothing short of scandalous.[36]

An offshoot of the NNC founded in 1937, the SNYC similarly "focused special attention on fighting for the dignity and rights of black women." Acting on the commitment issued in its "Proclamation of Southern Negro Youth" "to improve the status of Negro girls—the future Negro womanhood of the South," the SNYC organized a sit-down strike of mostly Black female tobacco workers in Richmond, Virginia; supported the case of Recy Taylor, an African American woman who had been gang-raped by white men in Alabama; and cultivated grassroots leaders such as Sallye Davis (Angela Davis's mother) and Florence Valentine, an official of the Miami SNYC.[37]

SNYC leaders Louis Burnham and Esther Cooper Jackson took care to frame civil rights and women's rights in an international, anticolonial context. Burnham was influenced by Du Bois's pan-Africanism and by Gandhian resistance, while Jackson's representation of the SNYC at the Soviet-sponsored World Youth Conference in 1945—where she befriended Du Bois and encountered delegates from Africa, Asia, and the Caribbean—moved her to see race and gender in increasingly global terms.[38] As editors of *Freedom* and *Freedomways,* respectively, Burnham and Jackson would continue to play pivotal roles within the post–World War II anticolonial Left and to create responsive venues for its Black internationalist feminism.

▫ ▫ ▫

During and immediately after World War II, the Black anticolonial Left revolved around the Council on African Affairs (CAA), previously the International Committee on African Affairs (ICAA). The ICAA had been founded by two leading African American radicals: Max Yergan, who had spent fifteen years in South Africa as a social worker and missionary before assuming leadership of the NNC, and Paul Robeson, the renowned performer and activist. After the ICAA was reorganized in 1942 with a militant anti-imperialist and anticapitalist orientation as the CAA, two more key figures came on board: pioneering pan-Africanist and civil rights crusader W. E. B. Du Bois and literary scholar and organizer William Alphaeus Hunton, the latter of whom was primarily responsible for making the CAA one of the most important organizations concerned with Africa at the time.

Articulating the CAA's stance, Robeson asserted that "our fight for Negro rights here is linked inseparably with the liberation movements of the people of the Caribbean and Africa and the colonial world in general."[39] In the mid-1940s, this position was shared by "the full range of black American liberals, church leaders, and professional and middle-class organizations" with which the CAA constructed an anticolonial popular front.[40] With the outbreak of World War II, the burgeoning of Third World independence, and the end of formal, direct imperialism, African Americans had adopted an internationalist perspective on movements for democracy and civil rights.

The organ of Harlem's anticolonial popular front in the 1940s was the leftist *People's Voice* (1942–1948), which founder Adam Clayton Powell Jr. once called the "Lenox Avenue edition of the *Daily Worker.*"[41] Yergan assumed co-ownership after Powell was elected to Congress, and Du Bois and Robeson contributed regular columns. The paper thus had strong ties with the CAA and the NNC, and it covered a broad range of issues pertaining to civil rights and anticolonialism. Along with exposing the "domestic fascism" of Jim Crow laws and antilabor and anticommunist elements, the *People's Voice* supported Indian independence and the Chinese Communist Party and (thanks to Du Bois's "Pan Africa" column) featured "some of the most informed writing about the history and contemporary politics of the Belgian Congo, South Africa, Kenya, and Ethiopia."[42] More than the CAA, the *People's Voice* enlisted the skills of African American women writers, editors, and artists—Ann Petry, a reporter and the editor of the women's pages; Fredi Washington, the theatrical columnist; and Marvel Cooke, the assistant managing editor who effectively ran the paper. Negro Women Inc., the community activist group that Petry organized with Audley Moore and other pro-Communist allies, was supported by the paper and met in its office.[43]

Although the 1940s began auspiciously enough for Black anticolonial alliances, they unraveled in just a few years as a result of co-optation and persecution by anticommunist forces set loose by the Truman Doctrine. For the next decade, African American liberals delinked decolonization movements abroad from domestic civil rights struggles and viewed both in terms of the United States' "rightful" leadership of the "free world."[44] Cold War anticommunism's destructive impact on the Black Left ended careers and lives, drastically suspended civil rights, and made exile necessary for a number of radicals.

Yet we must not go too far in assuming that the Black anticolonial Left and its legacy were ultimately extirpated.[45] Radical anticolonialism survived the peak of Cold War persecution due in no small part to Black Left feminists who clarified the stakes of the national question in conjunction with the woman question in the mid-1940s. Their positions on anticolonialism, race, and gender found support within the Left as it broke from the wartime accommodationism espoused by CPUSA general secretary Earl Browder. In a compromise with liberal-bourgeois forces, Browder had abandoned the Black Belt Nation Thesis in 1944 and declared that capital and labor were no longer antagonistic. Responding to a renewed sense of worldwide revolutionary possibilities after the war, the CPUSA reasserted Black people's right to self-determination at the same time that it reaffirmed the importance of women workers—a juncture that critically shaped postwar Black feminism.[46]

After Browder was expelled from the CPUSA and William Z. Foster assumed leadership in 1945, progressive women revived and built on earlier efforts to organize independently, analyze women's oppression, and undertake their strongest work yet on the woman question.[47] Substantial parts of this work were led and carried out by Black women. With lifelong socialist and first-wave feminist Elizabeth Gurley Flynn, Claudia Jones helmed the newly restored Women's Commission, the party's national body responsible for planning and carrying out women's work and for publishing *Woman Today* (the new incarnation of *Working Woman*). Black women affiliated with the NNC, the SNYC, and the National Congress of Negro Women were involved with the Congress of American Women (CAW), the American branch of the antifascist, pro-Soviet Women's International Democratic Federation (WIDF), from the CAW's beginnings.[48] After the WIDF was founded at the International Congress of Women in Paris in 1945, the CAW's global orientation was expressed by African American radical Thelma Dale, who asserted that "the exchange of experience and program with women from the colonial countries, the Soviet Union and many other lands, will help us on our return to make a substantial contribution to democratic developments in the United States," particularly concerning "the up-hill struggle of Negro women in America."[49] In addition to campaigning against segregation and lynching, the CAW took a leading role in defending Rosa Lee Ingram, the Georgia sharecropper who had been sentenced to death with two of her sons for accidentally killing a white farmer who tried to rape her.[50] Left feminism was further spurred by Black women's vulnerability to layoffs from manufacturing jobs after the war; resisting efforts to return Black women workers to service and domestic positions was a key issue for the African American popular front.[51] As a result of Black women's militancy, the party's 1947 platform for women's rights demanded the "full equality of Negro women from segregation, discrimination, intimidation, poll tax, and downgrading in employment" and "election to office in legislative bodies, labor unions, and all public organizations of capable women, Negro and white."[52]

At this same moment in the mid-1940s when Left feminism was flourishing, the salience of the Black Belt Nation Thesis was being reestablished by the party's leading theorist on the woman question, Claudia Jones. The Trinidadian-born Jones had been politicized by the Left, by interwar anticolonialism, and by the African American popular front, all of which raised her awareness of gender oppression as well. Jones came to the CP through the Scottsboro campaign and was involved with the protests of Italy's invasion of Ethiopia: as a writer for a "Negro Nationalist newspaper" from 1935 to 1936, she developed "precis [*sic*] of the main editorial comments on Ethiopia from [the] general commercial press, Negro workers trade union press etc."[53] In a 1955 autobiographical letter to William Z. Foster, Jones related her experience at this paper as a struggle against male chauvinism and indicated how her role in rousing the Harlem masses against imperialism had been suppressed:

> To my amazement, on attending one of their meetings (of the nationalists), I saw my boss reading my precis to the applause and response of thousands of community people in Harlem, men and women. When the next day, he would come in and tell me what a "Big Negro" he was, I would challenge his facts. What he did was to read books on Ethiopia all day and fuse his accumulated knowledge with my precis which were listened to by thousands of people in the mass rallies held by nationalists in Harlem.[54]

Her stint for this paper, to which she also contributed a weekly column, marked the beginning of her lifelong career in radical journalism. In 1936, Jones joined the Young Communist League, within which she quickly assumed a leading position, and the following year she assumed associate editorship of its paper, the *Weekly Review*. Soon thereafter, Jones became involved with the NNC and the SNYC, which, as we have seen, promoted Black women's leadership and fought their triple exploitation as Blacks, women, and workers.

Harry Haywood claims that it was "Jones's discussion article that kicked off a huge debate in the summer of 1945, attacking Browder's ideological and political stand on the Black national question."[55] After Browder abandoned the Black Belt Nation Thesis, the CP had opposed anti-imperialist and anti-racist struggles, such as the Double V campaign the African American press initiated to fight for civil rights at home and democracy abroad, on the grounds that these struggles were detrimental to national unity and the war effort. While Communists Black and white continued to support, participate in, and lead coalitional civil rights groups such as the NNC and the SNYC, the party's official capitulation to imperialist powers caused the desertion or expulsion of such prominent Black members as Richard Wright, George Padmore, and Richard Moore. Jones took advantage of the postwar reversal in Left strategy to launch her attack on "the revisionist class-peace policy advocated by Browder."[56] Jones's bold stance, which was published in the CP's theoretical journal *Political Affairs*, rejuvenated her comrades. Haywood wrote, "I was withdrawn—still reluctant to become involved in the inner-Party struggle. But I had seen an article by Claudia Jones . . . [that] had greatly stimulated my interest."[57] Only months later, Thelma Dale, then executive secretary of the NNC, added her exhortation to Communists to fight for the equal rights of African American workers, troops, veterans, and residents of the Black Belt, while noting that Black women bore the "major brunt of the lay-offs in the present period."[58] Dale concluded by warning of the "serious weakness" caused by the "lack of any fundamental theoretical analysis of the Negro question at the recent national and state conventions."[59] Jones addressed this lack in her January 1946 article, "On the Right to Self-Determination for the Negro People in the Black Belt," which maintained the salience of the Black Belt Nation Thesis for attaining African Americans' full economic, political, and social rights and beyond that, worldwide socialism.[60]

Jones's work on the national question was central to "An End to the Neglect of the Problems of the Negro Woman!" (1949), her article that irrevocably shifted the Left's gender and race politics in the context of postwar advancements on the woman question. Jones's Black feminist intervention—including her claims that women's liberation rested on "the Negro proletarian leadership of the national liberation movement" and that Black women held a rightful place within this leadership—was catalyzed by two events of 1948. That year Betty Millard, a CAW member and an editor of the Communist cultural journal *New Masses*, published "Woman against Myth," a two-part article (subsequently reprinted as a pamphlet) that impelled the party to address gender more complexly. Millard drew on Engels to establish historical materialist bases for women's subordination while challenging economic views that reduced women's oppression to a product of class exploitation and foresaw women's equality as an inevitable outcome of proletarian revolution. Millard argued that it was necessary to analyze the cultural dimensions of women's oppression and to root out male chauvinism both within and outside of the party.

However, Millard's "fail[ure] to address African American women's condition in any meaningful way" was made urgently apparent by the Rosa Lee Ingram case.[61] Ingram was a Black sharecropper and the widowed mother of twelve in Georgia who in 1948 was sentenced to death along with two of her sons by an all-white jury for defending herself from being raped and killed by a white sharecropper. Ingram's plight quickly became a major campaign among Left, Black, and women's organizations, including the CAW, the Sojourners for Truth and Justice, and the Civil Rights Congress. However, male radicals such as Harlem councilman Benjamin Davis and *Daily Worker* writer Harry Raymond elided the intersections of gender and race in their discussions of Ingram. Davis spoke of her as an ungendered representative of "the Negro people," while Raymond compared Ingram to the Scottsboro boys.[62] While there were outstanding similarities between the Scottsboro and Ingram cases that exposed the depth of institutionalized racism's grip on the South, the fact that the former involved young Black men and the latter centered on a Black woman produced key differences that Davis and Raymond suppressed with their references to the "Negro people" and "another Scottsboro."

Both white women who analyzed gender and Black men who analyzed race were unaware the "special oppressed status" of Black women. This lack of awareness is what led Jones to pen "An End to the Neglect of the Problems of the Negro Woman!"[63] Jones did more than simply analogize the Ingram and Scottsboro cases, as Harry Raymond had done. Instead, she foregrounded Ingram's relevance to Black and white women, whose concerns had been ignored or outright suppressed by the Left's anti-lynching Scottsboro rhetoric. Pointing out "the hypocritical alibi of the lynchers of Negro manhood who have historically hidden behind the skirts of white women when they try to cover up their foul crimes" in the name of chivalry, Jones demonstrated that it was in the interests of white women "to challenge this lie and the whole system of Negro oppression." White male paternalism was implicated in a form of national oppression that resulted in the lynching of Black men and in the rape and super-exploitation of Black women. It was "only to the extent that we fight all chauvinist expressions and actions as regards the Negro people and fight for the full equality of the Negro people" that "women as a whole [could] advance their struggle for equal rights"—and "the Negro woman . . . [was] the vital link to this heightened political consciousness."[64]

Because Black women were decisive in the battles against national and gender oppression yet had been neglected by party theory and practice, Jones devoted much of her essay to analyzing Black women's economic and social status. In 1940, Jones pointed out, two of every five Black women worked for a living (as opposed to two of every eight white women) "by virtue of their majority status among the Negro people" and "the low-scale earnings of Negro men." Black women's super-exploitation was manifest in their low wages—"less than half the pay of white women"—and their relegation to the most menial, undercompensated jobs in domestic, agricultural, and nonunionized manufacturing work. This was worsening under the postwar reconversion of the economy, which stripped women of their wartime employment gains in industry (symbolized by iconic figure of "Rosie the Riveter"). Black women suffered the most in this transition: the majority of them were being forced to return not only to their own homes but also to the homes of other women. Domestic service, in addition to being hard labor that was vastly underpaid, revived Black women's dehumanization under slavery by forcing them to seek employment "in virtual 'slave markets' on the streets." Jones linked this exploitation to Western imperialism and fascism through her discussion of legislative proposals in New York to fingerprint domestics, of which she wrote, "here we clearly see the imprint of the African 'pass' system of British imperialism (and of the German Reich in relation to the Jewish people!)."[65]

Jones's dialectical thought and personal experience led her to argue that the onslaught of postwar fascism could only accelerate Black women's militancy. Drawing heavily on Marxist historian Herbert Aptheker, Jones traced the roots of this militancy to the Black mother in African and slave history.[66] According to Jones, African cultural practices of property control and mothering and the denial of legal marriage under slavery led African American women to play a dominant role in their own families and in the community as a whole. In the present, their leadership was evident in the involvement of approximately 2.5 million African American women in clubs and organizations such as the National Association of Negro Women, the National Council of Negro Women, and the National Federation of Women's Clubs. (Jones's own work with the NNC, the CAW, and other groups involved with the Ingram case gave her additional firsthand evidence of Black women's activism.) Jones also reminded her readers that Black women had been crucial to strikes of sharecroppers and tobacco workers and to strikes in the automobile, packing, and steel industries.

Jones argued that the vibrancy and strategic import of Black women's revolutionary struggles made it incumbent on the party to eliminate the lethal combination of male chauvinism and white supremacy. While she acknowledged "the basic need for Marxist-Leninist understanding which our Party gives to all workers, and which enhances their political understanding," she distinguished this guidance from "chauvinist disdain for the organizational talents of new Negro members," which often resulted in "attempts to 'blueprint' them into a pattern." Black women, in other words, were invaluable to the party as Black women. Their "special oppressed status" and experience as mothers, club women, union organizers, and peace activists was precisely what endowed them with their "rightful place in the Negro proletarian leadership of the national liberation movement."[67]

The publication of "An End to the Neglect of the Problems of the Negro Woman!" was instrumental in moving party leaders in the 1950s to recognize Black women's special modes of oppression and resistance and to put them at the center of work on the woman question and the Negro question. The party escalated its efforts to recruit Black women while supporting their struggles through existing women's groups such as the Sojourners for Truth and Justice, the Congress of American Women, and American Women for Peace and through labor organizations including the Hotel and Restaurant Workers Union, the National Trade Union Conference for Negro Rights, the Domestic Workers' Union, and especially the National Negro Labor Council, an important labor organization of the Cold War era that fought for Black women's employment and leadership; the talented African American radical Vicki Garvin was one of its vice presidents. Although these efforts never persuaded large masses of Black women to become Communists, "in the racist and sexist environment of the United States in the 1950s, [the CP] became a center of writing and thought about the experiences of African American women and a source of support for some of their efforts to 'lift' as they 'climbed.'"[68]

Jones continued to make the CP a wellspring of writing and thought about African American women after writing "An End to the Neglect of the Problems of the Negro Woman!" As co-editor with Peggy Dennis of the "Woman Today" section of the Sunday edition of the *Daily Worker,* Jones regularly published articles by and about Black women as part of a 1950 overhaul of the woman's pages in response to readers' demands that the paper replace dress patterns and recipes with articles about the history and political struggles of women. Maude White became a frequent contributor, while Elizabeth Gurley Flynn, Dora Johnson, Jo Willard, and Eugene Feldman also addressed Black women's triple oppression and resistance. Jones herself wrote a column, "Half the World," which covered women's global "fight for peace, equality, security in the home, on the job, in the nation," as its subtitle conveyed.[69] She thus helped engender multiethnic and multinational analyses by feminists of color that addressed Mexican, Puerto Rican, Asian, and Jewish American women from the late 1940s to the mid-1950s.[70]

Meanwhile, Alice Childress and Lloyd Brown were applying the programmatic and theoretical relevance of the nationalist internationalism that Jones had been so crucial to reclaiming to Black cultural workers in the leftist journal *Masses and Mainstream.* Childress's "For a Negro Theatre" (1951) articulated aspects of the nationalist aesthetic that would be developed a decade later by the Black Arts movement. She called for schools that would teach Negro art forms, techniques, and themes arising out of Africa and everyday African American life. At the same time she expressed an internationalist vision for a Negro people's theatre that would draw from Chinese, Japanese, and Russian drama to "create a complete desire for the liberation of all oppressed peoples."[71] Brown's two-part essay "Which Way for the Negro Writer?" (1951) revisited the Black Marxism of Richard Wright's "Blueprint for Negro Writing." Against the false universalism of "'Americanization' as conceived by the American Legion and the Ku Klux Klan, the 'melting pot' where all so-called inferior cultures must be re-molded to conform to the Anglo-Saxon ideal," Brown posed a "true global viewpoint" based on "the great surging sweep of the anti-imperialist forces of the world."[72] This perspective was the basis for "universal art based on a universal theme uniquely expressed" by African Americans as an oppressed nation—"a *people* with special problems and interests common to all that were distinct from other Americans."[73] Brown concluded that "for the Negro writer, the true new direction is that which leads toward his own people and *through* them, *with* them, to the true internationalism which is sweeping the world."[74]

The convergence of nationalist internationalism and cultural radicalism that Childress and Brown championed would be developed in the years to come by African American women writers drawn to the postwar anticolonial Left. These writers built upon the analyses and activism of Maude White, Louise Thompson, Thelma Dale, Claudia Jones, and numerous other Black women radicals who brought nationalism, Marxism, and feminism to bear on each other in the first half of the twentieth century.

▫ ▫ ▫

Major institutions of the Black Left influenced writers' efforts to undo the combined depredations of heteropatriarchy and racist imperialism and to explore the salience of African American women's experiences for social transformation on a global scale. These include Paul Robeson's newspaper *Freedom*, the journal *Freedomways*, the Harlem Writers Guild, and the Cultural Association for Women of African Heritage.

From 1951 to 1955, *Freedom* bravely carried Black internationalism into the escalating Cold War under editor Louis Burnham, former executive secretary of SNYC, and general manager George B. Murphy Jr. In conjunction with covering anticolonial struggles and the civil rights, labor, and peace movements, the newspaper—which shared office space and staff with the

Council on African Affairs—provided lively cultural commentary in the form of interviews with performers such as Ruby Dee; reviews by John O. Killens and Lorraine Hansberry of fiction, plays, and film; and a column by Alice Childress. According to James Smethurst, *Freedom* was "the most visible African American Left cultural institution during the early 1950s."[75]

The staff at *Freedom* was a wealth of Black female leadership and talent. These individuals produced a distinctly protofeminist internationalist orientation that was expressed in an unsigned preface to the story "Women of Nigeria Meet in a Historic National Conference":

> Wherever national liberation movements are on the upswing in colonial lands, women are surging forward to a new position in society. The national consciousness which drives a people to take their destiny into their own hands naturally dictates that women be freed from the fetters imposed on them by feudal and imperialist domination.
>
> Thus women everywhere take their places in the front ranks of the struggle against foreign oppression and for self-determination.[76]

Shirley Graham, who had been instrumental in introducing her husband W. E. B. Du Bois to the Left, served on *Freedom*'s editorial board. Another founding board member was Vicki Garvin, the leading labor organizer who would build Afro-Asian anticolonial solidarities through her extended stays in Ghana and China.[77] Among the paper's contributors were Childress, Dorothy Burnham, and Eslanda Goode Robeson. The staff was additionally blessed with the presence of Thelma Dale, who had been at the vanguard of the African American popular front and the CP's work on women.

These women had an enormous impact on staff member Lorraine Hansberry, whose affiliation with *Freedom* provides a vivid example of how the postwar anticolonial Left supported Black women writers and their development of feminist praxis. Hansberry came to *Freedom* from the University of Wisconsin, where she had joined the CP and chaired the campus campaign for Henry Wallace's presidential bid. Quickly advancing at the paper from subscription clerk, receptionist, typist, and editorial assistant to associate editor, Hansberry covered local, national, and international issues that took her to D.C., Mississippi, and Montevideo, Uruguay. She spoke at rallies and other events, including the Intercontinental Peace Congress in Montevideo on behalf of Robeson while he was barred from international travel. Hansberry's journalism reinforced the conjunctions between Black freedom, Third World national liberation, working-class struggle, and women's rights that *Freedom* regularly represented. Reporting on anti-imperialist women's movements in Egypt, Argentina, China, Korea, Brazil, Kenya, and Jamaica, Hansberry redefined concepts of "the people" and "popular struggle" by placing women at their center.[78]

Alice Childress's cultural politics also found a platform in *Freedom* and contributed to its Black internationalist feminism. Her column, "Conversations from Life," which appeared in the paper more than thirty times from October 1951 to 1955, took the form of a dramatic monologue by the fearless Mildred Johnson, a domestic worker. Addressing her silent interlocutor, Marge, over each other's kitchen tables, Mildred applied her vernacular internationalist feminism to unionization, civil rights, the commodification of femininity, gender roles in the movies, and the links between African American and South African liberation. Consequently, the conversations between Mildred and Marge illustrated how *Freedom*'s politics were lived, or could be lived, by Black working-class women and men in the United States.[79] For example, in "Good Reason for a Good Time," Mildred tells of forming a club with friends over drinks, dancing, and a barbeque. Along with holding teas, parties, and other social events, the club would support Black writers and groups that are "tryin' to make things better for everybody" and sponsor talks about matters of concern around the world, beginning with Africa and the West Indies. In Childress's column, organizing around progressive, pan-Africanist politics was organic to everyday life; not only did the idea for the club come up informally at a party but Mildred recruited Marge over coffee and eggs while recounting her weekend: "Of course, I can get you in, Marge. . . . I particularly want you to join and, of course, whenever we give affairs anybody can come if they'll let us soak them five dollars. . . . Yes, your boyfriend can join too!"[80] The notion that organizing was an activity in which Black women participate was reinforced by the dramatic monologue form, which enlists the reader who assumes Marge's position of addressee/interlocutor through the openings created by the frequent ellipses.

Along with including the reader in her column's implied dialogue between Black women, Childress brought *Freedom*'s issues to bear on readers' lives through creating a "dialogic relationship" between the columns and the other stories in the paper, as Mary Helen Washington notes.[81] This dialogic relationship is vividly realized in the June 1953 African independence issue of *Freedom,* in which Mildred talks about attending a meeting where "someone explained all about African art and sculpture, and they showed us beautiful photographs of the things." As usual, the political stakes of culture are foregrounded; Mildred clarifies that "we didn't get to see any of the real stuff. How could we when it's all in the British Museum?" However, the end to this cultural imperialism appears imminent, for Mildred learns that "South Africans are breakin' the Jim Crow laws! . . . Just like if you was to walk in a Mississippi waitin' room, tear down the 'white' sign and sit yourself down!" The column ends with Mildred berating the Western speakers for equivocating on what Africans want: "All of a sudden I jumped straight up and hollered, '*There ain't no mystery about that! Africans want to be free!*'"[82] In the context of the column's internationalist feminism linking civil rights struggles to the anti-apartheid movement, this was a declaration of African American independence—"Just like if you was to walk in a Mississippi waitin' room, tear down the 'white' sign"—and an instantiation of Black female militancy. Childress's column thus complemented the surrounding articles on African art and culture, the map explaining the continent's history of colonialism, and an essay profiling African independence leaders entitled "Let Africans Speak for Africa!" by depicting these issues as ones of deep concern to the masses of working Black women in the United States.

To be sure, Mildred's militancy represented an ideal, but Childress's dramatic work from this period revealed that this character was by no means exceptional or wholly romanticized. As in Hansberry's reportage, the courage and resistance of non-elite Black women was a central theme of two historical revues written by Childress, a leading playwright of the Black Left as well as an accomplished actress who connected *Freedom* with the left-wing Committee for the Negro in the Arts (CNA). Childress's CNA-sponsored *Gold Through the Trees* (1952) presented a diasporic panorama of Black history connecting the enslavement of Africans, the Haitian Revolution, slavery in the United States, anticolonialism in the British West Indies, and the 1950s African National Congress's Defiance Campaign against Unjust Laws (for which *Gold Through the Trees* raised funds).[83] As Hansberry recounted in her review of the drama for *Freedom,* Childress portrayed the struggles of female slaves, peasants, and workers through sketches involving Harriet Tubman giving succor to "a young girl whose hands are bruised and weary from the hard work needed to raise money for the abolitionist movement" and a Haitian market woman (played by Childress) who, "between shouting out her wares for sale, brings news and materials for the Haitian rebellion led by 'Father Toussaint.'"[84] The revue's South African scene showed how the freedom fighters who started the Defiance Campaign came from the masses living in tar-paper shacks; the revolutionaries tellingly consist of one man and two women who agree that "we want all the women to go forward with [the campaign,] for what could we do without them? . . . We would be lost . . . for we know that those who give life can defend it the strongest."[85] This point is underscored by the narrator, another woman, who names and commemorates several of these women who engaged in civil disobedience. The same year that *Gold Through the Trees* was produced, Childress collaborated with Hansberry on another revue to celebrate Negro History Week in tandem with *Freedom*'s first anniversary. This dramatic event similarly presented a history from below that emphasized Black women's militancy and concluded triumphantly with the activism of the Sojourners for Truth and Justice, the civil rights and peace group made up of African American women that Claudia Jones hailed as "one of the most heartening developments of the Negro liberation movement."[86]

The internationalist feminism that *Freedom* fostered was supported by its successor, *Freedomways* (1961–1986), which carried on the work of covering the U.S. civil rights movement, liberation movements around the world, and developments in Black culture for domestic readers and international audiences in Africa, the Caribbean, Canada, Australia, and England, and throughout Asia and Latin America.[87] The magazine's global vision can be traced to the work of its founders and editorial board members for *Freedom* and within the CAA (Shirley Graham, *Freedomways*' first general editor; Dorothy and Louis Burnham; Alphaeus Hunton; George B. Murphy; John O. Killens) and/or in the SNYC (Esther Cooper Jackson, Augusta Strong, the Burnhams). In addition, Graham, Hunton, and novelist Julian Mayfield connected *Freedomways* to Africa and Black American expatriates in Ghana. Graham in particular kept in touch with *Freedomways*' editors and facilitated their access to African political and cultural figures such as Tom Mboya of Kenya, Oliver Tambo of South Africa, Julius Nyerere of Tanzania, and Leopold Senghor of Senegal.[88]

Although *Freedomways*' mission statement in its first editorial did not specifically address women's issues, the journal functioned, in Erik McDuffie's words, as "an important but often overlooked 'parent' of modern black feminism."[89] This was due in no small part to the fact that Esther Cooper Jackson served as the journal's managing editor through nearly its entire twenty-five year existence. As SNYC's executive secretary from 1942 to 1946, Jackson had been one of the many remarkable Black female leaders to emerge from the African American popular front. Under her guidance, *Freedomways* published and reviewed the work of veteran Black women radicals (Graham, Eslanda Robeson, Maude White, Louise Thompson), their political daughters on the anticolonial Left (Rosa Guy, Sarah E. Wright, Lorraine Hansberry, Paule Marshall, Jean Carey Bond), women of the Black Arts Movement (Mari Evans, Nikki Giovanni, Sonia Sanchez), the pioneers of the second renaissance of

African American literature (Audre Lorde, Alice Walker, Barbara Smith, Toni Morrison, June Jordan), and Marxist feminist revolutionary Angela Davis. As I show in the introduction, *Freedomways* ushered the legacy of Black internationalist feminism into the 1970s and critically responded to literary developments in the contemporary Black women's movement.

Another significant institution for African American women writers of the anticolonial Left was the Harlem Writers Guild, founded in 1950 by novelists Rosa Guy and John Oliver Killens and historian John Henrik Clarke, all of whom met through the Committee for the Negro in the Arts. The Harlem Writers Guild was crucial to engendering the second renaissance of African American literature and of African American women's literature in particular. Among those who participated in Guild workshops and events were Sarah Wright, Paule Marshall, Maya Angelou, Julian Mayfield, Alice Childress, Ossie Davis, Lonnie Elder, Louise Meriwether, Richard Moore, Audre Lorde, Toni Cade Bambara, and Terry McMillan. (Guy has claimed that over half of all African American writers were associated with the Harlem Writers Guild between 1950 and 1970.)[90] Many critically acclaimed novels by African American writers passed through Guild workshops, where they met, in Sarah Wright's words, "the searing judgment of [their] peers, merciless in [their] demand for truth, but supportive of every sign of talent," including Killens's *Youngblood* and *And Then We Heard the Thunder,* Angelou's *I Know Why the Caged Bird Sings,* Elder's *Ceremonies in Dark Old Men,* Guy's *Bird at My Window,* Wright's *This Child's Gonna Live,* and Meriwether's *Daddy Was a Number Runner.*[91] With the New School for Social Research, the Harlem Writers Guild co-sponsored a 1965 conference, "The Negro Writer's Vision of America," a highlight of which was the panel "The Negro Woman in American Literature." At this event that heralded the rise of contemporary African American women's literature, Alice Childress, Paule Marshall, and Sarah Wright presciently criticized the degrading representations of Black women in literature and popular culture and condemned the predication of the recovery of Black manhood upon the scapegoating of Black women. The Harlem Writers Guild further promoted feminist cultural critique by throwing a book party for Toni Cade Bambara's landmark anthology, *The Black Woman* (1970), which featured several Guild members, including Bambara herself.

Complementing its literary concerns, the Harlem Writers Guild fostered what Guy characterizes as "a broad understanding of what was happening in the world in terms of the exploitation of black countries and the relationship of such exploitation to the plight of blacks in the United States."[92] Workshops were clearinghouses for news and actions of relevance to the anticolonial Left: sit-ins in the U.S. South; Southern Christian Leadership Conference fund-raisers; Malcolm X's latest speech; freedom struggles in South Africa, the Congo, Angola, and Mozambique; and the first delegation of artists to revolutionary Cuba sponsored by the Fair Play for Cuba Committee, whose membership heavily overlapped with that of the Guild. (In addition to Harold Cruse, Robert Williams, and LeRoi Jones, Guild members Julian Mayfield and Sarah Wright took the trip. Killens, Childress, and Langston Hughes, who had contributed to an issue on "Los Negros en USA" for the Cuban cultural magazine *Lunes de Revolucion,* had been invited but declined.)[93]

Guild co-founder Rosa Guy was also a driving force, with Maya Angelou and singer Abbey Lincoln, within the Cultural Association for Women of African Heritage, which organized artists and entertainers in support of civil rights. Angelou paraphrases CAWAH's charter thus: "Since the entire power of the United States was arrayed in fury against the very existence of the Afro-Americans, we, members of CAWAH, would offer ourselves to raise money for, promote and publicize any gathering sincerely engaged in developing a just society."[94] Most notably, CAWAH instigated an event that became pivotal in the revival of Black nationalist consciousness in the United States, the 1961 demonstration at the United Nations to protest the CIA-sponsored assassination of Patrice Lumumba, the first elected prime minister of the Congo. Bringing future Black Power/Black Arts activists together with the older anticolonial Left, the demonstration led Sarah Wright and fellow novelist and Harlem Writers Guild member Calvin Hicks to form On Guard for Freedom to solidify the coalition.[95]

In his assessment of "the new Afro-American Nationalism" that resulted from the protest of Lumumba's assassination, John Henrik Clarke downplayed CAWAH's role and used masculinist terms to eulogize Lumumba as "the symbol of the black man's humanity struggling for recognition."[96] Recent accounts of Black radicalism have similarly relegated CAWAH organizers to the status of participants instead of acknowledging their leadership.[97] However, the women instrumental in fomenting the demonstration understood themselves to be leading Black men—and women—into more expansive forms of revolutionary consciousness. As late as 1988, Rosa Guy and Maya Angelou insisted on their place at the forefront of this change:

> R.G.: It was really a fantastic demonstration. Also, it was a turning point, I feel, even though Malcolm X did not come with us. Malcolm was a fantastic person, I believe, because he was in the process of growth. . . .

M.A.: He certainly changed. And it was wonderful to see it and to be a part of the time in which one could see that kind of growth, and to know it is possible, is encouraging as well. I look at some of the men of the time and think of how they grew. . . .

R.G.: Would you say they grew because of us? We sort of forced it on them. Because everyone was sitting back. . . .

M.A.: Yes, us, but us in a very large way because while we happened to be in New York and close to media, there were young men and women at the time who were doing some pretty brave things in other parts of the country.

R.G.: Not at that time. Not at that particular time. After. Because one of the things that we saw very clearly at that point: everybody was upset by the death of Patrice Lumumba. Young people in Central America were protesting. Students in Africa, in Europe, in China, but not one in the U.S. After our demonstrations there was a ground swell of students in the United States coming out in support.

M.A.: That's true. I hadn't thought about that. The Civil Rights Movement in this country was very active and very inspirational, but was really focused on American civil rights.

R.G.: After we demonstrated a group of young students came in from Boston. I remember that particularly. *Freedomways* was being launched. Its reception was given at the home of Du Bois. I met the Boston group outside and they said "You are Rosa Guy!" To them I was a heroine. Really. I mean, they could have put me on their shoulders.

M.A.: They almost did that with us in Harlem everytime we'd go.[98]

As this exchange indicates, the organizational efforts of African American women writers, although often underappreciated and forgotten, enabled postwar Black anticolonialism to survive the ravages of the Cold War and inspire a new generation of activists and artists. Importantly, Guy and Angelou saw themselves as heroically leading the challenge to the liberal U.S.-centered paradigms that had constrained the civil rights movement for the past decade and "forcing" the men of the time, such as Malcolm X, to grow. Such militancy emerged from the long-standing tradition I have delineated of African American women who, beginning in the interwar period, were radicalized by Left nationalism and its internationalist trajectories and retheorized these two political strands around Black women's "special oppressed status."

The chapters that follow turn to the literary efforts of Black women on the Left to think through sexuality as well as gender, subjectivity as well as politics, in order to expand the emancipatory potential of nationalist internationalism. The semi-autonomous realm of literature gave African American women writers a means of developing internationalist feminism in directions that were discouraged if not explicitly prohibited by Black Left institutions. In particular, the creative work of Black Left women writers undermines heteronormativity in ways that could not be attempted through their organizational work. While this queer perspective did not inform the literary writing of all women affiliated with the postwar Black Left, it is significant that the creative output of four of the authors I study—Hansberry, Childress, Guy, and Lorde—was concerned, often centrally, with the mutual imbrications of heteronormativity, patriarchy, and imperialism. These writers represented the everyday lives of lesbians and gay men, transgendered people, and heterosexual Blacks as relevant to and transformative of internationalist projects in ways that disturbed the very categories of race, gender, and sexuality leading to their marginalization. Such political aesthetics entailed the revision of established forms and conventions that exerted generic pressures to conform to hegemonic (and even counterhegemonic) ideologies and expectations with respect to marriage, individual triumph, masculine heroism, and feminine effacement. Consequently, the work of African American women writers of the postwar anticolonial Left is crucial to theorizing feminist and queer of color critique and to appreciating the scope and genealogy of contemporary African American women's literature.

2

Lorraine Hansberry's Existentialist Routes to Black Internationalist Feminism

Soon after arriving in Harlem, Lorraine Hansberry began writing for Paul Robeson's anti-imperialist and anticapitalist newspaper *Freedom.* With offices in the same building as the Council on African Affairs, the most visible anticolonial organization in the first years after World War II, *Freedom* put Hansberry in the midst of a vibrant Black Left network that included Robeson, W. E. B. Du Bois, Louis Burnham, Shirley Graham Du Bois, and Alice Childress.[1] For *Freedom,* Hansberry covered the outrage of African and Asian attendees at a World Assembly of Youth convention marred by paternalism; the trip to Washington, D.C., the Sojourners for Truth and Justice, a group of Black women activists, made to demand world peace and social justice; the jailing of Labor Youth League secretary Roosevelt Ward; Kwame Nkrumah's election as prime minister of the Gold Coast (soon to be Ghana); anticolonial struggles waged by Egyptians and Kenyan Kikuyus; the Intercontinental Peace Congress that brought North and South Americans together against "Yanqui Imperialismo"; and the murder of an African American graduate student who demanded that white students take down the image of a Black woman used as a dart target at a university fund-raiser. The range of Hansberry's articles alone speaks to the postwar Black Left's internationalist understanding of the linkage between Third World movements for national liberation and domestic antiracist and civil rights struggles, a point Hansberry's report on Nkrumah's political victory reiterated:

> The promise of the future of Ghana is that of all the colored peoples of the world; it is the promise of freedom.

> The people of Ghana clearly see their struggles and victories in connection with black folk on the rest of their continent as well as in the United States. A U.S. Negro reporter for the Pittsburgh *Courier* commented not long ago: "Whenever I make an interview in Accra it is a two-sided affair. I ask questions about events in the Gold Coast and they ply me with questions about the Willie McGee case, the Cicero, Illinois riot, Dr. Ralph Bunche and topics American Negroes are discussing today.[2]

The internationalism of the Black Left, and the *Freedom* group in particular, crucially shaped Hansberry's gender and sexual politics. Although the paper was not explicitly devoted to women's issues, key staff and contributors were at the vanguard of advancing Black women's concerns within progressive circles, and the paper regularly covered African American and Third World women's militancy. Through *Freedom,* Hansberry was exposed to the Black internationalist feminism of actress and playwright Alice Childress, leading popular front and women's rights organizer Thelma Dale, and the Sojourners for Truth and Justice. Reporting on anti-imperialist women's movements in Egypt, Kenya, China, Korea, Brazil, Argentina, and Jamaica, Hansberry redefined concepts of "the people" and "popular struggle" by placing women at the center of them: a caption likely written by Hansberry for a photo accompanying her article "Egyptian People Fight for Freedom" stated, "This young Egyptian woman is a member of her people's 'Liberation Battalions' organized to wrest Egyptian soil from foreign interests. She symbolizes the Egyptian people's part in the spirit of liberation that is sweeping all Africa. Along with their activity in the national liberation struggle, Egyptian women are fighting for their right to vote and hold public office." Demonstrating that anticolonialism gives rise to and entails struggles for gender equality, Hansberry located the Third World roots of the women's movement in Egypt, "the traditional Islamic 'cradle of civilization,' where women had led one of the most important fights anywhere for the equality of their sex."[3]

Within this milieu Hansberry also wrote a review panning Richard Wright's novel *The Outsider* (1953). Asserting that Wright's protagonist, Cross Damon, "is someone you will never meet on the Southside of Chicago or in Harlem" and that "Wright has been away from home a long time," Hansberry reiterated wider critical views that the exilic Wright had applied foreign, inauthentic existentialist ideas to the Black American experience, with aesthetically and politically disastrous results. Hansberry concludes, "He exalts brutality and nothingness; he negates the reality of our struggle for freedom and yet works energetically in behalf of our oppressors; he has lost his own dignity and destroyed his talent."[4]

Paul Gilroy questions such dismissals of Wright's existentialism, which "have generally preferred to stay within the boundaries of nationality and ethnicity and have shown little enthusiasm for connecting the life of one movement with that of another. What would it mean to read Wright intertextually with Genet, Beauvoir, Sartre, and the other Parisians with whom he was in dialogue?"[5] A version of Gilroy's question about Wright must be asked with regard to Hansberry, given her involvement with the Black anticolonial Left, her sustained engagement with different strands of postwar European and American existentialism, and the intertwining of these two political and intellectual commitments in her Black internationalist feminism.

Hansberry's review of *The Outsider,* in other words, is a key to understanding the intersections of feminist, queer, and anticolonial thought as they developed throughout her artistic and political career. At *Freedom,* Hansberry's global coverage of women's movements expanded Black internationalist discourses linking African Americans to nations of color. After leaving *Freedom* to focus on playwriting, Hansberry's Black internationalist feminism evolved to explore lesbian desire as a site for undoing the intertwining of militarization, U.S. Cold War nationalism, and heteropatriarchy. The play that is the culmination of Hansberry's dramatic vision of internationalism, *Les Blancs,* is a feminist and queer exploration of African national liberation.

The intersections of Hansberry's anticolonial nationalism, feminism, and queer politics have generally been missed, ignored, or undertheorized.[6] For example, Lisbeth Lipari asserts, "that Hansberry thought intersectionally [was] evident in all her writings" but then argues incorrectly that after her 1957 letters to the lesbian periodical *The Ladder,* "Hansberry never again publicly returned to issues of sexuality and sexism, focusing her remaining time and energy instead on the increasingly pressing battles against racism." Several aspects of Lipari's claim are troubling: If Hansberry was publicly devoted to battling racism but not sexism, this would not be "intersectional" work. And given that Hansberry *did* return publicly in her later work to issues of sexuality and its articulation of and by race, how is it that Lipari, a scholar concerned with Hansberry's "vital lesbian political ethos," can miss this in her plays?[7] Hansberry's feminism is also elided in Fanon Che Wilkins's study of her "critical nationalism," which demonstrates that Black anticolonialism survived McCarthy-era persecution but does not engage with gender and sexuality.[8]

The nuances of Hansberry's Black internationalist feminism are illuminated by her sustained engagements with existentialism. The depth and range of Hansberry's investment in existentialist thought and literature is much greater than current scholarship acknowledges in its discussion of her critique of absurdism.[9] For Hansberry, existentialism encoded, politicized, and dramatized racial and sexual identities (because Jean Genet and Norman Mailer represented Blacks, gays, and prostitutes who exposed the falsities upon which modern life was scaffolded) but it denied the historical material conditions that gave rise to both oppression and social change. In confronting the impasses of Genet's and Mailer's influential views, Hansberry found Simone de Beauvoir's existentialist feminism integral to rearticulating the meanings of and relationships between sexual, racial, and national liberation.

Hansberry's review of Wright, then, was only an early salvo in an argument with the work of Genet and Mailer as well as that of Albert Camus, Samuel Beckett, and Edward Albee over human existence, responsibility, and freedom. While these writers and thinkers presented diverse, even incommensurable world views, Hansberry understood them to be linked by an intellectually, politically, and morally bankrupt nihilism and solipsism.[10] Rather than leading to freedom, their view of the modern condition led to despair, apathy, or undirected anger. Hansberry willingly conceded that playwrights could not deny "the tenacity of the absurd in both human and natural affairs," which often confronted one with the senselessness of one's actions. Nonetheless, Hansberry insisted, "attention must be paid in equal and careful measure to the frequent triumph of man, if not nature, *over* the absurd. Perhaps it is here that certain of the modern existentialists have erred."[11]

This faith in human triumph over the absurd had become, as Hansberry put it, "the accoutrement of the most outlandish, utter 'square.'"[12] Whether or not Hansberry was square was undeniably a question in a *Village Voice* exchange among Hansberry, Norman Mailer, and avant-garde filmmaker Jonas Mekas over Jean Genet's acclaimed absurdist play *The Blacks*.[13] In response to Hansberry's indictment of what she called the "new paternalism" of Genet and Mailer, Mekas wrote,

> Mailer makes mistakes, yes, but his search comes from an inescapable Existential need (no cheap term), a need that is a matter of life or death to man and society today: not to the Negro man or the white man, but, simply, all men. . . . If Jean Genet, with all his pyrotechnics of decadence, sums up the present civilization of Europe, so Norman Mailer with all his Dostoevskian compassion sums up the new man of America.

> If Miss Hansberry rejects the compassion and anxiety of the most sincere and most intelligent (in the truest sense) of her contemporaries, she has to re-evaluate, rethink for herself. She is in danger of being left alone in a white suburban house, with all those nice neighbors (they will be really nice by then).[14]

The persistent aspirations and hard-won moral victories of the Younger family, poised at the end of Hansberry's *A Raisin in the Sun* to move out of their tenement into a house, are reduced here to assimilation into the spiritual and political wasteland of the white bourgeoisie. By contrast, *The Blacks*, with its exploration of power's tendency to corrupt within the context of African decolonization, spoke to the anomie and anxieties of Cold War life under the threats of totalitarianism and mass annihilation.

The Blacks' importance to the cultural moment was evidenced further within African American cultural politics after the U.S. production commenced in 1961. The first U.S. cast of *The Blacks* featured an array of dramatic talent that included James Earl Jones, Roscoe Lee Brown, Louis Gossett, Cicely Tyson, Godfrey Cambridge, Maya Angelou, and Abbey Lincoln, many of whom were friends and associates of Hansberry (Gossett had just appeared in *Raisin*; Jones would later play the protagonist of *Les Blancs*).[15] *The Blacks* also drew numerous race radicals into its orbit: in addition to Angelou and Lincoln, the play's music was composed by jazz percussionist and Black militant Max Roach, and Ossie Davis and James Baldwin served as informal advisors who attended rehearsals and conducted cast meetings. (Baldwin had gotten to know Genet in France.)

The involvement of so many leading Black artists and intellectuals with Genet's play heightened their fierce debates over it. These debates centered on two related issues: the play's suggestion that power universally corrupts, regardless of the race of those in power; and the effectiveness of the play's exposure of white racism. *The Blacks* was criticized on these counts in a symposium on "The Negro Writer in America," which raised the question of why "the [white] hordes keep coming on to be insulted" by Black actors. John O. Killens argued that the idea of Blacks coming to power and oppressing whites—a notion that Amiri Baraka derided as "the master's lie" in a different discussion of the play—let "white people a little off the hook."[16] Ossie Davis contended that white audiences watched *The Blacks* "to be exposed to [racial hostility] in the safest possible fashion."[17] Davis's claim finds support in Maya Angelou's autobiography, which concludes its chapter about performing *The Blacks* by describing Angelou's encounter with a white woman who expresses support and comprehension of the play but recoils when Angelou pointedly asks, "Would you take me home with you? Would you become my friend?" The white woman's negative response leads Angelou to inform her, "You can accept the insults if I am a character on stage, but not in person."[18]

At the same time, a range of Black leftists, nationalists, and liberals lauded Genet's play. As cast and audience members, many African Americans appreciated the play's expression of Black anger at a time when formal civil rights could not eradicate white supremacist violence and racial inequities. The actors, who were allowed to ad lib, referred to the 1955 lynching of Emmett Till and the 1963 Birmingham church bombing, as when James Earl Jones substituted the line, "Four little girls who died in a Birmingham church" for the line "One hundred thousand youngsters who died in the dust."[19] Jones admired Genet's conscience and the relevance of the play to the civil rights struggle, and according to Angelou, Max Roach passionately believed that "Genet understood the nature of imperialism and colonialism and how those two evils erode the natural good in people."[20] Angelou's husband at the time, South African revolutionary Vusumzi Make, was impressed by Genet's insight into the nature of power, a view shared by Roscoe Lee Brown, who in a retrospective panel on *The Blacks* noted the play's prescience given the failures of African political leadership.[21] And on a pragmatic level, *The Blacks* was welcomed for its serious, high-profile roles at a time when these were few and far between for African American actors.

Hansberry, however, stood with those who decried *The Blacks*' cynical view of national liberation, and this critique ultimately framed her own play about African anti-colonialism, *Les Blancs.*[22] African liberation had become a passion for Hansberry under the influence of her uncle, Leo Hansberry, a pioneering Africanist at Howard University. Her education continued with her immersion in the Black Left associated with the CAA and *Freedom,* when she studied with Du Bois. This trajectory led Hansberry to believe, in her words, that "the ultimate destiny and aspirations of the African people and twenty million American Negroes are inextricably and magnificently bound up together forever."[23]

Hansberry gave dramatic form to this claim in her first produced play, the internationally successful *A Raisin in the Sun* (1959). While most audiences missed its radical pan-Africanism, one viewer who picked up on it was the FBI agent assigned to "review" *Raisin.* Of all the characters in the play, it is Asagai, the Nigerian anti-colonial intellectual, who receives the most attention in the agent's report. In the late 1950s, Africa was being prioritized within the

Eisenhower administration: a new Bureau of African Affairs was established, and the United States for the first time voted for a UN resolution condemning South African apartheid.[24] The FBI review of *Raisin* acknowledges Africa's increasing role within the Cold War global arena; dispassionately and without overt commentary, the review summarizes Asagai's lines and actions, focusing especially on his desire "to educate himself so that he can return to teach and raise the level of the people of his village" so they can "overthrow the rule of European nations, find political freedom, improve themselves economically and educationally, and make their own future." Despite the radicalism of these ideas, the agent saw no cause for concern, since "relatively few [in the audience] appeared to dwell on the propaganda messages."[25] Yet the disparity between the attention the FBI devoted to Asagai and the fact that the character appears in far fewer scenes than Ruth, Walter, and Beneatha Younger suggests how much Asagai's vision mattered to the state.

These anticolonial, pan-African strands in *Raisin* became the focal point of *Les Blancs,* which, according to Robert Nemiroff, her literary collaborator and former husband, Hansberry considered "potentially her most important play."[26] In the last five years of her life, Hansberry worked on *Les Blancs* concurrently with several other plays, including *The Sign in Sidney Brustein's Window*; a play about Toussaint L'Ouverture; and a teleplay, *What Use Are Flowers?,* a response to Samuel Beckett's *Waiting for Godot.* These works reveal confluences between Hansberry's internationalist vision of Black liberation (the Toussaint play; *Les Blancs*), and her concern that existentialism would fuel the Cold War backlash against diverse forms of liberatory politics (*What Use Are Flowers?*; *Sidney Brustein*; *Les Blancs*). This confluence attains special clarity in the epigraphs Hansberry used in *Les Blancs.* She paired Genet's epigraph from *The Blacks* ("But what exactly is a black? / First of all, what's his color?") with an excerpt from Frederick Douglass's 1857 speech "The Significance of Emancipation in the West Indies"—including its oft-quoted line, "If there is no struggle, there is no progress"—which underscored the significance of West Indian slave revolt to Americans slave and free. *Les Blancs* illuminates the significance of African national liberation to Americans Black and white and examines the implications of Genet's existentialism in fighting (neo)imperialism.

Hansberry situated the political stakes of existentialism within a transnational cultural context in a *Village Voice* essay on *The Blacks*:

> At this moment, on both sides of the Atlantic, certain of the best of men have sent up a lament which is much concerned with the disorders of a civilization

> which they do not really believe in their hearts are to be set aright by invocation of either fresh "frontiers" or antique "*grandeur.*" Sensing the source of the disorders to be deeper than any of that, they have willfully turned to the traditional route of history's more serious nay-sayers. They have elected the spirit and fraternity of what the balance of society is always pleased to hope are "the damned": prostitutes, pimps, thieves, and general down-and-outers of whatever persuasion.[27]

Hansberry proceeded to trace the romanticizing of Blacks in particular to Norman Mailer's infamous essay "The White Negro: Superficial Reflections on the Hipster" (1957). Here Mailer celebrated the (straight, white male) hipster who affirms life in a death-ridden world through having "absorbed the existentialist synapses of the Negro," the exemplary psychopathic personality incapable of restraining his violence or need for erotic gratification.[28] As James Baldwin saw it, Mailer turned the Negro into a "walking phallic symbol" who "pays, in [his] own personality, for the sexual insecurity of others."[29]

Thus, despite claims of fraternity with "general down-and-outers of whatever persuasion," existentialist writers made of them inferior objectified Others—projections of white, male Selves. Their constructions of Blackness, Hansberry wrote, emerge from "the anticipations of white men" who "shall be disappointed if the blacks really do give more attention to building steel mills and hydroelectric plants throughout Africa than to slitting a few hundred thousand criminal throats."[30] Referring to the Volta River project Nkrumah championed as a symbol of independent Ghana's development, Hansberry argued that the racist existentialist fantasies of whites denied the historical and material progress Blacks had made.

This racial as well as sexual Othering manifested the solipsism that Hansberry identified as a key weakness in existentialist thought. In *The Blacks,* this solipsism precludes communication and solidarity across boundaries of race, nationality, gender, sexuality, and class. As one of Genet's "Blacks" tells the white audience, "We shall even have the decency—a decency learned from you—to make communication impossible."[31] This obstruction and denial of communication was an affront to Hansberry's commitment to nonseparatist, non-exclusionary forms of identity politics that sought to bring about the transformative social change exemplified by African independence and modernization.

Yet even in her unwavering criticism of existentialism, Hansberry did not dismiss it: she was strongly influenced by the existentialist feminism of Simone de Beauvoir's *The Second Sex,* which she called a "*great* book" that might "very well be the most important work of this century."[32] When its first English translation was published in 1953, she devoted "months of study" to it before "placing it in the most available spot on her 'reference' shelf."[33] Her essay "Simone de Beauvoir and *The Second Sex*: An American Commentary" (1957) reveals that this book presented Hansberry with a world view that countered the solipsism that marred Wright's novel and that Hansberry would continue to attack in the work of Mailer and absurdist playwrights such as Genet and Edward Albee. As Sonia Kruks asserts, *The Second Sex* built upon insights from de Beauvoir's earlier works that "link[ed] Sartre's individualistic existentialism with their shared commitment to the egalitarian and solidaristic values of socialism."[34]

By discussing two early feminist plays by Hansberry in tandem with her essay on *The Second Sex,* I will clarify how de Beauvoir helped Hansberry interrogate dominant views of tragic lesbians, represent lesbianism as an existential choice, and critique heteropatriarchal norms. Furthermore, I argue, Hansberry took note of de Beauvoir's analysis of lesbianism as a site of reciprocal recognition that transcends individualism and solipsism. Studying the influence of Beauvoirean existentialism on Hansberry is thus crucial to interpreting Nemiroff's assertion that Hansberry's homosexuality "was not a peripheral or casual part of her life but contributed significantly on many levels to the sensitivity and complexity of her view of human beings and of the world."[35]

Hansberry's later work, including and following *Raisin,* muted the feminism of her earlier work, as she replaced the female protagonists she had originally planned for *The Sign in Sidney Brustein's Window* and *Les Blancs* with male ones. Hansberry continued to explore homosexuality in these plays, but she now created gay male instead of lesbian characters. These changes in Hansberry's work can be seen as forms of silencing and self-censorship, as Adrienne Rich has claimed.[36] I do not discount the weight of sexism and homophobia, especially as they combined with the racism and anti-Communism of the 1950s and 1960s.[37] Nonetheless, we can also read Hansberry's "substitution" of women with men, including lesbians with gay males, as a strategy or opening through which she continued to develop an emancipatory political aesthetics committed to critiquing heteropatriarchy in conjunction with racialized imperialism and capitalism. From this perspective, we can perceive continuities with as well as differences between her earlier and later work.

This approach illuminates the anticolonial diasporic vision of *Les Blancs,* which is informed by Hansberry's debate with the racialized, sexual politics of existentialist thought. In repudiating existentialist solipsism and nihilism, Hansberry dramatized the ideas of reciprocal recognition that her study of de Beauvoir had helped her develop. Furthermore, *Les Blancs* enacts a critique of heteropatriarchy in conjunction with imperialism that Hansberry had sharpened in her earlier, feminist plays and in her reportage for *Freedom.*

▫ ▫ ▫

In 1955 Hansberry completed two feminist plays clearly influenced by de Beauvoir's discussion of woman as the Other through whom the male subject transcends himself but also as an "existent" in her own right seeking freedom. The first of these plays to be finished, "The Apples of Autumn," is a somewhat unwieldy depiction of the trials confronting young modern women, including sexual harassment, limited career options, and impotent forms of revolt that impede self-actualization.[38] In her notes to this play, Hansberry borrows liberally from de Beauvoir to describe the patriarchal social order that constitutes the situations of her female characters. Paraphrasing de Beauvoir's discussion of man's myth of woman—in de Beauvoir's words, a "representation of the world . . . which [men] confuse with absolute truth"—Hansberry writes,

> Women's body is [an] object or commodity to be appraised, studied, purchased with gift or marriage. Her mind is the source of witchcraft, "contrariness," gossip, mother wit, intuition and seduction, or so say the myths of male supremacist ideology. And thus, man being subject, being the source of all human values, so says the same myth, is befuddled, conjured, and at war with this creature. Thus, she is "the Other" in life; thus she is something short of a human being.[39]

Tellingly, Hansberry first raises de Beauvoir's existentialist feminism in these notes with respect to the play's lesbian character, Connie. Here Hansberry draws on the groundbreaking definition of lesbianism in *The Second Sex,* which interprets it as a "choice, arrived at in a complex total situation and based upon a free decision."[40] Consequently, de Beauvoir asserts,

> Like all human behavior, homosexuality leads to make-believe, disequilibrium, frustration, lies, or, on the contrary, it becomes the source of rewarding experiences, in accordance with its manner of expression in actual living—whether in bad faith, laziness, and falsity; or in lucidity, generosity, and freedom.[41]

Along these lines, Connie, "in the words of Simone de Beauvoir, has had . . . the concept of 'the Other' imposed on her since childhood," and as "a woman of special sensitivities, [she] has rebelled" by becoming a lesbian.[42]

While impressed by de Beauvoir's analysis of lesbianism, Hansberry ultimately portrayed it in "The Apples of Autumn" as a limited, even perverse rebellion compared to the authenticity of the straight protagonist's self-realization. Lesbianism, Hansberry writes in her notes to the play, is a "social problem" comparable to "alcoholism or dope addiction or prostitution or any number of things" that show how "the brutality of our lives can hammer perfectly good decent human beings . . . into the depths of degradation." Although Hansberry claimed that she "did not want ["Apples"] to become a play about homosexuality," its negative depiction of that topic is hardly incidental. If Connie is the "device for Julie's resolution" that Hansberry wanted her to be, it is because Connie is a tragic lesbian. In "the depths of [her] degradation," Connie lies about being raped by the boyfriend of the straight protagonist, Julie, in a failed bid for her love. Unable to bear this unrequited love, Connie leaves for parts unknown. Meanwhile, Julie's ability "to transcend the pressures against her sex" is affirmed at the play's end through the promise of a healthy marriage to a man of Marxist principles.[43]

Another early play, "Flowers for the General," similarly depicts a tragic and immature lesbian character to enact its feminist critique. As in "The Apples of Autumn," the play features an intelligent, ethical young female protagonist, Maxine, confronted with the "problem" of a close female friend, Marcia, who is in love with her. When she is outed by another woman in their college dormitory, Marcia tries unsuccessfully to commit suicide; she, like Connie in "Apples," becomes a tragic lesbian. As Maxine comforts her, Marcia shares her knowledge that Maxine herself is in love with another woman. However, whereas Marcia (whom the play consistently infantilizes) refuses to recognize her lesbianism as a passing phase, the more mature Maxine vows to repress same-sex desire and marry her boyfriend.

Yet despite its troubled lesbians, "Flowers" differs markedly from "Apples" in approximating de Beauvoir's view of homosexuality as a choice that can be authentic *or* inauthentic, leading to freedom or flight.[44] Tellingly, Marcia—derisively called "Sappho" by another character—and not the closeted Maxine is the visionary poet (in "Apples," the straight protagonist Julie is the poet who will "be among the first to tell [the world] about what [women] really feel—about wars; and work;—and love").[45] Marcia's clear-sightedness comes to the fore during a debate among the women students over an ROTC beauty pageant, the queen of which will present a war hero with a bouquet. Maxine succumbs to peer pressure and supports this celebration of Cold War heteropatriarchy, even though she finds it obscene. Marcia, however, resolutely condemns it and functions as Maxine's conscience. Maxine's betrayal of her values in supporting the pageant is mirrored in her flight from her feelings for Elly, the ROTC beauty queen engaged to a soldier.

Unlike "Apples," in which heterosexual marriage signals the protagonist's transcendence, "Flowers" critiques the intertwining of marriage with militarization, masculinity, homophobia, and Cold War nationalism. Far from celebrating Maxine's impending marriage, the play questions her willingness to make peace with a society that engenders "so much fuss about flowers for a general and so much hatred because of a little love" between women. Responding to Maxine's resignation to the status quo, Marcia says, "There must be millions who live like that; most people in fact. How very ugly. I don't know that I care very much for such a world."[46]

Marcia repudiates this world view fostered on the college campus by going "home to Mama."[47] Although this once again infantilizes Marcia, going home to Mama also signifies entering a feminine space more liberating than the women's dormitory—a space where Marcia can be "*Tochter aus Elysium,*" or Daughter of Elysium, as she calls herself while exiting to Beethoven's Ninth Symphony. Schiller's "Ode to Joy," to which Beethoven's music is set, declares that Joy, Daughter of Elysium, "binds together / What tradition has strongly parted," implying a repudiation of the patriarchal, heteronormative traditions that separate Marcia from Maxine and Maxine from Elly. Although the play emphasizes the indeterminacy of the outcomes of Marcia's and Maxine's choices, it can be read as a meditation on de Beauvoir's claim that "like all human behavior," homosexuality can be pursued "in bad faith, laziness, and falsity" (in Maxine's case) "or in lucidity, generosity, and freedom" (in Marcia's).

As we see, de Beauvoir's notion of lesbianism as an existential choice shaped Hansberry's feminist thought. De Beauvoir's conceptualization of lesbianism as a site of intersubjectivity also appealed to Hansberry. This idea is central to a key passage demystifying U.S. heteropatriarchy in Hansberry's essay "Simone de Beauvoir and *The Second Sex*: An American Commentary" (1957). Also that year, Hansberry separated from Robert Nemiroff and wrote letters to *The Ladder*—the journal of the first U.S. all-lesbian organization, Daughters of Bilitis—in which she connected homophobia with patriarchy and examined the social and economic pressures on women to marry. The following year, Hansberry began writing what is perhaps her only play with an entirely lesbian cast of characters, "Andromeda the Thief," featuring Sappho as its protagonist.

Hansberry's essay on *The Second Sex* seeks to debunk "the most devastating anti-equality myth of all," the "American myth of the *already* liberated American woman of all classes."[48] To illustrate how the modern world has (incorrectly) accepted "the woman of the United States as the symbol of the 'free woman,'" Hansberry relates the following anecdote:

> The writer is reminded of a time in Buenos Aires when she was in the company of a young Argentinean woman lawyer who, though not out of her twenties, had circled the world a couple of times and was currently playing a major and politically important role in the peace movement of her nation. Preparing to make a meeting somewhere I drew on a suit jacket and tossed a shoulder strap bag across my shoulders and stood waiting for our departure in low-heeled plain pumps. . . . I will not forget the eyes of the Argentine woman traveling the length of my frame (I am not a tall woman, really) and noting the outfit, and perhaps the stance, and saying aloud finally from the reaches of her shawls and earrings and long, flowing hair: "*Ah, la norteamericana tipica!*" [a typical North American woman] It was neither a compliment nor altogether an insult; it was a remark of wonder. Multitudes of United States women would have been offended by the association of my particular unattractive outfit of that afternoon with the *essence* of North American womanhood, and with good reason. Yet for all of it, there was a kernel of the recognition of a characteristic that is not without foundation. The tailored suit, the shoulder strap bag and the flat-heeled or low-heeled shoe is the mark of the fashion-indifferent woman who desires freedom and utility of movement and service in wearing apparel. It is the mark of women in the past who have believed they had something to do in the world other than "sit around and look pretty." It is not an empty stereotype in that such modes of costume have in the past been inextricably identified with the feminist; the woman professional; the radical woman; and, of course, the lesbian.[49]

The passage evokes Sartre's concept of the look, which produces one's subjectivity in relation to the Other: "The Other's look fashions my body in its nakedness, causes it to be born, sculptures it, produces it as it is, sees it as I shall never see it." While the Other objectifies me by looking at me, she also reveals that I am responsible for my being. To recover it, I must "assimilate the Other's freedom."[50]

In *The Second Sex,* however, de Beauvoir argues that a conflictual Hegelian dialectic is not the only possible relationship between individuals. There can be reciprocity and mutual recognition between equal consciousnesses, which de Beauvoir associates with travel and contact zones and perspectives:[51]

> Following Hegel, we find in consciousness itself a fundamental hostility toward every other consciousness; the subject can be posed only in being opposed—he sets himself up as the essential, as opposed to the other, the inessential, the object.
>
> But the other consciousness, the other ego, sets up a reciprocal claim. The native traveling abroad is shocked to find himself in turn rejected as a "stranger" by the natives of neighboring countries. As a matter of fact, wars, festivals, trading, treaties, and contests among tribes, nations, and classes tend to deprive the concept *Other* of its absolute sense and to make manifest its relativity; willy-nilly, individuals and groups are forced to realize the reciprocity of their relations.[52]

De Beauvoir elaborates on this idea of reciprocity later:

> It is possible to rise above this conflict [between master and slave] if each individual freely recognizes the other, each regarding himself and the other simultaneously as object and as subject in a reciprocal manner. But friendship and generosity, which alone permit in actuality this recognition of free beings, are not facile virtues; they are assuredly man's highest achievement, and through that achievement he is to be found in his true nature.[53]

Hansberry's encounter in Buenos Aires with the Argentinean woman exemplifies this reciprocity with the "native traveling abroad." True to de Beauvoir's account, Otherness is relativized through travel; Hansberry is not (only) a native Self but to the Argentinean is a foreign Other—"*la norteamericana tipica*"—and consequently can exist "simultaneously as object and as subject in a reciprocal manner." The Argentinean's look of (mis)recognition not only objectifies Hansberry, à la Sartre, it also allows Hansberry to validate aspects of her identity not readily accepted by a homophobic and patriarchal U.S. national community: "the feminist; the woman professional; the radical woman; and, of course, the lesbian."

Although implicit, the recognition and flow of lesbian desire are integral to the reinscription of American womanhood in this encounter. According to Sartre, "The Other holds a secret—the secret of what I am."[54] For Hansberry, the secret revealed by the Argentinean's look is a "kernel of the recognition of a characteristic that is not without foundation." This characteristic, Hansberry explains, is that of the liberated American woman of the past. However, the complex grammar of her previous statement, with its doubly negative "not without" and shifting verb tense, suggests the presence and absence of another related characteristic that the Argentinean "sees" in Hansberry. This other characteristic, I submit, is the last category of womanhood once "inextricably identified" with Hansberry's mode of dress: the lesbian, who, like the feminist, woman professional, and radical woman, "desires freedom and utility of movement and service in wearing apparel." Here Hansberry draws on de Beauvoir's discussion of the lesbian who "commonly dresses in mannish fashion," since (according to de Beauvoir)

> nothing is less *natural* than to dress in feminine fashion; no doubt masculine garb is artificial also, but it is simpler and more convenient, being intended to facilitate rather than to hinder activity; . . . Every active woman likes low heels and sturdy materials. . . . The heterosexual feminists were formerly as intransigent in this matter as the lesbians: declining to make themselves into merchandise, offered for sale, they affected severe tailor-made suits and felt hats.[55]

Hansberry eroticizes the looks that she and the Argentinean woman exchange, as she recalls "the eyes of the Argentine woman traveling the length of my frame," culminating in an ejaculation—"*Ah, la norteamericana tipica!*"—erupting "from the reaches of her shawls and earrings and long, flowing hair." This visual caress makes reciprocity possible, following de Beauvoir:

> Between women love is contemplative; caresses are intended less to gain possession of the other than gradually to re-create the self through her; separateness is abolished, there is no struggle, no victory, no defeat; in exact reciprocity each is at once subject and object, sovereign and slave; duality becomes mutuality.[56]

Like travel, lesbian eroticism can produce reciprocity. For Hansberry, both experiences rupture the confined meaning of "American" womanhood.

Also relevant to Hansberry's commentary on gender, sexuality, and nationhood is the implicit context of her episode with the "young Argentinean woman lawyer who, though not out of her twenties, had circled the world a couple of times and was currently playing a major and politically important role in the peace movement." This individual was most likely Leonor Aguier Vasquez of Buenos Aires, a 26-year-old lawyer whom Hansberry had met at the 1952 Intercontinental Peace Congress in Uruguay. As Hansberry relates in her coverage of the congress for *Freedom,* Vasquez had investigated atrocities committed during the Korean War, a subject of especial concern to Uruguayans under pressure to shore up U.S. forces in Korea.[57] By incorporating Vasquez's antimilitarism into the queering of American womanhood in her essay on *The Second Sex,* Hansberry contests hegemonic Cold War American femininity and heteropatriarchy. Indeed, like the relationship between the heroines of "Flowers," Hansberry and Vasquez's lesbian intersubjectivity (as portrayed by Hansberry) counters the *intertwining* of sexism, heteronormativity, and U.S. imperialism.

The feminist existentialism and representations of same-sex desire in Hansberry's largely unpublished, unproduced early work take different and muted forms in her later work, the subject of the following section. Yet despite the disappearance of female protagonists and lesbian characters from the later plays, they extend—even consummate—Hansberry's internationalist, queer, and feminist vision. In *The Sign in Sidney Brustein's Window*, Hansberry's overt engagement with existentialism focuses on critiquing its articulations of sexual and racial Others. In challenging this Othering in Genet's vision of anticolonial struggle, *Les Blancs* invokes ideas of mutual recognition that Hansberry had developed in thinking through gender and sexuality via de Beauvoir. Furthermore, the intersections of race with sexuality and imperialism, which Hansberry downplayed in her early plays, are central to *Les Blancs*.

▫ ▫ ▫

Hansberry's subtitle for a 1963 draft of *Sidney Brustein* was "*Up Yours, Ed Albee*," one of several allusions to *Who's Afraid of Virginia Woolf?* (1961), in which the retort expresses the meaninglessness of the effort "to make communicable sense out of natural order, morality out of the unnatural disorder of man's mind."[58] The spokesperson for existentialism in *The Sign in Sidney Brustein's Window* is a gay absurdist playwright, David Ragin, who evokes Albee.[59] Albee, a contemporary of Hansberry (both made Greenwich Village home, and they experienced their first theatrical successes at roughly the same time), was the leading American dramatist of absurdist theatre. Albee helped spread the influence of the European absurdists through his own work and by producing their plays, including Genet's *Deathwatch*. Of special interest to Hansberry would have been Albee's *The Death of Bessie Smith* (1959), which depicts the Jim Crow South as a cauldron of sexual desire and repression that emptied itself to reveal social stasis and decay.

In *The Sign in Sidney Brustein's Window*, Hansberry portrays the immoral and tragic consequences of existentialist nihilism and its representation within absurdist drama. These consequences are vividly portrayed in the play's climactic "absurdist orgy." The hero, Sidney, has been betrayed by the political candidate on whom he had pinned his hopes for social reform; his nadir coincides with that of his sister-in-law, Gloria, who has been betrayed by her fiancé, Alton, a Black Marxist who hypocritically deserts her upon learning that she is a prostitute. Together, Sidney and Gloria admit the meaningless of life, a surrender that is formally paralleled by the scene's "denaturalization" as it assumes the conventions of absurdist drama:

> When each speaks it is stiffly and unnaturally, intoned with a heightened, fragmented delivery beyond sense or sequence, as if lucidity no longer required logic. An absurdist orgy is being created in front of us—a disintegration of reality to parallel the disintegration in SIDNEY's world.[60]

David's entrance positions him as the writer or director literally behind the scene: he "slowly descends the stairs" but "stops halfway down to light a cigarette and stands—in silhouette—thoughtfully smoking, while the dialogue continues," and then "continues down and stands just inside the door, watching GLORIA and SIDNEY as the sensual heat mounts between them." David joins them, and the three parrot absurdist tenets while drunkenly dancing and engaging in ritualistic and sensual behavior that recalls *Who's Afraid of Virginia Woolf?*; Sidney, Gloria and David even sing "in disjointed unison," "Oh, who's afraid of Absurdity! Absurdity! Absurdity! / Who's afraid of Absurdity! / Not we, not we, not we!"[61] Sidney passes out, and David asks Gloria to facilitate sex between him and another man by watching them. David's request, capping a lifetime of abuse by men, leads Gloria to kill herself.

Characters like David, and like Willy and Eric in *Les Blancs,* have troubled critics because of their unsympathetic portrayals of gay men.[62] Certainly the pervasive homophobia of Cold War America, which extended to anti-Communists, Communists, African Americans, and countercultural artists such as Mailer and Jack Kerouac, engendered contradictions and silences in Hansberry's work. Yet the fact remains that in the face of such repression, Hansberry continued to create gay characters. These characters can be seen as fictional representations of publicly gay playwrights such as Genet or Albee. Unfortunately, they also can be read as "tarring" existentialism through its association with homosexual decadence.

However, Hansberry's gay characters are not one-dimensional. On the contrary, Hansberry strove for complexity in them to refute what she saw as the "deistic celebration" of gays, Blacks, and the lumpen proletariat by "Genet, Mailer, and the New Paternalism," as she titled her response to Mailer's review of *The Blacks.*[63] In *Sidney Brustein,* David's treatment of Gloria reveals the dire results of his "deistic celebration" of "the damned." Upon meeting him, Gloria is outraged by David's presumed fraternity with her:

> Look, little boy—*(Sudden strong, throaty tones)* I've never met you before, but I have met them like you a hundred times and I know everything you are about to say; because it's been asked and written four thousand times . . .

> anything I would tell you, you would believe it and put it down and feel like you'd been close to something old and deep and wise.[64]

Refusing to be the object of David's fantasies, Gloria resists his efforts to exploit her pain for his art. At this moment the play conveys the material reality of prostitution; as Gloria stands up to order David to leave, she winces from bruises inflicted by a sadistic client. Prostitution, Hansberry makes clear, is not the life-affirming sexual excess that existentialists imagine; it is a means of survival that is produced by and propagates patriarchal capitalism. To deify prostitutes, or gays or Blacks, is to deny their subjectivity and contribute to their oppression. Hansberry's negative representation of her gay absurdist playwright thus challenges an existentialist conceptualization of homosexuality as, in Sidney's words, "something that only the deepest, saddest, the most nobly tortured can know about."[65] David is not Saint Genet.

Genet's "Blacks" are analogously reduced to projections of white fantasy; as one Black character asserts, "We are what they want us to be. We shall therefore be it to the very end, absurdly."[66] While this might be read as subversive, *The Blacks*' ritualistic enactment of a "clown show" (the play's subtitle) thwarts political action as well as communication across the racial divide. Archibald, who directs the *clownerie,* tells the (white) audience: "In order that you may remain comfortably settled in your seats in the presence of the drama that is already unfolding here, in order that you be assured that there is no danger of such a drama's worming its way into your precious lives, we shall even have the decency—a decency learned from you—to make communication impossible."[67] The play thus portrays the isolation and entrapment of whites and Blacks within their own desires and nightmares.

Moreover, the new paternalists constructed an eroticized as well as an exoticized racial Other. The interpenetration of racial and sexual discourses in *The Blacks* extends beyond the transgression committed by a Black man, Village, who rapes and then strangles a white woman. Adding to the grotesqueness of the "murder by fornication" (as Mailer called it), the Black vicar Diouf is made to take the role of the victim in a ritualistic reenactment for white audiences. Conjoining the myth of the Black male rapist with transvestism and bisexuality (Diouf conspicuously dresses as the white lady in reenacting the rape with Village), Genet creates a drama that "make[s] communication impossible" between Blacks and whites: the white audience merely sees in "the Blacks" the oversexed, deviant Others it desires and expects. It is as sexually deviant, transgendered racial Others that Genet's Blacks portray anticolonial violence not as progressive or emancipatory but, in Nemiroff's words, as "doomed ultimately to repeat the same cycle that Europe has gone through."[68]

Les Blancs sharply opposes this view. Like Fanon, Hansberry believes that in risking their lives in violent struggle, the colonized can become psychologically as well as politically liberated subjects.[69] To return to Douglass's dictum in the epigraph for *Les Blancs*: "If there is no struggle, there is no progress."[70] Unlike Fanon, however, Hansberry explores forms of interracial reciprocity possible even within the Manichean colonial world. This reciprocity, I submit, returns us to de Beauvoir's contention that "wars, festivals, trading, treaties, and contests among tribes, nations, and classes" can lead to mutual recognition as well as conflict, because they "tend to deprive the concept *Other* of its absolute sense and to make manifest its relativity."[71] Furthermore, *Les Blancs* recalls Hansberry's earlier feminist work by representing homosexuality as a site of intersubjectivity across races and nations, thus denying the sexualized, racial Othering that underpinned Genet's cynicism about anticolonial struggle.

In contrast to Hansberry's earlier feminist work, *Les Blancs*, which is about an African male intellectual's anguished decision to rejoin the struggle for national liberation, features no lesbian characters or central female protagonists. Nonetheless, the play's gay male characters extend the critique of heteropatriarchy from Hansberry's earlier work into her analysis of racialized imperialism. Indeed, Hansberry concluded her notes to "The Apples of Autumn" by ruminating that while "homosexuality in women does differ from masculine homosexuality insofar as it is a form of protest and rebellion against the insanities of feminine oppression . . . I suppose also that homosexual males revolt from the artificial imposition of what is or is not 'feminine' or 'masculine' as set down by society."[72] *Les Blancs* portrays this kind of revolt within its exploration of the formation of Black revolutionary nationalist consciousness. In doing so, the play critiques what Roderick Ferguson describes as "the racialized investment in heteropatriarchy [that] bequeathed itself to liberal and revolutionary projects, to bourgeois and revolutionary nationalisms alike."[73]

The racialized investment in heteropatriarchy crucially informs the protagonist Tshembe's plight. Tshembe's departure from the independence struggle in his country (which is based on Kenya in the play) has been precipitated both by his exposure to French existentialism and his marriage to a white European woman. Evoking the existentialist revelation in the park of Antoine Roquentin in Sartre's *Nausea*, Tshembe tells us,

> One day, sitting on a bench in Hyde Park—watching the pigeons, naturally—it came to me as it must to all men: I won't come this way again. Enough time will pass and it will be over for me on this little planet! And so I'd better do the things I mean to do. And so I got up from that bench and went to meet the girl I had been wanting to marry but had not, you see, because of—(*On his fingers, deliberately mocking the words*)—the liberation! the Movement! "AH-FREE-KA!"—and all the rest of it. Well, I was, as Camus would have it . . . (*Ironically, with a small introspective laugh, for he does not in any sense feel the "freedom" he boasts about*) . . . a "free man" in that moment because I "chose" freely.[74]

Wishing nothing more than to return to his "dim little flat off Langley Square, watching the telly with my family," Tshembe seeks shelter from political responsibility in the arrangements of the nuclear family.[75] But his roots in Europe, secured by heterosexual union and reproduction, are queered from the play's outset by his gay and biracial brother, Eric, soon after Tshembe returns to Africa for their father's funeral. "Critically" studying a photograph of Tshembe's wife, Eric poses a series of questions that defamiliarizes the conventions, and hierarchies, of sexual and national relations:

> ERIC: How old is she? . . .
> TSHEMBE: (*Amused—at both ERIC and the custom*) That is something one is not supposed to ask.
> ERIC: Why?
> TSHEMBE: It is a custom among her people not to.
> ERIC: Why?
> TSHEMBE: (*Absurdly*) Because it is.
> ERIC: She's not very handsome.
> TSHEMBE: . . . It is also not the custom to say such things about other people's wives!
> ERIC: She looks older than you do.
> TSHEMBE: She isn't. Europeans—wrinkle faster. . . . She is handsome. And she has eyes that talk.[76]

And so on in this comic exchange that forces Tshembe to defend his wife's features with platitudes about feminine beauty. The exchange can be read superficially as a culture clash between African and European norms and customs, between the ignorant African and his knowledgeable, westernized brother. More compellingly, Eric's dismissive comments are not a sign of lack (of maturity, civility, manhood) but an interrogation of the white, Western, and heterosexual conventions of romance through which Tshembe's estrangement from Africa and political commitment has taken place.

Eric's critique of Tshembe, even in light-hearted banter, stems from his queering of boundaries of race and nationality.[77] Eric's biracialism—the result of the rape of the national liberation leader's wife by the head of the colonial army—makes him the "testament to three centuries of rape and self-acquittal" and "the living denial" of the missionaries' civilizing claims.[78] Eric also bears the open secret of his sexual relationship with Willy DeKoven, a white doctor at the missionary hospital who supplies him with alcohol and at whose request Eric wears makeup. Consequently, the sexual violence of colonialism initially appears to take new form in Eric and Willy's relationship, especially from Tshembe's heteropatriarchal perspective. Eric's transvestism and homosexuality subordinate him under and assimilate him into the colonizer's world, as Tshembe accuses Willy of making Eric his "white woman" and "playtime little white hunter."[79] Even when Eric decides to join the anticolonial revolt, Tshembe discredits him on the basis of Eric's transgression of racial, national, and sexual boundaries:

> TSHEMBE: (*Enters*) You are half European. Which part of yourself will you drive into the sea!
>
> ERIC: I am African enough not to mock when my people call!
>
> TSHEMBE: And what will you do when your doctor [Willy] calls, Eric? It takes more than a spear to make a man.[80]

However, Eric's response—"What does it take, Tshembe? . . . A white wife and son?"—once again interrogates the centering of heterosexuality within the yoked constructions of black manhood and national identity.[81] The first of his brothers to join the uprising, Eric challenges homophobic ideologies of Black nationalism.

Furthermore, Eric's relationship with Willy depicts the interracial reciprocity that Hansberry valued and that repudiated the sexualized, racial Othering that she criticized in existentialist literature. As Stephen Carter argues, "Willy is indisputably attached to Eric and may, in part, have gained his insights into the African view of colonization from the relationship."[82] By virtue of Willy's sexual if not racial difference from "*les blancs,*" he gains critical distance from his own dominant group. Consequently, Willy demystifies reactionary views of anticolonial struggle, which Nemiroff articulates in his notes on *Les Blancs* as "this theme of the 'death of the West' as opposed to the virile rise of the 'uncomplicated' and the 'primitive'—it is only doomed ultimately to repeat the same cycle that Europe has gone through, and on and on into doom and gloom, a la Jean Genet and 'The Blacks.'"[83] Willy comments ironically on this idea:

> [The natives] will murder us here one day. . . . All of us. And the press of the world will send a shudder through men everywhere. It will seem the crowning triumph of bestial absurdity. We pillars of man's love for man rewarded for our pains: our very throats slit ear to ear by rampaging savages. And whole generations will be born and die without knowing any better.[84]

Willy interrupts the homogeneity of *les blancs* as both a sexual and a racial order through the double entendre "we pillars of man's love for man rewarded for our pains." The "we" here refers to white missionaries like himself, whose philanthropy only exacerbates colonial exploitation and repression. However, it secondarily and covertly alludes to Willy's homosexuality, thereby complicating the heteropatriarchal ideologies of "*les blancs*" that sanction the sexual violence of colonization Eric embodies: the rape of the resistance leader's wife by the British officer. Thus, in proceeding to debunk the perception of the "bestial absurdity" of anticolonial violence, Willy queers the Manichean opposition between black natives and white colonizers: "Do not let the drums, the skins and the mumbo jumbo fool you. The sun really *is* starting to rise in the world, so we might just as well stop pretending it is the middle of the night. *They* are quite prepared to die to be allowed to bring it to Africa. It is *we* who are not prepared."[85] Unlike either the benevolent missionaries or the colonial army (both of which he understands to occupy the same position vis-à-vis the Africans), Willy does not fully inhabit the colonial "we"; indeed, when he was completing *Les Blancs* after Hansberry's death, Nemiroff had considered giving this speech, except for the last line, also to Tshembe, the reluctant African revolutionary.[86] Like Tshembe, Willy sees through "the drums, the skins and the mumbo jumbo"; he recognizes the autonomy and freedom of the black Other.

In his insight and doomed love for Eric, Willy also inhabits a larger pattern in Hansberry's work that would seem to be autobiographical to some extent and that draws a further connection between *Les Blancs* and Hansberry's early feminist work. Carter has eloquently described this pattern as "the plight of intellectuals coerced by physical passion into making painful compromises with their ideals and rational approach toward life," and this is the theme of Hansberry's lesbian play, "Andromeda the Thief."[87] Its heroine Sappho abolishes slavery on Lesbos and as a result loses the love of Atthis, who has asked Sappho for a particular slave girl. Despite her love for Atthis,

Sappho refuses to make an exception to her decree ending slavery. Through a technicality, the Ethiopian Andromeda gives the slave girl to Atthis, thereby stealing her love from Sappho. At the end of the play, Sappho is alone in her wisdom and nobility, paralleling Willy's position. *Les Blancs* of course does not explore homosexuality to nearly the same extent as Hansberry's early work; a sign of the play's ambivalence toward homosexuality is that Eric and Willy almost never share the stage. Nonetheless, through these characters we see how a critique of heteropatriarchal racial and national identities and an interrogation of traditional gender norms are integral to the play's anticolonial nationalism.

These gay male characters complement the allegorical, unnamed African woman warrior (called simply "The Woman") in *Les Blancs* who transgresses boundaries of gender and sexuality. The Woman appears at the beginning of the play "suspended in the sky in a characteristic African dance pose. Black-skinned and imposing, cheeks painted for war, her wiry hair rounded by a colorful band, she wears only a leather skirt and, about her waist, a girdle of hammered silver."[88] Through her pose and subsequent gestures, the Woman is an allegory for the East African world view.[89] At the same time, she celebrates Black women's beauty and strength in an internationalist spirit of all women who lead their people to freedom. As Tshembe tells Charlie, the American journalist, "When you knew her you called her Joan of Arc! . . . Queen Esther! Columbia! La Pasionara!" The Woman embodies a distinctly feminine militancy, but like Joan of Arc, she disrupts the opposition between female and male—rendering sexual difference indeterminate and sexuality polymorphous. Toward the end of the Prologue, the Woman pulls out the spear planted in the earth in front of her "with great strength" and "raises it high in symbolic appeal to resistance."[90] After the death of Tshembe's father, it is the Woman who possesses the phallus; she is the source and holder of African culture and history who "circles in movements symbolic of the life of the people" and "signifies the slaughter, the enslavement."[91] Consequently, in signifying on Hamlet, Hansberry has not the ghost of Tshembe's father but rather the Woman appear to Tshembe to ask him to address injury.

As the play progresses, the Woman comes to inhabit "the other bisexuality" of Genet; that is, "each one's location in self (*répérage en soi*) of the presence—variously manifest and insistent according to each person, male or female—of both sexes, non-exclusion either of the difference or of one sex, and from this 'self permission,' multiplication of the effects of the inscription of desire, over all parts of my body and the other body."[92] However, the Woman wrests this bisexuality away from racist, neocolonial desire for the

Other and invests it with a Black nationalist subjectivity. This is evident in her calls to Tshembe to take up arms against the settlers when she appears to him in recurring visions that combine sexual and political potency. Tshembe tells us,

> I have known her to gaze up at me from puddles in the streets of London; from vending machines in the New York subway. Everywhere. And whenever I cursed her or sought to throw her off . . . I ended up that same night in her arms! . . . Even when I held my bride, she lay beside me, her arms on my thighs caressing, insisting that I belonged to her![93]

The Woman threatens Tshembe's complacency and eroticized identification with the metropole not only by inserting herself as the "Other Woman" in a ménage à trois but by destabilizing heterosexuality itself. For "her" arms on his thighs are the arms of the warriors, male and female, whose dance she performs, "beckoning urgently, insistently" before "she sweeps up a spear and thrusts it before him." It is no coincidence that only after the Woman's final appearance in the play do we have the appearance of Ngago, the leader of the resistance and the "poet-warrior invoking the soul of his people," who "moves with a dancer's grace."[94] The disappearance of the Woman at this time suggests that Ngago now embodies her spirit, as does Tshembe himself by the play's close. An incarnation of the "passionate brotherhood" of the nation, the Woman suggests the dissolution of the division between "'proper' homosociality" and "more explicitly sexualized male-male relations," two modes of interaction the nation has sought to keep separate.[95] Instead, revolutionary Black nationalist consciousness opens onto plural sexualities and genders that defy the heteronormative and patriarchal ideologies through which colonial and neocolonial social orders have been secured.

▫ ▫ ▫

Like Richard Wright, Hansberry must be read within a transatlantic conversation with writers who intimately shaped her understanding of diasporic Blackness and anticolonial struggle. In crucial ways, Hansberry's work supports Paul Gilroy's non-essentialist paradigm of a Black Atlantic, which explodes boundaries of race and nation along with national ideologies of gender and sexuality. At the same time, Hansberry's location within the postwar Black Left enjoins us to rethink the diasporic critiques of nationalism that Gilroy's influential work has spawned.

Michelle Wright's study of female subjectivities that *The Black Atlantic* marginalized is relevant here. Wright questions the heteropatriarchal worldview of Black nationalist narratives—ranging from Du Bois's *Souls of Black Folk* through the Négritude and Black Arts movements—that posit a dialectic of the Black male subject. Wright argues that Black women writers such as Audre Lorde and Carolyn Rodgers contest their negation within this dialectic by moving away from the nation toward a dialogic formation of diaspora in which heterogeneous subjects have "far greater power . . . to connect with others and *recognize* their subjectivity"; "difference becomes the means by which one can speak with, recognize, and thus be recognized by a variety of subjects."[96] This dialogic model has much in common with de Beauvoir's concept of mutual recognition; both models challenge the master-slave dialectic as the primary form of intersubjectivity.

Although we can see this diasporic dialogism in Hansberry's work, Hansberry crucially did not reject nationalism but rather was grounded in the Black Left's nationalist internationalism. As Neil Lazarus argues, Gilroy's Black Atlanticism brushes aside this internationalism along with Marxism as a totalizing economistic theory.[97] Michelle Wright's critique of Marxism is different but leads to a similar bracketing of nationalist internationalism. Wright shows the Marxist dialectic to participate in the exclusion of the Black female subject and posits dialogism in its stead, thereby opening up the Black Atlantic to gender and sexuality in ways that are conspicuously absent from Gilroy's study. Nonetheless, it and other postnationalist accounts fail to see the Black internationalist feminism developed by Hansberry and her sisters on the anticolonial Left, for whom feminism and nationalism were at times in tension but were ultimately not mutually exclusive. In the next chapter, I examine Alice Childress's recuperation of Garveyite nationalism for a Black feminist, queer, and transgender politics of liberation that illuminates the evolution of postwar Black Left feminism in the 1970s.

3

Rosalind on the Black Star Line

Alice Childress, Black Minstrelsy, and Garveyite Drag

In 1951, as Alice Childress was securing her reputation within the Left as one of the foremost playwrights and promoters of Black drama, she published an essay, "For a Negro Theatre," in the left-wing journal *Masses and Mainstream* and in the Communist Party's newspaper *The Daily Worker* (where it was more radically titled, "For a Strong Negro People's Theatre"). Drawing on her own efforts to establish Black theater at Harlem's Club Baron with the support of the leftist Committee for the Negro in the Arts, Childress articulated crucial aspects of the nationalist aesthetic that would be developed over ten years later by the Black Arts movement. She called for schools to teach Negro art forms, techniques, and themes arising from Africa as well as from "our neighbors, the community, the domestic workers, porters, laborers, white-collar workers, churches, lodges, and institutions." At the same time she expressed an internationalist vision for a Negro people's theatre: "Its work is too heavy, its task is too large to be anything other than a great movement. It must be powerful enough to inspire, lift, and eventually create a complete desire for the liberation of all oppressed peoples." To that end, "we shall take advantage of the rich culture of the Chinese, Japanese, Russian, and all theatres. We shall study oppressed groups which have no formal theatre as we know it, but we must discover theatre as they know it."[1]

The following year, Childress executed her diasporic vision for Black drama in "the first professionally produced play written by an African American woman," *Gold Through the Trees* (1952), which became the latest example of CNA-sponsored theater at the Club Baron.[2] In the pages of Paul Robeson's anticolonial newspaper *Freedom*, Lorraine Hansberry praised Childress's use of African, West Indian, and African American dance and music to depict a pan-African history of struggle "in four different parts of the world, in five different times in history—Africa, 300 years ago; Haiti, during the overthrow of the French planters and Napoleon's army in 1849; the British West Indies today; and the United States during slavery."[3] In the *Daily Worker,* John Hudson Jones lauded the "successful artistic blending of the African and Negro peoples' struggles" in a scene about the 1951 execution of seven young Black men accused of raping a white woman in Martinsville, Virginia. The play linked the plight of the Martinsville Seven to apartheid in a scene in which "the bars of a U.S. prison were shadowed across the face of the huge African mask background."[4] The drama culminated with the contemporaneous anti-apartheid struggle; in fact, the African National Congress and South African Indian Congress launched important demonstrations on April 6, 1952, the day before *Gold Through the Trees* premiered. The play raised money to support these anti-apartheid organizations.[5]

Incorporating music, dance, and sketches, *Gold Through the Trees* was a revue. As such, it had roots in vaudeville and blackface minstrelsy. In the 1950s, however, associating blackface minstrelsy with the anti-colonial pan-Africanism espoused by Childress and her comrades on the Left would have met with outrage. For in the era of desegregation heralded by *Brown vs. the Board of Education,* what many African Americans and white progressives indignantly saw as blackface was being revived by the debut of *Amos 'n' Andy* on television in 1951, the year before *Gold Through the Trees* was produced.[6] As a Black playwright and public intellectual, Childress was in the thick of left and liberal criticism of the show. The Committee for the Negro in the Arts—the cultural wing of the Harlem Left, the theater division of which Childress chaired—voiced its disgust at "hundreds of thousands of dollars [being] spent to insult Negroes for 30 minutes once a week."[7] Covering the NAACP-led boycott of the show and its sponsors in *Masses and Mainstream,* only months after Childress's "For a Negro Theatre" had appeared in the journal's pages, John Hudson Jones compared *Amos 'n' Andy* to the lynching of the Martinsville Seven and the persecution of Black Left leaders Benjamin Davis, W. E. B. Du Bois, Alphaeus Hunton, Claudia Jones, and William Patterson. In the June 1951 issue of *Freedom,* Lorraine Hansberry wrote that the "false and vicious impression of Negroes" served up by *Amos 'n' Andy* and *Beulah*—the latter of which starred the great African American singer and actress Ethel Waters in a mammy role—made it "easier to justify economic and every other kind of discrimination, so rampant in this country."[8] Childress's 1955 play, *Trouble in Mind,* has been read as a protest against the mainstream entertainment industry's degrading roles for African Americans.[9] But what especially brought the controversy over these shows home to Childress was her marriage to actor Alvin Childress, who played Amos. (They officially divorced in 1957, although the relationship had frayed years before then.)[10] As Alvin's wife, Alice got a firsthand view of the revulsion *Amos 'n' Andy* inspired, such as the *Chicago Defender*'s refusal to go through with arrangements for the show's cast to ride in its annual parade, which the Childress family subsequently watched from the street.[11]

Despite or perhaps because of the furor over *Amos 'n' Andy*, Childress was committed to recuperating the oppositional political and artistic legacy of Black minstrelsy. In a "Brief History of the Minstrel Show and It's [*sic*] Form" (undated but probably written in the late 1950s, given its references to Ghanaian independence and civil rights struggles), Childress goes so far as to suggest that the highest expression of a strong Negro theatre could be a Black minstrel show. Childress traces its origins to the medieval English minstrels who "composed and sang verses to *honor* the chiefs of their tribes" and "sang of *brave deeds* and battles" and to the Welsh bards hanged by King Edward I of England "because their songs inspired the people with a spirit of rebellion." While acknowledging that white actors in the United States had "turned [the minstrel show] into such a vicious instrument that the Negro turned against the 'minstrel' and struggled to abandon the form," Childress understood it to be a highly adaptable, potentially subversive dramatic genre that could revive its earlier purposes of commemorating a people's courage and inspiring rebellion.[12] To those ends, Childress suggested that

> we observe Negro History [Week] in the nite club with a sparkling revue which carries us from the past to the present. . . . Small's Paradise will be the first night club to hold such a celebration. It will top many other celebrations because it will not be a heavy show but a light and sparkling one. It will take in Negroes in the variety fields. It will reach back for the best memories and touch upon the present.
>
> I propose that the show be titled . . . *ONCE UPON A TOMORROW*. . . . We will bring back memories of the CAKE WALK, Camp Fire circle, Bert Williams, Florence Mills, the Southernaires, early jazz forms etc.[13]

Black minstrels and performers with roots in minstrelsy such as Williams and Mills were forebearers of Black theater as well as participants in early civil rights struggles. Childress thus did not find it inconceivable to suggest that a scene built around the legendary Afro-Caribbean blackface minstrel Bert Williams could be dedicated to the contemporary civil rights movement (the Montgomery bus boycott, the desegregation of Clinton High School): "Another production number may touch on Montgomery, Alabama (Maybe this could be the Bert Williams number.) 'I know about Kentucky Home, the old folks there and so we'll weep no more my lady. . . . But I've yet to hear a song about Montgomery or dear old Clinton, Tennessee!'" Childress's politicized minstrel theater promoted Left internationalism by yoking U.S. civil rights with African liberation: "We should have one number on Africa. I think it should hit on 'Ghana.' . . . Since the independence of Ghana there hasn't been any song that has reached my ears concerning it. . . . Here the Olio [the acting portion of the minstrel show] could give us background on how the independence came about."[14] This proposal in fact presents a version of what Childress accomplished with *Gold Through the Trees* and another revue co-written with Lorraine Hansberry to celebrate Negro History Week in tandem with *Freedom*'s first anniversary.[15]

Childress was able to imagine this international spectacle because of Black minstrelsy's cosmopolitan context of labor migration, overseas touring, intraracial conflict, African emigration and recolonization projects, and pan-African activism. In particular, the elaborate musicals of the West Indian–born Bert Williams and his African American partner, George Walker, featured African and Caribbean settings and characters that, despite their exoticism and travesty of Blackness, "introduced a much more respectful and accessible vision of Africa" to Black and white audiences in the United States and England. Williams and Walker's minstrelsy developed a diasporic sensibility that in its "attention to the tensions, differences, and incommensurabilities beneath the skin of racial typology" complemented but also critiqued the pan-African nationalisms of Marcus Garvey and W. E. B. Du Bois.[16]

In the 1970s and 1980s, Childress revisited the worldly Black minstrelsy of Bert Williams as well as comedian Jackie "Moms" Mabley to develop the Black aesthetic she had outlined in "For a Negro Theatre": one that represented everyday Black life, studied and used the cultures of oppressed peoples, and served emancipatory aims. As she contends in *Moms: A Praise Play for a Black Comedienne* (1987), the complexly subversive legacy of Black minstrelsy was an antidote to the stereotypes that were associated with it. Childress elaborates on this idea in an interview from the early 1980s, in which she considers the possibility of a blackface comedian "turning," or subverting, a classic misogynistic joke in order to defamiliarize the sexual norms of racial segregation:

> The only white face in a minstrel show is Mr. Interlocutor, the questioner. He asks the blackface comedian, "Who was that lady I saw you with last night?"

> He answers, "Dat was no lady, dat was my wife!" The reliable joke brings a reliable laugh. The humor would fall flat on the ears of some revelers if it turned, ever so slightly: "Dat was no lady, dat was *your* wife!"[17]

This "turned" humor represents the tradition of resistant Black minstrelsy that Childress incorporated in *A Short Walk* (1979), her Pulitzer Prize–nominated novel, and its "intertext," *Moms. Moms*'s portrait of pioneering Black comedian Jackie "Moms" Mabley built upon *A Short Walk*'s depiction of Black minstrelsy—which in turn drew on Bert Williams's pan-African spectacles—in order to depict Mabley's professional roots in minstrelsy, her struggles over Black female identity, and the intertwining of these two issues.[18] Separately and together, Childress's novel and play represent Black minstrelsy as a crucial site for revising heteropatriarchal gender roles precisely because it engaged with global affairs and foreign policy. Minstrelsy bridged the fields of comedy and international political analysis that often lay on opposite sides of the racial divide, as Childress observed:

> The Black artist finds most opportunity and reward in the field of ludicrous comedy, refuge in laughter. That labeled "serious and controversial" is silently considered dangerous ground. We usually wait for whites to interpret global affairs and form government policy toward foreign countries. That "minority" leadership which shows independence of thought and action is often silenced, imprisoned, or mysteriously murdered.[19]

Minstrelsy, however, did not have to be a ghetto for Black artists forced to channel their myriad talents into humorous entertainment; it could be their vehicle for presenting dangerous and controversial perspectives on foreign affairs to a Black public sphere.

The global critique of race Bert Williams and "Moms" Mabley enacted was useful to Childress in examining the legacy of Garveyism, which was shaped by Black minstrelsy's spectacles and rhetoric. Garvey, Robert Hill writes, was a "man given to enigmatic twists, dazzling histrionics mixed with constant role-playing . . . a master manipulator of the visual image."[20] Through appropriating and satirizing the spectacles of imperialist nationalism, Garvey invested and invented modern political subjects of a "black empire."[21] It was not just European nations that inspired Garvey's use of titles, uniforms, pageantry, and parades, however: as Louis Chude-Sokei shows, Garvey must be read in the context of the visual vocabulary of Black nobility, African sovereignty, and pan-African identification that Williams and Walker's musicals developed. The connections between Garveyism and minstrelsy even shaped criticism of the charismatic leader: "the description of Garvey as clown, charlatan, minstrel, or as masquerade artist . . . [ran] throughout the entire period of his presence upon the Harlem stage."[22]

Childress was grappling with Garveyism as it was bearing fruit and regaining favor as a result of the new independence of Ghana and other African nations, the growth of Black Power in the United States, the renewed repatriation movement in Jamaica, and the publication of writings by and about Garvey, including John Henrik Clarke's collection *Marcus Garvey and the Vision of Africa* (1974), in which the pioneering left nationalist historian asserted that the Garvey revival had become "something of an epidemic."[23] Although Clarke was arguably the most committed and influential of the Black leftists to acknowledge, study, and promote Garvey's legacy, he was not the only one. Childress, Rosa Guy, and Paule Marshall, who had all been exposed to Garvey's Universal Negro Improvement Association (UNIA) at an early age, discussed its impact on their identities and wrote about it in their fiction.[24] In the mid-1960s, Childress began work with composer Irving Burgie (renowned for writing the song "Day-O" and the national anthem of Barbados) on a musical drama about the Garvey movement called *Song of the Storm*. Childress and Burgie's play could have been a worthy follow-up to *Big White Fog* (1937), Theodore Ward's landmark social drama about the UNIA. (Childress acknowledged Ward's influence in "For a Negro Theatre," in which she tells him, "I hope you blaze the way in helping to build such a theatre.")[25] For unclear reasons, *Song of the Storm* was never finished, but it got a second life, so to speak, in *A Short Walk*. In a sustained, vivid section that Alice Walker and John O. Killens have singled out for praise, *A Short Walk* presents an account of the UNIA and especially Garvey's vision that a fleet of ships, the Black Star Line, would create Black jobs and capital by competing in the shipping industry, facilitate communication throughout the Black world, and make it easier to emigrate to Africa.[26]

This section of Childress's novel critically rethinks Garveyism's separatism and territorialism, a contemporaneous articulation of which Marcus Garvey Jr. made in "Garveyism: Some Reflections on Its Significance for Today," in which he elaborates on the necessarily "separatist nature of the Garvey movement." The younger Garvey contends that "in every strong nationalism which the world has witnessed there has been an element of racial exclusiveness and a desire for national privacy," hence his advocacy of race purity against the "race suicide" of miscegenation. This logic leads to the goal of "an African superstate equipped with modern weaponry and disposing massive military force." In contrast to the U.S.-based Black Power movement, Garvey Jr. argued that community empowerment within a country where Blacks comprise a political minority was a false solution.[27] Like his father, the younger Garvey believed that a politically effective Black community could be built only in an autonomous Black-majority nation.

In contrast to Garveyism, Childress demonstrates that nationalism is consistent with the Black project of reclaiming America. Her representations of Black minstrelsy in *A Short Walk* and *Moms* underscore that while it is myopic to posit the U.S. nation-state as "the sole arbiter of universal values and legitimate political aims" for people of color, "it would be a mistake to overlook the political inventiveness, collective irony, and socially significant identity that have resulted from black people's struggles to make the U.S. nation-state their own."[28] Childress presents examples of such political inventiveness, irony, and identity reformulation through minstrel drag, which enables Black women, men, and transgender people to expose and reenvision the violently normative roles that underpin U.S. liberal democracy's putative freedoms.

Childress also rejects Garvey's opposition to internationalism, or the "progressive and positive" Black nationalism espoused in an essay on Garvey by Richard B. Moore, a founding member of the African Blood Brotherhood and an early Black Communist. Moore argues that nationalism should express "the right of the African, *as of all other peoples,* to self-determination, self-government, and self-realization." Nationalism is thus "marked by due regard for the rights and liberties of other nations and peoples while cherishing, promoting, and defending the best interests of one's own nation." Moore contended that in the 1920s, this progressive nationalism "gave way in Garvey's consciousness more and more to unrestrained and reactionary nationalism . . . evident in the selfish and ruthless disdain for the freedom and welfare of other nations and their people, and in the elevation of the supposed interests of a particular nation above those of all others."[29] Childress adopts Moore's critique in *A Short Walk*: what the novel's most prominent male Garveyite finds "hardest to understand" about his lover—more than her bootlegging, gambling, and involvement with blackface comedians—is the fact that she is promiscuously "mixed up with attending parties where Chinese, Cubans and other aliens socialize."[30] Childress explicitly links this "reactionary nationalism" with Garveyism's heteropatriarchal, bourgeois propriety while she locates progressive, internationalist nationalism within the sphere of feminist and queer racial politics.

A Short Walk does not reject Garveyism, however; it recuperates its investment in Black transnational mobility, which Childress represents as the movement's key contribution to realizing Black freedom dreams, more so than its concerns with the reclamation of territory and nation building. Of all the aspects of the UNIA, *A Short Walk* devotes the most attention to the Black Star Line. But because of Garveyism's heteropatriarchy, Childress argues that the traveling minstrel show grants Black women more opportunity than the Black Star ships to create mobile, emancipatory roles. Of course, as Childress acknowledges, Black performers in the United States were subject to considerable racial violence because their mobility was curtailed by efforts of whites to reassert their supremacy using curfews and passes. In addition, Black women confronted sexual harassment, condemnation of women stage performers, and stereotypical roles that required women to have male partners. Nonetheless, touring and performing in "minstrelsy and vaudeville provided welcomed alternatives for the black female, professional entertainer," who was "no longer restricted to the church, domestic work, or prostitution."[31]

In *A Short Walk* and *Moms*, Black minstrel or minstrel-based performances pose an alternative to Garveyism's heteropatriarchal, imperialist, and separatist political theater by enacting what Daphne Brooks terms "Afro-alienation." Afro-alienation illuminates

> the hypervisibility and cultural constructions of blackness in transatlantic culture. . . . Just as Brecht calls for actors to adapt "socially critical" techniques in their performances so as to generate "alienation effects" and to "awaken" audiences to history, so too can we consider [performers of Afro-alienation] as critically defamiliarizing their own bodies by way of performance in order to yield alternative racial and gender epistemologies.[32]

Childress specifically portrays the need to defamiliarize and reappropriate the pervasive mammy role, which undoes the dichotomy between the worldly minstrel show and the world outside the show tent. While *Moms* explores how Jackie Mabley challenged sexist, racist, and imperialist ideologies through a comic act that revolved entirely around reenacting the mammy stereotype, *A Short Work* represents progressive Black internationalism and transnationalism through a drag queen's reinterpretation of the mammy as church mother. The deconstructive critique of the mammy's minstrel drag constitutes a feminist and queer politics of Black liberation.

▫ ▫ ▫

Decades before writing *A Short Walk* and *Moms*, at the height of her immersion in the Left during the early 1950s, Childress presented a feminist, anticolonial reappropriation of the mammy role in her column "Conversation from Life" for Robeson's revolutionary *Freedom* newspaper.[33] The column's speaker, a witty, militant Black domestic named Mildred, pointedly repudiated the mammy stereotype perpetuated by the contemporaneous television show *Beulah,* which "depicted an ideal suburban world in which whites and black *servants* lived in harmonious acceptance of the status quo."[34]

Mildred's antiracist, anti-imperialist feminine militancy echoes throughout Childress's drama from this period. *Gold Through the Trees* depicts the anticolonial resistance of Black peasant and working-class women such as the Haitian market woman played by Childress herself. An unproduced play, *Copra: A West Indian Drama,* examines the intersections of patriarchal oppression and colonial exploitation through a white, peasant-born wife of a plantation owner and her Black female servant, who urges other workers to go on strike.[35]

These explorations of women-led revolt arose out of Childress's involvement with the postwar anticolonial Left and its global positioning of Black struggle.[36] Along with her aforementioned work with *Freedom* and the CNA, Childress belonged to the speakers' bureau of the left-wing National Council of the Arts, Sciences and Professions, through which she was "available for subjects pertaining to History of the Negro Artists in America, Negro Women in America, Outstanding Figures in Negro History, and Cultural Backgrounds, America, West Indies and Africa."[37] Indeed, Childress's expertise in African history as well as her penchant for meticulous research is evident in her 27-page "Report on the Gold Coast," an anticolonial history of West Africa that began in 400 B.C. with the Carthaginian expeditions to colonize the west coast of Africa and ended with the release of Nkrumah from jail after his election as prime minister of the newly independent nation of Ghana. Childress was also a founding member of the Sojourners for Truth and Justice, which sent a delegation of 100 Black women to Washington, D.C., in 1951 to demand world peace and social justice.

Even after Childress markedly curtailed her radical activism after the mid-1950s with the demise of both *Freedom* and the Council on African Affairs and the exile or deaths of its leaders, she participated in major activities sponsored by the Black Left, often in conjunction with artists and organizations of the Black Arts Movement. With Paule Marshall and Sarah Wright, she contributed to a well-received panel on "The Negro Woman in American Literature" at a Harlem Writers Guild–New School for Social Research conference, "The Negro Writer's Visions of America," in 1965. Their presentations were published in *Freedomways,* as a result of which *Présence Africaine* contacted Childress about writing an essay on "The Blacks—Women—Men—Children, in American Film."[38] Childress was a panelist at another Guild-sponsored conference in 1981, "The Responsibility of the Black Writer to the Community," that affirmed the need for both universal liberation and Black self-determination. Childress represented the Guild on the 1971 trip to the Soviet Union with the delegation George B. Murphy Jr. organized. While Childress was critical of Soviet color-blindness, which she called "admirable in one sense . . . but not applicable in to [*sic*] our situation at home," she was impressed by socialist planning, especially its benefit to women and children and the "darker peoples" of the Central Asian republics the delegation visited.[39] Through this trip and a subsequent one to China in 1973, Childress made good on her proposal in "For a Negro Theatre" to "take advantage of the rich culture of the Chinese, Japanese, Russian, and all theatres."[40] She adapted for the stage a film she had seen in China, *The White-Haired Girl*, by Ting Yu and Ho Chin-Chih, and proposed a film about "the relationship between Africans and Afro-Americans, and their relationship to all others in the world community of peoples." to be potentially produced in the Soviet Union by Africans, African Americans, and Soviets.[41]

Thus, although *A Short Walk* was written nearly two decades after the peak of Childress's involvement with the Black Left, it is part of the less visible yet persistent pattern of anti-imperialist, internationalist activism that she pursued in the 1960s and 1970s and that continued to inform her sustained concern with Black women's issues. Building on the postwar anticolonial Left's global analysis of race, *A Short Walk* examines twentieth-century Black female subjectivity and the project of Black liberation as they are shaped by the legacy of slavery—Jim Crow segregation, racial terror, discrimination in housing and employment—and colonialism in Africa and the Caribbean. For Childress, Black minstrelsy is a site for articulating anticolonial pan-African politics that break with the heteropatriarchal norms that restrict both Black (trans)national and U.S. national identities. Exposing the performativity of race, gender, and sexuality, Black minstrels in *A Short Walk* engage in "Afro-alienation acts" that denaturalize hegemonic and counterhegemonic identities and enact new ones. Childress shows these performances to have material consequences in the world beyond the minstrel tent—or, more precisely, she undoes the dichotomy between the world and the minstrel tent, revealing that the worldly Black minstrel show shapes and is determined by global race politics.

Because the minstrel show is not confined to the tent or the stage, it quickly emerges as the primary classroom for Cora, the protagonist of *A Short Walk*.

We first encounter her on the way to see a black-on-black minstrel troupe for her fifth birthday with her father, Bill. This momentous occasion leads Cora to ask Bill, "What is life?" to which he replies, "I heard that life is just a short walk from the cradle to the grave." Bill and Cora's own walk illustrates his metaphor when Cora pleads with Bill to detour into a park designated for whites only and they are caught by a policeman. To protect Cora, Bill enacts the type of docile, comical "darky" performance that they are on their way to see under the minstrel tent; his act is greeted with the "sound of police laughter [that] follows them as they hurry down the street." Bill's degradation supplements his existentialist metaphor: life is not just a short walk with a set path for African Americans but a minstrel show with set roles. When Cora expresses her delight with the troupe by proclaiming, "I'd like to spend my whole life in a minstrel show," Bill wryly responds, "You just might, darling, it be that way sometime."[42]

If the world is a minstrel tent writ large, the minstrel tent is a microcosmic "double-aisled world of colored and white," a formative space wherein Cora "begins to decipher the true language of [her] world—realizing that words do not always mean what they seem to say. She notices. There are many things to be noticed at a minstrel show." One of the most striking things that Cora notices is that Black womanhood itself is a minstrel role. Within the segregated audience, Cora is fascinated by the rear section for the Black "fancy-women" who perform under a surreptitious white male gaze in tandem with the minstrel show, "toss[ing] themselves about, intentionally showing off a shaking bosom or a calf and ankle" whenever a joke is told. This unbridled Black female sexuality is echoed onstage by Mandy-the-cook, a plantation mammy performed in blackface drag by a man who "wears balloons under his great, wide skirts," which two other minstrel men flip up to expose "baggy underdrawers made from flour sacks."[43]

Blackface minstrelsy's misogynistic and racist nostalgia for slavery is imbricated in colonial constructions of race and sexuality. In a final draft of the novel, an image of Mandy-the-cook that greets the audience as they enter the tent is paired with a hawker's spiel on the show's "gen-u-wine SENEGAMBIANS" and "captive dancin girls . . . brought for your pleasure from neath the palm trees of Egypt! Full blooded, dark eyeded, untouched, innocent maidens, leavin nothing to the magination of a full grown, natural-natured man."[44] Childress's juxtaposition of plantation "darkies" and exotic "Africans" suggests that the erotics of empire feed the projection of the slaveholder's sexual domination onto the hypersexualized Black female slave, and vice versa.

Given the intertwining of patriarchy, colonialism, and U.S. slavery and Jim Crow segregation, when the Black minstrels in *A Short Walk* call for freedom and racial justice, it is a diasporic call reverberating beyond the borders of the United States. This subversive act repurposes the minstrel form during the olio, "'Chief Boo-Roo of Kookalanki,' a story of justice in far-off darkest Africa."[45] With its plotline and authorship (we learn that the act was written by the Black actor playing Boo-Roo), "Chief Boo-Roo of Kookalanki" alludes to the back-to-Africa musicals of the early twentieth century, especially to the show that made this genre popular, *In Dahomey* (1902), "the first full-length musical written and played by blacks to be performed at a major Broadway house."[46] *In Dahomey* starred Bert Williams as Shylock Homestead and George Walker as Rareback Pinkerton, two detectives hired by the president of a colonization society to find a missing heirloom. After various escapades, Homestead, Pinkerton, and their entourage wind up in Dahomey; they ultimately choose to relocate there and build a "broadway in the jungle."[47] As Louis Chude-Sokei argues, shows such as *In Dahomey* "dragged minstrelsy from the plantation and Jim Crow topos where it stagnated and forced it to speak to the also emergent black counterglobalization that was pan-Africanism."[48]

Childress invokes Williams and Walker's minstrel pan-Africanism with "Chief Boo-Roo of Kookalanki," which features a Black American comic duo, Rastus and Bones. Roughly following *In Dahomey*'s plotline, Rastus and Bones travel to Kookalanki to "discover gold for America and also to free all good Africans from the cannibal rule of wicked Chief Boo-Roo." Boo-Roo threatens to cook them unless they marry his "crude" daughter, Ross-a-jass, an African counterpart to Mandy-the-cook. However, Boo-Roo's beautiful second daughter, Rosalinda, intercedes on their behalf, and "all in a twinkling, there is no longer a minstrel show" as she sings, "Let them be free, let them be free; Oppression, dear father, is slaver-eeee."[49] Breaking with the minstrel mammy role, Rosalinda confuses and incenses the white audience with the diasporic reach of her cry for freedom for all people of African descent:

> "And what's all this singin about freedom? They *are* free, aren't they?"
> "They mean back in Africa, Lorina, not here."[50]

Rosalinda's song expresses the pan-African solidarity produced when Black Americans step "out of place" and travel—however imaginatively—to Africa. Countering the degrading image of Black womanhood perpetuated through Mandy-the-cook, Rosalinda breaks not only with racist and sexist ideologies but also with their articulations of and by imperialism.

The radical possibilities of travel first presented to Cora by the Black minstrel show are taken up by her childhood sweetheart, Cecil, with whom she comes to see Black freedom and autonomy in terms of physical mobility across the ocean. As World War I is waged, Cora and Cecil meet to "count how many ships are in the harbor and . . . wave welcome at any Negro sailors coming ashore"; they even cut out pictures of ships in the papers to "paste in notebooks, . . . know each one by heart and pretend [to] own them." In addition to the prospect of travel, the appearance of the traveler matters to Cecil; part of his excitement about being in the navy is the prospect of donning its "blue uniforms with decorations for the sleeve," and his fantasy of working on a passenger liner includes "wear[ing] white coats, dark trousers and black bow ties."[51]

The promise of fulfilling these two components of Black liberation—the opportunity to travel on one's own ships and to dress the part of the traveler, or, to put it another way, to engage in the theater of travel—comes when first Cecil and then Cora finds Marcus Garvey's UNIA and Black Star Line, the fleet of ships with which Garvey intended to unite and uplift the African diaspora through international trade.[52] Although the ships failed as a business venture, they were spectacularly successful as propaganda. Along with Garvey's deployment of elaborate military and scholarly dress, titles of nobility, parades, pageants, and other forms of court display, the ships constituted an appropriation and satirization of the trappings of European imperial nation-states.[53] To display Black (trans)national power was to engender its possibility: "Garvey's spectacles of black statehood allowed his black and colonial spectators to envision the impossible—the virtual or imagined fulfillment of their desires for inclusion within the world order of nation-states in construction after World War I."[54]

It was not just the power of national spectacle on which Garvey drew, however, but also the power of minstrel spectacle. As Louis Chude-Sokei compellingly argues, "so much of [Garvey's] use of symbols, icons, costumes, and Africentric iconography was made possible by the proto-pan-African spectacles of the Williams and Walker shows," such as *In Dahomey*.[55] Cecil alludes to Garvey's pan-African minstrelsy when he tells Cora that in their finery on the Black Star liner—including Cecil's "dark blue uniform with red trouser stripes, a dress sword at [his] side, a white plumed hat, [and] epaulets" that are "Garvey's adaptation of the British field marshal's uniform"—she will finally "be like Miss Rosalinda when she stepped out onto the stage at the minstrel show, beautifully dressed and singing."[56]

The Black Star Line provides another stage for Rosalinda's call for international unity when the ship is docked outside Havana, where it is besieged with visitors. One of the visitors, a female voudoun practitioner, becomes possessed by a girl named Rosa who

> had the gift of second sight and healin. . . . Now her musical little voice comes back through a medium, singin a song, blessin our ship, and promisin that someday we who are downtrodden will rise in the light. Every color shall then live as one—because of the Black Star Line.
>
> [Cora] wept. The voice of poor little Rosa took [her] back to childhood and the Rabbit Ears Minstrel, and [her] papa's voice: "When will Rosalinda sing?"

Rosa(linda)'s song, however, does not reach Cora's ears: "I . . . long to hear some spirit voice, but all I hear is the buzz of a bee stealin sweetness from a flower on the ship's rail."[57] Part of the reason for this is that for all of its symbolic power, Garvey's maritime spectacle is illusory: the ship is rotting, its financial mismanagement is appalling, and Garvey cannot compete with the established European shipping lines.

An equally pressing reason for the deferral of Rosalinda's song of liberation is that women of color are suppressed and excluded by Garvey's pan-African spectacle of nobility, including his use of royal titles.[58] Garvey's collusion with heteronormative bourgeois norms becomes clear when Cecil falsely represents Cora as his wife, Lady Green, because they "must show respect if [they] are to travel together." To this end, he has printed "a marriage certificate with the goldest seal and the reddest ribbon" that Cora has ever seen.[59] The counterfeit marriage certificate yokes spectacular heteropatriarchy to a spectacular race radicalism for which Black Star Line stock certificates become a key prop. The fungibility of these two certificates is evident when Cecil presents Cora with five UNIA shares in front of Garvey as a token of love after announcing their marriage. Finding Cecil's presentation lackluster, Garvey supersedes it with a masterful display of political theater:

> Garvey throws the door open and straddles the threshold. Black, stalwart and proud, he speaks to all within hearing distance. "I hold in my hand shares in a universal government, absolutely our own! . . . Fulfill your own destiny! Become a power, a power, a power, a power." . . .
>
> In the room outside, the word is repeated softly. A murmuring wave of sound soon sweeps down two flights of stairs and out to the street. " . . . a power, a power, a power." . . .
>
> Garvey paces in and out of both rooms, no longer addressing only those gathered, but calling to Africans, West Indians, South Americans, Fiji Islanders.[60]

While Garvey's global stagecraft creates the appearance of endlessly multiplying Black power, it has the opposite effect of negating Black female subjectivity through multiplying the oppressive roles through which it is enacted. As "Lady Green" to Lord Cecil Green, Cora does not find in this new role the means to "become a power"; instead the role is an obstacle to self-knowledge and self-representation. She tells Cecil, "My real mother was Johnson, and she died and I became 'James,' then Kojie turned me into 'Anderson.' Now you say 'Mrs. Green,' 'Lady Green'—I never seem to know who I am!"[61]

The titles of nobility conferred by the UNIA thus carry roles that prove to be as degrading as that of the plantation mammy, which Garvey's movement is incapable of shedding. Laverne, a Jamaican-born Black Star nurse who is rewarded for her exemplary sale of UNIA stock with a berth on Garvey's ship and the title "Countess of the Congo," literally struggles to free herself from this role as she changes out of her royal attire. The descriptions of Laverne's stomach "criss-crossed with welts," the "deep grooves" pressed into her shoulder by the corset's straps, and the shoe that "has cut through the silk stocking, into the flesh, and raised blisters" evoke marks of slavery that result from Garveyite masquerade. In fact, these signs of slavery in the flesh confirm that the role of the plantation mammy lurks underneath that of the countess: "I'm big-boned, stout and . . . sort of a muddy brown, so I got a harder row to hoe. Them funny picture postcards—Oh, it seems so mean to call us 'mammy' and 'auntie,' all because of the flesh, y'know?" Laverne's reflections spur Cora to recall the minstrel show, where "men stuffed balloons beneath their clothes, and wore big red bandanas to make sport of fat black women." Laverne pointedly clarifies that "it ain't just a show. The 'minstrel' is not confined to a tent."[62]

The burden of the mammy role also becomes Cora's after leaving the UNIA. Having become the manager and co-owner of a gambling club, Cora discovers that the wealthy white man who finances the business, Mr. Simeon, is sexually drawn to her because she is getting to be "built like a postcard Mammy." Although reluctant, Cora begins to accept Simeon's advances, since he has been liberal with his money and racial views and has become to Cora "the dearest Mister Interlocutor there ever was." Nonetheless, when they are about to make love, "tambourines jingle in [her] head," and she imagines herself "*jiggin across a stage with a glass a water on [her] head—and then [she is] Ross-a-jass, cutting carrots and onions in the big pot.*" Rejecting this colonial racist fantasy, Cora refuses to engage in intercourse with a white man, even one so liberal as Simeon—a private feminine act of Black empowerment no less valid than Cecil's public masculine displays: "I don't preach on the street corner, but my nationalism is right here in this room."[63]

However, it is through Black minstrelsy itself—and its successors, the vaudeville circuit and drag ball—that the mammy role is most powerfully challenged and rearticulated in a way that makes space for feminine and queer expressions of Black power. After leaving the Garvey movement, Cora supports herself by touring the Theatre Owners Booking Association (TOBA) circuit, which showcased Black entertainers and catered to Black audiences from 1907 through the 1930s and presented "the principal stage for the transition from minstrelsy's rigidly maintained stereotypes to a performance style that more accurately reflected the majority tastes of the black community."[64] Cora first tours the TOBA as part of a comedy and dance act with her lover, Nappy, then as the manager of her own vaudeville troupe. As a "respectable colored transient," she finds more of the freedom that was only partly attainable on the Black Star Line because of Garvey's investment in bourgeois ideologies of womanhood. Whereas Cecil accuses Cora of failing her gender and her race by "go[ing] off dancing and acting the fool for that buffoon of a man [Nappy]," Rosalinda (Cora's Aunt Francine, who further complicates the minstrel show's boundaries by being called "Rosalinda" even after retiring from the stage) applauds Cora for precisely these reasons, which allow her to "stay free." By contrast, Rosalinda regrets her own lack of freedom in the bourgeois arrangements of marriage that are at odds with the traveling minstrel show. When her husband points out that "you'da had to shake and shimmy for a living—that ain't atall becoming to you," she retorts, "I'd be better off shakin on the road than slowly turning to dust on a Charleston piazza."[65]

Even as Cora faces violence and discrimination on the TOBA, she demands and gets racial and gender equality in ways that were not open to her on the Black Star Line and in her own marriage before she joined the UNIA. Rather than stoically enduring inferior meal service on a train as the Black bourgeoisie do, Cora threatens to give a "performance" if she is not allowed into the dining car; a Black waiter who has seen her act puts her tab on the house. At a theater in Georgia, Cora responds to the white manager's refusal to pay in advance and provide decent changing facilities with an outburst that commemorates the resistance of female performers such as Ethel Waters and Bessie Smith to exploitative work conditions: "Fuck Georgia law, I ain't made it! . . . Throw me in jail, lynch me—I'm ready to die! This is my last stop on the Jim Crow line! Pay up and open the dressin rooms, you white-ass, cheatin sonofabitch, *or I ain't goin on!*"[66] Cora is also in charge of her finances and sexuality in ways that were denied to her on Garvey's ship or in her former husband's house: she hires a young male lover and sets the terms of their relationship. Meanwhile, the troupe's co-manager, another Black woman, takes a female lover on the vaudeville circuit.

Along with the freedom that touring the TOBA circuit offers Black women, Childress indicates that performing its minstrel-based acts can revamp heteropatriarchal nationalisms by engaging in political protest made possible by Black minstrelsy's multiple maskings. This subversive minstrelsy culminates in a performance given by a "heavyset but very ladylike" West Indian man named Marion who recuperates the mammy's minstrel drag in order to disrupt hegemonic identities and engender a feminine and queer anticolonial public sphere.[67] Marion's act is illuminated by what I argue to be the drag of Jackie "Moms" Mabley, as portrayed in Childress's *Moms: A Praise Play for a Black Comedienne* (1984). Mabley, a groundbreaking TOBA performer with professional roots in minstrelsy, provided a historical model for *A Short Walk*'s examination of "the black woman's life as a minstrel show."[68] At the same time, Cora's and Marion's struggles with(in) the ubiquitous mammy role were rehearsals for Childress's subsequent depiction of Mabley's successful stage act as a wise and maternal older woman arrayed in tattered housedresses, floppy hats, and oversized men's shoes—an outfit "designed to suggest the clown, the fool, as well as the slave granny, the mammy."[69] Drawing on the oral history provided by Mabley's adopted son, Charles Aiken, Childress suggests that Moms's outfit and the mammy role it signified were denaturalized by Mabley's cross-dressing, which exposed the ambiguities, contradictions, and crises of Black/American identity produced by U.S. racist imperialism. I now turn to the queer and feminist anticolonial critique expressed by Moms Mabley's Black minstrel drag in order to illuminate its significance to the exploration of Garvey's legacy in *A Short Walk.*

▫ ▫ ▫

Mabley, the "first distinctive black female comic star able to run an act on her own," drew on her roots in minstrelsy throughout her career, "differentiating the formula and appropriating it to fit her audience and her times."[70] Mabley alienated African Americans in the 1950s who strove to distance themselves from the subservience embodied in the mammy figure. Yet Mabley's shrewd deployment of this stereotype had empowered her to break with vaudeville's gendered and racial limits. In the 1920s, she became one of the few female vaudevillians to perform alone by assuming the mammy persona that she would eventually call "Moms." Moms's familiar, unthreatening guise allowed Mabley to overcome the patriarchal norms that paired vaudeville's women with men instead of allowing female solo acts.[71] (Among the actors with whom Mabley was teamed was Tim Moore, who would later play Kingfish on the *Amos 'n' Andy* television series.) The mammy guise helped Mabley slip past the racist conventions that had prevented Black comics from directly addressing white audiences before the 1950s, since, according to Mel Watkins, a "black performer who demanded a personal response [from whites] would have transgressed a boundary by suggesting an equality intolerable to most non-blacks."[72] As Moms, Mabley became one of the first Black comics to employ the monologue, which she used to pioneer comic social satire that was aimed at targets ranging from southern segregationists to international heads of state, positioning herself as interlocutor to each group.

Mabley's reappropriation of the mammy role extended to its multiple minstrel masks, which are illustrated by one of the best-known incarnations of this figure, Aunt Jemima. "Old Aunt Jemima" was a popular song written and performed by the celebrated Black minstrel Billy Kersands. Kersands' song was eventually appropriated by a white blackface minstrel in drag (at this time, most minstrels were men), who inspired the owner of a flour mill searching for a brand for his pancake flour. The Davis Milling Company acquired the Aunt Jemima trademark and at the 1893 Columbian Exposition in Chicago "turned [it] into a real person. The flour millers hired Nancy Green, a fifty-nine-year-old domestic worker who had been born into slavery on a Kentucky plantation, to portray Aunt Jemima. She greeted guests and cooked pancakes at Davis's booth, an exhibit designed to look like a giant flour barrel." Green, a "real" Black domestic, portrayed not herself but a mystified image of a Black domestic inspired by a white man's performance of a Black woman based on a song by a Black man exploiting a white nostalgic vision of Black culture—thereby branding not only a commercial product but a white supremacist image of America itself, as Karen Sotiropoulos implies: "Aunt Jemima was as well-known as the Pledge of Allegiance by the fair's end."[73]

Activating the multiple masks of the minstrel mammy, Mabley undermined reified static categories of race and gender that underpinned hegemonic and counterhegemonic national identities. With the broad, toothless smile with which Mabley began her act, she put into play the iconic blackface mouth's plural and contradictory meanings. Yoking maternity and infancy, the blackface mouth symbolized the white fantasy that Blacks gladly and docilely produced bounty for whites who were at once masters and children to serve. White men cross-dressing as Black women in the postbellum minstrel show created another layer of meaning, displaying the gaping blackface mouth to convey and contain the threat of feminine sexual and political power.[74] The words issuing from Mabley's grinning mouth juxtaposed these different identities—the down-home mother to all of her "children," as she called her audience, irrespective of race; the lecherous old woman yearning for a young man; and the militant preacher speaking truth to power as she "move[d] easily from folksy homilies to ribald double entendres and on to social and political satire."[75] Inhabiting all of these identities without prioritizing any one of them, Mabley did not necessarily supplant an inauthentic mammy role with an authentic Black female identity, be it an incarnation of the strong and loving grandmother after whom she modeled "Moms" or a "gritty ethnic quality" in line with the values of the Black cultural nationalism that contributed to her recognition in the 1950s and 1960s. Rather, her performance induced the "category crisis" that Marjorie Garber ascribes to "the extraordinary power of transvestism to disrupt, expose, and challenge, putting in question the very notion of the 'original' and of stable identity."[76]

It is not (co)incidental that Mabley regularly cross-dressed on the road, onstage, and in private and that the blurring of boundaries between these spheres was a product of her cross-dressing. Although best known for her frumpy old woman's outfit, Mabley also wore men's attire—jackets, shirts, shoes, and boxer shorts—both onstage and off.[77] Mabley's cross-dressing exploded discrete gender and sex roles, as Charles Aiken indicates:

> [Mabley] was my mother, someone I use [*sic*] to hang around with, my star. Above all, always dressed in her male attire, she was my father. Alice, a beautiful red-headed black woman who looked like Alice Faye, was my mother. I've had many different mothers throughout my life. . . . But mother was my only father.[78]

If Mabley adopted a masculine subject position through her cross-dressing and lesbianism, then Moms was a drag performance—a female role inhabited by an actor in a male role itself undermined by Mabley's androgyny. Moms was thus, like Aunt Jemima, composed of multiple masks.

Drawing heavily on Aiken's oral history for her play, Childress depicted Mabley's resignification of the mammy role through her cross-dressing and lesbianism.[79] In *Moms,* the mammy stereotype is central to the climactic argument between Mabley and her pianist, Luther. Frustrated with what he perceives to be Mabley's emasculation of him, Luther accuses her of wanting to "play BIG-MAMA and be MIGHTY-MAMMY." His recourse to the mammy stereotype and its counterpart, the strong Black matriarch, in an effort to assert Black male dominance is problematized by Mabley's stand-up act immediately following their fight. As Moms, Mabley transforms the mammy's maternal embrace of all races into an embrace of all genders and sexualities: "Thank you, children . . . all of you out there, male, female, heteros, homos, transvests, trans-sex, bi-sex, and anything new that Moms may not have heard bout." As Mabley tells Luther in response to his effort to ascertain whether she is gay: "Like the good Lord, Moms Mabley tried to love EVERYBODY." Queering Black maternal love, Mabley repudiates exploitative images of the nurturing, self-abnegating mammy and the emasculating Black matriarch by undoing the heteropatriarchal frame of reference for these identities. That is, the male-headed nuclear family (white or Black) gives way to nonbiological bonds between Moms and her "children" that do not center on reproducing a patriarchal, capitalist, and/or white supremacist social order. As a result, Mabley claims other roles besides "big mama" and "mighty mammy" that confound the narrow binaristic identities that Luther knows best: when he asks Mabley whether she is "gay . . . I mean Lesbian," he stumblingly elaborates that "it is a contradiction . . . I mean her having four children AND being a Lesbian. . . . I mean, IF you [Mabley] are, or ever WERE Gay . . . (lamely) . . . you couldn't have been very . . . dedicated."[80] Of course, Mabley was a very "dedicated" lesbian who also had male lovers and raised children. Her rejection of the mutual exclusivity of these roles and of the dominant ideologies of gender, sexuality, and race that deem them to be mutually exclusive was effected through, not in spite of, her repurposed Black minstrelsy.

Childress's depiction of Mabley's transvestism pursues the implications of her minstrelsy. Appearing in a "well tailored man's suit" over "lacey 'Teddies'" after her Moms act, Mabley announces that she has been at a "wear-what-you-want, say-what-you-want, do-what-you-want-but-know-what-you-doin kinda place" where she "[feels] perfectly at home." Childress's euphemistic language need not be read as mere coyness. More to the point, it signifies Mabley's sense of belonging within a space that is not strictly gay or straight, male or female (indicated further by Mabley's masculine *and* feminine dress). Mabley's transvestism echoes the fluidity increasingly evident in Moms's catalog of "male, female, heteros, homos, transvests, trans-sex, bi-sex, and anything new that Moms may not have heard bout."[81]

As that "apparently spontaneous or unexpected or supplementary presence of a transvestite figure in a text . . . that does not seem, thematically, to be primarily concerned with gender difference or blurred gender," Mabley manifests "a *category crisis elsewhere,* an irresolvable conflict or epistemological crux that destabilizes comfortable binarity, and displaces the resulting discomfort onto a figure that already inhabits, indeed incarnates, the margin."[82] The "elsewhere" of Mabley's minstrel drag is her fictive traversal of the contested borders of the U.S. nation-state as a worldly interlocutor of heads of state. This shtick became so popular that the titles of three of her comedy albums refer to it—*Moms Mabley at Geneva Conference* (1961), *Moms Mabley at the UN* (1961), and *Moms Mabley at the White House Conference* (1966).

Childress incorporated some of Mabley's monologue from this genre into her play:

> Harlem's still got a little magic for me . . . and a lotta memories. Over, yonder, is the Hotel Theresa. I was livin there when Fidel Castro and Nikita Kruschev came up to visit Harlem. Sure I spoke to em. . . . After all, if the big blow comes, no tellin what Country my butt might land in. (With a wink) I told Krusch . . . you wanta fight? Fight me. I'll fightcha . . . in Mississippi, Georgia, Alabama, or any other foreign country.[83]

Citing a highlight of anticolonial Left history—Fidel Castro's decampment to Harlem's Hotel Theresa, where he met with other world leaders—Mabley challenges racism on international terms. She jokingly yet defiantly asserts that Blacks are free to relocate to Cuba or the Soviet Union, which are no more foreign than the deep South due to the fact that U.S. racism radically questions what is American and what is foreign, what is patriotic and what is treasonous.

Moms explores the ambivalence toward and ambiguities of national identity that arise from the conjunctions of U.S. racism and imperialism by recovering the repressed anti-war, anti-lynching militancy of Bert Williams's blackface minstrelsy.[84] Williams's militant legacy is represented by Mabley's former lover and vaudeville partner, Jack Mabley, whose name she took for her stage name in what we might see as another act of cross-dressing. In the play, the hospitalized and terminally ill Jack laments that he never got to perform "I'm Gone Before I Go," Bert Williams's song about African Americans in the Mexican revolution: "Political stuff always got cut out of shows," Jack tells Moms. "I put that number in one-a my acts. And I never made it." Against this silencing, Moms urges Jack to "do your Bert Williams," and he becomes "suddenly, angrily in need of performing." This moment becomes Jack's stand against the historical and ideological forces that have contributed to his impending death, including mainstream America's disavowal of racist exploitation and racial critique. His defiant performance becomes the counterpart to Mabley's resistance to the mammy stereotype by "claim[ing] her right to exist" and proclaiming, "I am here!" Yet Jack's performance of "I'm Gone Before I Go," like Mabley's Moms act, does not really entail self-revelation: he tellingly calls his version of this song an "imitation of the great Bert Williams"—that is to say, the imitation of a Black West Indian who imitated a Black American as a blackface minstrel.[85] Instead of authenticity, we have artifice; instead of self-affirmation, we have self-negation: "I'm Gone Before I Go" recalls "Nobody," Williams's "great paean to self-negation" for which he was (and still is) best known.[86] However, the minstrel self-effacement of "I'm Gone" functions differently from that of "Nobody." By exposing the racial terror and imperialist warfare at the heart of American universalism, "I'm Gone" negates the negation of Black subjectivity created by the physical and epistemic violence of racial subjugation.

To unpack this "Afro-alienation act," some background on Williams's song is in order. Bert Williams recorded "I'm Gone" in July 1916, only months after segregated African American troops—the same "Buffalo Soldiers" charged with massacring Native Americans to defend Anglo-American life and property along the U.S.-Mexico border—pursued Pancho Villa into Mexico in the disastrous "Punitive Expedition." As the Mexican Revolution, with its "profound anticlericalism, far-reaching land reform, deep-seated hostility to U.S. imperialism, and democratic promise," threatened U.S. political and economic interests, African American troops became increasingly important. It was believed that unlike soldiers of Mexican origin and certain European immigrants, African Americans "did not have an allegiance to the real or imagined foes of Washington." Yet for all their perceived patriotism (or at least lack of allegiance to another country), African Americans were treated no better than before, leading many of them to see in the revolution not a threat but a hope for a social order that recognized the rights and dignity of people of color. Consequently, whereas the mainstream media depicted Pancho Villa as a terrorist, the Black press celebrated him as an African-blooded folk hero who could give the United States and its white supremacy a run for its money.[87] Further fueling the publicity around Villa and the Punitive Expedition was its coincidence with the emerging popularity of motion pictures (D.W. Griffith's *The Birth of a Nation* had been released the previous year). Elaborately reenacted footage of the fighting "added to the perceived heroism of the combatants on all sides."[88] Trading on Villa's currency in the cultural marketplace, Williams satirized the revolutionary in the Ziegfield Follies. But as Childress indicates in her play, he apparently never got to satirize American patriotism on the Follies stage with "I'm Gone Before I Go."[89] Nonetheless, using the title as a catchphrase, Williams alluded to the topical song and its exposure of the racial terror that rendered Americanness unattainable for people of African descent.

"I'm Gone" ironizes the triumph of American truth and might celebrated in the "Battle Hymn of the Republic," to which Williams's refrain is sung. Williams begins by intoning, deadpan, "Patriotism always has been uppermost with me / I used to row out every day just to kiss Miss Liberty."[90] The second line of the couplet deflates the high-minded patriotism professed in the first line and flirts with the sexualized and racial limits of American freedom by representing it through the explosive image of a Black man kissing a white woman (Miss Liberty).[91] The song continues to disclose the difference that race makes to official U.S. nationalism by substituting Black founding fathers and heroes for white ones: Williams sings of a friend, Sam Brown, who goes to fight in Mexico so that "his name would always live in history / like Washington—he meant Booker T." Then Sam Brown replaces John Brown as Williams modifies the words of "John Brown's Body" (another song set to the tune of the "Battle Hymn of the Republic"): "Sam Brown's body lies a-mouldin in the ground / I guess I'm gone before I go." Instead of the martyred white abolitionist calling Union soldiers to fight as "his soul goes marching on," the martyred Black soldier symbolizes the futility of African American military service ("I'm gone before I go").

Even more radically, the song replaces Andrew Johnson in its pantheon of great Americans with Black heavyweight boxing champion Jack Johnson, thereby positing a Black subject position outside any country. This substitution occurs in the second half of the song, which describes a second, unnamed friend's plan to go to Mexico as a spy instead of a soldier so that "his name would always live in history / like Johnson—he was talkin bout Jack." Having defeated several white boxers, including James Jeffries in 1910, Johnson was one of the most visible and successful challengers to white supremacy. Johnson thus mirrored Pancho Villa in the Black popular imagination, a pairing that would gain more substance when in 1919 Johnson went to Mexico, where he set up a land company that ran ads in Black newspapers inviting "you who are lynched, tortured, mobbed, persecuted and discriminated against in the boasted 'Land of Liberty'" to "OWN A HOME IN MEXICO where one man is as good as another."[92] Furthermore, echoing the image of Williams kissing Miss Liberty, Johnson challenged the sexual logic of white supremacist U.S. national identity: he had been infamously married to two white women by the time "I'm Gone" was recorded in 1916, and a relationship with a third resulted in his seven-year exile beginning in 1913 after his conviction on trumped-up charges of violating the Mann Act, which prohibited the transportation of women across state lines for immoral purposes.[93] In following the footsteps of the exiled Johnson by becoming a spy, Williams's friend unmoors himself from national ties. He rationalizes that while "the fallen heroes paid for all the victors that the others made . . . the gumshoe men were the ones found the plans the enemies laid," and so "the clever men were the ones that used the eagle eye / And never had on a uniform." Significantly, Williams doesn't specify which side his friend spies for. What is clear is that such ambiguity was intolerable, for "they hung my friend to a sour apple tree."

Jack's performance of "I'm Gone" in *Moms* omits the spy and sings only of a soldier who meets the spy's dishonorable, violent end.[94] In doing so, Jack's version suggests that within a white supremacist state, the African American soldier is no different from the spy, insofar as his race puts him irredeemably at odds with the national body. *Moms* alludes to Williams's own exemplification of this conundrum through Mabley's eulogy at the conclusion: "A flower for [Jack's] friend, Bert Williams . . . (To audience) A West Indian comedian and an officer in the 369th Infantry."[95] Williams had joined the Colored Regiment of the New York National Guard in the fall of 1916 (after recording "I'm Gone Before I Go" that summer), when the general sentiment among African Americans was that they needed to support the war effort to achieve racial equality. Nonetheless, Williams became increasingly disillusioned with the persistent limits to American democracy he had exposed in "I'm Gone." The following year, Camille Forbes writes, he

> started to speak more openly about his experiences in America and in the *Follies*, garnering attention for his offstage pronouncements. His words would take on a darker tone, even as he aimed to remain optimistic. By this time, he would have heard about the violence and near-riot that occurred in July when his friend, musician Noble Sissle, was in South Carolina for training and did not remove his hat fast enough to satisfy a store manager standing behind a counter.[96]

As Jack's version of Williams's song suggests, wearing the country's uniform was not enough to bring the Black soldier, who was still subject to the violence meted to the spy, into the country's fold. We might thus read *Moms*'s characterization of Williams as "[a] *West Indian* comedian and an officer in the 369th Infantry" as reintroducing the spy's national ambiguity: Williams was never fully Americanized despite his (largely symbolic) military service or even his naturalization two years later.

In *A Short Walk*, Childress reintroduced Black minstrelsy's critique of imperialist nationalism and heteropatriarchal articulations of Blackness through the drag ball, the minstrel show's analogue. These two spaces are connected in several ways. The androgynous name of Cora's friend Marion, who wins first prize at the ball, invokes one of Black minstrelsy's great composers and a co-writer of *In Dahomey*, Will Marion Cook. Meanwhile, the MC of the ball, "a smooth, handsome cat in a full dress suit," is a "black interlocutor," and the fact that he is "black as shinola polish" suggests minstrelsy's racial artifice. Cora even encounters a drag Rosalinda in the ball's perennial winner, a white man who has come as a "peacock" with rhinestone earrings, feathers, golden slippers, and "[t]wo attendants in lavender tights . . . bearin gold bowls from which they sprinkle a carpet of rose petals as he slowly struts around the floor." Cora thinks, "He reminds me of something I've long tried to do—rise above it, above everything that's tryin to hold us back," calling to mind Rosalinda in the minstrel show of Cora's childhood "serenely stand[ing] above and beyond the ugly limitation of a patched tent and the double-aisled world of colored and white."[97]

Childress suggests, however, that such transcendence is ultimately impossible because all the world—even Garvey's worldly UNIA—is a minstrel stage. Consequently, Black empowerment is engendered not through the ethereal beauty of Rosalinda rising "above and beyond the ugly limitation" of the minstrel tent but through the mammy figure of "Madame Marion," "big as all outdoors," redeploying minstrel drag in the vein of "Moms" Mabley:[98]

> Hefty and middle-aged, he wears a proud, patient look on his face. . . . He looks out at the crowd, kindly, with love. One woman calls out from a box, "Mother!" Someone titters, then is hushed by others. Marion walks forward, almost timidly. People begin to clap in time to his stride. . . . He is what he claims to be—a representative of that spirit which is seen and felt at Wednesday testimonial. The spirit of those who've been through some rough trials.[99]

Like Rosalinda, Marion has a freedom song, a spiritual that turns the drag ball into a "church meetin" and that reveals the other face of the denigrated mammy to be the powerful and revered church mother whose "'children' are often religious and political leaders who owe their power and authority to the sponsorship of such women."[100] These women were central to the necessary work of uniting the race, as Childress wrote the year after *A Short Walk* was published:

> There is a great tradition of strong leadership coming from the Black church . . . particularly mature Black women. The Black community has come through a long period of seeing poor communication between themselves . . . of fragmentation[,] and the people are in great need of seeing some togetherness in understanding.[101]

With his spiritual, Marion unites a diasporic congregation of queens—including Cleopatra, the Queen of Sheba, and the African Rain Queen—who "can't help but join along, clappin, singin, cryin."[102] Their song, "On My Journey: Mount Zion," evokes Garvey's back-to-Africa platform along with the drag ball's spectacle of global power, which reprises Garvey's appropriation of the costumes, titles, and pageantry of imperialist nationalism. In addition to "Madame Marion" and the aforementioned African royalty, European powers are represented by Madame de Pompadour, Queen Elizabeth, and the Duchess of Alba. However, the heteropatriarchal, imperialist nobility Garvey had fetishized is replaced by the grassroots, feminine, and queer Black leadership of Marion's church mother.

Carrying forth this tradition of Black female race leadership, Marion is no "mere" impersonator; "he is what he claims to be—a representative of that spirit which is seen and felt at Wednesday testimonial." The effect of Marion's singing on his audience, who "join along, clappin, singin, cryin," is no less authentic than Cora's shout at Wednesday testimonial, which makes the church come "alive with [her] sound as all fly higher and higher on the wings of [her] prayer."[103] Although Marion cites Cora as his inspiration while accepting first prize at the ball, by the end of the novel it is Cora who imitates him, as we will see.

Like Moms Mabley—herself a secular church mother—Marion's drag denaturalizes the essentialist and originary constructions of gender that are often supported by the essentialist logic of racism, as illustrated by Cora's meditation on churchwomen's hats:

> Years back, down in New Orleans, durin slave days, they had a law which forbid any slave women to wear a hat—had to be a kerchief. Explanation was: so they could tell white women from mixed bloods who looked white. Lotta mess-ass laws. Right now, down in Mississippi, if a white man marries a colored woman both can be fined ten thousand dollars each and be put in jail for ten years. If they just sleep together, with no marriage, that only calls for thirty days' hard labor and a scoldin. The black man will be lynched for mixin. Strange laws and lawmakers.
>
> I'm thinking a hat is a silly idea, with flowers, ribbons and bows. It's the law of the church that women cover their heads and men uncover theirs.[104]

Cora's genealogy ties the gender segregation that is "the law of the church" to the "strange laws" of racial segregation, which create a visible marker of racial difference in the face of racial admixture. The hats are symptoms of legal and cultural systems that seek to inscribe clear categories of gender and race. Similarly, Garvey's separatism, according to Richard B. Moore, signaled his acceptance of "the European colonial concept of 'race' as valid, natural, fundamental, and requiring the separation of so-called 'races' in order to maintain 'race purity.'"[105]

By contrast, Cora's befriending of a white woman, May, not only crosses the color line but dispenses with its binarism; May introduces Cora to her Filipino husband, Apolinario, and their Chinese, Cuban, African, and West Indian friends, who are seagoing men. Preferring that Cora associate only with those in her race, Cecil disparages these men as "aliens." Yet in the novel Apolinario and his friends prefigure the Black Star Line's goals of transnational mobility as "seamen from all over the world . . . who left home to labor their way around the world," a fraternity of aliens exercising their right to "go ashore and stay ashore anyplace in the world."[106] The Third World solidarity and transnationalism Cora's friendship with the seamen symbolizes is revisited by Marion's performance of "dark" rather than Black womanhood, capped with her rousing rendition of "On My Journey: Mount Zion." For Marion and the other queens, who "wouldn't take nothin for [their] journey now," the freedom to travel is no less important than the project of reclaiming a homeland.

The complexity of reclaiming a homeland is such that Childress's novel never allows African emigration to become more than an abstract idea, despite its centrality to Garveyism. Instead, *A Short Walk* is more interested in reclaiming America. Cora thinks about this even on the Black Star Line:

> Water is churnin by as we pass the Statue of Liberty holding her lamp high and clutching the lawbook. I try not to think about Jim Crow laws—for a moment I know what it's like to feel patriotic, and U.S.A. becomes my very own country as our black ship tugs past the white woman wearing her crown of spikes like Jesus' thorns.[107]

Like the ambivalent and tragic outcomes of Black military service that Bert Williams sang about and lived, Cora's paradoxical claim on the United States only in leaving its shores is symptomatic of the contradiction between American universalism—its color-blind extension of freedom and democracy to all, monumentalized by the Statue of Liberty "holding her lamp high and clutching the lawbook"—and the racial and gendered limits of this universalism, which turns Liberty into "the white woman wearing her crown of spikes like Jesus' thorns." The drag ball spectacularly restages the contradictions of U.S. liberal democracy as well as the limits of Garvey's separatism. Liberty's dystopic image, "the white woman wearing her crown of spikes like Jesus' thorns," is captured in the novel by the white peacock's winning performance at the previous year's ball, when he had come as the Statue of Liberty with a gold spiked crown, a sequined lawbook, and a "red lamp that flashed on and off with each step."[108] The nation's utopic promise of inclusivity is rendered by the West Indian Marion with his "corsage of bright red American Beauty Roses" who unites the multiracial, multinational drag ball in song.[109] Marion's spiritual is evidence that Black culture "presents a compelling and particular universalism that paradoxically provides more secure, normative foundations for forging a common political life among diverse peoples than those varieties of universalism simply dubbed 'American.'"[110] Indeed, the Black universalism represented by Marion at the drag ball recreates the political vision of another pageant that stirred its audience to sing "On My Journey: Mount Zion": the cultural festival Childress and Hansberry wrote to celebrate Negro History Week and the first anniversary of Robeson's *Freedom* newspaper. ("On My Journey" was a central song of Robeson's repertoire.)[111] Featuring a reading of "A Call to Negro Woman" issued by the Sojourners for Truth and Justice, Childress and Hansberry's program showcased Black women's leadership in demanding the application of American democracy to all:

> We insist that only when our government abolishes the lynch justice of Mississippi, when it does away with the Ciceros and Peekskills [sites of white mob violence], only when it moves to enforce the 13th, 14th and 15th amendments to the Constitution of the United States . . . then and only then can it speak as a free nation for a free world.
>
> We call upon the government to prove its loyalty to its fifteen million Negro citizens.[112]

Marion's drag restages this testament to Black women's struggles to transform America by denaturalizing and rejecting reified categories of both womanhood and Blackness. By foregrounding the performativity and constructedness of these roles, Marion frees them from the narrow identity politics of authenticity and routes them instead through a politics of emancipation that cannot but spill into the world's stagecraft.

Thus, beyond the ball, Cora reprises Marion's emancipatory enactment of dark womanhood on the eve of her death, when for the last time she works within and against minstrelsy's script. Her stout figure dressed simply yet elegantly in black, Cora is a copy of Marion in drag as she makes her way to meet him at the Broadway theatre district. However, she first steps into a souvenir shop to select for Cecil "a comic postcard with a big fat black woman standing in front of an outhouse Underneath is printed *I Love You No Matter Where I Am!*" The postcard is not wholly ironic; rather, it acknowledges that the Mammy role has followed and defined Cora wherever she has gone. Even her death on Broadway reenacts the antics of Mandy-the-cook that had delighted her as a child, when the minstrel man playing Mandy lifted "her" skirt to show "her" undergarments. Cora's last moments repudiate minstrelsy's exposure and abjection of the Black female body, as passersby are compelled to maintain her dignity after she collapses on the street: "A woman pulls down Cora's dress to cover the glimpse of thigh which spills over the top of her stocking. Another hand places her purse on her stomach."[113]

Cora's final performance of dark womanhood culminates the novel's vision of reclaiming Garvey's nationalist and transnational politics of Black liberation: her death merges into the Black Star Line's spectacle of free mobility as Cora, carried into an ambulance, imagines its siren to be a ship's whistle and the paramedics to be "captains in their white coats [who] lean over her and lift her toward the gangplank—'Oh, Joy!'"[114] Childress's notes on this scene say "and now Rosalinda will sing."[115] Cora's death on a New Year's Eve in the midst of World War II marks not only an end but a beginning when, in Michelle Stephens's words, "the blackface of the decline of empire would be the rise of new racial nationalisms and colonial liberation movements in Africa, Asia, and the West Indies, movements that Garveyism both predicted and prefigured."[116] To extend this apt characterization of Third World radicalism, the drag of Garveyism that Cora and Marion's subversive minstrelsy exemplified would be the feminist and queer pan-Africanism and anticolonialism that postwar Black women writers developed.

In retrieving Garveyism's investments in transnational mobility and political theater, Childress envisioned anew the movement's prophetic relevance to the circuits linking Black Power in the Americas to African redemption. The elements that generated Garvey's unprecedented mass appeal—the Black Star Line, the pageantry, the performance of racial self-government—also confined it within imperialist and heteropatriarchal ideologies. Childress insisted that these ideological bounds be broken within the revival of interest in Garveyism that the post–World War II Black Left promoted and debated. Like Richard B. Moore, Childress challenged Garvey's essentialist "reactionary nationalism" with nationalist internationalism. Going even further, she reimagined Garveyism through a Black internationalist feminist lens: rescripting the minstrel roles that Garvey's imperial performances adapted, she destabilized pervasive hierarchies and hegemonic norms of gender and sexuality.

The promise of Childress's rehabilitated Garveyism and of other forms of race radicalism was called into question by Rosa Guy's novel, *The Sun, the Sea, a Touch of the Wind* (1995). As the next chapter investigates, Guy was positioned in the mid-1990s to assess Black radicalism's failures of leadership and political tactics. Although unsparing in her portrait of patriarchy, hubris, and voluntarism within the Black left, Guy retained its anti-imperialist critique to counter the U.S. exceptionalism of contemporary Black feminist discourses of empowerment. In doing so, Guy represented transnational queer and feminist subjectivities in the vein of Hansberry and Childress while departing from these writers in grappling with the erosion of revolutionary movements in the United States at the dawn of the twenty-first century.

4

Rosa Guy, Haiti, and the Hemispheric Woman

To frame the Black feminist intervention of Rosa Guy's *The Sun, the Sea, a Touch of the Wind* (1995), I want to discuss a contemporaneous novel that shares with Guy's the theme of African American female rejuvenation and empowerment through Caribbean romance—Terry McMillan's bestseller and pop culture phenomenon, *How Stella Got Her Groove Back* (1996). Because McMillan is one of the most widely known authors who defines Black feminism today,[1] it is worthwhile to consider how her work takes up Carole Boyce Davies' salient questions: "How do United States Black women/women of color, often the most dispossessed on the ladder of social and economic resources, pursue their own liberation? Is it through alliance with oppression or in resistance?"[2] As I will argue, the influential yet problematic version of Black women's liberation popularized by McMillan's novel—with its reliance on the interlocking ideologies of heteronormativity and U.S. exceptionalism—is countered by Guy's examination in *The Sun, the Sea, a Touch of the Wind* of Black internationalism's meanings for African American women in the late twentieth century.

In McMillan's *Stella,* the eponymous heroine is a successful but weary African American financial consultant who finds rejuvenation through dating a winsome younger man from Jamaica, Winston, whom she meets while vacationing on the island. After overcoming myriad obstacles, Stella and Winston reunite in the United States with the promise of marriage. In the words of Oprah Winfrey, this was "a story based on real life that gave millions of lonely women hope" as they avidly consumed McMillan's "intimate details of her own steamy romance with a man 23 years younger" in Jamaica.[3]

The novel's "real life" basis and unfolding in the form of McMillan's marriage to Jonathan Plummer fueled the *Stella* phenomenon, including the movie based on the novel starring Angela Bassett and Taye Diggs.

However, *Stella*'s compelling narrative of romance relies upon and promulgates U.S. exceptionalism. What matters is not only that Stella and Winston marry but that they marry in the United States, figured as the land of opportunity through blissful inattention not only to the exploitative tourist industry that has brought the happy couple together, but to the role of the United States in engineering the economic, political, and social crises (the crippling debt, trade deficit, poverty, widening income gap, and deteriorating social services) that have left Jamaica overreliant on tourism for its gross national product.[4] That *Stella* briefly but directly addresses slavery and domestic racism only foregrounds its blindness to U.S. imperialism and raises the question of why this lacuna seems so necessary within the generic imperatives of popular romance fiction—a topic I return to in the conclusion.

Rosa Guy's *The Sun, the Sea, a Touch of the Wind,* published just one year before *Stella,* starts from the opposing premise that demystifying and challenging U.S. imperialism is essential to Black feminist narratives of empowerment—and that Black feminism redefines anti-imperialist and anticolonial struggles for sovereignty. In Guy's novel, the ongoing legacy of Haiti's "colonial, imperial slave past" is embedded not only in the country's landscape, which is "devastated by the United States government's futile attempt to produce substitute rubber for World War II," but also, and just as importantly, in the psyche of its African American female protagonist, Jonnie Dash.[5] Jonnie travels to Haiti in the 1970s thinking that rekindling romance with an old lover there will heal her psychic wounds. However, Jonnie Dash's very name (and she is frequently called by her full name) alludes to the paradoxical nature of free movement for African Americans, especially women, a result of the ways that "state violence directed at peoples of color [in the United States] not only defines U.S. democracy but also provides an insidious blueprint for U.S. imperial designs."[6] Although Jonnie is regularly described as "dashing around," her agency is undermined by her inability to move on, physically or psychologically, from the violence to which she has been subjected as an African American woman and the increasingly clear international dimensions of that violence.[7] While she has purposively traveled from the United States to Haiti and from Port-au-Prince to the idyllic mountain village of Fermath, unresolved pain and anger from her past lead to a blackout during which she returns to the Port-au-Prince hotel where she had first stayed upon arriving in Haiti. Her unconscious return to the Old Hotel, an outpost of American and European tourists and expatriates with dreams of possessing Haiti, signals the constraints that imperialism and colonialism set upon free movement for people for color: until Jonnie confronts her traumatic past of "domestic" racial conflict and the new forms it takes within this "foreign" site, she will not be free.

This confrontation is set in motion by Jonnie's introduction to a white U.S. diplomat, Charles McCellan, whose immediate hostility toward her bespeaks the racial limits and contradictions of U.S. liberal democracy:

> What threat did this young redhead, with his character, already screwed up behind his plastic diplomat mask, imagine that she posed to him and his country because she wore her hair natural? Did he really see her as a rebel? A terrorist? An enemy of the system? Terrifying to think that those in control of gunboats offshore, those who covertly represented the power on this tiny island and the surrounding islands saw a Black American woman's hair, worn natural, as a threat.[8]

Even while the representative of U.S. interests in—and power over—Haiti projects the threat of subversion onto Jonnie and her Black Power–signifying Afro, it is he who terrorizes the local population by exploiting his office to procure a Haitian boy, Lucknair, for his sex slave. Jonnie's reluctant involvement in this morass sutures the exigencies of U.S. imperialism to her experience of racist police brutality in New York: after hiding Lucknair in her room, Jonnie is appalled to find Tonton Macoutes members ransacking the hotel in search of the boy. The dedication of "this independent Black country's soldiers . . . doing the bidding of this ordinary-looking bastard [McCellan]" painfully reminds her of "those white cops beating on the head of another little Black boy [her childhood friend, Boysie] on a New York street."[9]

Saving Lucknair enables Jonnie to work through the trauma of losing both Boysie and her son, Emmanuel, to the punitive racist U.S. state. Whereas she had been unsuccessful in challenging a New York City court that had unjustly sentenced Emmanuel to jail, Jonnie effects Lucknair's escape through the kangaroo court that is summoned when she crosses another high-ranking American official in Haiti. While being interrogated by several American expatriates—"judges and juries of crimes done to, or by, American citizens"[10]—Jonnie wins the approbation of her accusers by announcing her decision to adopt Lucknair. In doing so, Jonnie exploits her status as a U.S. citizen, with all the formal rights that status entails. However, what the novel affirms is not the triumph of American liberal democracy—Jonnie punctures Lucknair's dreams of the United States as a safe haven or land of opportunity for Black people—but anticolonial diasporic solidarity.

▫ ▫ ▫

The roots of this solidarity are intimated by the novel's acknowledgements, in which Guy first thanks the Harlem Writers Guild, "the organization that I helped found and in which I spent many years perfecting my gift as a writer." This expression of gratitude, comprising over half of the acknowledgements, signals the grounding of Guy and her novel in the postwar Black Left, within which Guy played a dynamic but overlooked part. As a cultural wing of the Black Left, the Guild held an anticolonial, internationalist outlook that Guy characterized as "a broad understanding of what was happening in the world in terms of the exploitation of black countries and the relationship of such exploitation to the plight of blacks in the United States."[11] Many associated with the Guild, especially its core members, tenaciously continued the work of the Council on African Affairs and Robeson's *Freedom* newspaper after they had been dissolved in 1955. Guild members were also involved with *Freedom*'s descendant, *Freedomways,* the Fair Play for Cuba Committee, and the Cultural Association for Women of African Heritage. Guy, who had close ties with the Congolese UN delegation and had met with Patrice Lumumba, was instrumental in moving CAWAH to recognize and act on the interconnections between struggles for civil rights in the United States and struggles for national liberation across the globe.

Guy's Black internationalism informed her "hemispheric consciousness," the result of "having been born in the West Indies and having suffered the injustices of the North American continent."[12] A major influence on this hemispheric consciousness was fellow Trindadian C. L. R. James, who had given her literary career an early boost; after they met in Trinidad in 1960, he published her first literary work—two short stories, one about Carnival, the other based on her experiences working in a New York brassiere factory—in *The Nation,* the Trinidadian newspaper of the People's National Movement party. Of particular importance to Guy's politicization was James's groundbreaking study of the Haitian Revolution, *The Black Jacobins.* When it was first published in 1938, *The Black Jacobins* had broken the historiographic silence on Haiti's successful struggle for independence, which had brought into being the Western hemisphere's second independent republic and first Black nation, as well as the hope—or threat, depending on one's perspective—of the death knell of slavery and colonialism in other countries. In 1962 James appended an essay, "From Toussaint L'Ouverture to Fidel Castro," that "attempt[ed] [to accomplish] for the future of the West Indies, all of them," what *The Black Jacobins* had done to "stimulate coming emancipation" of

Africa.[13] Guy used this essay's analysis of Haitian national consciousness in "Haiti: The Enigma of the Caribbean," her article for a 1964 special issue of *Freedomways*, "People of the Caribbean Area."

However, whereas James, in making the case for West Indian federation, emphasizes the teleological development of the "Caribbean quest for national identity" begun by the Haitian Revolution and culminating in the Cuban Revolution, Guy is concerned with Haiti's lack of national unity and its suspended progress. The "enigma" that Haiti presents to Guy is that "*the clock of history was stopped for [the peasants] some one hundred and fifty years ago, and in the long lists of presidents that have fought and juggled for power, not one has seriously made a concerted effort to get it moving again.*"[14] Guy revisits this enigma in *The Sun, the Sea, a Touch of the Wind,* in which a British aristocrat with "dreams of empire" muses that "in Haiti all things remained constant—the inevitable overthrow of governments, its lofty mountains, its peasants shackled to the past in the slow movement of time."[15] In commenting on Haiti's political and social stagnation, the result of instability, exploitation, corruption, and sabotage, these passages introduce a concept akin to Benjamin's notion of "homogeneous, empty time" of the linear progressive history of capitalism, which precludes social transformation through its devastating sameness.[16]

The Sun, the Sea, a Touch of the Wind disrupts this stagnant homogeneity by demonstrating that it gives rise to what Benjamin calls "Messianic" temporality, in which "the present is not a transition, but in which time stands still and has come to a stop. For this notion defines the present in which [the historian] himself is writing history." This involves a "cessation of happening, or put differently, a revolutionary chance in the fight for the oppressed past," such that control over history's telling can be wrested from the ruling classes.[17] As the novel's self-described Black revolutionary puts it,

> Do you know the greatest mystery in the world today? It's that Haiti still exists. Every great European power from the nineteenth into the twentieth century tried to blow her out of existence, singly and collectively.
>
> The only reason they haven't is because on this island time goes so goddamn slow. . . . Since the Yankee marines nailed Charlemagne to the cross, [Haitians] been waiting for him—or Jesus Christ—to come back and deliver them. Damballa answers their prayers by holding the sun in the sky longer than he got the right to, so Charlemagne and Christ think they got nothing but time. But whatever they think, the sun always got to rest.[18]

In revisiting the history of the first U.S. occupation of Haiti (1915–1934) to which this passage alludes, *The Sun, the Sea, a Touch of the Wind* reconstructs the meanings of Haitian independence for Black emancipatory thought in the late twentieth century. In line with *The Black Jacobins* and the broader radical tradition of literature about the Haitian Revolution James's work anchored, Guy is concerned with what David Scott calls "the conceptual problem of political presents and . . . how reconstructed pasts and anticipated futures are thought out in relation to them."[19] The political present of Guy's novel included the second U.S. occupation of Haiti (1994–2000) in order to return Jean-Bertrand Aristide to power after the brutal Cédras regime, whose coup the U.S. had covertly supported, became an embarrassment. *The Sun, the Sea, a Touch of the Wind* can be read as exposing the contradictions of "Operation Restore Democracy," as the second U.S. occupation was called, by exploring the legacy of earlier efforts to establish U.S. hegemony in the Caribbean.

Among these earlier U.S. efforts, which include the construction of the Panama Canal, the occupation of the Dominican Republic, the colonization of Puerto Rico, the purchase of the Virgin Islands from Denmark, and support for the Batista-led coup that ousted populist president Ramon Grau of Cuba, the first U.S. occupation of Haiti resulted in the creation of a puppet government, a new constitution, and a takeover of the country's finances.[20] When the corvée system of forced labor was revived to build roads the occupation forces needed, the resulting growth of native insurgency was led by Charlemagne Masséna Péralte, who was slain by U.S. marines in 1919. Invoking Péralte (or Charlemagne, as the novel refers to him) more so than Toussaint L'Ouverture as its historical-mythical hero, *The Sun, the Sea, a Touch of the Wind* foregrounds the history of U.S. occupation and represents it through a Benjaminian Messianic temporality that interrupts the teleological concept of progress held by American neocolonial forces.[21] The novel's insistent memory of the first U.S. occupation chafes against what Guy calls the "determined innocence" of white America's denial of its role in creating the very economic underdevelopment and political instability that it attempts to alleviate on its own terms.[22] Furthermore, *The Sun, the Sea, a Touch of the Wind* shows that this ongoing history of neocolonialism intimately shapes and is shaped by the oppression of African Americans.

But at the same time that Guy's novel comes out of a radical tradition of literature about the Haitian Revolution that was committed to redeeming or elevating the past in order to understand and transform the present (and that was inspired in part by left agitation against the first U.S. occupation), it breaks with this tradition's heteropatriarchal ideologies. Assessing the line of radical writing about or inspired by revolutionary Haiti, which includes Guy Endore's *Babouk* (1934) and Arna Bontemps' *Black Thunder* (1936) and

Drums at Dusk (1939) in addition to *The Black Jacobins,* Hazel Carby writes that Haiti and Toussaint L'Ouverture serve as models of "black male autonomy, self-government, and patriarchal black nationhood."[23] *The Sun, the Sea, a Touch of the Wind* focuses on how these masculinist ideals intersect with a nondialectical Black messianism and its notion of "a manifest destiny or a God-given role to assert the providential goals of history and to bring about the kingdom of God on earth." In *Black Messiahs and Uncle Toms: Social and Literary Manipulations of a Religious Myth,* Wilson Jeremiah Moses identifies four major patterns of messianism, two of which are especially relevant to *The Sun, the Sea, a Touch of the Wind*: first, the "expectation or identification of a personal savior—a messiah, a prophet, or a Mahdi"; and second, "journalistic and artistic presentations of certain black individuals as symbolic messiahs" who "may be created by the press or the public imagination without his conscious cooperation."[24] To these patterns we can add messianic androcentrism and its naturalization of male leadership, as seen in John Henrik Clarke's representative portrait of Lumumba, "this 'best son of Africa,' this 'Lincoln of the Congo,' this 'Black Messiah.'"[25]

Guy elaborates on the messianic legend of Charlemagne's revolt against and "crucifixion" by U.S. marines not only to represent a signal aspect of Haiti's revolutionary history that illuminates the establishment of U.S. hegemony in the Caribbean but also to critique the "erotic and phallic form of masculinity [that] was assumed and subsumed in representations of the black male rebel."[26] For Guy, messianic masculinism yokes the violent suppression of Black female subjectivity with a nondialectical relationship between revolutionary leadership and the masses that forestalls social transformation even as it posits a progressive march of history. Struggling through oppressive relationships with men portrayed as Charlemagne's descendants and claiming her own vision as an African American artist, Guy's protagonist Jonnie Dash recasts masculinist projects of "'author[ing]' revolution through fiction" that remake the Caribbean, "literally and figuratively, in the image of Caribbean man."[27]

In Guy's novel, messianism is also the linchpin between diasporic and domestic discourses of heteropatriarchal Blackness. Along with contesting the masculinism of radical representations of Haiti, Guy criticizes the constraining deification of womanhood within U.S. Black messianic nationalism exemplified by Albert Cleage Jr.'s enshrinement of the Black Madonna. The Black Madonna is the flip side of the demonized matriarch of Daniel Moynihan's 1965 report *The Negro Family,* which influentially proposed androcentric conceptions of racial hardship and advancement. *The Sun, the*

Sea, a Touch of the Wind critiques the ideologies of gender and sexuality circulated by domestic discourses of race, in the spirit of Toni Cade Bambara's challenge to revolutionaries to "creat[e] a new identity, a self, perhaps an androgynous self, via commitment to the struggle."[28] Like Bambara, Guy insists that challenging the heteropatriarchy of Black internationalism is a necessary extension of connecting the oppression of Third World nations to the oppression of African Americans in the United States.

▫ ▫ ▫

Conveying the disintegration of Black female subjectivity wrought by messianic masculinism, the novel begins chaotically and graphically with Jonnie regaining consciousness after a blackout, only to remain lost within a nightmarish hallucination:

> Golden phallus slashing the flesh of her stomach. Guts, hot, gushing over her thighs. Womb flaccid, empty, falling to her feet. . . . Now he ascended. Bright-as-the-sun body soaring, hard-as-gold phallus burning. Christ-like he ascended, streaking up out of the dark earth leaving her charred, mutilated in the silent earth.[29]

The Christian and psychoanalytic symbolism of this passage resurfaces with the revelation of Jonnie's past, which entails a self-destructive lifelong search for a father/savior/lover. This search, we learn, is instigated by a primal scene involving Jonnie's rescue from a tenement fire by her father and, as she sees it, his subsequent abandonment of her when he dies trying in vain to save her mother, "the woman he's fucking." Excluded from her parents' mutual desire, Jonnie spends her life compensating for the loss of her father by obsessively sketching penises and engaging in sexual relationships that repeatedly end in abandonment. In particular, Jonnie's rape by her spiritual father, a priest who flees his parish after molesting her, prefigures her exploitation by her mentor and lover, the radical Haitian intellectual Gérard Auguste. Championing her artistic talent and exposing her to Négritude and Marxism, Gérard expands Jonnie's horizons, but the violence of his will to re-create her in his image "like some modern-day Pygmalion" is manifested in Jonnie's nightmare of being torn open by the phallus of a "Christ-like" demon.[30]

Guy's Christian typology links the messianic Gérard with the historical Haitian rebel Charlemagne Masséna Péralte, who led the 1918 peasant revolt against the first U.S. occupation of Haiti, established a provisional government, and called upon Haitians to liberate themselves and their land. After killing Péralte, the marines distributed pictures of his corpse strapped to a door in an unsuccessful effort to demoralize the resistance. This led to rumors that Charlemagne had been crucified, to which *The Sun, the Sea, a Touch of the Wind* alludes:

> Even the United States, itself a newly liberated colony, adapting to the customs and mores of the existing world, on the brink of industrialization and in need of cheap labor, refused to come to the aid of a fledgling nation—fearful that the glorious independence of a Black nation would arouse the passions of its own slaves. And so, like Christ's, Haiti's glory became her cross to bear, exemplified by Charlemagne being nailed to his cross by the American marines who occupied the island from 1915 to 1934.[31]

The crucified Charlemagne is the novel's mythic touchstone, focusing attention on the confluence of U.S. domestic racism and imperialism rather than emphasizing European imperialism at the risk of perpetuating historical amnesia about U.S. efforts to subjugate the Caribbean.

The Christian symbolism of Charlemagne's legend also conveys Guy's critique of top-down leadership and hero worship that renders the masses passive. As the novel's alternative to revolutionary messianism, Black revolutionary Maxie Gardener, tells Jonnie, "Since the Yankee marines nailed Charlemagne to the cross, [the peasants] been waiting for him—or Jesus Christ—to come back and deliver them." Such passivity is paralleled in Jonnie's relationship with Gérard, who views her as inert material—"that bright-eyed Black girl with so much talent [who] can be molded" by him. As the masses await their savior, Jonnie "had waited and longed and prayed" for Gérard's return after he had left New York for Haiti, had waited for him "as had the students who sat at his feet worshiping him, eager to welcome back their god, a new leader. Waited for him to ascend his throne." While linking Jonnie's struggles as a Black urban worker with those of the Haitian peasantry has "made her part of the great world movement," Gérard maintains his own separation from and superiority to both Jonnie and the peasantry (a sector of which works his family land).[32]

Gérard's disconnection from the majority of Haitians leads him to romanticize them and, in the process, deny any role for intellectual leaders. When Jonnie asks Gérard about Haiti's "bright young people, the thinkers and artists," he crudely dismisses them—"What do we need with intellectuals? Was Toussaint an intellectual? Was Dessalines an intellectual?" Gérard revels in a vision of spontaneous mass uprising that is quickly unveiled as "dreams and lies":[33]

"When the French kidnapped Toussaint and took him away to die in the dungeons of France, Toussaint said to them, 'In overthrowing me, you have cut down only the trunk of the tree of liberty. It will spring up again for its roots are numerous. . . . That is why I am so happy that you have come, Jonnie, *chérie*. . . . We shall go among the people. We shall talk to them. Look at you—you can inspire—when I tell them that you were poor just like them." He clasped her to him, held her against his chest—and broke the spell.

She pulled away from his arms, the feel of his flaccid flesh. Then watched his face in fascination. One moment it was flushed with the spirit of youth, revived, the next its flesh had fallen into its folds of weary resignation.[34]

Gérard's sexual impotence betrays the political impotence of his masculinist messianism and its assumptions of inevitable mass revolt.

The Sun, the Sea, a Touch of the Wind depicts the uncertainty of such revolt by displacing it onto nature: it is not a popular uprising but a fierce climactic storm that disrupts the neocolonial development plans of an American entrepreneur and that symbolically demolishes the protective boundaries of the Old Hotel that separate its wealthy Western guests from the Haitian urban poor. This figuration of nature as an agent of change is presaged in Jonnie's encounter with Haitian seamstresses doing piecework on an estate. As Jonnie gazes upon their bent shoulders, she recalls her own oppressive experience working in New York sweatshops and acknowledges that "one had to choose sides. And the side Jonnie had chosen was not on the side of [the owner of the estate]." However, the "ceaseless struggle being waged around the seemingly bare yard" is not between workers and bosses but between the surrounding jungle and "the restraining fence that had been made strong, damned near impregnable, to hold it back."[35] Although Jonnie perceives that she shares interests with Haitian women workers under neoliberal capitalism, she forms no relationship with them but only "notice[s] with satisfaction that around these stalls the forest was succeeding. Vines thick and luxurious had spread out over the stalls, providing a shield for the women against the sun that beamed down on the galvanized tin roofs. The vines wrapped around the supports and down to the ground—a victory of sorts." The storm that wreaks havoc on the Old Hotel is similarly "a victory of sorts," causing "the collapse of the bougainvillea covered [hotel] walls, their disintegration accompanied by the shouts and cries of the homeless who had been clinging to the other side for shelter and now came rushing over the grounds . . . demanding to be let in."[36] But these attacks on symbolic sites of neocolonialism not only are out of human hands, but they also suggest the pyrrhic victory evoked by the gothic image of Haiti with which Guy closes her 1964 *Freedomways* essay. She depicts the country as "a fragile old estate" in which "the ghosts of great men abound, [and] the echoes of greatness pervade[,] but with further decay, a loud shout will bring down the ruins, burying its greatness beneath piles of useless debris."[37] While depicting the untenability of Haiti's current state of affairs and its historical roots in imperialist hostility, Guy resists radical narratives of salvation by a Black messiah embodied by either a great (male) leader or the militant masses who inadequately grasp the nation's crises.

Thusly critiquing the Black messianic tradition associated with revolutionary Haiti, Guy connects its patriarchal ideologies with those underpinning conceptualizations of African American oppression and liberation within the United States. Guy explores this connection through Jonnie's son, Emmanuel. Another Christ figure ("Emmanuel," Hebrew for "God is with us," refers to the prophesied Messiah), Jonnie's son is crucified by U.S. racism: caught in a cycle of drugs, theft, and a judicial system that sentences him to prison immediately after dismissing a white boy facing similar charges, Emmanuel is killed by police after trying to steal a chalice and shooting the priest who catches him. Guy shows these punitive measures to "constitute powerful forms of state violence that echo colonial practices and produce forms of individual alienation that can either impede or ignite political resistance."[38]

If Emmanuel is a Black American Christ in concrete, Jonnie bitterly casts herself as the virgin mother of "the second Immaculate Conception" as she recollects her marriage and her son's birth.[39] In doing so, she ironizes messianic narratives of African American redemption such as those articulated by the Rev. Albert B. Cleage Jr., founder of the Shrine of the Black Madonna in Detroit. In his collection of sermons *The Black Messiah* (1968) and the talks and seminars selected for *Black Christian Nationalism: New Directions for the Black Church* (1972), Cleage expounds upon the true gospel of Jesus, whose "whole ministry was going about among a Black Nation preaching to them about the things that had to be done if they were to find freedom from oppression by a white nation, Rome."[40] This nation building relies upon traditional gender roles whereby Black mothers bear and raise male warriors, as expressed by the primary iconography of Cleage's church: "The Black Madonna is a black woman standing there with a little black child in her arms. . . . He's *our* child, and that's what we're fighting for. Because he has to carry on the Nation."[41]

For Jonnie, however, messianism's deification of the Black Madonna turns into misogynistic sexual violence. In her hallucinated violation with which the novel begins, the "Christ-like" demon's "hard-as-gold phallus" disembowels her womb. Later, in a fit of madness, Jonnie accuses Emmanuel of having "destroyed" her: "No, he's no Immaculate Conception, just a fucking thief! . . . From my womb into the drugs! Stealing my life! He joined in the conspiracy against me."[42] Jonnie's paranoia exposes the misogyny behind nationalist discourses of the Black Madonna, which have compounded her traumatization by U.S. racist state violence.

As a result of its patriarchal expression of race redemption, the deified Madonna went hand in hand with the demonized Black "matriarch" who entered public discourse with the publication of *The Negro Family: The Case for National Action* (1965) only three years before *The Black Messiah*. The Moynihan Report, as it is popularly called after its author, sociologist and future senator Daniel Patrick Moynihan, located the roots of racial inequality in the "matriarchal" and hence "pathological" and "disorganized" Black family structure.[43] The sexism and heteronormativity of Moynihan's analysis intensified nationalist accusations that Black women were emasculating Black men by denying them their rightful place at the head of the family and the race.[44]

This heteropatriarchal assessment of racial adversity permeates Guy's first novel, *Bird at My Window* (1966), published one year after the appearance of the Moynihan Report. *Bird at My Window* centers on Wade Williams, a Black man with a crippling attachment to his family and especially his mother, which is a primary factor in his inability to realize either his freedom or his genius. Wade's mother passes her fear of whites on to him in a way that sets "his limits, his boundaries, forever." Wade's opportunity to free himself comes while serving in France during World War II, when he confronts and kills a white American officer who calls him an "African monkey all dressed up like an honest-to-goodness U.S. soldier." Killing the officer "change[s] the hell out of him," negating his own as well as his father's emasculation by women both Black and white. Wade's mother, however, undermines this triumph when she prevents him from leaving Harlem for France by spending the money he had asked her to set aside for him. Wade learns that "she had spent half of his life holding him in a trap while she spent the other half punishing him for being caught in it." Shackled to the ghetto, Wade is driven to kill his mother and, inadvertently, his beloved sister after realizing that his dutifulness to his family has advanced none of them. With its indictment of institutional racism, *Bird at My Window* does not entirely repeat Moynihan's scapegoating of the Black matriarch. Nonetheless, Wade's mother is undeniably an agent of oppression who has hypocritically used Christianity to socialize her children into the racist status quo: "Mr. Charlie had forced her to her knees a long time ago and she had made [her children] pay with her prayers."[45]

The Sun, the Sea, a Touch of the Wind confronts the sexist ideologies underpinning nationalist articulations of both the Madonna and the matriarch by examining racial oppression and resistance from the perspective of an African American woman who has been traumatized by these configurations of Black motherhood. It rescripts motherhood as a site of Black female liberation as well as oppression rather than as a means of Black male emasculation or heroization: Jonnie heals the wounds of her traumatic past when she avenges the police shooting of her son by adopting the Haitian peasant boy Lucknair. She thereby saves him from being prostituted to the white American diplomat, McCellan, who represents the interests of the racist state that had taken Emmanuel's life. Jonnie's relationship with Lucknair radically revises the destructive mother-son relationship at the center of *Bird at My Window*. Not only is biological motherhood foreclosed for the menopausal Jonnie, but her adoption of Lucknair is only nominal. While Lucknair is poised to fulfill the revolutionary potential that was thwarted in Emmanuel and Gérard, Jonnie neither nurtures him nor hinders him in the manner of the emasculating Black matriarch. Her role is to pursue her own artistic ambitions. Consequently, after ensuring Lucknair's safety, she hands him over to Maxie Gardener.

Like Jonnie, Maxie unravels the messianic nationalism that has proven so damaging to Black women. The son of a Russian Jewish Communist father and a "Black nappy-headed lady who does not know, nor could she ever fit into, your Black bourgeoisie," Maxie has become disillusioned by the systemic elimination and co-optation of Black national liberation and civil rights leaders: "Toussaint had to die, just as King had to die, as Malcolm had to die. Patrice Lumumba, Charlemagne, Jesus Christ—all dreamers."[46] Against this moribund messianic line of male "dreamers" of a free Black nation or a truly democratic United States, Maxie positions himself as a "revolutionary" who "lay[s] claim to this whole hemisphere" as a result of his transnational as well as biracial roots/routes:

> Look, my great-grandfather came from Africa and landed in Brazil. His brother landed here in Haiti. The youngest brothers were taken to the States. Baby, folks in this hemisphere got to screwing and carrying on so that we don't look African no mo. We look American. Sure those in power try to hang on to outdated aristocracy—Spanish, Portuguese, British. But they can't tell their kids one from another.[47]

The entangled roots of the Americas, Maxie implies, will produce revolutionary openings, and it is in search of these openings—which he predicts will come to racially hybrid Brazil—that he "travel[s] up and down [the] coasts [of this hemisphere], talking to all who want to listen."[48]

Breaking with Jonnie's "landlocked" sense of possibilities, Maxie's migratory subjectivity is an extension of the androgyny indicated by his ambiguously gendered name (similar to Jonnie's). Commingled with a campy masculinity ("'Sh—i-i—it, you fuck. You know you fuck. And you know that you and me, we gonna get it on.' . . . He moved his penis deliberately to entice her") is the maternal presence of his fleshy body, including a "protruding stomach" that Jonnie calls a "built-in incubator." Unlike Jonnie's white British male lover, who is bothered that she is past childbearing age and hence incapable of continuing his patrilineage, Maxie wants children "whichever way" and plans to instill his migratory worldview in them through his own maternal abilities: "Yes, I want my kids to learn at sea—boys, girls, I want them with me, holding them to me. Why you think I got these'—he touched his fat chest—'bosoms?'" Even the intimacy and desire that Maxie elicits from Jonnie take strikingly maternal forms: "Lasting tenderness came with bosoms, with ovaries—things like that. Maxie. She had to get to Maxie"; "enfolded in his embrace, pressed into his soft bigness, his breasts—a mother's breasts against her cheeks—waves of tenderness washed up from her curling toes to tingle her body, spreading through her, spreading through her."[49] In becoming Lucknair's adoptive parent, Maxie in effect takes on and revises the role of the Virgin Mother, the Black Madonna, that had been Jonnie's cross to bear. In this way, Maxie counters the tendency in Black revolutionary narratives to have heroic males "appropriate the reproductive power of the female body to bring forth an act of rebellion," even as "feminization alone can only mark the abject."[50] Instead, Maxie's desire to produce rebellious political subjects is also the desire and ability to fill the traditionally feminine role of raising children.

In a further departure from the Black messianic narrative of revolution, Guy explores the political solidarities engendered through same-sex desire between Jonnie and a white British aristocrat, Jessica Winthrop. Jessica's blithe chauvinism initially casts her as a female embodiment of imperialism akin to George Lamming's "Old Dowager," Mrs. Gore-Brittain, in *Water with Berries* (1971) or the English patroness in Paule Marshall's *The Chosen Place, the Timeless People* (1969) Such figures represent "the seductions . . . of the maternal bond between England and the Caribbean in England."[51] Lamming's Mrs. Gore-Brittain is an emasculating force that the male West Indian painter/revolutionary, Teeton, must kill. And in Marshall's novel, the patroness yokes homosexuality with perversion and imperialism by maintaining a sexual and financial hold on her Afro-Caribbean protégée that sabotages the latter's redemptive marriage to a Ugandan nationalist.

The Sun, the Sea, a Touch of the Wind takes a markedly different approach to this vilified white female figure by exploring interracial desire between women as a conduit for political solidarities.[52] In doing so, the novel counters the heteropatriarchy of narratives that predicate Black liberation on the male conquest and/or obliteration of white women who allegorize imperialism while erasing Black women's stories. Appearing initially as an arrogant "heir to all the stolen wealth" of the British empire as well as Jonnie's sexual rival for the attention of Jessica's male consort, Jessica reveals her own affection for and attraction to Jonnie while helping her through a severe bout of depression. Jessica's desire for Jonnie grows out of colonial eroticism that nonetheless acknowledges Black passion for freedom:

> Jessica looked out at the picture-perfect mountains. They put her in mind of Jonnie's chiseled face. Her face superimposed itself against them. Jessica blinked to clear the vision, then stood staring up at the lofty, indestructible creations.
>
> Haiti. She loved the island. Slavery and imperialism had created its poverty and its glory—the enigma, the metaphor of the Americas. Here, in Haiti, where slaves had mounted the only successful slave rebellion to win their independence, all the great powers—Britain, France, Germany—had converged to prevent her progress. Even the United States, itself a newly liberated colony . . . [was] fearful that the glorious independence of a Black nation would arouse the passions of its own slaves.[53]

Jessica's reverie is broken by "strong fragrances, herbal perfumes. . . . She turn[s] to see Jonnie standing before the mirror applying oils over her firm, muscular body," and as "their eyes [meet] in the mirror . . . an electrical charge bristle[s] from one to the other." While Jessica's "hunger" for Jonnie's "smooth darkness" conjures up fetishistic colonial eroticism, interracial desire also makes possible alliances across boundaries of nationality, race, and class. Jessica's great love had been a Black Senegalese doctor whom she had assisted in Gabon, "giving vaccinations, performing operations, or caring for vexing diseases," and her interest in Jonnie—who reminds Jessica of her doctor—produces other forms of interracial collaboration. Not only is Jessica incapable of "colonizing" Jonnie, sexually or otherwise, but their relationship is increasingly marked by mutual respect and reciprocity. After Jessica saves Jonnie from the recurrence of her manic depression, Jonnie saves Jessica from an American swindler. Jonnie also forces Jessica to see the limits of her white liberal feminism, her privilege and blindness to matters of race and class, such that Jessica finally admits that while "dreams of empire die hard . . . no one can make of Haiti their dynasty."[54] Tellingly, the novel ends with Jonnie choosing against sailing away with Maxie and Lucknair and thereby reconstituting a nuclear family (albeit an untraditional, transnational one) that represents the rejuvenated Black race. The novel ends instead with Jonnie and Jessica's reunion, thus looking forward to an interracial feminine partnership in the next phase of Jonnie's life as a hemispheric woman:

> "Jonnie, what say I go home, get this head cleared up, and after your rites for your boy, we hook up in Brazil?"
>
> "Jessica," Jonnie said, groaning. "Do you think that Brazil can stand the two of us?"
>
> "At any rate, my dear Jonnie, after us Brazil will never be the same."[55]

In challenging Black heteropatriarchal narratives of revolutionary nationalism, *The Sun, the Sea, a Touch of the Wind* might be read as presenting a queer and feminist "discrepant cosmopolitanism," to use James Clifford's term for diasporic "cultures of displacement and transplantation . . . inseparable from specific, often violent histories of economic, political, and cultural interaction."[56] As Jonnie extricates herself from her search for a Black messiah, she asserts her identity as a mobile artist poised at the end of the novel to return only temporarily to the United States to commemorate her son before leaving for "another country, in this hemisphere" to create her masterpiece inspired by Haiti.[57] Jonnie's self-imposed exile from the United States and transformation into a hemispheric woman positively reimagines her orphaned status and calls to mind those Black Atlantic cosmopolitans who "begin as African-Americans or Caribbean people and are then changed into something else which evades those specific labels and with them all fixed notions of nationality and national identity."[58]

However, it is more accurate to say that Black America's global dimensions do not supersede racial and national histories and identities in Guy's novel but instead reactivate them as sites of struggle. Even as Guy demonstrates that Blackness exposes and strains against the limits of U.S. liberal democracy, she posits the nation-state as a necessary terrain of struggle and identity formation, as exemplified by the traumatic repetition of U.S. racial domination in Haiti that Jonnie is forced to confront in order to work through her depression and blackouts. Jonnie's embrace of a migratory hemispheric subjectivity is thus predicated on her return to the United States to erect a gravestone for Emmanuel that reads, "SON OF JONNIE DASH, *BLACK AMERICAN ARTIST*."[59]

Indeed, *The Sun, the Sea, a Touch of the Wind* does not easily support postnationalist perspectives, as it maintains a vision of Third World national unity to be realized by the Black woman artist at the same time that it critiques messianic nationalism and questions the conditions for Haitian mass struggle. This utopic vision appears to Jonnie as a storm destroys the walls protecting the Old Hotel. As Haiti's urban poor flood into the hotel's ballroom, Jonnie is captivated by the sight of

> bodies wedged together, bodies curving into bodies, rich, poor, guests, workers, beggars, hair, clothes, faces, all covered with masks of mud and sand blown in by the rain, indistinguishable one from the other. A tableau to be done in bronze—awesome.[60]

The storm's momentary erasure of difference creates an epiphany of unity, the lack of which Guy had called "the greatest paradox of Haitian life" in her *Freedomways* essay: "this country where the division of classes is the most stringently drawn is the country that has less reason [for such division], for the people share alike in this history" of slave revolt and independence.[61] The image of national unity inspires Jonnie's plans for her masterpiece, a "tableau to be done in bronze" called *The Storm* that mirrors her personal development. From her early obsession with painting penises spurred by her search for a father/lover/savior, Jonnie moves on to a portrait of a Haitian peasant while under the influence of Gérard's paternalistic anticolonialism and his romanticization of the people. Her decision to work in a different medium signals her break with messianism so that she can issue her own vision of the national transcendence to come with Haiti's storm of gross inequalities and political instability that will sweep everyone up in its wake.

Although it might seem paradoxical that Jonnie must leave Haiti to create her vision of its unity, this is in keeping with Guy's refusal to oppose Third World national and international struggles: as Guy writes, Haiti's "legacy of a colonial, imperial slave past" constitute "the shackles from which *the Western Hemisphere* kept struggling to be free."[62] Thus, Jonnie's bronze is a bellwether for the larger storm brewing throughout the Americas as a result of "the afterlife of slavery."[63] The novel grapples with the failures of national revolution, including Haiti's, not by giving up nostalgic, enfeebled, and exhausted anticolonial longings for revolution (as David Scott urges us to do in his reading of *The Black Jacobins*) but by remaining open to revolution as a historical possibility, as expressed in Maxie's theory about Brazil:

> Corruption's the accepted rule of this hemisphere. Only difference—Brazil ain't had their revolution—yet. That's what I'm searching for. Revolution. The only way for a revolution to succeed is to be there to grab the chance. Keep it what it started to be.
>
> Brazil's up for grabs right now. When they get it all together, that's gonna be the richest, freest country in this hemisphere—or the most screwed up. But then they'll only be joining the world—know what I mean?[64]

Sure enough, it is to Brazil that Maxie sails with Lucknair at the end of the novel, which also closes with Jonnie and Jessica's planned rendezvous there. The novel does not present a historical analysis of the conditions for social upheaval in Brazil, but as I see it, it makes the case that Haiti's legacy of revolution is a hemispheric legacy without guarantees—and precisely for that reason, revolution remains something for African Americans, including and especially African American women, to reenvision and fight for.

□ □ □

Guy wrote of her heroine, "Jonnie Dash, born in despair, despair framing every inch of her growth and development, had only tales that evoked shame in her and made others turn from her."[65] In its full significance Jonnie's story was indeed one that made reviewers of *The Sun, the Sea, a Touch of the Wind* turn away from the novel. As Eugene McAvoy lamented,

> Were this simply Jonnie's story, the tale of a woman's discovery of her identity and freedom from the abuses of 'these mother's children calling themselves men," Guy would have a stronger novel. But her heavy-handed push for social importance renders the book an often incoherent meandering through good intentions.[66]

McAvoy picks up on the parallels between Jonnie's and Haiti's struggles, which he even enumerates among the novel's strengths.[67] But he ultimately argues that the story of individual feminine empowerment should be delinked from historical and social critique—the latter of which degenerates into "an ill-articulated political ideology." This is the general sentiment of two other critics who similarly find fault with Guy's anti-imperialism and anticolonialism. Opal Moore's review (unpromisingly titled "An Allegorical Hodgepodge of Haiti") characterizes *The Sun, the Sea, a Touch of the Wind* as, among other things, "a tired 1960s-style revolutionary tract" serving up "Haitian colonial-guilt history." Consequently, "the novel attempts both too much and too little," as its "allegorical aspects," though "complex enough," "confine the action and flatten the characters." And Sandra Adell's introduction to the 2001 edition of

Bird at My Window complains of the engagement of *The Sun, The Sea, a Touch of the Wind* in "1960s rhetoric about racism, imperialism, and colonialism to the point of tedium."[68]

While I am sympathetic to criticisms of the style and characterization of *The Sun, the Sea, a Touch of the Wind,* which hinder both the narrative of Jonnie's self-discovery and its allegorical meaning, my fundamental disagreement is with these reviewers' dismissal of the novel's anti-imperialist and anticolonial critique. It seems odd that this critique would be viewed as dated or at odds with "the tale of a woman's discovery of her identity and freedom," since two of these reviewers acknowledge "the urgency and potency of Haitian history and current events."[69] This raises the question of how that "urgency and potency" is being understood, and I would venture that these critics do not simply find *Guy's* anti-imperialism and anticolonialism to be outmoded but that they assume that such politics are irrelevant altogether. Thus, Moore and Adell situate the novel's radicalism in the 1960s, that emptied-out signifier of rebellious days long gone. These critics ignore that the novel, set in the 1970s, in fact grapples with the messy unraveling of civil rights, Black Power, and Third World liberation movements instead of rehashing their tenets (which is perhaps what renders the novel ideologically "ill-articulated" for McAvoy). It is precisely this assumption of "postcoloniality"—the sense that we exist "after" colonialism—that *The Sun, the Sea, a Touch of the Wind* seeks to disprove by exploring the hemispheric impact of national oppression on an African American woman.

If, on the other hand, we stripped the anticolonial internationalism from Guy's novel, we would have something closer to Terry McMillan's *Stella,* the mainstream's preferred vision of African American female empowerment not only because it offers contemporary yet formulaic romance but also because it maintains U.S. superiority and innocence. Having discussed *Stella* as predicating Black feminism on a U.S.-centric and exceptionalist worldview, I want to return to the question I posed earlier of why McMillan's narrative of romance depends on this ideology. I want to propose in conclusion that *Stella* presents a recent, widely circulated expression of the mutual imbrications of U.S. exceptionalism and racialized heteronormativity: the generic pressures on the novel to culminate in marriage (or the promise of marriage) are informed by the role normative sexuality plays in defining and defending U.S.-Americanness against racial/national others. This role is heightened in *Stella* due to the Black foreignness of Stella's Jamaican suitor, and its perniciousness is displayed by the disintegration of McMillan's marriage to Jonathan Plummer after he came out as gay. In tracing the damaging consequences of the heteronormative constitution of U.S. exceptionalism, I reaffirm the stakes of Guy's Black internationalist feminism, which makes the undoing of fixed gender/sex roles central to anticolonial critique.

Both *Stella*'s Winston and the man who inspired him—McMillan's husband before he came out—represent an exotic Caribbean presence made assimilable through demonstrating heterosexuality, rugged self-reliance, and monogamy. Before proposing to Stella, Winston informs her that if he were to stay in America,

> I would apply to school and work on becoming a certified chef with a specialization so that it would be easier for me to get work in this country and I would work doing anything until such time, as I am not the type of man who could tolerate being taken in by a woman, you know, I mean I would have to earn my own way and help out in the household, you know?[70]

Once Plummer revealed that he was gay, however, McMillan linked his homosexuality to foreignness, HIV/AIDS, promiscuity, parasitism, and criminality (what McMillan referred to as "terrorist behavior" in a 2006 court document).[71] His coming out and subsequent efforts to revoke his prenuptial agreement with McMillan in order to obtain alimony prompted her to say in her first major interview concerning the divorce,

> He has risked my life having sex with men for years. He has gotten to become a U.S. citizen because of his affair with me, his relationship with me. And he's trying to get sympathy for himself, and he's an habitual liar, and he's a sociopath. . . . I don't care about him being gay, but he risked my life. What if I'm sitting here HIV positive? I can't be—I can't be—I can't get rid of that, and he wants my money? He should get a job.[72]

In her ongoing legal and publicity battles with Plummer, McMillan continued to harness the powerful associations of AIDS with homosexuality, dependency, criminality, and foreignness.[73] One 2006 court declaration in particular exploits fears of contamination by the foreign and the homosexual, as evidenced by McMillan's recounting of receiving a hand-delivered invitation to an AIDS health forum featuring Plummer. McMillan read this gesture as "meant to incite not only my anger at his so-called 'celebrity' status, but to arouse my fears and curiosity as to why he was appearing at anything having to do with AIDs unless he was, in fact, also infected with the virus." The detail that the invitation was hand-delivered to one of McMillan's friends further connotes the threat of contamination, which McMillan amplifies by connecting it with immigration; she described how Plummer had used her to obtain a green card for his mother, who had "been in this country working illegally for several years." Vocalizing fear of the commingled influxes of Third World immigrants, AIDS, and homosexuality upon a besieged American body politic allegorized by McMillan herself (see below), this example of Plummer's "harmful and degenerative behavior" is listed right before an inventory of his gay pornography.[74] McMillan's disingenuous denial of the relevance of Plummer's homosexuality to her legal case—a denial made partly in response to Plummer's allegations of her homophobia, buttressed by phone message transcripts in which McMillan repeatedly called him a "fag"—only underscores the centrality of the homo/heterosexual binary to the intertwined discourses of race, gender, and nationality through which the *Stella* phenomenon unfolded.[75]

More precisely, McMillan's divorce proceedings lay bare the mobilization of sexuality to promote a cohesive American identity distanced historically and geopolitically from oppression. In fighting Plummer's financial claims on her, McMillan's wielding of her authority and priority as a U.S.-born citizen extends the exceptionalism that underpins *Stella*:

> If this Court does not finally prevent Mr. Plummer from harassing me . . . I will be forced to go to the ACLU and the media and complain about how my rights as a U.S. citizen have been violated in favor of someone who has been granted the privilege of citizenship and yet shown no respect for the laws of this country he so coveted, not to mention those of his ex-wife's, the person responsible for his being a citizen and providing him with the freedom to live openly as a gay man.[76]

As in *Stella,* in McMillan's court filings the United States represents the land of freedom and opportunity, in contradistinction to Jamaica with its virulent homophobia. Plummer himself contended that he did not know he was gay "until [he] came to [the United States] and realized that there's a freedom of speech."[77] Yet the homosexuality to which America is putatively open is what McMillan paranoiacally exploits to represent Plummer's gay Black Jamaican body as a source of disease, immorality, and illegality and hence a prime target of the punitive state to be jailed or deported. (She claims to have spoken with Bill Clinton, members of Congress Maxine Waters and Barbara Lee, and the FBI about Plummer's acts of fraud and extortion.) Sexuality is thus a pivotal and contradictory site for displaying U.S. liberal democracy's selective openness to Caribbean difference *and* for constructing national borders against the threat this difference ultimately poses.[78] Rearticulating discourses of sexuality, American exceptionalism suppresses histories of neocolonial domination through direct and covert military operations, economic and political destabilization, the imposition of neoliberal policies, immigration law, and other acts that belie the universalism of U.S. democracy.

If *Stella* and its attendant controversy exploit the interlocking of nationalism and homophobia, then *The Sun, the Sea, a Touch of the Wind* shows that rethinking such "landlocked" formulations is integral to a Black feminism that rejects the specious, ultimately self-defeating privileges of identifying with the United States at the expense of wider solidarities. Exploring alliances against neocolonialism, *The Sun, the Sea, a Touch of the Wind* maintains the internationalism of the postwar Black Left from which it emerged. Guy's novel is very much a product of the Harlem Writers Guild and discourses of Caribbean radicalism circulating through *Freedomways,* groups such as the Fair Play for Cuba Committee, the work of C. L. R. James, and literature about the Haitian Revolution. Guy resignifies the left's masculinist messianism that foreclosed the existence of Black radical women artists such as Jonnie Dash and Guy herself. Through her heroine's triumphs, Guy intimates the nonteleological possibilities of national liberation that are bound up in the feminine erotic as a source of creativity for hemispheric women *and* men. But in the wake of the repression and attenuation of Black freedom struggles, Guy conjoins without reconciling the internationalist Left's faith in revolutionary nationalism and postmodernism's skepticism about progressive narratives of the nation.

Audre Lorde, one of the foremost theorists of postmodern Black feminism, similarly responded to the neoconservative backlash against race rights by revisiting the anticolonial Left internationalism that had nurtured her poetics and praxis. More so than Guy, Lorde posits the historical and theoretical salience of revolutionary nationalism as she casts her gaze on battles for self-determination in Grenada, South Africa, New Zealand, and Australia. The next chapter considers how Lorde extends Claudia Jones's Black internationalist feminism through essays and poetry that articulate identity politics with struggles against neoliberalism and that define difference and intersectionality in the context of national liberation movements. Perhaps more than any other writer, Lorde allows us to see how the postwar Left's gender and sexual radicalism shaped contemporary feminisms of color.

5

Audre Lorde Revisited

Nationalism and Second-Wave Black Feminism

Let me begin by juxtaposing Audre Lorde with another Black revolutionary whose nationalist investments have been misunderstood and repressed. In "On National Culture," Frantz Fanon reflects that

> humanity, some say, has got past the stage of nationalist claims. The time has come to build larger political unions, and consequently the old-fashioned nationalists should correct their mistakes. We believe on the contrary that the mistake, heavy with consequences, would be to miss out on the national stage. If culture is the expression of the national consciousness, I shall have no hesitation in saying, in the case in point, that national consciousness is the highest form of culture.[1]

I would guess that many readers familiar with Lorde would contrast her feminist diasporic politics of difference with Fanon's anticolonial nationalism. Indeed, they might position Lorde with those who believe that "humanity . . . has got past the stage of nationalist claims." This latter assumption drives much Black and Third World feminist scholarship, which contends that nationalism, with its investments in heteropatriarchy, homogeneity, normativity, and territory, can no longer be seen as liberatory, especially for women of color. The postmodern subject of Third World feminism, according to Inderpal Grewal, is a heterogeneous and inclusive one that "provides a constant critique of nationalist and even insurgent agendas."[2] Revolutionary nationalism's political failures are traced to the corruption of neocolonial elites who follow the bidding of First World governments and transnational corporations; the inability of Third World nations to establish democratic, equitable societies; the adoption of Enlightenment and colonial ideologies and their constitutive sexism and heteronormativity; and the increasingly complex movements of people, ideas, and capital with little regard for national borders. As postnationalist theorists of race, gender, and sexuality formulate alternatives to nationalist thought, they often cite Lorde to support their claims, and their work indelibly shapes how she is read: the essentialism and normativity that afflict nationalism are exposed, criticized, and replaced by her embrace of multiple and simultaneous differences as a Black lesbian socialist feminist with transnational commitments.[3] Lorde's work represents a path beyond national struggle whereby she locates liberation in the erotic, the body, and the act of "working through a discourse of difference to build coalitions and communities with others."[4]

Postnationalist critics validate their readings of Lorde by focusing on her cultural and spiritual ties to Africa rather than her political ones. This approach draws on selective discussions of *Zami*, the poems in *The Black Unicorn*, and certain essays from *Sister Outsider* such as "The Uses of the Erotic."[5] In particular, Lorde's "biomythography," *Zami: A New Spelling of My Name*, lends itself to postmodern feminist analyses of hybridity and boundary crossings.[6] "Zami," the "Carriacou name for women who work together as friends and lovers," has come to exemplify a Black lesbian feminist subjectivity that is diasporic as well as postnationalist.[7]

Yet *Zami* is only one moment (albeit a clearly important one) within Lorde's larger process of reclaiming Caribbean identity. Another phase of this reclamation is marked by her essay "Grenada Revisited," which Carole Boyce Davies calls "one of the best evaluations of the implications of the United States invasion of Grenada and, as I see it, a fitting conclusion to the journeys embarked on in *Zami*."[8] Whereas much scholarship on Lorde delinks her anti-imperialist critique of U.S. hegemony from her theorization of identity, Davies reminds us that this critique is crucial to Lorde's diasporic feminism.

Nonetheless, even scholars such as Davies and Michelle Stephens who attend to Lorde's anti-imperialism obscure the analyses of national liberation and national identity that became increasingly central to her thought. For Davies and Stephens, the heteronormative and patriarchal ideologies of nationalism serve to discredit entirely its liberatory potential. Davies, for example, establishes early in *Black Women, Writing and Identity* that beyond acknowledging that nationalism was a "management 'trap'" invented by Europeans,

> we may want to go further and ask, as a number of feminist scholars are beginning to do, if the concept of "nation" has not been a male formulation. This may explain why nationalism thus far seems to exist primarily as a male activity with women distinctly left out or peripheralized in the various national constructs.[9]

Along these lines, in reading "Grenada Revisited" as a "shadow narrative of empire," Michelle Stephens writes,

> From the windows of her own oppression, by both nationalisms and internationalisms, the Caribbean woman of color may have the clearest eye on the United States' role in the world at large. The Carriacou woman asks us to consider, what are the ways in which we understand our own desires for national affiliation and community, and can these be fulfilled without the interpellations of the state? What does it mean to imagine black love and its related terms, black femininity and masculinity throughout the diaspora, without the securities of home, nation, and heterosexuality?[10]

These are crucial questions for those in the United States for whom national affiliation means assenting to and supporting institutions, laws, and beliefs that exploit and brutalize people of color throughout the world. Furthermore, it initially appears as though Stephens does not foreclose the potential that "desires for national affiliation and community" can be viable and important, as she distinguishes, in E. San Juan's words, "between the referents of nation (local groups, community, domicile, or belonging) and state (governance, machinery of sanctioning laws, disciplinary codes, military)."[11] This distinction is necessary because, as San Juan argues, "state violence and assertion of national identity need not be automatically conflated so as to implicate nationalism—whose nationalism?"[12] However, Stephens moves away from distinguishing between oppressor and oppressed nations, as she yokes nation and home with heterosexuality. Because national affiliations are circumscribed by heteronormativity, Stephens bemoans "the dominance of the newly independent nationalist state" and values instead "insurgent attempts to imagine alternative forms of multiracial, multinational social community."[13]

Stephens's dismissal of anti-imperialist revolutionary Black nationalism goes against the spirit of "Grenada Revisited," as Davies points out:

> Lorde's connectedness to the Caribbean has its impetus in revolutionary Grenada (not colonial Grenada) and the sense of possibility and challenge which it held. For Lorde, cultural identification has to be addressed along with an overtly anti-hegemonic discourse. She therefore moves the discussion beyond a Pan-African identification as in[,] say[,] [Paule] Marshall, to a fuller acceptance of a gendered relationship to history and an ideological consciousness of the meaning of Grenada's thwarted revolution within the context of power, powerlessness, and empowerment.[14]

Despite Davies' predominantly postnationalist paradigm, she acknowledges that an "anti-hegemonic discourse" of Grenadian independence, one that presents "a gendered relationship to history," is integral to Lorde's evolving sense of self and/in history.

Davies' conclusion serves as my starting point. In my reading of Lorde,

"Grenada Revisited" is not "a fitting conclusion to the journeys embarked on in *Zami*," as Davies writes, but the beginning of a new leg of Lorde's political development. Turning to her poetry and prose from the mid-1980s on, after the invasion of Grenada, we see that independent Black nationhood becomes an important political goal for Lorde, one not yet superseded by "free" mobility or exilic diasporic communities. This is the case in poems from *Our Dead Behind Us* (1986) and the essays "Grenada Revisited" (1984), "Turning the Beat Around: Lesbian Parenting 1986," "A Burst of Light: Living With Cancer" (1986), "Apartheid U.S.A." (1988), and a 1990 chronicle of Hurricane Hugo's devastation of St. Croix. While "Grenada Revisited" has received minor critical attention, these other essays have largely been overlooked.[15] Yet it is in Lorde's post-invasion prose and poetry that she most explicitly and consistently explores a nationalist internationalism positing that African Americans are morally and politically bound to support Third World and indigenous struggles for national sovereignty and that anticolonial struggles illuminate and impact African Americans' situation in the United States as an oppressed people.

It is analytically useful to distinguish the nationalist internationalism of Lorde's writing after the invasion of Grenada from what I call the "cultural nationalism" exemplified by *The Black Unicorn* and *Zami*—even as this cultural nationalism extends into and is recreated by her later prose and poetry. By cultural nationalism, I refer to Lorde's feminist recovery and recreation of African spirituality and myth, a project facilitated by her 1974 trip to Africa, which introduced her to Dahomean and Yoruban deities such as Seboulisa, Mawu-Lisa, and Aido Hwedo.[16] In *The Black Unicorn, Zami,* and essays from *Sister Outsider* such as "Scratching the Surface: Some Notes on Barriers to Women and Loving," Afrocentric epistemologies and spirituality allow Lorde to consider how differences rethink and energize monadic identity politics of race, gender, and sexuality. The politics of difference articulated in these texts, however, are largely unconnected to Third World struggles for national sovereignty. Lorde first notably registers the importance of national political liberation in "Grenada Revisited," which surveys the meanings of national sovereignty for women workers, mothers, and wives. In subsequent essays collected in *A Burst of Light,* and especially in poems from *Our Dead Behind Us,* Lorde's "cultural nationalist" recovery of Dahomean women warrior traditions creates conceptual, rhetorical, and stylistic bases for her feminist engagement with national liberation.

This later work after the invasion of Grenada reveals that national liberation is key to fostering socially transformative coalitions and decolonizing forms of difference. The fact that the terms "difference" and "coalition" continue to appear regularly in the later texts might camouflage the shift in Lorde's thought that I seek to define; one might assume that the consistency in terminology reflects a consistency in meaning.[17] However, Lorde retheorizes "difference" and "coalition" as national struggle becomes increasingly central in her work. Far from including national liberation as one among many struggles, let alone moving away from it, essays and journal entries from *A Burst of Light* privilege national liberation as a central goal for people of color—one that has been redefined by women, lesbians, and gays. These writings thus complicate postnationalist claims that 1970s and 1980s Black feminism opposed nationalism and enjoin us to reevaluate our histories of Black feminist thought.[18]

For in appreciating how and to what extent Lorde adopts key ideas of nationalist internationalism regarding culture, reclamation of land, solidarity with anticolonial movements, and internal colonialism, we must recognize that the U.S. invasion of Grenada in 1983 was not a singular event responsible for shifting Lorde's Black feminism. Rather, the invasion crystallized certain tendencies already present in Lorde's thought due to the influence of U.S.-based Black movements centered on national liberation. Despite their homophobia and sexism, these movements crucially nurtured and shaped Lorde's Third World solidarity and her socialist anti-imperialist critique—along with her literary talent. The post–World War II Black Left, through the Committee for the Negro in the Arts and the Harlem Writers Guild, first picked up on and encouraged Lorde's poetic abilities when she was still in high school. The Guild's journal, the *Harlem Writers Quarterly*, published an early poem by Lorde in its spring 1952 issue, and Guild cofounder and pioneering Africana scholar John Henrik Clarke was an important mentor who "taught [her] wonderful things about Africa."[19] Other figures of the Black anticolonial Left whom Lorde encountered included Langston Hughes, Rosa Guy, and Julian Mayfield. Lorde wrote to the latter, "I owe more than I can say here as a Black woman and writer, to the encouragement, stimulation and insights gathered in those [Harlem Writers Guild and Committee for the Negro in the Arts] meetings through the lean years."[20] Later, the presses and publications of the Black Arts movement reviewed and published Lorde's poetry; Dudley Randall's Broadside Press published *From a Land Where Other People Live* (1973) and *New York Head Shop and Museum*(1974). And in addition to befriending Sonia Sanchez, Lorde met other Black nationalists and leftists such as Addison Gayle, June Jordan, and Toni Cade Bambara through City College's SEEK Program.[21] In reconstructing this history, I am not denying that Lorde, as she often said, could not find a home in these and other institutions with nationalist politics.[22] However, I want to suggest that we oversimplify and distort in rigidly opposing Lorde's feminism to Black nationalism's multiple incarnations and affiliations in the mid- to late twentieth century.

In the 1980s through her untimely death in 1992, Lorde's feminist alliances with Black and Third World oppositional nationalisms were encouraged by women activist-writers involved with the anti-apartheid movement. Gloria Joseph, a "Black revolutionary spirited feminist" and Lorde's partner in the last period of her life, was the main force behind the 1984 formation of Sisterhood in Support of Sisters in South Africa (SISA), which recognized "the emerging South African women's self-help movement as a form of political resistance to apartheid" and which "signified a powerful, contemporary example of the international links between the quest for black liberation in America and in Africa."[23] Through SISA, Lorde established a lasting friendship with Ellen Kuzwayo, a leading South African feminist writer and revolutionary, and in 1986, as Lorde struggled with liver cancer, a high point was the time she spent with the Zamani Soweto Sisters, one of the organizations SISA supported.[24] Along with Michelle Cliff, June Jordan, Alice Walker, and Sonia Sanchez, Lorde articulated the significance of anti-apartheid struggles to racial oppression in the United States and to Black feminist thought.[25] With these sisters in arms, Lorde acted on women's issues that were irreducible to but also inseparable from nationalist struggle.

Lorde's engagements with national identity and liberation were further informed by indigenous activism in New Zealand and Australia in which women assumed leading roles. Inspired by U.S. civil rights struggles, the indigenous movements in these countries fundamentally challenged the white settler state by insisting on their rights to their land, to cultural autonomy, and to political representation.[26] Rejecting multicultural strategies of accommodation to existing state structures, Maori and Aboriginal people stressed their special claims as original inhabitants and "nations within" that were distinct from minority and migrant groups. As Menno Boldt observed in 1993, indigenous movements made up a new wave of Third World national liberation that succeeded the upswell of decolonization after World War II.[27] Struggles for Maori and Aboriginal self-determination spurred Lorde to reframe her politics of difference to account for resistant nationalisms that challenge hegemonic nation-states instead of positing an oppositional consciousness that supersedes the homogenizing tendency of all nationalisms.

Lorde's later writings, then, testify to important historical and theoretical continuities between second-wave Black feminism and the nationalist internationalism of the postwar Black Left and the Black Power movement. Lorde presents us with a Black feminist analysis of Fanon's warning against "the mistake, heavy with consequences," of "miss[ing] out on the national stage."

▫ ▫ ▫

While "Grenada Revisited" is the first prose text to demonstrate Lorde's concern with Third World national liberation, she registered the importance of the issue in an earlier essay, "Learning from the 60s," which examines the political possibilities beyond the impasses of Black Power nationalism. For Lorde, Malcolm X's legacy lies not so much in his work within the Nation of Islam (which Lorde cannot take seriously "because of [its] attitude toward women as well as because of [its] nonactivist stance") but in his recognition in the last year of his life of "difference as a creative and necessary force for change" and his examination of "the societal conditions under which alliances and coalitions must indeed occur." While acknowledging the "raw energy of Black determination released in the 60s," which "is still being felt in movements for change among women, other peoples of Color, gays, [and] the handicapped," Lorde urges her readers to confront and transcend the limitations of nationalism: "We must face with clarity and insight the lessons to be learned from the oversimplification of any struggle for self-awareness and liberation, or we will not rally the force we need to face the multidimensional threats to our survival in the 80s."[28] All of this is in keeping with postnationalist claims that second-wave Black feminism, of which this essay is an example, exposes and breaks with essentialist and regulatory Black nationalist politics.

Yet we should not ignore the essay's emergent nationalist internationalism, which Lorde developed and theorized more deeply in subsequent writings. This position is expressed mainly in a section marked by Lorde's anger over the U.S. invasion of Grenada in 1983, an event that was so significant for her that she added commentary about it in the published version of this piece after it had originally been given as a talk in 1982:

> We are Black people living in a time when the consciousness of our intended slaughter is all around us. People of Color are increasingly expendable, our government's policy both here and abroad. We are functioning under a government ready to repeat in El Salvador and Nicaragua the tragedy of Vietnam, a government which stands on the wrong side of every single battle for liberation taking place upon this globe; a government which has invaded and conquered (as I edit this piece) the fifty-three square mile sovereign state of Grenada, under the pretext that her 110,000 people pose a threat to the U.S. Our papers are filled with supposed concern for human rights in white communist Poland while we sanction by acceptance and military supply the systematic genocide of apartheid in South Africa, of murder and torture in Haiti and El Salvador.[29]

Lorde's reflections on Black consciousness amplify U.S. Third World discourses of internal colonialism, as she compares the "slaughter" of Black people in the United States to "the systematic genocide of apartheid in South

Africa" and other instantiations of U.S. foreign policy intended to liquidate left-wing national liberation movements in Southeast Asia and Central America. Lorde pursues this notion of the internal colony—what she calls "Apartheid U.S.A." in a later pamphlet—as she describes socioeconomic conditions that render African Americans a nation within a nation in the 1980s: "Washington, D.C. has the highest infant mortality rate of any U.S. city, 60 percent of the Black community under twenty is unemployed and more are becoming unemployable, lynchings are on the increase, and less than half the registered Black voters voted in the last election."[30] In "Apartheid U.S.A.," Lorde explicitly framed such conditions in terms of the institutionalization of South African apartheid, thereby claiming that African Americans comprised not merely a citizenry of ethnic minorities but a colonized population subject to super-exploitation and state-supported extermination. "Learning from the 60s" represents a move toward theorizing African American national oppression at the same time that it critiques the sexism and homophobia undergirding Black Power nationalism's flawed insistence on unity. That is to say, while Lorde urges her audience to learn from and go beyond U.S. Black nationalism in order to confront multiple intersecting oppressions, she does not foreclose the radical potential of nationalism. Instead, she underscores both the importance of Third World movements for self-determination and their bearing on the social conditions of African Americans.

Lorde fully elaborates her nationalist internationalism in "Grenada Revisited," which counters U.S. state discourses "calculated to reduce a Black nation's aspirations in the eyes and ears of white Americans already secretly terrified by the Black Menace [and] enraged by myths of Black Progress." Revisiting the internal colony model, Lorde claims that the invasion serves to warn African Americans that they, no less than the Grenadians, are a "conquered people."[31]

A first reading of "Grenada Revisited" might confirm the view that nationalism is characterized by heteronormative patrilineage, homogeneity, and incompatibility with feminist analysis. In praising the People's Revolutionary Government (PRG) under Prime Minister Maurice Bishop for unifying Grenada's "highly stratified society," Lorde foregrounds the colonial legacies of "colorism and classism" as primary divisions but does not explicitly address gender inequalities such as the fact that the state is a male domain. However, the essay describes Grenadian nationhood by drawing mainly from the experiences of women and children; in Basil Davidson's terms, Lorde emphasizes the social aspects of anticolonial struggle impacting the majority of Grenadians rather than narrowly national issues pertaining primarily to male elites. In doing so, she foregrounds the impact of independence and (neo)colonialism on women and children. In her conclusion, she situates

Grenada's future in a popular struggle embodied by peasant and working-class women, not one that is in the hands of a few privileged males.[32]

"Grenada Revisited" begins by recalling Lorde's first trip to the island in 1978, "eleven months before the March 13, 1979 bloodless coup of the New Jewel Movement," the popular organization opposing the reactionary regime of Eric Gairy.[33] Among the images Lorde catalogs are children on their way to school and women driving sheep, frying fish, and walking along the beach. It is these women and children—not the conservative or revolutionary male heads of state—who represent Lorde's vision of Grenada and its potential. To illustrate progress under the PRG, Lorde showcases its programs (free medical care, the Center for Popular Education) that primarily benefit women and children. The situations of women also make evident how much Grenada stands to lose as a result of U.S.-backed neoliberal restructuring. Lorde asks, "How soon will it be Grenadian women who are going blind from assembling microcomputer chips at $.80 an hour for international industrial corporations?"[34] Passages such as these make clear the gendered stakes for "Grenadians who dared to believe that they could have a right to define themselves and the future of their nation independent of the United States."[35]

Lorde concludes her essay by once again typifying "the people" through women like her mother:

> I . . . came for reassurance, to see if Grenada had survived the onslaught of the most powerful nation on earth. She has. Grenada is bruised but very much alive. Grenadians are a warm and resilient people (I hear my mother's voice: "Island women make good wives. Whatever happens, they've seen the worse"), and they have survived colonizations before. I am proud to be of stock from the country that mounted the first Black english-speaking People's Revolution in this hemisphere. Much has been terribly lost in Grenada, but not all—not the spirit of the people. *Forward Ever, Backward Never* [the slogan of the Grenadian Revolution] is more than a mere whistle in the present dark.[36]

While Stephens's reading of this essay emphasizes the domination of Grenada by U.S. imperialism and looks forward to non-national forms of political community, Lorde concludes by suggesting that the dream of the revolutionary nation-state has not been quelled. Lorde celebrates the country's claim to be "the first Black english-speaking People's Revolution in this hemisphere"—something the U.S. invasion cannot erase—and does not locate its independence in an obsolete past. Instead, she holds out independence as a path, however tenuous, out of the "present dark." Furthermore, Lorde subtly contests forms of nationalism that "exist primarily as a male activity with women distinctly left out or peripheralized in the various national constructs."[37] While men may have led the "People's Revolution," the "island women" are its "people"; Grenada is not a merely symbolic "she." Grenada's women are a source of its resiliency, its power to endure and once again overthrow imperialism, for under it they have nothing to lose but their chains. Even Lorde's mother's adage that "island women make good wives," which seemingly positions them within a heteropatriarchal national community,[38] strains against this meaning when read intertextually with *Zami,* which commences with this saying. *Zami* clarifies at the end of its first chapter that these island women

> survived the absence of their sea-faring men easily, because they came to love each other, past the men's returning.
>
> *Madivine. Friending. Zami. How Carriacou women love each other is legend in Grenada, and so is their strength and their beauty.*[39]

The good island woman is not confined to the heteropatriarchal role of wife but has autonomy from the "sea-faring" man within a community of women-loving women: *zami.*

This feminist revolutionary nationalist stance is internationalist and diasporic: Lorde connects the invasion of Grenada with the efforts of the United States to suppress the independence movement of the Vietnamese, the U.S. government's support of the apartheid regime in South Africa, and racist U.S. foreign policies with respect to other Caribbean nations. At the same time, this diasporic perspective diverges from deconstructive postnationalist perspectives that "challenge the very meaning of specific identity and placement."[40] While postnationalist studies of Lorde posit a "transnational, inter-island legacy" to be reclaimed, the essay's most striking vision of inter-island movement conveys not freedom or the plurality of difference but imperialistic violence. Lorde speaks of "the Grenadian bodies shipped back and forth across the sea in plastic bodybags from Barbados to Grenada to Cuba and back again to Grenada" as part of an effort to hide evidence of the invasion.[41]

Even if "Grenada Revisited" explores the "migrations between identities or the articulations of a variety of identities . . . central to our understandings of the ways in which [Black women] writers express notions of home," the essay is at least equally invested in Lorde's situatedness as an American, or specifically a "Grenadian-american," as she calls herself here.[42] As Stephens writes, "though [Lorde] too adopts the stance of the conscientious reporter [associated with the cosmopolitan stranger/outsider] she also rigorously attempted to place herself, *as an American citizen,* in relationship to United States imperial actions and the life of the Carriacou women."[43] For Lorde, identifying as a U.S. citizen, as opposed to inhabiting only or primarily an exilic, in-between status that disavows national affiliation, did not mean identifying *with* the U.S. nation-state; it meant *dis*identifying with its racist, homophobic, and imperialist forms of domination. As a Grenadian-american, Lorde used her relative situational privilege from within the First World to analyze and speak out against acts of global depredation.[44]

Claiming one's nationality and accepting its attendant responsibilities are integral to Lorde's anti-imperialist internationalism, and this tenet reappears regularly in entries from her second published set of cancer journals, which she wrote in the wake of the invasion and collected in *A Burst of Light*. For example, Lorde's entry of February 18, 1984, just weeks after her fact-finding mission to Grenada in late 1983, pursues the implications of using one's position and relative power as an American:

> Last night I gave a talk to the Black students at the University about coming to see ourselves as part of an international community of people of Color, how we must train ourselves to question what our Blackness—our Africanness—can mean on the world stage. And how as members of that international community, we must assume responsibility for our actions, or lack of action, as americans. Otherwise, no matter how relative that power might be, we are yielding it up to the opposition to be used against us, and against the forces for liberation around the world. For instance, what are our responsibilities as educated Black women toward the land-rights struggles of other people of Color here and abroad?[45]

Lorde's internationalist conceptualizations of Blackness—its meaning "on the world stage" for African Americans, who belong to a global community of people of color—are informed by racial identity on the national level, whereby citizenship gives African Americans some leverage as well as the moral and political imperative to resist U.S. imperialism.[46]

Lorde's solidarity with the land-rights movements cited in this diary entry further exemplifies her efforts to link national/nationalist and internationalist modalities of Blackness. Her concept of African American national oppression, specifically land dispossession, fed and was reinforced by land reclamation movements of Maori and Aboriginals. While she was planning trips to New Zealand and Australia to meet with indigenous feminist activists such as Donna Awatere, author of *Maori Sovereignty* (1984), Lorde wrote her most cogent analysis of African American national oppression, "Apartheid U.S.A."[47] The essay expands on an entry from "A Burst of Light" that expresses "the tragedy of being an oppressed hyphenated person in America, of having no land to be our primary teacher."[48] Lorde's awareness of the importance of land to African Americans, a perspective that was informed by her adoption of the internal colony model, prompted her to view indigenous land-rights movements as a priority for "educated Black women."

Lorde pursued this priority in her keynote address at a women writers conference in Melbourne, which she dedicated to Black Australian women's land rights struggles. This speech, a portion of which is transcribed in "A Burst of Light," used the 150th anniversary of the state of Victoria to call attention to the fact that it was "built upon racism, destruction, and a borrowed sameness." Elaborating on the speech's title, "The Language of Difference," Lorde challenged the audience of primarily white Australian women to hear this language as it was voiced by "the Aboriginal women of this land who were raped of their history and their children and their culture by a genocidal conquest in whose recognition we are gathered today."[49] While Lorde thus indicted the violent homogeneity of settler nationalism that had resulted in the eradication of Aboriginal heritage, her call for a language of difference did not condemn nationalism in toto. Lorde's conceptualization of difference was rooted in her solidarity with Aboriginal nationalism: attending to difference, for example, meant lobbying white Australians to support land-rights legislation. In this context, "difference" is not attained through postnationalist cosmopolitan hybridity but through support for indigenous movements for self-determination that would challenge the "racism, destruction, and a borrowed sameness" of the settler nation. In calling attention to the violence of Australian nationalism, Lorde refused to conflate it with the resistant nationalism of the oppressed.

Lorde's encounters with indigenous feminists amplified her conclusion in "Grenada Revisited" that women were integral to national struggles. As she wrote in an October 1985 journal entry, "Wherever I go, it's been so heartening to see women of Color reclaiming our lands, our heritages, our cultures, our selves—usually in the face of enormous odds."[50] This entry suggests that "our real work as Black women writers of the Diaspora" requires an internationalist consciousness of anticolonial nationalist struggles:

> For me as an African-American woman writer, sisterhood and survival means it's not enough to say I believe in peace when my sister's children are dying in the streets of Soweto and New Caledonia in the South Pacific. Closer to home, what are we as Black women saying to our sons and our nephews and our students as they are, even now, being herded into the military by unemployment and despair, someday to become meat in the battles to occupy the lands of other people of Color?
>
> How can we ever, ever forget the faces of those young Black american soldiers, their gleaming bayonets drawn, staking out a wooden shack in the hills of Grenada? What is our real work as Black women writers of the Diaspora? Our responsibilities to other Black women and their children across this globe we share, struggling for our joint future?[51]

This last question about the responsibilities of Black women writers of the diaspora "to other Black women and their children across this globe" was one that Lorde sought to answer in essays and poetry from this period that examined and redefined liberatory struggle through Black women's experiences of motherhood and parenting.

Perhaps her most sustained prose response to this question lies in "Turning the Beat Around: Lesbian Parenting 1986," also in *A Burst of Light*. For Lorde, the act of raising children as "warriors rather than cannon fodder" could contribute critically to liberatory struggles if parents developed "some cohesive vision of that world in which we hope these children will participate, and some sense of our own responsibilities in the shaping of that world." This "coherent vision" situated U.S. lesbians and gays of color "as citizens of a country that stands on the wrong side of every liberation struggle on this globe," especially insofar as it "publicly condones and connives with . . . apartheid South Africa."[52] Lorde made Black South African self-determination central to lesbian and gay parenting through her discussion of the 1976 Soweto uprisings, when nationwide demonstrations were ignited by the gunning down of schoolchildren who were protesting a decree to make Afrikaans the primary medium of instruction. Lorde's poem "The Evening News"—one of several that invoked Soweto—asks, "what does it mean / our wars / being fought by our children?"[53] The response provided by her essay on lesbian parenting is that this tragedy constitutes the "lesson we must teach our children, that difference is a creative force for change, that survival and struggle for the future is not a theoretical issue."[54] As does her keynote speech defending Aboriginal land rights, "Turning the Beat Around" grounds "difference" in the efforts of oppressed people to reclaim their land and culture. The "creative force for change" is embodied by the children "who stuff their pockets with stones in Soweto and quickstep all the way to Johannesburg to fall in the streets from tear gas and rubber bullets in front of Anglo-American Corporation"; children for whom revolution is "the very texture of [their] lives" because they follow their parents' example.[55] Lorde argues that raising warriors to support such struggles for self-determination is a primary goal for gay and lesbian parents of color in the United States because of the conditions in which they live: "We are Gays and Lesbians of Color at a time in that country's history when its domestic and international policies, as well as its posture toward those developing nations with which we share heritage, are so reactionary that self-preservation demands we involve ourselves actively in those policies and postures."[56]

While this analysis grows out of Lorde's earlier work, it also differs markedly from the earlier intersectional feminism for which she is better known. A brief comparison with "Learning from the 60s" from *Sister Outsider* is instructive here. "Learning from the 60s" shares rhetoric with "Turning the Beat Around," such as "the question of difference as a creative and necessary force for change." This earlier essay, however, focuses its critique on sexist and homophobic U.S.-based Black nationalist movements that pursue a homogeneous identity politics that is inadequate for the task of confronting multiple levels and sites of oppression. As Lorde cogently states in her rejection of this mode of resistance, "There is no such thing as a single-issue struggle because we do not live single-issue lives."[57] But the main object of critique—the enemy of difference—shifts in "Turning the Beat Around," which indicts "white racist profit-oriented sexist homophobic america" and its policies of "classic" as well as internal colonialism. Lorde suggests that these forms of colonialism occupy a heteropatriarchal spectrum of oppression "stretch[ing] from the brothels of Southeast Asia to the blood-ridden alleys of Capetown to the incinerated Lesbian in Berlin to . . . grandmother Eleanor Bumpurs shot dead in the projects of New York." While Lorde's analyses in "Learning from the 60s" and "Turning the Beat Around" are largely complementary, it is much more so the case in the latter essay (as in Lorde's other work from the mid-1980s onward) that Lorde does not limit nationalism to a critique of sexist U.S.-based Black identity politics but embraces Third World liberation movements that extend to African Americans as an internal colony. Lorde privileges her nationalist internationalism in her later work as a position that supports and is supported by Black lesbian feminism. Thus, whereas "Learning from the 60s" refrains from hierarchizing struggles in order to avoid suppressing difference—a point exemplified by the rhetorical question, "Can any one [*sic*] here still afford to believe that the pursuit of liberation can be the sole and particular province of any one particular race, or sex, or age, or religion, or sexuality, or class?"—"Turning the Beat Around" posits the centrality of anticolonial nationalist struggle to lesbians and gays of color.[58]

The sexual politics of "Turning the Beat Around" in fact complements the analysis of internal colonialism and national liberation in "Apartheid U.S.A.," published in *A Burst of Light*. "Apartheid U.S.A." had originally been published in 1986 (the year Lorde wrote "Turning the Beat Around") by Kitchen Table: Women of Color Press together in a single pamphlet with a speech by the socialist feminist Merle Woo, "Our Common Enemy, Our Common Cause: Freedom Organizing in the Eighties." Woo's and Lorde's texts are both concerned with the anti-apartheid movement; Woo focuses on campus organizing and Lorde investigates the connections between South African apartheid and U.S. racial oppression. As Lorde claims, "The political and social flavor of the African-American position in the 1980s feels in particular aspects to be analogous to occurrences in Black South African communities in the 1950s, the period of the postwar construction of the apparati of apartheid, reaction, and suppression." Her observation in her cancer journals excerpted in "A Burst of Light" regarding African Americans' lack of a land base is reiterated in "Apartheid U.S.A." to explain why "a militant, free Africa is a necessity to the dignity of African-American identity." As she was writing, national liberation seemed imminent in the context of the growing unrest in reaction to a new constitution the South African government implemented in 1984 that further entrenched apartheid rule. Lorde interprets this unrest as "Black South Africa [taking] center stage on the world platform," paraphrasing writer, feminist, and anti-apartheid movement leader Ellen Kuzwayo.[59]

Lorde examined the world historical centrality of the revitalized Black South African struggle, including its pressing relevance to African Americans, in terms of the meaning of parenthood for lesbians and gays of color in "Turning the Beat Around." She emphasized that sexual and familial relations cannot be shunted off to the realm of the private or seen as part of the superstructure. At the same time, Lorde insists that gay and lesbian parenting is not revolutionary in and of itself: "It would be dangerous as well as sentimental to think that childrearing alone is enough to bring about a livable future in the absence of any definition of that future."[60] Individually and together, the texts from *A Burst of Light* define a livable future through struggles for self-determination that set the sociopolitical horizons for people of color in the United States, especially women, lesbians, and gays of color, in critical ways. This Black internationalist feminism also informs the themes and aesthetics of Lorde's poetry in *Our Dead Behind Us* (1986), to which I will now turn. This poetry builds upon Lorde's reimagining of West African religions and histories in order to redefine nationalist internationalism through Black motherhood and the erotic.

▫ ▫ ▫

In charging lesbian and gay parents of color with raising warriors, "Turning the Beat Around" rearticulates the cultural nationalism of *The Black Unicorn* and *Zami,* with their Black lesbian feminist re-visions of African spirituality. More precisely, the essay recalls the Dahomean tradition linking mothers and warriors, which Lorde describes as follows:

> It is the West African women of Dahomey who have the legend . . . and who demonstrate . . . that there is not a contradiction between the taking of lives and the giving of life, and the making of war, so that you have your Dahomeyan amazons who were the fiercest warriors of the king. It is very important to have that, because, in fact, in the lives of so many Afro-American women, my mother, my mother's generation, I saw that these women were nurturing, they were cher-

> ishing, they were loving, but they were also really tough warriors, you know. . . . This is why I think it is so necessary, I think, to weave myths into our world.[61]

These warriors are incarnate not only in African American women but in African women freedom fighters: "It is affirming to me when I see now images of the Zambian women, the women who fought in Zimbabwe, the Angolan women with a gun on their shoulder and the babies in their arms as they patrol."[62] This Dahomean tradition is present in Lorde's essay on gay and lesbian parenting, which speaks of the South African children who die fighting imperialist and colonial domination because "somewhere their parents gave them an example of what can be paid for survival."[63] In this feminist rendering of revolutionary national culture, traditions of African parenting and legends of the Dahomean Amazons attain contemporary significance as they illuminate Black women's centrality to and agency within Third World nationalist struggles.

Black feminist revolutionary national culture lies at the heart of Lorde's poetry in *Our Dead Behind Us,* as evidenced by the cover of the first edition.[64] It presents what Lorde describes in the poem "Beams" as "a snapshot of the last Dahomean Amazons / taken the year that I was born / three old Black women in draped cloths / holding hands."[65] This photo is superimposed on an image of a demonstration of South African freedom fighters, a visual counterpart to Lorde's claim that Amazonean foremothers are "behind" Black South African national liberation, in the sense that the present is beholden to an insurgent Black female past. Lorde picks up and refracts aspects of this theme in multiple ways throughout *Our Dead Behind Us,* but it is arguably the first poem, "Sisters in Arms," that most cogently reinterprets national struggle and international solidarity through Black women's experiences and traditions.[66]

"Sisters" invokes both the West African mother warrior figure and the Afro-Caribbean idea of *zami* ("women who work together as friends and lovers") as the poem thematically and formally draws attention to state violence against women of the Black diaspora and to their relationship to revolutionary national struggle. The poem portrays the political and sexual relationship between an African American woman (the poem's speaker) and a South African female revolutionary whose daughter is tortured to death by the police. Lorde conjoins the struggle for self-determination with Black female experiences of eroticism and motherhood: "The edge of our bed was a wide grid / where your fifteen-year-old was hanging / gut-sprung on police wheels." At the same time, Lorde makes it clear that there is no inherent connection between political radicalism and Black womanhood (and, by extension, no homogeneous definition of Black womanhood), as the speaker is unable to return with her lover to South Africa to bury her daughter and join her revolt. Instead of "plant[ing] the other limpet mine / against a wall at the railroad station," the speaker buys her lover a ticket to Durban with her American Express card, using her relative privilege as an African American in complicity with U.S. capitalism's past and present ties to colonialism[67] rather than blowing up its infrastructure. National differences engender political differences between the two women.

Yet even as the poem's speaker does not act on her connection with South African liberation, she cannot escape its relevance to her life. In the second stanza, while tending her garden, she finds a mere "half-page story" in the *New York Times* that "finally mentions [her lover's] country." Events, however, are distorted by the U.S. mainstream media's focus on "the first white south african killed in the 'unrest'" and its neglect of the massacre and imprisonment of Black children like the lover's daughter. It is not just the violence of the apartheid state that devastates the speaker but the repression of this violence both within the speaker's individual life (her inability to join her South African lover's revolt) and within U.S. national life, represented by the *New York Times*' fleeting, distorted coverage. The very absence of U.S. recognition of apartheid's violence constitutes its own form of racist and colonial violence against the African American subject, devastating the speaker: "my hand comes down like a brown vise over the marigolds / reckless through despair."

What Megan Obourn calls Lorde's traumatic aesthetics is evident in the *apo koinou* in these lines. *Apo koinou* is a rhetorical term for a word or phrase shared between two distinct syntactic units; consequently, the syntax is irregular and disorienting, producing a traumatic effect as "the poem's meaning seems to exceed language's ability to hold, represent, and narrate it."[68] In the lines quoted above, such disorientation is produced by the way that "reckless through despair" modifies both the speaker alone in her garden in the United States and the speaker and her lover during their last night together in South Africa. The poem thereby registers the return of the repressed—apartheid state violence and the forms it takes against Black women and children—by segueing seamlessly from the narrative present to the past that maintains its claim on the speaker despite its geographical and temporal distance:

> my hand comes down like a brown vise over the marigolds
> reckless through despair
> we were two Black women touching our flame
> and we left our dead behind us
> I hovered   you rose   the last ritual of healing
> "It is spring," you whispered
> "I sold the ticket for guns and sulfa
> I leave for home tomorrow"

and wherever I touch you
I lick cold from my fingers
taste rage
like salt from the lips of a woman
who has killed too often to forget
and carries each death in her eyes
your mouth a parting orchid
"Someday you will come to *my* country
And we will fight side by side?"

Eroticism initially promises to transcend the bloody past—"we were two Black women touching our flame / and we left our dead behind us." But the dead cannot be left behind, for they are embodied in the speaker's lover, "who has killed too often to forget / and carries each death in her eyes." History and the erotic are enmeshed in the lover, who tastes of rage. Her words associate spring and rebirth with her decision to return to the struggle for liberation, a decision financed by the speaker's token of complicity with apartheid—the ticket to Durban.

The lover's question—"Someday you will come to *my* country / And we will fight side by side?"—remains just that; the poem offers no clear response or resolution. At the same time, the poem does not foreclose representations of either reality or revolution in the process of registering trauma, political uncertainty, and Black women's multiple identities.[69] Like the essays and journals from *A Burst of Light*, "Sisters" grounds difference and multiplicity in national struggle. This can be seen in the stanzas following the lover's parting question, which denotes not only her lips opening to speak and kiss ("your mouth a parting orchid"), but the pair's parting from each other. This separation of the speaker and her lover is represented in the stanza immediately following the lover's question:

Keys jingle in the door ajar   threatening
whatever is coming belongs here
I reach for your sweetness
but silence explodes like a pregnant belly
into my face
a vomit of nevers.

Whether these violent, imagistic lines present the silence of the lover's departure or her death (keeping in mind the poem's telescoping of times and places), sisterhood and intimacy are negated in "a vomit of nevers."

Yet this negation gives way to a third meaning of the lover's parting question in the poem's final stanza centering on the image of the nineteenth-century

South African warrior Mmanthatisi leading men into battle. In this stanza, the question of fighting side by side in South Africa can be read as parting the two women into multiple selves. This division of the subject is manifest in the pronoun slippage from "you" to "her" as the speaker compares her lover to "a woman / who has killed too often to forget / and carries each death in *her* eyes" (elsewhere in the poem, the lover is referred to and addressed in the second person). This woman to whom the speaker refers in the third person can be interpreted to be Mmanthatisi, who comes to embody the speaker and her lover in the final stanza. Like the lover, Mmanthatisi is both mother and warrior, bearing arms and children. Given the final lines, which describe Mmanthatisi "dream[ing] of Durban" as she "maps the next day's battle," we can also read this woman as an avatar of the speaker, who perhaps does eventually rise to her lover's challenge to join her in battle. In other words, Mmanthatisi is not a relic of the past but a dynamic figure of the present and of possible futures still to be won and written with "our dead behind us." As "warrior queen and leader of the Tlokwa (Sotho) people during the *mfecane* (crushing), one of the greatest crises in southern African history," according to Lorde's footnote, Mmanthatisi presents an alternative history of and model for African liberation, one that calls upon Black women's multiple and simultaneous roles as mothers, lovers, and leaders of their people.

This figure of the African woman warrior/ancestor/mother/sister/lover reappears in various forms throughout *Our Dead Behind Us*, preparing the ground for the last poem's "Call" to Aido Hwedo, the Dahomean deity representing "all ancient divinities who must be worshipped but whose names and faces have been lost in time."[70] "Call" deploys the spiritual ritualistic qualities of *The Black Unicorn* to re-member sisters in arms and recuperate their power: "she who scrubs the capitol toilets"; "Thand[i] Modise winged girl of Soweto"; a jailed guerrilla soldier with the Umkhonto we Sizwe, the military wing of the ANC; the goddesses "Oya Seboulisa Mawu Afrekete"; civil rights leaders Rosa Parks and Fannie Lou Hamer. The diasporic "Call" speaks to a Black internationalist feminism that is sustained by and sustains battles led by women: "On worn kitchen stools and tables / we are piecing our weapons together / scraps of different histories / do not let us shatter / any altar." "Worn kitchen stools and tables" ingeniously yokes domesticity and feminine militancy, including coalitional U.S. Third World and anticolonial struggles led by women. The image calls up Kitchen Table: Women of Color Press, which Lorde co-founded in 1980 with Barbara Smith. Devoted to publishing all women of color, the grassroots press allowed them to "piece . . . together" "different histories," weapons against their erasure by mainstream institutions and histories. The stool in the poem alludes to the Ashanti (Akan) warrior queen Yaa Asantewa, who waged war against the British after they demanded the golden stool symbolizing Ashanti sovereignty.[71] In the poem, U.S. Third World feminism and anticolonial nationalism are not antagonistic but are intertwined and conjoined with civil rights struggles led by women: "Rosa Parks and Fannie Lou Hamer / Assata Shakur and Yaa Asantewa / my mother and Winnie Mandela are singing / in my throat / the holy ghosts' linguist / one iron silence broken / Aido Hwedo is calling."

Lorde's Black internationalist feminism shifted yet again after she joined what she termed the U.S. colonial community of St. Croix.[72] No longer identifying primarily with African Americans on the U.S. mainland, Lorde adopted an Afro-Caribbean islander perspective that in many ways completed the political trajectory of her later years. Having made national liberation central to her Black feminist thought and aesthetics, Lorde became part of the Cruzan colonial community fighting for self-determination against U.S. hegemony. From this position, Lorde began to grapple with some of the limitations of the internal colony model that had been central to her analysis of national oppression as she became aware of the need to break geographically as well as ideologically with the U.S. mainland/mainstream.

▫ ▫ ▫

Increasingly and then permanently, Lorde made the U.S. Virgin Island of St. Croix her home with Gloria Joseph from the mid-1980s until her death. During the time Lorde lived on the island, it was populated mainly by native-born Crucians (nearly half the population) and other West Indians of African descent. Technically U.S. citizens, the people of St. Croix nonetheless could not vote in presidential elections and had only a nonvoting delegate to Congress. Like the economy of many other Caribbean islands, that of St. Croix was geared toward tourism and was largely controlled by outside white interests.[73] Cut off from their land, the impoverished native-born majority existed in what Lorde called "a frankly colonial relationship to the United States," one that would allow it to "[ram] through the territorial government of the Virgin Islands, an okay to build a catalytic cracker" that could not be built on the continental United States due to environmental and safety concerns.[74]

This direct colonial relationship was magnified in 1989 when Hurricane Hugo hit the island. In a scenario that was tragically repeated sixteen years later with Hurricane Katrina's devastation of African American communities in the southern United States, the residents of St. Croix received only limited humanitarian assistance from FEMA, and what they did get was inefficiently administered. The U.S military and the FBI descended on the island with the primary goal of protecting U.S. economic interests in oil and tourism.

This military presence also muzzled growing pro-independence sentiment on the island.[75] To Lorde, "the U.S. military takeover of St. Croix reminded me of nothing so much as the U.S. military invasion of Grenada."[76]

After Hugo, Lorde claimed St. Croix as home for political and personal reasons, situating herself within "the U.S. colonial community." This placement was not exclusive; Lorde emphasized that she was "part of many communities," including "the international community of people of color" and "the Black women's community."[77] At the same time, as we have seen with Lorde's previous work, this multiple diasporic self-positioning was internationalist rather than postnationalist. It did not break with anticolonial nationalism; it asserted a fundamental struggle between oppressor and oppressed nations while proclaiming the need to rebuild, reclaim, and redefine home instead of exchanging it for what Lorde called the "safety of exile."[78]

The extent to which Lorde was serious about reclaiming home and land in St. Croix, thereby establishing a rooted rather than routed diasporic presence, can be seen in her rhetoric of identification with the island's colonial community. In an interview she gave not quite a year after Hugo, Lorde declared, "When I say we, I mean the indigenous people of [the Virgin Islands] as well as those of us who have chosen to make the Virgin Islands home."[79] Lorde's identification with the people of St. Croix rather than with mainland Americans is also a predominant feature of her contribution to the anthology that she co-edited with Gloria Joseph and Hortense Rowe in answer to the racist and paternalistic media coverage of Hugo's devastation of the island, *Hell Under God's Orders: Hurricane Hugo in St. Croix—Disaster and Survival.* Lorde's essay, "Of Generators and Survival—Hugo Letter 12/89," shares with "Grenada Revisited" the goals of providing investigative reporting and anti-imperialist analysis. "Grenada Revisited," however, takes care not to impose Lorde's views as a (sister) outsider on Grenadians: "Grenada is their country. I am only a relative. I must listen long and hard and ponder the implications of what I have heard, or be guilty of the same quick arrogance of the U.S. government in believing there are external solutions to Grenada's future."[80] But the very form of Lorde's Hugo letter explicitly positions her as an insider who endures the hurricane with other Cruzans and who exposes the depths of the situation to a U.S. mainlander "Friend." Her constant invocation of "we," especially in the refrain "We are rebuilding," contrasts markedly with the references to Grenadians (as in "the average Grenadian") in "Grenada Revisited." While Lorde has the option to be "evacuated in those huge grim triple-decker C-140's," she firmly stays put: "We are rebuilding. This is our home."[81]

Lorde's rooted islander perspective put pressure on the internal colony model that had become central to her thought in the wake of Grenada's invasion in essays such as "Grenada Revisited," "Turning the Beat Around," and especially "Apartheid U.S.A." On the one hand, Lorde continued to use this analysis to expose the forms of oppression that African Americans shared with Black Crucians: "Whether it's oil and land in California and Georgia or creating an oil plantation out of St. Croix, the issues of exploitation by a white militaristic economy are essentially the same, although expressed differently in different locales." Lorde insisted that "what happens on [the Virgin Islands] is directly involved with what is going on with Black people on the mainland and all over the world."[82] On the other hand, Lorde became more attuned to the limitations of analogizing and drawing continuities between the conditions of First World minorities and those of Third World national majorities. As Cynthia Young writes about the use of Third World rhetoric and discourse, including theories of internal colonialism, by U.S. leftists of color, "the elision of specific historical conditions and their attendant consequences makes certain political and cultural possibilities available, but it also closes down others."[83] Among other things, the internal colony model "cannot fully address the situational privilege First World national minorities have vis-à-vis Third World national majorities; . . . and it cannot account for the different forms of colonialism or the differences between colonialism and imperialism."[84] Lorde's relocation to St. Croix forced her to confront more sharply than before the relative privilege of African Americans on the U.S. mainland, which obstructed diasporic solidarities with native- and West Indian–born Crucians:

> As Black people on the continental U.S., we have become used to considering ourselves part of the mainstream—that is to say, it matters on the national stage, or at least in the national media, what happens in New York or L.A., even to Black people. . . . But when Hurricane Hugo smashed the "minor outlying islands" totally destroying the homes and livelihood of 66,000 people, when our communities were in upheaval, that was not of particular interest to Detroit, Chicago, California, or New York. And Black people in those places don't realize that these are Black communities that were decimated.[85]

This gap between Black Crucians who are subjected directly to U.S. colonialism and African Americans sheltered at least partially from its effects is one that Lorde takes care to both mark and bridge in her Hugo Letter. As an insider addressing a distanced friend in the mainland/mainstream of the United States, Lorde is positioned to expose the "costly lesson of what it really means to be in a colonial relationship to a super power"—the U.S. military's brutalization and criminalization of the people it should be protecting, the FEMA aid directed to the tourism industry instead of to families or the elderly, the overriding of territorial governance in the interests of the oil industry.[86]

Precisely because of the substantial differences between the structural situations of the Third World national majority in St. Croix and the African American First World national minority, Lorde cast her lot with the former, which enabled her to take yet another stand for Black national self-determination through the project of rebuilding the island. Lorde even imagines her readers joining her and Gloria in St. Croix at the close of her Hugo Letter:

> My friend, I wish you were living down the road. Rocky as it may be, it is still also the most beautiful. Gloria and I would take our walking sticks after a long day's work, and the three little bluefish Curtis just brought by, and go clean them down on the beach, throwing the guts to the seabirds. We'd bring the fish over to your house, and we'd all sit around and have a fish-fry over driftwood coals, swapping stories of how it was, and how it is, and how it is surely going to be.[87]

Lorde's fanciful, idyllic invitation nonetheless poses the serious notion that disidentifying with U.S. neocolonialism can take place most fully only by becoming part of the Third World majority, not as a tourist or visitor but as a member of an (inter)national community rooted on its own land. This utopic vision fulfills the longing expressed in "Bicentennial Poem #21,000,000":

> I know
> the boundaries of my nation lie
> within myself
> but when I see old movies
> of the final liberation of Paris
> with french tanks rumbling over land
> that is their own again
> and old french men weeping
> hats over their hearts
> singing a triumphant national anthem
>
> My eyes fill up with muddy tears
> that have no earth to fall upon.[88]

For all its nostalgia, the poem has no illusions about the forces arrayed against the realization of national self-determination within the Third World. The "french tanks / rumbling over land / that is their own again" deny sovereignty to African and Southeast Asian countries. Consequently, the "final liberation of Paris," which is heralded with "a triumphant national anthem," is not only contrasted with but predicated on the speaker's "muddy tears / that have no earth to fall upon." Nonetheless, Lorde refused to abandon revolutionary nationalism on grounds that it was not feasible or that it derived from Western modernity with its contradictory propagation of violence and progress.[89] As we see in the Hugo Letter, Third World national (be)longing came to instantiate Lorde's "use [of] the energy of dreams that are now impossible, not totally believing in them nor their power to become real, but recognizing them as templates for a future within which my labors can play a part."[90]

Lorde's nationalist internationalism positions her ideologically and historically as a descendant of the postwar Black Left. Although her involvement with it was peripheral and brief compared to the other writers discussed in this book, its politics, culture, and activism permeated her involvements with the Black Power movement and the Black women's movement. Thus, Lorde's writing displays a Marxist, pan-Africanist, and feminist worldview that in her later years reprised the Black internationalist feminism of Claudia Jones. Jones challenged monadic, androcentric formulations of race by accounting for the triple burden of Black working-class women. But rather than positing open-ended intersections of race, gender, and class, she argued that "every aspect of Negro oppression in our country stems from the existence of an *oppressed nation*" under U.S. imperialism.[91] Within this oppressed nation, Black women constituted a vanguard that would lead the way to "a Socialist America—the final and full guarantee of woman's emancipation."[92] Lorde's later essays and poetry expand Jones's thought to address sexual, gender, and racial identities under late capitalism. In the work discussed in this chapter, Lorde theorized the leadership and concerns of women of color within national liberation movements that would advance the rights of other women, lesbians, and gays. For Lorde, sexual and racial difference could not thrive under a neoliberal/neocolonial global order. Therefore, battles for self-determination, national culture, and land reclamation were principal bases for validating intersectionality and heterogeneity. Like Jones, Lorde conceptualized a dialectical rather than an oppositional relationship between national liberation and internationalism, which accounted for the agendas of radical feminists of color throughout the world such as the Afro-German women Lorde encountered while teaching poetry in Berlin, the leaders of the anti-apartheid and indigenous land rights movements, and other Black women writers such as Paule Marshall, Michelle Cliff, June Jordan, and Ntozake Shange who decried the depredations of U.S. imperialism.

Tracing its lineage to Jones's work on the Negro question and the woman question, Lorde's revolutionary praxis indicates the role of the postwar anticolonial Left in shaping late-twentieth-century Black feminism and critiques from queer women of color. In chapter 6, I meditate on the presence and influence of this Left internationalist feminism within contemporary U.S. culture more broadly.

6

Reading Maya Angelou, Reading Black Internationalist Feminism Today

In reflecting on the relevance of African American women writers of the postwar anticolonial Left today, it is useful to look closely at the work of Maya Angelou. Not only has she attained the most mainstream visibility and commercial success of all the women affiliated with the African American Left, but her Black internationalist feminist autobiography, *The Heart of a Woman* (1981), has become part of U.S. mass culture. Although this attests to the co-optation of radicalism, Angelou's autobiographical series (composed of five other volumes) should also be examined as a site of contestation over national identity, race, and the goals of feminist and queer critique.[1] For as I will argue, these texts reproduce competing claims of postcolonial citizenship versus multicultural nationalism and of Black internationalist versus liberal feminism. The fact that these oppositional narratives exist within a body of work that has so visibly shored up hegemonic Americanism indicates the residual influence of postwar Black internationalist feminism and its salience to the challenges twenty-first-century race radicals face.[2]

The Heart of a Woman, the fourth volume of Angelou's autobiographical series, was selected by Oprah Winfrey for her Book Club in 1997. This was in many ways a logical choice. The woman-centered topics that often recur in the books Oprah selects—paralleling the topics that frequently appear on her shows—include "love, motherhood, friendship, self-discovery, overcoming adversity, negotiating difference, surviving."[3] While some of the books she selects are socially engaged, their relevance is generally framed by a focus on the individual rather than the collective, on interpersonal rather than structural sources of oppression. Oprah's books are not politically revolutionary: it is unimaginable that we would find among them the autobiographies of Angela Davis, Assata Shakur, or Elaine Brown, much less that these women would host a televised pajama party in their homes for Oprah's viewers to discuss their books, as Angelou did. By contrast, Angelou's life story, pivoting around "the joys and burdens of a black mother in America," was prime material for the liberal feminism of a show "focuse[d] on identity and self-help," one that "discourage[d] broader social critique or efforts at political change."[4]

Angelou's iconic American status has given her the presence she has had within the Oprah brand.[5] The enormous success of *I Know Why the Caged Bird Sings*, the first volume of Angelou's autobiography, set the stage not only for five subsequent volumes and numerous awards and honors but also for Angelou's metamorphosis into one of the country's most beloved prophet-poets, a wise maternal figure uniting the nation at large.[6] Tellingly, Angelou was appointed by Gerald Ford to the American Revolution Bicentennial Council, a group of twenty-five prominent Americans who traveled the country to find ways to celebrate its birthday. Angelou is one of the few African American women who seemingly transcend race to embody the American dream. Her compelling narrative of overcoming adversity has generated its own success story by launching a lucrative career that has included a partnership with Hallmark to develop a line of greeting cards filled with the pithy, folksy aphorisms for which her autobiographies are known. Testifying to her place in the national imaginary, Bill Clinton chose Angelou as the poet for his presidential inauguration, making her the first African American and the first woman to assume this role. Angelou's 1993 inaugural performance of "On the Pulse of the Morning" obtained the largest audience for poetry in history, and in addition to becoming a bestseller and canonical work of literature in its own right, the poem increased the sales of *I Know Why the Caged Bird Sings* by nearly 500 percent.[7]

Caged Bird and "On the Pulse of the Morning" situate Angelou squarely within a U.S. national(ist) framework. *Caged Bird*, about Angelou's childhood in Arkansas, Missouri, and California, is often read as an affirmation of American self-reliance and individual fulfillment.[8] Indeed, crucial to the book's success was the fact that it was published just a few years before the development of U.S. multicultural nationalism in the wake of the civil rights and Black Power movements and the mobilization of other racial groups and women, lesbians, and gays. The radical demands of these movements for economic and social justice were met with a multicultural Americanism that the state supported in an effort to shore up its legitimacy while co-opting the militancy of the new social movements.[9] Multiculturalism emerged as a double-edged ideology that revised Eurocentric and patriarchal formulations of citizenship—for example, by incorporating works like *Caged Bird* into school curricula nationwide—while mystifying the intensification of structural racism evidenced by deindustrialization, deregulation, capital flight, and the evisceration of welfare. A multiculturalist text such as "On the Pulse of the Morning" (which, like *Caged Bird*, has become a staple of primary and secondary school reading lists) expanded the racial, ethnic, sexual, and classed norms of nationhood to encompass "the Asian, the Hispanic, the Jew / The African, the Native American, the Sioux"; "The Gay, the Straight, the Preacher, / The privileged, the homeless, the Teacher." And in combining these distinct and disparate names within its nationalist rhyme scheme, the poem reaffirmed ideologies of American progress, diversity, and inclusion that occluded forms of political protest and affiliation that go beyond and fundamentally challenge the nation-state.[10]

Although Angelou is best known through these lenses of liberal feminism and multicultural Americanism, I want to work against their repression of radical history and politics to recover the revolutionary Black internationalist content and perspective of the last three volumes of her autobiography, especially *The Heart of a Woman*. Acknowledged by critics to be the most political of Angelou's autobiographical works, it centers on her involvement with the Harlem-based internationalist Left—a context that has gone largely unnoticed.[11] Covering 1957–1962, the book richly documents the development and persistence of postwar Black anticolonialism with vignettes about the Harlem Writers Guild, Castro's stay in Harlem, Martin Luther King Jr. and the SCLC, Malcolm X, and the demonstration at the United Nations against Lumumba's assassination.

From this angle, Angelou can be productively read within the genre of Black Power autobiographies alongside autobiographical works by Malcolm X, George Jackson, and Huey Newton and especially writings by women radicals such as Angela Davis, Assata Shakur, and Elaine Brown.[12] *The Heart of a Woman* and the volumes that follow it, *All God's Children Need Traveling Shoes* and *A Song Flung Up to Heaven*, speak to the paradigm-shifting efforts of the new Black Power studies to rethink the periodization, geographical scope, and ideological configurations of twentieth-century race radicalism.[13] Angelou illuminates both the fluidity and the conflicts between Black Left, civil rights, and nationalist activists and organizations. Overly rigid distinctions between moderate and militant, domestic and global Black freedom struggles are undone by her simultaneous involvement in groups with roots in the anticolonial Left while organizing with the SCLC and attempting to draw support from Malcolm X and the Nation of Islam.

Angelou's Americanism, then, assumes a very different meaning when examined through the later volumes of her autobiographical series. The journeys described therein affirm but also redefine Americanness through pan-Africanist routes: *All God's Children,* which recounts Angelou's sojourn in Ghana from 1962 to 1965, portrays Angelou's desire to belong to America and concludes with her decision to return. The book fundamentally troubles the exceptionalist terms of assimilation into the dominant U.S. social order that "On the Pulse of the Morning" celebrates. Instead, the integrationism of *All God's Children* resembles Malini Johan Schueller's concept of "Post-Colonial citizenship," which maintains anti-imperialist solidarities and "activist racial politics at once grounded in the nation and looking beyond it, but a nation the very idea of which is reconfigured through both antiracist and anti-imperialist struggles."[14] Unlike hegemonic multicultural nationalism, postcolonial citizenship exposes and challenges the structural inequalities produced by the nation-state through racist domestic and foreign policies.

In *The Heart of a Woman,* Angelou investigates the possibilities of postcolonial citizenship from a Black internationalist feminist perspective that weaves together her maturation as a writer, a woman, and a revolutionary. However, mainstream and critical readings have denied the interrelationship of Angelou's feminine and political development: Oprah's Book Club privileges the story of Black motherhood, postcolonial scholar and African Americanist Selwyn Cudjoe emphasizes the book's focus on political subjectivity while ignoring its feminism, and literary critic Mary Jane Lupton treats gender issues and feminist readings separately from the volume's concerns with racial and national liberation.[15] The text itself poses this divide between the political sphere and the struggles of womanhood as a problem:

> Somewhere after sunset and before I reached Brooklyn, the glorious magic disappeared. When I stepped off the subway at Park, I was no longer the bright young woman executive dedicated to Justice, Fair Play for Cuba and a member of the Harlem Writers Guild. I was an unmarried woman with the rent to pay and a fifteen-year-old son, who had decided that anything was better than another dull evening at home with Mother.[16]

The split between anticolonial politics and the private sphere is exacerbated by the patriarchal Black internationalism depicted in Angelou's recounting of her oppressive romance with a South African revolutionary. Against narrow conceptions of gender and race that divorce anticolonialism from feminine experience, Angelou negotiates her public activism through her subjectivity as a woman, mother, and wife (and reconstructs womanhood out of her radicalism). Ostensibly unrelated narratives of racial political awakening and feminine empowerment are juxtaposed as a result of the book's episodic structure, thereby suggesting their mutuality. Although this narrative form and the theme of Black female self-discovery permeate Angelou's autobiography as a whole, *The Heart of a Woman* recasts the previous volumes' examination of Black womanhood by accessing intersectional analysis of racism and sexism through Black Left anticolonialism.[17]

In this regard, *The Heart of a Woman* must be recognized as a Black internationalist feminist text—but if this is so, what do we make of its prominence within the world of Oprah's Book Club? Certainly Angelou has distanced herself from the Black Left, and this is reflected in the autobiography's attenuation and displacement of Black internationalism. Closure is effected through romanticized portraits of homecoming and redemption in Africa (in *All God's Children*) and depoliticized personal triumph (in *The Heart of a Woman* and *A Song Flung Up to Heaven*). Running alongside and in conflict with representations of the self in dialectical relationship to global Black revolutionary movements, individualist narratives prove amenable to liberal U.S. multiculturalism. Nonetheless, I propose that this duality in Angelou's autobiography speaks more broadly to the fate of Black internationalist feminist writing. Despite the fact that it has been diluted, misrepresented, and repressed, the feminism of women writers on the anticolonial Left circulates within and questions dominant U.S. culture while sharing affinities with new directions in African American women's political activism in the twenty-first century. As a result, recovering Black internationalist feminism is an effective means of rethinking dominant conceptions of race and nation and of undoing their restrictive hold on organizing today.

▫ ▫ ▫

Like the poem by Georgia Douglas Johnson that gives the volume its title, *The Heart of a Woman* explores the tensions between Black women's free movement and captivity within "some alien cage," to quote Johnson.[18] From the outset, feminine mobility/immobility is yoked to the contradictory movement of the nation in the throes of the civil rights era: the prologue opens with the lyrics of a spiritual—"The ole ark's a-moverin' along"—that, according to Angelou, "could have been the theme song of the United States in 1957. We were a-moverin' to, fro, up, down and often in concentric circles."[19] Citing the progress and setbacks of school desegregation, efforts to derail the Voting Rights Bill, and the symbolic weight of Sugar Ray Robinson's wins and losses, Angelou presents a domestic framework for civil rights struggle that reflects her understanding of it in the narrative present. But her involvement with the Harlem Black Left leads her to a global view of U.S. racial conflict, and for her, the "concentric circles" of the nation's trajectory are always expanding and intersect with Third World liberation movements.

Within this context of political turmoil, Angelou's personal evolution is intertwined with her momentous decision to become a writer—to "spell my name: WOMAN." This decision, which opens the first chapter and effectively fuels the volume's major developments, is shown to be made possible by figures of the Harlem Left: performer Abbey Lincoln, jazz musician Max Roach, and novelist John Killens, Angelou's primary source of inspiration and mentorship. Although Angelou does not name the Black Left as such, she extensively depicts her friends' internationalist radicalism:

> In the Killens' home, if entertainment was mentioned, someone would point out that Harry Belafonte, a close family friend, was working with a South African singer, Miriam Makeba, and South Africa was really no different from South Philly. If the West Indies or religion or fashion entered the conversation, in minutes we were persistently examining the nature of racial oppression, racial progress and racial integration.[20]

Initially put off by this "unrelenting diatribe" against whites, Angelou believed that "California blacks were thousands of miles, literally and figuratively, from those Southern plagues" of segregation and lynching.[21] However, this notion is undermined by Killens's rejoinder: "If you're black in this country, you're on a plantation."[22]

Angelou reinforces the naïveté of her belief by juxtaposing it with the previous scene in which her mother, Vivian Baxter, desegregates a hotel in Fresno, "a middling town with palm trees and a decidedly Southern accent." Having chosen to meet Angelou at a venue where the color bar has been lifted for only a month, Baxter reveals a pistol in her purse, "half hidden by her cosmetic case," and informs her daughter, "The Desert Hotel better be ready for integration, 'cause if it's not, I'm ready for the Desert Hotel." She then shares her plans to desegregate the Marine Cooks and Stewards Union: "I'll put my foot in that door up to my hip until every woman of color can walk over my foot, get in that union, get aboard a ship and go to sea." Civil rights struggle is thus refracted through the mother-daughter relationship that runs throughout the autobiographical series, connecting the narratives of racial radicalization and Black womanhood. Angelou represents her mother as a feminist counterpart to Robert Williams, who, as she later explains, "encouraged black men to arm themselves and protect their homes and families" and who would later globalize the battleground for race rights from exile in Cuba and China.[23] Baxter, however, does not need protection by Black men and is capable of defending herself and her daughter against white supremacists.

Angelou's narratives of politicization and feminine self-discovery continue to unfold in tandem with her artistic development as she enters the Black Left through the Harlem Writers Guild, where discussion of craft segues into debate over how to support Castro against the United States. In this context, we should not be surprised to learn that Angelou's first published story appears in the Cuban magazine *Revolución.* At the same time, the first manuscript she subjects to the Harlem Writers Guild's rigorous criticism, a play titled "One Love. One Life," indicates the importance of the genre of women's romance to her authorial aspirations and metatextually gestures toward the fact that her own romance narrated in *The Heart of a Woman* emerges, like her play, out of engagement with Black internationalism.

Angelou's singing, too, is instantly transformed by her radicalization, as she sadly contrasts her night club career with the marriage of art and antiracist anticolonial politics that Lincoln, Roach, Killens, and celebrities such as Lorraine Hansberry, James Baldwin, and Harry Belafonte accomplished. Consequently, Angelou incorporates the interactive African freedom song "Uhuru" into her act at the Apollo. Despite being warned by the white manager that audiences won't go along with it, "Uhuru" solicits passionate participation from Harlemites energized by the Nation of Islam and televised spectacles of African independence. As Angelou writes, "Black people in Harlem were changing, and the Apollo audience was black. The echo of African drums was less distant in 1959 than it had been for over a century."[24]

Angelou further represents the revival of pan-African and Third World anticolonialism through her struggles with motherhood, inflecting this "private" narrative with the shift in Black public opinion. In the wake of Castro's meeting with Khrushchev during the former's sojourn at the Hotel Theresa in Harlem, Angelou depicts both the collective and the individual impact of this signal event in U.S. Third World Left history. Describing the sentiment of the African American throngs cheering the encounter, Angelou writes,

> Some white folks weren't bad at all. The Russians were O.K. Of course, Castro never had called himself white, so he was O.K. from the git. Anyhow, America hated Russians, and as black people often said, "Wasn't no Communist country that put my grandpappa in slavery. Wasn't no Communist lynched my poppa or raped my mamma."[25]

This decisive break with liberal discourses of race is reiterated on the personal level of Angelou's relationship to her son, Guy, after she publicly chastises him for skipping school so he can witness Castro's visit to Harlem. Taking umbrage with her short-sighted infantilization of him, Guy tells her,

> To me, a black man, the meeting of Cuba and the Soviet Union in Harlem is the most important thing that could happen. It means that, in my time, I am seeing powerful forces get together to oppose capitalism. I don't know how it was in your time, the olden days, but in modern America this was something I had to see. It will influence my future.[26]

Aligning his independence from his mother with Cuba's display of autonomy from Cold War America, Guy implicitly provokes Angelou to do the same. Accepting her son's rebuke, Angelou retreats into her office. She concludes the chapter by noting that "Abbey [Lincoln], Rosa [Guy] and I decided what was needed was one more organization. A group of talented black women who would make themselves available to all the other groups."[27] Not until four chapters later does Angelou actually discuss this new organization, the Cultural Association for Women of African Heritage, which harnesses Harlem's resurgent anticolonialism by planning the demonstration at the UN against Patrice Lumumba's assassination. But by framing the group's formation as a response to Guy's reflections on U.S. Black–Third World solidarity, Angelou registers that her relationship to her son is a site of politicization that fuels her own self-perception in relation to rising nations of color.

In addition to Angelou's experiences as a daughter and a mother, romance is another arena of feminine subjectivity that reflects her political milieu and intimately shapes her radicalism. Specifically, the patriarchal arrangements of marriage pose obstacles to Angelou's activism even as she leaves her first prospective husband, a bail bondsman, for a South African freedom fighter, Vusumzi Make. Wedded to traditional sex roles—the dutiful wife and helpmate within the home; the breadwinning revolutionary husband out on the frontlines—Make and his comrades reproduce the gendered public/private split: "When other Africans visited, Vus would insist that Guy sit in on the unending debates over violence and nonviolence, the role of religion in Africa, the place and the strength of women in the struggle. I tried to overhear their interesting conversations, but generally I was too busy with household chores to take the time."[28]

While critiquing male chauvinism through her oppressive marriage to Make, Angelou articulates Black feminist revisions of patriarchal nationalism. When she and the other "wives of freedom fighters [who] lived their lives on the edge of screaming desperation" are left out of a pan-African conference in London, they construct an alternative feminist public sphere in which they question their exclusion ("Have we been brought here only as portable pussy?"); testify to their militant anti-imperialism ("We, in Kenya, are not just wombs. We have shown during Mau Mau that we have ideas as well as babies"); and share Black women's traditions of resistance ("I told about black American organizations, remembering the . . . secret female organizations with strict moral codes. . . . The African women responded with tales of queens and princesses, young girls and market women who outwitted the British or French or Boers"). Despite "the distances represented and the Babel-like sound of languages," diasporic unity is affirmed through Black womanhood, as Angelou's dramatic rendition of Sojourner Truth's "Ain't I a woman?" closes the gathering and brings the African women to their feet, crying and "proud of their sister, whom they had not known a hundred years before."[29]

This feminist pan-African solidarity among Black West Indian, African, and American women in London carries over into the United States with the founding of CAWAH by women of the Harlem Left. Through CAWAH, Angelou represents the struggle over the scope of African American civil rights, which is brought to a head for the group by Lumumba's assassination. Political identification with the slain leader of independent Congo is disdained by members who had supported Black cultural identity through planning "an immense fashion show based on African theme and showing African designs." However, it is the Left internationalism expressed by Rosa Guy that prevails: "We've got to let the Congolese and all the other Africans know that we are with them. Whether we come from New York City or the South or from the West Indies, that black people are a people and we are equally oppressed."[30] Against historical amnesia about African American women's militant leadership, Angelou extensively details CAWAH's instigation of the demonstration at the UN over Lumumba's murder, including her role in turning the group's original plans for a "dramatic statement" by six women into a mass protest that would galvanize nationalist consciousness.

Complementing but also somewhat diminishing its representation of Black female collective work, the volume soon turns to the deleterious effects of masculinist Black internationalism and women's acquiescence to it. In the wake of the CAWAH demonstration, Angelou and Rosa Guy attempt to shift the responsibility for building its momentum onto Malcolm X and the Nation of Islam. However, Malcolm disagrees with CAWAH's "integrationist" strategy of making demands on the UN, insisting instead that Harlemites follow Islam and the path to separation.[31] The women's disappointment and anger over Malcolm's patronizing dismissal sets the stage for Angelou's disillusionment with the paternalism she encounters in her marriage to Make.

After vividly documenting Robert Williams's armed defiance against North Carolina white supremacists, the formation of SNCC, the Freedom Rides, the awarding of the Nobel Prize to Ralph Bunche, and the numerous achievements of Black Left artists, Angelou anti-climactically concludes by noting that she "was becoming a good African wife"; "Vus traveled to and from East Africa, West Africa, London and Algeria, and I sat at home." Angelou's retreat from activism colors her travel to Africa with her husband and son. Despite the growth of Black American solidarity with African independence that she herself had striven to nurture, Nasser's Egypt is mere Orientalist fantasy—"the setting for two contemporary lovers" where she can be "the heroine in a novel teeming with bejeweled women, handsome men, intrigue, international spies and danger."[32] Invoking conventions of romance fiction in depicting her isolating marriage, Angelou exposes revolutionary nationalism's uncritical inheritance of bourgeois patriarchal norms.

In keeping with Black internationalist feminism, however, Angelou does not reject nationalist struggle. Describing Make's efforts toward South African freedom, Angelou notes that she "still admired and appreciated him" even though she was no longer in love with him.[33] Still aligned with anticolonial nationalism, Angelou obtains work as an associate editor of the Nasser-friendly *Arab Observer* in the process of disentangling herself from Make. Her reclamation of female autonomy in the private sphere is thus tied to her reclamation of Black internationalist commitments in the public sphere.

Most crucially, Angelou's separation from Make leads her to Ghana, "an exciting country at an exciting time. Kwame Nkrumah was the African hero. He had wedded Marxism to the innate African socialism, and was as loved by black people all over the world as he was hated and feared by whites in power."[34] In Ghana she encounters and eventually joins the African American expatriate community connected to the U.S. Black anticolonial Left through W. E. B. and Shirley Graham Du Bois and Alphaeus Hunton and through a younger generation of radicals that included Julian Mayfield, Vicki Garvin, Alice Windom, and Max and Jean Carey Bond.[35] Nkrumah, Angelou explains in *All God's Children,* "had let it be known that American Negroes would be welcome to Ghana. He offered havens for Southern and East African revolutionaries working to end colonialism in their countries."[36] As part of this pan-Africanist community, Angelou participates in a challenge to the U.S. Cold War liberal framework for African American identity that severed its solidarities with Third World decolonization.

At the same time, Angelou begins to signal ambivalence toward Black internationalism. Ghana is not Angelou's intentional destination; she does not leave Egypt with the purpose of joining the expatriate community in support of Nkrumah, as she had no contacts in Ghana. Emphatically representing her sojourn in Ghana as a matter of chance rather than political conviction, she distances herself from the African American expatriate radicals there. Stopping in Accra only to establish Guy at the University of Ghana, Angelou is headed to Liberia to take a government post when his involvement in an automobile accident derails her plans. In focusing on Guy's recovery and departure for university, the final chapters foreground the personal narrative of the mother/son relationship in a way that delinks it from the social narrative of Black internationalist struggle. When Guy leaves for his dormitory, Angelou

> wait[s] for the wave of emotion to surge over me, knock me down, take my breath away. Nothing happened. I didn't feel bereft or desolate. I didn't feel lonely or abandoned.
>
> I sat down, still waiting. The first thought that came to me, perfectly formed and promising, was "At last, I'll be able to eat the whole breast of a roast chicken by myself."[37]

Ending with these reflections, the volume leaves Angelou triumphantly alone so that she can affirm herself after having given away so much to her husband and son. This private, individual narrative of feminine self-discovery suppresses the unfolding of pan-African anticolonial subjectivity, including the formation of radical Black feminine collectives such as CAWAH and the group of women militants married to African freedom fighters.[38]

This is not to deny the narrative logic of the preceding chapters, which illustrate how "the heart of a woman" was profoundly shaped by the confluence of civil rights, nationalist, and radical movements; the revival of African American global consciousness; and feminist challenges to the patriarchal ideologies that hamstrung national liberation movements.[39] It is certainly not incidental that Angelou's hard-won self-sufficiency and optimism at the conclusion come to her in Nkrumah's Ghana. Her journey to female autonomy undeniably takes place *through* involvement with the dynamic symbiosis of Black liberation struggles.

Furthermore, in covering her three years in Ghana in the next volume, *All God's Children Need Traveling Shoes,* Angelou unequivocally positions herself within the radical expatriate community that finds common cause with Ghanaians in "denunciations of American capitalism, American imperialism, American intervention, and American racism."[40] If the home of Julian Mayfield and his wife, Ana Livia Cordero, becomes expatriate headquarters, then the second most popular place of congregation is the bungalow that Angelou shares with Vicki Garvin, the radical labor leader, and Alice Windom, a younger woman with a master's in sociology and a strong commitment to African revolution.

All God's Children takes as its central theme (expressed, as in *The Heart of a Woman,* in the dedication) the search for home, especially as it was conducted "passionately and earnestly" by "Julian and Malcolm and all the fallen ones." For the expatriate "Revolutionist Returnees" this search is a personal and political one complicated by the tensions between their enthusiasm for Ghana and their exclusion from its social and political circles, between their radicalism and the realpolitik of Nkrumah's neutralism, and between their support for African American struggle and their geographical distance from it. These tensions are resolved through the reformulation of liberal democratic citizenship during the expatriates' demonstration at the U.S. embassy in Ghana in support of the March on Washington of August 28, 1963. As the expatriates denounce two soldiers raising the U.S. flag, Angelou reflects on the painful contradictory knowledge that this "symbol of hypocrisy and hope" was "[their] flag and [their] only flag" and that their invectives "did not hide [their] longing for full citizenship."[41] What they long for, however, is not assimilation into the dominant U.S. society "which had rejected, enslaved, exploited, then denied us."[42] Within the context of the expatriate demonstration's linkage of African American and African struggle, full citizenship calls for a transformative relationship to the nation that would undo its racist hierarchies while reaching beyond its boundaries to affirm anti-imperialist alliances.

This full or postcolonial citizenship is elaborated in the next section, which describes Malcolm X's arrival in Ghana to solicit support from African leaders to petition the UN on behalf of African Americans. Using the framework of human (rather than civil) rights, Malcolm looks beyond U.S. citizenship to posit the colonial oppression of African Americans. Angelou paraphrases him: "If South African Blacks can petition the U.N. against their country's policy of apartheid, then America should be shown on the world's stage as a repressionist and bestial racist nation."[43] It is on these Black internationalist terms, not out of faith in the exceptionalism of American democracy, that Angelou decides to return to the United States: Malcolm urges her to "bring [Africa] home and teach our people about the homeland" by working for the Organization of Afro-American Unity, Malcolm X's effort to engender a pan-African liberation movement.[44]

Angelou thus elaborates on the personal and political stakes of the search for home, but she also crafts a narrative of African homecoming that is pointedly stripped of internationalist commitments. Toward the beginning of *All God's Children,* she writes that

> while Ghana's domestic and foreign policy were stimulating, I was captured by the Ghanaian people. Their skins were the colors of my childhood cravings: peanut butter, licorice, chocolate and caramel. Theirs was the laughter of home, quick and without artifice.[45]

This passage proves to be paradigmatic of the conclusion, which replaces concern with Ghana's sociopolitical landscape with a depoliticized personal narrative of African return:

> I had continually and accidentally tripped over [the roots of my beginnings]. . . . Once I had been taken for Bambara, and cared for by other Africans as they would care for a Bambara woman. Nana's family of Ahantas claimed me, crediting my resemblance to a relative as proof of my Ahanta background. And here in my last days in Africa, descendants of a pillaged past saw their history in my face and heard their ancestors speak through my voice.[46]

As does *The Heart of a Woman, All God's Children* concludes by privileging self-affirmation over Black anticolonialism. Consequently, diasporic identity ultimately appears to be routed less (if at all) through the internationalist challenge to the racist and imperialist U.S. state than through romantic visions of "Africa's maternal welcome" that Angelou had so scathingly subjected to materialist critique earlier in the book.[47]

Angelou's internationalism is even more attenuated in the last volume, *A Song Flung Up to Heaven,* but it emerges at key moments. The volume begins by reminding the reader that the catalyst for Angelou's return to the United States is to work with the Organization of Afro-American Unity, which would not only "help us rid our country of racism once and for all" but would provide South Africans with inspiration and tactics for freeing their own country from white rule.[48] These hopes are shattered by Malcolm's assassination, but Angelou's sense of the interconnectedness of African American and African liberation returns to inform her representation of the Watts uprising:

> Certain political analysts observed that the people were burning their own neighborhood. Though few houses were set afire, the rioters considered the stores, including supermarkets, property of the colonialists who had come into the neighborhood to exploit them and take their hard-earned money.[49]

Connecting the freedom struggles of nations of color with the demands for jobs, child care, and health care that the Watts insurgency expressed, Angelou sees in it not the mindless and savage destruction of property but the resistance and rebirth of a race. As she testifies in her poem about Watts, "Our / YOUR FRIEND CHARLIE pawnshop / was a glorious blaze" that produced "whole blocks novae / brand-new stars / policemen caught in their / brand-new cars" and that would multiply into "a hundred Watts / Detroit, Newark and New York."[50] Attesting to her arrival as a writer, this poem, the only one by Angelou to appear in her autobiographical series, affirms the importance of Black nationalism and its internationalist implications to her art.

▫ ▫ ▫

Commenting on Angelou's performance as Clinton's inaugural poet, James Campbell writes that "the appearance of two children of Arkansas, born on opposite sides of the Jim Crow divide, standing on the same rostrum offered an alluring vision of racial hope. It also demonstrated, yet again, the extraordinary capacity of the American political system to metabolize dissent, to find nourishment for national myths in the struggles of the very people who have been excluded from the nation's bounty."[51] Corroborating the assimilation of dissent, Oprah's selection of *The Heart of a Woman* for her book club transformed a text on women's Black Left anticolonialism into a branded commodity. The fate of Angelou's radical commitments makes painfully clear how Black internationalist feminism has been enervated in the face of late capitalism and hegemonic Americanism.

Nonetheless, in reading *The Heart of a Woman* as a Black internationalist feminist text and situating Angelou's autobiography as a whole within the nexus of postwar Black Left/civil rights/Black Power movements, it's worth pausing to note that these alternative narratives of African American political subjectivity are the best-selling books of "the most visible black woman in the United States, save perhaps for her friend Oprah Winfrey."[52] Of course, Angelou's mainstream visibility is predicated on effacing her involvement with the Left. But as I have argued, the erasure has not entirely taken place: for all the downplaying, obfuscation, and denial of Angelou's radicalism by herself and others, at the heart of her life story is a Black feminist consciousness that emerged from within the Harlem Left and African decolonization movements. Assuming that Angelou's history with the Black Left is negated by her commercialization and liberalism oversimplifies her autobiography and concedes too much to dominant ideologies of racialized and gendered nationhood. Hegemonic meanings of Americanism and Blackness can be forcefully destabilized through the widely known work of a figure who has famously confined these terms within the paradigm of U.S. multicultural nationalism.

The multicultural canonicity of Lorraine Hansberry's *A Raisin in the Sun*—recently revived on stage and remade for network television to commemorate its fiftieth anniversary—affords another opportunity for disclosing Black internationalist feminism through a text that has been celebrated for its supposed liberal Americanism. Since the play's debut, audiences have understood the Younger family's acquisition of a house and their integration of a Chicago suburb to signify that African Americans are American too. *Raisin*'s Black internationalism is further watered down in the 2008 teleplay, which cuts both Walter Younger's epiphany regarding his African heritage and the anticolonial critique expressed by the Nigerian intellectual, Asagai (who in the teleplay instead trumpets his individual exceptionalism in coming to the United States to study). Reading against mainstream interpretations of *Raisin,* we find that in the play, African liberation movements fuse with Black American civil rights struggles: the Youngers' fight against racialized capitalism and segregation is on a continuum with Asagai's plans to defeat colonialism in Nigeria. Moreover, this revolutionary pan-Africanism is notably supported by subplots centering on the efforts of Walter's sister, Beneatha, to define herself as a Black woman. Such internationalist feminist visions haunt and give rise to contemporary U.S. culture as residual influences that "still seem to have some significance because they represent areas of human experience, aspiration and achievement, which the dominant culture undervalues or opposes, or even cannot recognize."[53] Precisely because *Raisin,* like Angelou's autobiographical series, continues to reach mass audiences, its radicalism can rearticulate dominant constructions of national identity within the public sphere.

Alice Childress and Rosa Guy, while not as well known today as Angelou and Hansberry, reintroduced Black internationalist feminism in the last quarter of the twentieth century. Although Childress downplayed her radical ties from the 1960s on, she did not stop associating with Leftists or writing from the perspective of her postwar anticolonialism. *A Short Walk* (1979) revises heteropatriarchal forms of left nationalism that flourished with Garveyism's revival beginning in the late 1950s, and her young adult novel, *Those Other People* (1989), depicts interracial alliances against homophobic witch hunts, reflecting its African American popular front orientation.[54] Guy's *The Sun, the Sea, a Touch of the Wind* (1995) rearticulates popular discourses of Black female empowerment in order to delink feminisms of color from U.S. exceptionalism and heteronormativity and to write back to the patrilineage of Caribbean revolutionary literature. These texts are representative of Childress's and Guy's cultural politics, but both writers produced a number of other novels dating from the 1970s renaissance of African American women's literature that await further investigation.[55]

The imprint of Black internationalist feminism on scholarship motivated by the intersections of race, gender, and sexuality is made evident by the work of Audre Lorde. Essays and poetry from the last decade of her life challenge U.S. imperialism and elaborate a politics of diaspora by championing the self-determination of oppressed nationalities, including African Americans. Although largely obscured because of the prevalence of feminist and postmodern critiques of nationalism, Lorde's nationalist internationalism—and that of other second-wave anticolonial feminist writers such as Paule Marshall, June Jordan, and Michelle Cliff—was foundational to the evolution of intersectional analysis concerned with heterogeneous identities.

Recovering this strand of Black feminism is a timely endeavor as feminist and queer scholars grapple with formations of gender, sexuality, and race in the wake of the new social movements' delimited successes in gaining sociopolitical recognition for people of color, women, lesbians, gays, bisexuals, and transgendered people.[56] As these populations have become delineated and mobilized by U.S. wars in the Middle East; the militarization of the U.S. economy, government, and police; and neoliberal globalization, the parameters of freedom have become increasingly marked with contradictions and costs. New concepts of homonormativity, queer liberalism, U.S. sexual exceptionalism, and the mainstreaming of women's liberation illustrate how struggles for sexual freedom and feminist empowerment collude with racist agendas for military intervention and occupation, privatization, prison growth, xenophobia, consumerism, and the curtailment of social welfare.[57] This morass can be navigated by Black internationalist feminism, which shares with much radical feminist and queer of color critique a materialist and global analysis of oppression that goes beyond narrow identity politics, ludic postmodernism, and elitist cosmopolitanism.

At the same time, Black internationalist feminism reinvigorates feminist and queer of color critique that has been stalled by postnationalism and nonhierarchical intersectionality. Postnationalist theory expands our analytical and political horizons by exposing the racial, heteropatriarchal, and essentialist investments of nationalist discourses and by recognizing that histories, cultures, technologies, and populations often cannot be described only in terms of the nation-state. But insofar as it rejects nationalism as potentially revolutionary, the postnationalist lens blinds us to progressive forces that conjoin national liberation and transnationalism. Such forces include the "border zone of Black nationalist feminism/Black feminist nationalism" in which Patricia Hill Collins locates politically active African American women today, including community workers, hip-hop feminists, and writers of Third Wave Black feminism.[58] This Black nationalist feminist/Black feminist nationalist space challenges white and western feminism by

> situating Black women's community work within global feminist nationalist frameworks. . . . Instead of viewing African American women's community work as the labor of a minority within a minority—the current treatment of African American women within the American race-relations framework—Black women's community work more accurately reflects similar struggles by women worldwide.[59]

Thus, in Collins's analysis, the feminist consciousness arising out of young Palestinian women's participation in national liberation struggle is comparable to that of African American women who, in solidarity with Black men, reconstruct "meanings of both nationalism and feminism within culturally specific contexts produced within postcolonialism and racial desegregation."[60] In building global feminist nationalism out of these conditions, activists would do well to study the women of the postwar anticolonial Left who eschewed total separation from revolutionary nationalist movements while vigorously critiquing the heteropatriarchy of those movements and insisting that Black women's distinctive forms of oppression should determine progressive platforms and leadership.

Black internationalist feminism, which recognizes multiple identities and oppressions, is imbricated to a significant degree with intersectionality. Not merely an additive approach to difference (for example, appending gender to race as if the two were discrete), intersectionality entails a qualitative change to how we view Black, transgender, and other identities. The intersections of these identities refer to their mutual constitutivity and the ways that they shape and are shaped by social, economic, and political processes. In this vein, African American women writers of the anticolonial Left understood gender and sexuality in relation to racialization, segregation, Cold War geopolitics, and national liberation. Nonetheless, Black internationalist feminism goes against the tendency of post-Marxist intersectional thought to avoid reestablishing hierarchies of identity and oppression. The post-Marxist fixation on nonhierarchical differences has prevented scholars from seeing what is distinct and generative about Black internationalist feminism: its robust theorization of the *priority* of national liberation for achieving substantive rights for women, gays, and transgender people and for working-class people and people of color. This hierarchical intersectionality, while paradoxical in postmodern terms, rigorously analyzes identity formation under capitalism and reminds us that confining intersectional thought to cataloguing and proliferating difference is not enough. The prominence of national struggle within Marxist-Leninist thought leads us to see that race, class, gender, and sexuality are effects and determinants of uneven development throughout the world, not multicultural units trapped within the U.S. social imaginary. By foregrounding the struggles between oppressor and oppressed nations, Black Left feminists made sexual liberation contingent on the destruction of racist capitalism and imperialism. But far from reducing the fight against heteropatriarchy to anticapitalist or anti-imperialist campaigns, Black Left feminists queered revolutionary nationalism and redefined its tactics and content around working women's needs. Consequently, the nationalist internationalism of Black women on the Left is crucial to historicizing and developing queer, feminist, and Black Marxisms and to articulating their interrelationships.

African American women writers of the postwar anticolonial Left did more than prefigure or help give rise to second-wave Black feminism; they produced an autonomous line of feminist thought that built on Marxist-Leninist internationalism to advocate truly universal freedoms and rights through the particularities of Black women's lives. Even when they were unable or unwilling to organize around queer politics, postwar Black Left women writers envisioned through literature new genders and sexualities wrought by revolutionary nationalist struggle. These visions remain relevant as the temptation to define one's own freedom at the expense of racialized, sexualized, and gendered others has intensified in the context of the latest crises of capitalism, the U.S. presence in Afghanistan and Iraq, and proposed new anti-immigrant legislation. Under such conditions, we urgently need materialist transnational perspectives that are not averse to the possibilities of national liberation; revolutionary nationalist politics centered on the experiences of Third World women and queers of color; and engagements not only with the culture of movements but also with movement culture, which in turn would enrich our abilities to read the resistance of women of color. The Black internationalist feminism elaborated by women writers of the postwar anticolonial Left can help us imagine and perhaps realize such alignments.

Notes

Introduction. Black Internationalist Feminism

1. Murphy, "Black Delegation Visits the U.S.S.R.," 3. On African Americans in the USSR and the importance of Soviet internationalism to the formulation of Black internationalism, see Baldwin, *Beyond the Color Line and the Iron Curtain.*

2. I borrow the term "nationalist internationalism" from Neil Lazarus, who uses it to describe Franz Fanon's 'dual revolutionary commitments to national liberation struggle *and* the wider struggle for socialist internationalism'; Lazarus, *Nationalism and Cultural Practice in the Postcolonial World,* 242. Baldwin argues that the contradictions and imperialist outcomes of Soviet internationalism cannot blind us to its functioning as a "narrative of possibility for non-Soviet others" (*Beyond the Color Line and the Iron Curtain,* 8). This narrative of possibility stems not only from Lenin's distinction between repressive and emancipatory nationalisms but also from his efforts to reconcile his implicit claim that the USSR embodied an emancipatory nationalist project with its interventions into its southern and eastern neighbors. For a discussion of Black internationalism from the second half of the eighteenth century to the present, see West and Martin, "Contours of the Black International."

3. A note on terminology: I use "Left" to designate Communist and Communist-affiliated individuals and groups. I use "left" to refer to the broader spectrum of radical movements beyond the Communist Party. I say more below about my focus on the Communist Left; for now, I acknowledge that this use of "Left" and "left" centers the Communist movement and diminishes the diversity of U.S. radicalism. However, insofar as the Communist-affiliated Black Left was a primary organizational and ideological "home" of postwar Black women writers (with all the fraught meanings that "home" carries for Black feminists), I strategically use this terminology to indicate the Communist Left's importance to these writers and to their Black internationalist

feminism. I see my study not as the final word on Black feminist radicalism but as part of a broader conversation that must continue to excavate but also look beyond the Communist Party.

4. The persistence of the influence of the Black Belt Nation Thesis in the 1970s is also evident in Nelson Peery's *The Negro National Colonial Question* (1972), "probably the most widely read defense of black self-determination in Marxist-Leninist-Maoist circles at the time"; Kelley, *Freedom Dreams,* 101. However, Communists theorizing African American nationality in the early 1970s no longer distinguished between African Americans in the rural Black Belt and those in urban communities.

5. Biondi, *To Stand and Fight,* 275.

6. Murphy, "Black Delegation Visits the U.S.S.R.," 6.

7. Another figure associated with the Black delegation and its postwar Black anticolonial feminism was Thelma Dale, a popular front figure prominent in the National Negro Congress and Civil Rights Congress and a leader of the Congress of American Women, the first all-women's organization to be endorsed by the CPUSA. Dale had wanted to join the delegation but was unable to do so.

8. To clarify, Black internationalist feminism was concerned with the intersections of sexuality as well as the intersections of gender with race. Hansberry, Childress, Guy, and Lorde were deeply invested in lesbian and gay rights, the relationship of sexuality to radicalism, and challenges to heteronormativity. I argue that the writings of Hansberry, Childress, and Guy enact the queer of color critique for which Lorde is better known.

9. Childress interviewed in Murphy, "Black Delegation Visits the U.S.S.R.," 10.

10. Gaines, "From Center to Margin," 297.

11. See for example Mullen, *Popular Fronts*; Smethurst, *The Black Arts Movement*; Gaines, *African Americans in Ghana*; and Joseph, "An Emerging Mosaic."

12. Black women on the Left have been studied by Martha Biondi, Carole Boyce Davies, Angela Davis, Dayo F. Gore, Jeanne Theoharis, Komozi Woodard, Kevin Gaines, Gerald Horne, Robin Kelley, Alex Lubin, Erik McDuffie, William Maxwell, Bill Mullen, Mark Solomon, James Smethurst, Judith Smith, Mary Helen Washington, Fanon Che Wilkins, and Cynthia Young.

13. Michelle Stephens (on interwar Black transnationalism) and Kate Baldwin (on African American writers in the Soviet Union) by no means preclude rich analysis of gender and sexuality as a result of focusing on male intellectuals. Nonetheless, sustained attention to the cultural politics of Black women is missing.

14. Young, *Soul Power,* 17.

15. Theoretical discussions of Black feminism include Gloria T. Hull, ed., *All the Women Are White, All the Blacks Are Men, but Some of Us Are Brave*; Barbara Smith, *Home Girls: A Black Feminist Anthology*; Audre Lorde, *Sister Outsider* and *Zami*; Angela Davis, *Women, Race and Class*; bell hooks, *Ain't I a Woman: Black Women and Feminism* and *Feminist Theory: From Margin to Center*; Hazel Carby, *Reconstructing Womanhood: The Emergence of the Afro-American Woman Novelist*

and "White Woman Listen! Black Feminism and the Boundaries of Sisterhood"; Patricia Hill Collins, *Black Feminist Thought: Knowledge, Consciousness, and the Politics of Empowerment*; Carole Boyce Davies, *Black Women, Writing, and Identity*; Joy James, *Shadowboxing: Representations of Black Feminist Politics*; and Michelle Wright, *Becoming Black*. Historical analyses of Black feminism include Kimberly Springer, *Living for the Revolution: Black Feminist Organizations, 1968–1980*; Benita Roth, "Race, Class and the Emergence of Black Feminism in the 1960s and 1970s" and *Separate Roads to Feminism: Black, Chicana, and White Feminist Movements in America's Second Wave*; and Anne M. Valk, *Radical Sisters: Second-Wave Feminism and Black Liberation in Washington, D.C.* On U.S. Third World feminism, see Cherríe Moraga and Gloria Anzaldúa, eds., *This Bridge Called My Back: Writings by Radical Women of Color*; Gloria Anzaldúa, *Borderlands/La Frontera*; Chela Sandoval, "U.S. Third World Feminism: The Theory and Method of Oppositional Consciousness in the Postmodern World" and *Methodology of the Oppressed*; and Grace Hong, *The Ruptures of American Capital.*

16. The pioneering Black feminists of the Combahee River Collective located their origins in the second-wave women's movement and movements for Black liberation of the 1960s and 1970s and did not acknowledge the earlier anticolonial Black Left (although they did mention the "white male left"). See the Combahee River Collective, "A Black Feminist Statement," 211. For recent studies of second-wave Black feminism that locate its primary roots in the civil rights and Black Power movements of the 1960s and 1970s, see Kelley, *Freedom Dreams*; Roth, *Separate Roads to Feminism*; and Springer, *Living for the Revolution.* For an important corrective to this genealogy of twentieth-century Black feminism, see Gore, Theoharis, and Woodard, *Want to Start a Revolution? Radical Women in the Black Freedom Struggle.*

17. The Cold War era and the Old Left in general are seen as inhospitable to feminism, a view that Kate Weigand challenges in *Red Feminism.*

18. On American exceptionalism, see Kaplan and Pease, eds., *Cultures of United States Imperialism.*

19. Biondi, *To Stand and Fight,* 272.

20. Important correctives to these tendencies include Singh, *Black Is a Country*; Kelley, *Freedom Dreams*; Biondi, *To Stand and Fight*; Smethurst, *The Black Arts Movement*; Gaines, *African Americans in Ghana*; Joseph, "An Emerging Mosaic"; and Gore, Theoharis, and Woodard, *Want to Start a Revolution?*

21. Killens, *Black Man's Burden,* 174.

22. Hansberry, *To Be Young, Gifted and Black,* 115.

23. Hong, *The Ruptures of American Capital,* xvi.

24. Mayfield, "Into the Mainstream and Oblivion," 33 and 31. The question and meaning of integration was central to this conference as a whole, which was dominated by the Black Left.

25. Schueller writes, "In order to retain a politicized sense of differentiated citizenship that can address the intersection of national racial and imperial structures by

participating in anti-imperial solidarities seen beyond the nation, I propose the idea of Post-Colonial citizenship. This citizenship speaks to the imaginative possibilities of an activist racial politics at once grounded in the nation and looking beyond it, but a nation the very idea of which is reconfigured through antiracist and anti-imperialist struggles"; Schueller, *Locating Race,* 5.

Michelle Stephens's assessment of Black radicals between World Wars I and II also applies to their political heirs in the post–World War II Black anticolonial Left: "Black subjects could strengthen their individual nationalist struggles through international racial formations, transnational, race-based networks.... Far from resorting to a disengaged cosmopolitanism or state of exile, these alternatives represented the hope for an engaged, Black internationalism that could generate *new conceptions of 'citizenship,' new conceptions of the meaning of a 'national community*'; Stephens, "Black Transnationalism," 605, my italics. See also Kevin Gaines's account of African American expatriates in Nkrumah's Ghana, who "enact[ed] a transnational American citizenship in solidarity with African peoples and in so doing participate[d] in the democratization of America"; Gaines, *African Americans in Ghana,* 76.

26. For a critical discussion of these "myths" about feminism, see Barbara Smith's introduction to *Home Girls,* xxvi–xxxi.

27. Ferguson, *Aberrations in Black,* 134.

28. Sandoval, *Methodology of the Oppressed,* 209, 184, Sandoval's italics.

29. Examples of postnationalist feminist scholarship include Kaplan, Alarcón, and Moallem, *Between Woman and Nation: Nationalisms, Transnational Feminisms, and the State*; Dubey, *Black Women Novelists and the Nationalist Aesthetic*; and Hong, *The Ruptures of American Capital.*

This feminist work overlaps with and feeds into the postnationalist turn in the Black Atlantic studies inaugurated by Paul Gilroy. Some scholars have taken up the "postnationalist" mantle in order to make interventions similar to those I wish to make. For example, in their introduction to *Post-Nationalist American Studies,* Curiel et al. state, "If the global is not progressively obliterating the national or the local today, but rather global, national, and local forces are articulating with each other in complex modalities, then the elucidation of these articulations rather than a celebration of them is the urgent task before us" (8).

I also draw on Marxist critiques of the postnationalist shift in postcolonial, cultural, and ethnic studies such as Lazarus, *Nationalism and Cultural Practice in the Postcolonial World*; Parry, *Postcolonial Studies: A Materialist Critique*; and San Juan, *Racism and Cultural Studies: Critiques of Multiculturalist Ideology and the Politics of Difference.*

30. Grewal and Kaplan, "Introduction: Transnational Feminism Practices and Questions of Postmodernity," 22.

31. See for example Hong, *The Ruptures of American Capital,* xix and xxix; Ferguson, *Aberrations in Black*; and Wright, *Becoming Black.* A number of critics recognize the need to avoid conflating different nationalisms. Timothy Brennan writes, "It

is the want of analysis on the varieties within that category [of ethnic particularism]—from, say, Ariel Sharon at one extreme to Ho Chi Minh at the other—that leads to many absurdities in the discourse on the nation and, as in the case of cosmopolitanism, the nation's end. . . . One can hold on to . . . a nonparticularist view politically, while retaining a nationalist position. It is, in fact, the only way to do so"; Brennan, *At Home in the World,* 24. And John Carlos Rowe has this to say about cultural nationalisms in the United States: "Within the United States, moreover it is important to distinguish between nationalisms which are aligned with the nation-state and those which challenge 'official' nationalism. . . . Despite their limitations, Black and Chicano nationalisms, for instance, are not identical with or reducible to U.S. nationalism. In other words, we need to critique the limits and exclusions of nationalism without forgetting the differences between nationalisms or throwing all nationalisms into the trash of history"; Rowe, *Post-Nationalist American Studies,* 2.

32. Alarcón, Kaplan, and Moallem criticize the "nostalgic longing for substance and presence through nationalist activism"; Alarcón, Kaplan, and Moallem, "Introduction: Between Woman and Nation," 4. For a similar critique, see Scott, *Conscripts of Modernity.*

33. Lazarus, *Nationalism and Cultural Practice in the Postcolonial World,* 120, Lazarus's italics.

34. Ahmad, *In Theory,* 34–35. Neil Larsen outlines "a general if highly uneven crisis of 'third worldist' or national-liberationist ideology stemming in turn from the progressive collapse of the strategic class and national alliance of third world bourgeoisie and third world labor underwriting this ideology"; Larsen, "Imperialism, Colonialism, Postcolonialism," 41. The indicators of this crisis include the 1973 overthrow of Allende in Chile; the economic decline and marketization of Vietnam in the mid-1970s; the counterrevolutionary turn of the People's Republic of China after the triumph of Deng Xiaoping; the 1979 Iranian Revolution; U.S. interventions against popular leftist states in El Salvador and Nicaragua; and the fall of the USSR.

35. Brennan, *At Home in the World,* 63.

36. The Combahee River Collective expressed intersectionality in this way: "We are actively committed to struggling against racial, sexual, heterosexual, and class oppression and see as our particular task the development of integrated analysis and practice based upon the fact that the major systems of oppression are interlocking. The synthesis of these oppressions creates the conditions of our lives. As Black women we see Black feminism as the logical political movement to combat the manifold and simultaneous oppressions that all women of color face"; Combahee River Collective, "A Black Feminist Statement," 210.

37. Parker, "Revolution," 242.

38. Ibid., 240.

39. Beal's ties to the Left can be traced in part through her mother, a Communist who remained involved with Old Left networks in the McCarthy era. However, Beal's knowledge of the postwar anticolonial Black Left is unclear; indicating its

weakening under Cold War anticommunism, she has stated that internationalism and pan-Africanism "didn't exist, at least at the time I left the States in 1960 because the Vietnam War had not yet come on. People's relationships to Africa had not been established." Beal interview by Ross, 24.

40. Beal, "Double Jeopardy," 110, 109, 113, 122, 120.

41. Jones, "An End to the Neglect of the Problems of the Negro Woman!" 120.

42. Beal, "Double Jeopardy," 116.

43. Ibid., 199, Beal's italics in first quote. Beal's feminist internationalism was shaped by her 1959–1966 sojourn in Paris, where she was politicized through encounters with African students and the Algerian independence movement while dealing with an oppressive marriage and at one point undergoing an illegal abortion. Beal interview by Ross, 29–30.

44. Springer, *Living for the Revolution,* 49.

45. Beal interview by Ross, 39.

46. Roth, "Race, Class and the Emergence of Black Feminism," 3.

47. Lorde, *A Burst of Light*, 70.

48. Lorde's and Toni Cade Bambara's dates of birth (1934 and 1939, respectively) give another indication of their roles in bridging the post–World War II Black left with the contemporary Black feminist movement. Both Lorde and Bambara were separated by about a decade or less from Black leftists such as Julian Mayfield and Maya Angelou (both born in 1928) and Lorraine Hansberry (born in 1930), as well as from pioneering Black feminists such as Gloria Hull (born in 1944), Barbara and Beverly Smith (born in 1946), and Cheryl Clarke (born in 1947).

49. On *The Black Woman,* see Griffin, "Conflict and Chorus."

50. Beyond *The Black Woman,* Bambara continued to work with women of the post–World War II Black Left. For example, she was part of a delegation of Black women writers to Cuba in 1985 with Rosa Guy and Audre Lorde, among others.

51. Super-exploitation refers to the extraction and maximization of profits through imperialism and heteropatriarchy. Racism and sexism drive down wages and create cheap labor power by making it possible for women and people of color to be exploited to a greater degree than white male workers in "core" regions where wealth is concentrated.

52. "Black Women: Internationalizing the Struggle," 5–6, italics in original.

53. Bond, the niece of Harlem Communist and city councilman Benjamin Davis, has maintained her Left commitments in the present through her involvement with the Black Radical Congress, which espouses a proletarian, internationalist, feminist, and antihomophobic program.

54. Bond, "For Colored Girls Who Have Considered Suicide," 187, 189.

55. As Calvin Hernton writes, outrage over Wallace's book was stoked after *Ms.* excerpted Wallace's book in an issue that declared on its cover that Wallace would determine the main issues for Blacks in the 1980s; Hernton, "The Sexual Mountain and Black Women Writers."

56. Bond and Gregory, "Two Views of *Black Macho and the Myth of the Superwoman*," 13, 20, 18, 14, and 21.

57. Ibid., 14–15.

58. Ibid., 18.

59. Hairston et al., "Black Writers' Views of America."

60. Bond and Peery, "Is the Black Male Castrated?"

61. Alan Wald and Michael Denning have criticized the centering of the CP within radical studies. My rationale for focusing on the Communist Left is that a major strand of Black internationalist feminism arose specifically out of Communist and Communist-affiliated institutions and politics. While radical African American women writers engaged with a spectrum of political thought, including Garveyism and Mao Zedong Thought, the Marxist-Leninist Left provided a distinct foundation for their feminism. The CPUSA's leading role in anti-racist and anti-imperialist activism dating back to the late 1920s and 1930s, discussed in chapter 1, enabled the party to maintain roots in the African American community in the second half of the twentieth century.

Moreover, focusing on the CP does not preclude examining its intersections with the diverse, sometimes conflicting Third World Marxisms of Kwame Nkrumah in Ghana, Fidel Castro and Che Guevara in Cuba, Mao Zedong in the People's Republic of China, Amilcar Cabral in Guinea-Bissau, and Ho Chi Minh in Vietnam. After all, the CPUSA and Third World Marxists have shared roots in a Leninist tradition that prioritized the revolutionary struggles of oppressed nations and placed them in an international context. See Wald, *Writing from the Left*; and Denning, *The Cultural Front*.

62. Smethurst, *The Black Arts Movement*, 18–19.

63. Among the numerous examples of the postwar Black Left's intersections with the civil rights and Black Arts/Black Power movements, consider Maya Angelou's (often simultaneous) activism with Martin Luther King Jr. and the Southern Christian Leadership Conference, the Harlem Writers Guild, the community of African American expatriate radicals in Ghana, and Malcolm X's Organization of Afro-American Unity. The Black Left's ties to Maoism, with its promise of leading the upsurge of Third World nations and maintaining Lenin's legacy, are evident in the careers of John Killens, Alice Childress, and especially W. E. B. and Shirley Graham Du Bois, all of whom experienced firsthand the Chinese socialism they extolled during visits to the People's Republic of China (Graham Du Bois even chose to live her final months there). Childress's 1973 excursion, undertaken with Sonia Sanchez and Earl Ofari Hutchinson and sponsored by the US-China Friendship Committee and the leftist *Guardian* newspaper, suggests the links between Maoism and the Black Left, Black Arts, and Marxist-Leninist New Communist movements. On the Black Arts/Left nexus, see Smethurst, *The Black Arts Movement*. On the Black Left and Maoism, see Elbaum, *Revolution in the Air*; Horne, *Race Woman*, 217–242; Kelley and Esch, "Black Like Mao"; and Killens, "Black Man in the New China."

64. I draw on James Smethurst's extensive study of postwar Harlem's relevance to Black cultural radicalism in *The Black Arts Movement,* 100–132; and Welch, "Black Art and Activism." As Smethurst observes, at the same time that Harlem was a primary site for and symbol of Black political and cultural life, the postwar anticolonial Left had bases throughout New York City. This was due in part to Harlem's housing shortage. Sarah Wright, for example, lived on the Lower East Side; W. E. B. and Shirley Graham Du Bois, Esther Cooper and James Jackson, and John and Grace Killens in Brooklyn.

65. American Labor Party, "ALP Facts: Negro-Americans in New York City," 1949, quoted in Biondi, *To Stand and Fight,* 54; Smethurst, *The Black Arts Movement,* 108.

66. Julian Mayfield, "A Challenge to a Bestseller: Crisis or Cruse," 13. On the antagonism between Communism and Black nationalism, see Cruse, *The Crisis of the Negro Intellectual*; and Hutchinson, *Blacks and Reds.*

67. Jones, "On the Right to Self-Determination," 77.

68. Davies, *Black Women, Writing, and Identity,* 4.

69. Biondi, *To Stand and Fight,* 280.

70. Plummer, "Castro in Harlem," 135.

71. UN petitions concerning U.S. civil rights became a strategy of the postwar African American popular front. Three such petitions were submitted by the National Negro Congress, the Civil Rights Congress, and the NAACP between 1946 and 1952. See Biondi, *To Stand and Fight,* 57–59.

72. Chapter 1 discusses this historical context for Jones's analysis.

73. Joseph Stalin, *Marxism and the National and Colonial Question,* quoted in Jones, "On the Right to Self-Determination," 69.

74. Jones, "On the Right to Self-Determination," 67, 69, 74. Jones's italics.

75. On Browder's liquidation of the right of Black self-determination, see Haywood, *Black Bolshevik,* 530–535.

76. Ibid., 72–74.

77. Jones, "An End to the Neglect of the Problems of the Negro Woman!" 120, Jones's italics.

78. Davies, *Left of Karl Marx,* 48.

79. Weigand, one of the few other scholars who discusses Jones, also elides the centrality of the national question to Jones's article. For example, Weigand skips over Jones's reference to the Black woman worker's "rightful place in the Negro proletarian leadership of the national liberation movement" and jumps to Jones's assertion of Black women's role in realizing a Socialist America; *Red Feminism,* 120. Weigand thus distorts Jones's feminism by omitting her contention that socialist internationalism could be achieved only through national liberation, which in turn required Black women's leadership and participation.

80. Jones, "An End to the Neglect of the Problems of the Negro Woman!" 108.

81. Chapter 2 elaborates on the gender politics of radical and progressive responses to the Ingram case.

82. See Maxwell, *Old Negro, New Left*, 141–149. Chapter 1 discusses more fully the racial and gender politics of Communist anti-lynching propaganda.

83. Jones, "An End to the Neglect of the Problems of the Negro Woman!" 120, 119, 109, 114–115. My italics.

84. Jones, "On the Right to Self-Determination," 69.

85. Jones, "An End to the Neglect of the Problems of the Negro Woman!" 122.

86. Jones, "International Women's Day and the Struggle for Peace," 33–34.

87. See Von Eschen, *Race Against Empire*; and Meriwether, *Proudly We Can Be Africans*.

88. Kelley, "Stormy Weather," 70.

89. Gaines, "From Center to Margin," 296, 302.

90. Weigand, *Red Feminism*, 3.

91. Clarke, "The New Afro-American Nationalism," 286.

92. Killens, *Black Man's Burden*, 102, 158, 169.

93. For Bakhtin, a "literary work's artistic unity in relationship to an actual reality is defined by its chronotope"; *The Dialogic Imagination*, 243. The chronotope, or "time space," allows "the representability of events" due to "the special increase in density and concreteness of time markers—the time of human life, of historical time—that occurs within well-delineated spatial areas" (ibid., 250).

94. Paule Marshall, whose work is foundational to Black internationalist feminism, is absent from my book due to the fact that her fiction and diasporic feminism have generated substantial critical study. See for example Davies, *Black Women, Writing and Identity*; Hathaway, *Caribbean Waves*; Edmondson, *Making Men*; Hall, *Mercy, Mercy Me*; McGill, *Constructing Black Selves*.

To this scholarship, I will only add that Marshall's Left affiliations constitute an important context for studying her art. Marshall's involvement in Black Left cultural politics is indicated by two events that attracted significant attention. As a member of the Association of Artists for Freedom, Marshall participated in a 1964 New York Town Hall debate on "The Black Revolution and the White Backlash," which the *New York Post* characterized as "a dialogue between 'white liberals' and Negro 'militants' about where men go from here in the civil rights battle"; quoted in Cruse, *The Crisis of the Negro Intellectual*, 196. The Association of Artists for Freedom was founded in response to the 1963 Birmingham church bombing that killed four Black girls. It was made up of Harlem Leftists such as Marshall, John O. Killens, Lorraine Hansberry, Ossie Davis, and Ruby Dee; LeRoi Jones, who had moved toward Third World Marxism and Black nationalism; and James Baldwin, who was staunchly anti-Communist but circulated within Black Leftist circles. The limits of white U.S. liberalism, which the association probed at the Town Hall, constitute a major theme in Marshall's novels, which reveal its inadequacies through Black transnational perspectives that reprise key tenets of self-determination.

Another event at which Marshall spoke was a watershed in postwar Black feminism: the panel on "The Negro Woman in American Literature" at the 1965 conference on "The Negro Writer's Visions of America," co-sponsored by the Harlem Writers' Guild and the New School for Social Research. An overarching concern of the panel (which also featured Alice Childress and Sarah Wright) was mainstream U.S. society's stereotyping of Black women as whores or domineering matriarchs. Marshall cogently argued that "the reason for this is simple and yet complex, and it has to do with the history of this country, a history grounded in slavery. The purpose . . . was to deny the Negro woman her humanity. For if she was less than human, all sorts of crimes could be committed against her and go unpunished"; Marshall quoted in Childress, Marshall, and Wright, "The Negro Woman in American Literature," 298. Marshall's assertion, and the panel as a whole, point to the postwar Black Left roots of contemporary African American women's literature, which Marshall's *Brown Girl, Brownstones* helped inaugurate.

95. Welch, "Gender and Power," 79.

96. Horne, *Race Woman,* 250. Welch calls for careful study of Graham Du Bois's cultural work in "Gender and Power," 77. In *Realism for the Masses,* Chris Vials recovers the Black feminist critique of mass culture in Graham Du Bois's play *I Gotta Home* (1939).

97. See Brown, "Which Way for the Negro Writer?" Wright produced her own literary manifesto, "The Responsibility of the Writer as Participant in the World Community." Wright's thoughts here on representing race and gender reiterate those of Jean Bond in her *Freedomways* review of *Black Macho and the Myth of the Superwoman,* discussed earlier:

> our torments, the torments of our people, and the very real torments of African-American women cannot be laid at the doorstep of the African-American male. It is not a matter of shutting one's eyes to the very real suffering that Black women and children suffer at the hands of Black men. It *is* a matter of *opening* one's eyes and the eyes of the writer's audience to the agony of being a Black man in America, an agony which so tragically is turned both inward and upon his loved ones in many cases. . . .
>
> And so the tracing of relations *in their totality*, in their context, here is one of the African-American writer's major responsibilities.

Bond, "For Colored Girls Who Have Considered Suicide," 36, Bond's italics.

98. Wright, *This Child's Gonna Live,* 179; Campbell, "'It's a Time in the Land,'" 219.

99. Campbell, "'It's a Time in the Land,'" 221.

100. Wright, *This Child's Gonna Live,* 179, Wright's italics.

101. Wright's organizational work complemented her literary commitment to national liberation around the world. She was a member of the Harlem Writers Guild, and she organized several major conferences of Black writers that brought art and politics to bear on each other. Wright also belonged to CAWAH, and its instigation of the UN demonstration against Lumumba's assassination led her to co-found On Guard for Freedom, which drew together Black Leftists and younger proto–Black

Arts cultural activists. As part of the Fair Play for Cuba Committee, Wright traveled with Julian Mayfield, John Henrik Clarke, LeRoi Jones, Harold Cruse, and Robert F. Williams to Cuba on a trip organized to enlist African American support for Castro. Wright's anti-imperialism never wavered; in her later years she protested the Vietnam War, South African apartheid, and the U.S. invasion of Iraq.

Chapter 1. The Negro Question, the Woman Question, and the "Vital Link"

1. Kelley, *Race Rebels,* 105.

2. Naison, *Communists in Harlem during the Depression,* 5–7. On the ABB, see also Solomon, *The Cry Was Unity,* 3–21.

3. Maxwell, *Old Negro, New Left,* 32.

4. Naison, *Communists in Harlem during the Depression,* 3–4.

5. Maxwell, *Old Negro, New Left,* 63–93; Solomon, *The Cry Was Unity,* 89. Kate Baldwin argues that McKay was centrally concerned with linking racial and sexual emancipation and that Soviet (and U.S.) marginalization of women's issues in advocating black self-determination bespeaks McKay's lack of influence; Baldwin, *Beyond the Color Line and the Iron Curtain,* 30, 57–85.

6. Quoted in Baldwin, *Beyond the Color Line and the Iron Curtain,* 42. See also Maxwell, *Old Negro, New Left,* 90.

7. On the Black Belt Nation Thesis, see Solomon, *The Cry Was Unity*; Naison, *Communists in Harlem during the Depression*; and Haywood, *Black Bolshevik.* Haywood, then the leading Party theorist of the "Negro Question," co-drafted the Black Belt resolution. On the resolution's cultural implications, see Foley, *Radical Representations,* 170–212, and Smethurst, *The New Red Negro,* 21–32.

8. Naison, *Communists in Harlem during the Depression,* 18. The theoretical and historical limitations of the Black Belt Nation Thesis have been well documented and criticized by scholars from a range of ideological positions. Anti-communist liberal historians Wilson Record and Theodor Draper have argued that the resolution's grounding in Soviet history and political imperatives rendered it irrelevant, even inimical to U.S. conditions. Showing that Soviet influence did not necessarily suppress the initiatives of African Americans, New Left historians Mark Naison and Mark Solomon have recovered the resolution's practical implications. However, they contend that it was only by ignoring or downplaying what Naison calls the "albatross" of the Black Belt Nation plank that Communists took a leading role in Black freedom struggles. See Naison, *Communists in Harlem during the Depression,* 18; Solomon, *The Cry Was Unity,* 85–89; and Smethurst, *The New Red Negro,* 24. Other scholars, such as New Left sociologists Michael Omi and Howard Winant and Marxist literary critic Anthony Dawahare, have pointed out the theoretical incoherency and weaknesses of the Black Belt Nation Thesis, factors that resulted in its inconsistent application, increasing marginality, and eventual demise. Marxist literary critic Barbara Foley

emphasizes that the call for Black self-determination "act[ed] as an important guide to the party's strategies for leading the class struggle in the United States" throughout the 1930s but notes the frequent confusion of "nation" and "class" and the "aura of segregationism surrounding the Black Belt proposal"; Foley, *Radical Representations,* 181–182.

However, key Black (and white) radicals did not view notions of a free Negro republic and of Black national struggle to be theoretically incoherent, obstructive, or incompatible with U.S. conditions or multiracial class unity. For many race radicals, the Black Belt Nation Thesis laid the grounds for understanding the irreducibility of race as well as its intersections with class in the United States; the role of Black culture (specifically rural, southern Black culture) in political struggle; the need for Black leadership and autonomy; and demands for full social, economic, and political rights within the United States in conjunction with the right of oppressed nations to self-determination. Even as the party officially abandoned the Black Belt Nation Thesis, Black leftists sought to revive it or pursue its implications for their work well into the late twentieth century.

9. On African American interest in the Second Italo-Ethiopian War, see Kelley, *Race Rebels,* 123–158; and Plummer, *Rising Wind.*

10. On African Americans and the Spanish Civil War, see Kelley, *Race Rebels,* 123–158.

11. Weigand observes that the touchstone texts on the woman question—Engels's *The Origin of the Family, Private Property, and the State,* Bebel's *Woman and Socialism,* and Lenin's *Women and Society*—reinforced the idea that women's emancipation was secondary to the emancipation of the proletariat. *Red Feminism,* 20.

12. Kelley, *Race Rebels,* 114, 121.

13. Smethurst, *The New Red Negro,* 57.

14. Shaffer writes, "It was . . . the restrictive family policy that the USSR instituted in the early 1930s—which included the outlawing of homosexuality, cessation of research on contraception, and the greater difficulty of obtaining divorce—that the American CP used as a guide to its own policies"; Shaffer, "Women and the Communist Party," 109. Also in the mid-1930s, the Soviet Union encouraged larger families and outlawed abortion; Dixler, *The Woman Question,* 19–28.

15. Foley, *Radical Representations,* 219. An example of Left representations of Black militancy influenced by heteronormative popular front ideologies of the nuclear family can be seen in the iconography of the Scottsboro mothers, discussed below.

16. McKay, *The Negroes in America,* 77. The Soviet State Publishing House commissioned *The Negroes in America* to develop McKay's "Report on the Negro Question" for the Comintern; it was published in Russian.

17. Maxwell, *Old Negro, New Left,* 88.

18. Baldwin, *Beyond the Color Line and the Iron Curtain,* 78. Baldwin argues that the story "The Mulatto Girl" in *Trial by Lynching* attempts to account for the specific conjunctions of racial and sexual violence against black women.

19. Smethurst, *The New Red Negro,* 57.

20. Solomon, *The Cry Was Unity,* 89.

21. Solomon, "Rediscovering a Lost Legacy," 7.

22. In an effort to demonstrate responsiveness to White's charges of racism, the CP put on trial August Yokinen, a custodian who had made a racist comment to several African Americans. Fifteen hundred people witnessed this show trial, which was less about Yokinen's "crime" than about the CP's efforts to prove its commitment to fighting white chauvinism. One year later, White charged a furrier with using abusive language against her, resulting in another well-attended trial that resulted in the party's vow to address racism substantially in the needle trades union instead of symbolically expelling individual members. See Solomon, "Rediscovering a Lost Legacy," 8.

23. Maxwell, *Old Negro, New Left,* 143.

24. Exemplifying the impact of women's lives on their political work, Thompson herself was unable to visit the socialist republics, as she was forced to return to the United States to care for her ailing mother, who had supported her radicalism. Thompson, "With Langston Hughes,"157.

25. Carter, *Scottsboro.*

26. Haywood, "The Scottsboro Decision," 296. Along similar lines, James S. Allen wrote that "the rapidity with which the Negro masses were aroused and large sections of them set into motion, reveals how deeply the roots of Scottsboro are embedded in the conditions of national oppression of the Negro people"; Allen, "The Scottsboro Struggle," 309.

27. See Maxwell, *Old Negro, New Left,* 137–141.

28. "Scottsboro mothers" Janie Patterson, Ida Norris, Viola Montgomery, Ada Wright, and Mamie Williams marched on the Capitol, spoke to the press on behalf of their boys and toured the United States and Europe to raise awareness and campaign funds.

29. Thompson, "And So We Marched," 6. See also Maxwell's discussion of Thompson's Scottsboro reportage for *The Crisis* for another example of how she wrote women's empowerment into narratives of Black liberation; Maxwell, *Old Negro, New Left,* 141–149.

30. The Third Period refers to the late 1920s and early 1930s, when the end of capitalism and imperialism appeared imminent. At this time Communists denounced liberals and non-Communist leftists while vigorously fighting for civil rights, inclusive unions, and national liberation.

31. Thompson, "Negro Women," 25–27, my italics.

32. Bill Mullen, James Smethurst, and Martha Biondi use the term "African American Popular Front" to refer to African Americans' continuation of anti-racist, anti-lynching, civil rights coalitional work after the official end of the Popular Front, often marked by the 1939 Nazi-Soviet Nonaggression Pact and the resulting widespread disillusionment among Communists and fellow travelers occasioned by Stalin's negotiations

with Hitler. As Smethurst argues, Black radicals were more concerned with the party's backpedaling on its racial militancy in favor of wartime national unity, and even here, "it is important not to overstate the impact of the CPUSA opposition to the 'Double V' [campaign for democracy abroad and racial justice in the United States] in terms of day-to-day work by its local organizations"; Smethurst, *The New Red Negro,* 46.

A smaller popular front group devoted to Black women's issues was the Harlem community organization, Negro Women Inc., co-founded by Audley Moore and Ann Petry.

33. McDuffie, "The March of Young Southern Black Women," 87. Rebecca Hill observes that "the Party's official position at this time was that women were only oppressed if they were members of the working-class [*sic*]"; Hill, "Fosterites and Feminists," 73.

34. "National Negro Congress Meets in Chicago," 110.

35. Inman, *In Woman's Defense,* 2–3.

36. Cuthbert, *Democracy and the Negro,* 20.

37. McDuffie, "The March of Young Southern Black Women," 85–86, 91–92.

38. Ibid., 89.

39. Robeson, "A Message from the Chairman to Members and Friends of the Council on African Affairs," 223.

40. Von Eschen, *Race against Empire,* 19.

41. Powell quoted in Hamilton, *Adam Clayton Powell, Jr.,* 105. For my discussion of the *People's Voice,* I draw on Kathleen Currie's interview with Marvel Cooke; Rachel Peterson's unpublished conference paper "The People's Voice: Anticommunism and the Progressive African American"; and Alan Wald's *Trinity of Passion.*

42. Lewis, *W. E. B. Du Bois,* 538. Fredi Washington refers to "domestic fascism" in her *People's Voice* column (see Black, "'New Negro' Performance in Art and Life," 61).

43. On Negro Women, Inc., see Wald, *Trinity of Passion,* 116.

44. Von Eschen, *Race against Empire,* 3.

45. Von Eschen has argued that the Cold War substantially decimated the anticolonial black Left. This argument is disputed in Biondi, *To Stand and Fight*; Welch, "Black Art and Activism,"; and Wilkins, "Beyond Bandung."

46. Weigand cogently contextualizes the departure from revisionist Browderism: "In late 1945, following the Allied powers' victory in Europe and Asia, the context for Communist and progressive activism began to shift dramatically once again. In the immediate postwar period national liberation struggles erupted in African and Asia, Communists and other leftists gained political influence all over Europe, American workers launched an unprecedented strike wave, and U.S. president Harry Truman proposed a program of reforms that included national health insurance and civil rights for African Americans. In part because of the opportunities for revolutionary change the postwar environment seemed to offer Communists around the world in 1945, the Comintern engineered the expulsion of the Party's Popular Front

leader Earl Browder and condemned his support for reformist politics"; Weigand, *Red Feminism*, 26.

47. Ibid., 27.

48. The New York branch of the CAW was formed by Jones, Thelma Dale, Ada B. Jackson, Halois Moorehead, and Charlotte Hawkins Brown. Jones, Dale, Jackson, and Moorehead were NNC members; additionally, Jackson and Moorehead belonged to the National Congress of Negro Women, which had been co-founded by Brown; Hill, "Fosterites and Feminists," 72.

49. Dale quoted in McDuffie, "The March of Young Southern Black Women," 90.

50. Weigand, *Red Feminism*, 60–61.

51. See Biondi, *To Stand and Fight*, 24–25.

52. Flynn, *Woman's Place in the Fight for a Better World*, 16.

53. Jones, "Dear Comrade Foster," 89.

54. Ibid.

55. Haywood, *Black Bolshevik*, 550. Haywood's 1948 book *Negro Liberation*, a landmark study of the African American national question, is thus indebted to Jones's earlier essays on this issue.

56. Jones, "Discussion Article," 718.

57. Haywood, *Black Bolshevik*, 543.

58. Dale, "Reconversion and the Negro People," 895. Rebecca Hill points out that the older Dale might very well have mentored Jones, a member of the NNC, which by 1936 had already argued that black women were "thrice exploited, as women, as workers, and as Negroes"; Mary Inman quoted in Hill, "Fosterites and Feminists," 73. After becoming executive secretary of the NNC in 1942, Dale "would consistently take a public stand for black women's rights, arguing for the unionization of domestic workers, and for an end to discrimination against Negro women" (ibid.).

59. Dale, "Reconversion and the Negro People," 901.

60. See the introduction for a discussion of "On the Right to Self-Determination for the Negro People in the Black Belt."

61. Weigand, *Red Feminism*, 101. On the Ingram case, see Horne, *Communist Front?* 204–212.

62. In his introduction to Raymond's pamphlet on the Ingram case, Davis wrote of "the special pro-fascist persecution of the Negro people in the South" as well as their place at "the vanguard in the struggle for democracy"; Davis, "Introduction," 3. Raymond quoted a southern NAACP official as saying, "This is another Scottsboro case and we have got to put everything we can muster behind it, legally, financially, and organizationally"; Davis, *The Ingrams Shall Not Die!* 10. Raymond later reiterated the comparison: "I am convinced Georgia Jimcrow justice will certainly prevail if the democratic people of the nation do not rally in a grand, mighty protest against this most brutal assault against the Negro people since the Scottsboro case" (ibid., 14). William Patterson was more perceptive yet still tentative in his opinion that the

Ingram case "verges on the woman question to a tremendous degree"; Patterson quoted in Horne, *Communist Front?* 204.

63. Weigand writes that "An End to the Neglect of the Problems of the Negro Woman!" was written "partly in response to 'Woman against Myth'"; Weigand, *Red Feminism,* 101, 119–120.

64. The impact of Black women on the analysis of racial oppression is also evident in W. E. B. Du Bois's brief on the Ingram case to the UN, commissioned by Mary Church Terrell, Maude White Katz, and other supporters of the Ingram campaign. Like Jones, whose essay would have come out shortly before or as Du Bois was writing the brief, Du Bois addressed the historical and structural oppression of African American women in denouncing Rosa Ingram's incarceration. He asserted that Rosa Ingram's "crucifixion" was "of one piece with Georgia's treatment of colored women"; excoriated the hypocrisy of the "reverence for womanhood" professed by a country in which women of African descent were slaves, "concubines," and "human brood mares"; and pointed out that African American women and their children bore the brunt of the sharecropping system, "where Southern slavery still lingers"; Du Bois quoted in Katz, "Learning from History," 84.

65. Jones, "On the Right to Self-Determination," 109–110, 116. Rebecca Hill observes that Black and white women radicals alike denounced the "fascist triple K"—*Kinder, Küche, Kirche*; children, kitchen, church—a slogan that linked women's oppression to "the Party's decision, under William Foster, that the US was subject to imminent fascist take-over"; Hill, "Fosterites and Feminists," 83. However, Black women activists "spent as much time discussing gender as discussing race. They reminded others in the Party that the cult of domesticity worked differently for them than it did for their white sisters on the assembly line" (ibid., 82).

66. Jones relied on Herbert Aptheker's essay "The Negro Woman" (*Masses and Mainstream* 2 [January 1949]: 10–17) for her historical account of Black women.

67. Jones, "An End to the Neglect of the Problems of the Negro Woman!" 123, 120.

68. Weigand, *Red Feminism,* 107.

69. Jones quoted in Davies, *Left of Karl Marx,* 79–80.

70. Jones briefly mentioned that Black, Puerto Rican, and Mexican women could be organized around the two issues of the fight against racist school curricula and the underfunding of schools that disproportionately impacted communities of color in two articles, "International Women's Day and the Struggle for Peace," and "For the Unity of Women in the Cause of Peace!" Weigand documents the coverage and discussion of women of color in the *Worker*'s "Woman Today" section; see Weigand, *Red Feminism,* 186n27.

71. Childress, "For a Negro Theater," 63.

72. Brown, "Which Way for the Negro Writer?" 61, 62–63.

73. Ibid., 53, 58, Brown's italics.

74. Ibid., 62, Brown's italics.

75. Smethurst, *The Black Arts Movement,* 45.

76. Preface to "Women of Nigeria Meet in a Historic National Conference," 6.

77. On Garvin, see Kelley and Esch, "Black Like Mao," 104–105.

78. I discuss Hansberry's reportage in chapter 3.

79. "Conversations from Life" subsequently appeared in the *Baltimore Afro-American.* Childress collected an edited version of the columns in a book, *Like One of the Family* (1956). Mildred can be considered a female counterpart to Jesse B. Semple of Langston Hughes's *Chicago Defender* column. Childress had adapted the character for the stage in 1950 with *Just a Little Simple.* Both Hughes's and Childress's columns display their authors' radical pan-Africanism.

80. Childress, *Like One of the Family,* 74–75. This account of organizing reflects the Black left's modus operandi of undertaking political work in "fluid and extra-institutional locations" such as parties and dinners at people's homes that nonetheless had serious underlying political motives; see Welch, "Black Art and Activism," 163. This mode of organizing had political and economical bases: it helped keep Black radical activity under the radar and also avoided the costs of renting a hall or office.

81. Washington, "Alice Childress, Lorraine Hansberry, and Claudia Jones."

82. Childress, *Like One of the Family,* 99–100. Childress's italics.

83. *Gold Through the Trees* was also the first play by an African American woman to be professionally produced on the U.S. stage; see Jennings, *Alice Childress,* 6.

84. Hansberry, "CNA Presents Exciting New Dramatic Revue," 7.

85. Childress, "A South African Scene from *Gold Through the Trees.*"

86. Jones, "Negro Women Launch New Movement for Peace and Freedom," 8.

87. Esther Cooper Jackson has stated that Ed Strong and Louis Burnham had conceived of *Freedomways* as a continuation of both *Freedom* and the Freedom Fund. See Ian Rocksborough-Smith, "'Filling the Gap,'" 12, 15. On the history of *Freedomways,* see also Esther Cooper Jackson's introduction to the *Freedomways Reader.* On the SNYC, see Smethurst, *The Black Arts Movement,* 321–326; and McDuffie, "The March of Young Southern Black Women."

88. Horne, *Race Woman,* 218.

89. McDuffie, "The March of Young Southern Black Women," 100.

90. Norris, *Presenting Rosa Guy,* 12–13.

91. Wright, "The Lower East Side," 593; Smethurst, *The Black Arts Movement,* 118. Harlem Writers Guild workshops were usually held in the home of one of the members on a rotating basis. Sarah Wright has described the weekly workshop as "a sacred although by no means always solemn occasion. It was a time for reading aloud our works-in-progress to one another"; Wright, "The Lower East Side," 593. On the Harlem Writers Guild, see also Cruse, *The Crisis of the Negro Intellectual*; Smethurst, *The Black Arts Movement,* 118–120; Angelou, *The Heart of a Woman*; and Welch, "Black Art and Activism," 78–82.

92. Guy quoted in Norris, *Presenting Rosa Guy,* 11.

93. See Angelou, *The Heart of a Woman,* 42, 67; Wright, "The Lower East Side," 594.

94. Angelou, *The Heart of a Woman,* 143.

95. On the demonstration at the United Nations and the founding of On Guard for Freedom, see Smethurst, *The Black Arts Movement,* 118–119.

96. Clarke, "The New Afro-American Nationalism," 286.

97. Tyson, *Radio Free Dixie,* Young, *Soul Power,* and Gaines, *African Americans in Ghana* have downplayed or overlooked CAWAH's role in instigating the UN protest; Smethurst's *The Black Arts Movement* is notable for acknowledging CAWAH with regard to this event. Guy's role in co-founding the Harlem Writers Guild has also fallen prey to scholarly amnesia.

98. Guy, "A Conversation between Rosa Guy and Maya Angelou," 229.

Chapter 2. Lorraine Hansberry's Existentialist Routes to Black Internationalist Feminism

1. On Hansberry and *Freedom,* see Smith, *Visions of Belonging.*

2. Hansberry, "'Gold Coast's' Rulers Go," 2.

3. Hansberry, "Egyptian People Fight for Freedom," 3.

4. Hansberry, "The Outsider," 7.

5. Gilroy, *The Black Atlantic,* 186.

6. On Hansberry's feminism and/or lesbianism, see Gomez, "Lorraine Hansberry: Uncommon Warrior"; Wilkerson, "Lorraine Hansberry: The Complete Feminist"; Wilkerson, "The Dark Vision of Lorraine Hansberry"; and Lipari, "The Rhetoric of Intersectionality."

7. Lipari, "The Rhetoric of Intersectionality," 224, 240, 221.

8. Wilkins, "Beyond Bandung."

9. On Hansberry's responses to absurdism, see Nemiroff, "A Critical Background"; Cheney, *Lorraine Hansberry*; and Carter, *Hansberry's Drama.*

10. As Martin Esslin observes, it does not make sense to lump absurdist playwrights into one category. Nonetheless, Esslin's generalizations are useful: he demonstrates that the absurdist theatre strove to express existentialist ideas through form as well as content. On the absurd, Esslin quotes Ionesco's essay on Kafka: "'Absurd is that which is devoid of purpose. . . . Cut off from his religious, metaphysical, and transcendental roots, man is lost; all his actions become senseless, absurd, useless'"; Ionesco quoted in Esslin, *The Theatre of the Absurd,* 5.

11. Hansberry, *To Be Young, Gifted and Black,* 176, Hansberry's italics. For a well-developed articulation of this argument, see Hansberry, "The Negro Writer and His Roots." As the editors of *The Black Scholar* note, this 1959 speech, delivered to a conference of black writers convened by the American Society of African Scholars, was "Hansberry's credo, a fundamental attempt to articulate the challenge to black writers, as she saw it, at the start of the 1960's." Editors' preface to Hansberry, "The Negro Writer and His Roots," 2.

12. Hansberry, "The Negro Writer and His Roots," 6.

13. The English translation of Genet's *Les Nègres* (1958), which I refer to as *The Blacks,* was published in 1960.

14. Mekas, "Movie Journal," 13. See also Mailer, "Mailer to Hansberry." Hansberry was exasperated that existentialism's influence extended even to Arthur Miller. Of Miller's *After the Fall* (1964), Hansberry wrote, "He is trying like hell for the respectability of fashionable despair"; Hansberry, "On Arthur Miller, Marilyn Monroe, and 'Guilt,'" 174.

15. *The Blacks* employed a wide range of actors, including "most of the cream of black actors," because of its longevity—it ran for four years and 1,408 performances—and its rotating cast. Hughes and Meltzer, *Black Magic*, 238; see also Warrick, "*The Blacks* and Its Impact on African American Theatre in the United States."

16. Killens, Davis, Dodson, and Baldwin, "The Negro Writer in America," 63–64. Killens reiterated and expanded his critique of *The Blacks* in his essay "The Black Writer Vis-à-Vis His Country." In fact, Genet and his play are invoked throughout Killens's essays in *Black Man's Burden* to signify the myopic assumption that Black liberation is doomed to follow the West's decline (116, 157). For Amiri Baraka's comment, see *Jean Genet's The Blacks: A Panel Discussion*, directed by James Briggs Murray. Featuring actors from the first U.S. production of *The Blacks* and its director, Gene Frankel, this at-times acrimonious panel discussion illuminates controversies surrounding the play.

17. Killens, Davis, Dodson, and Baldwin, "The Negro Writer in America," 63.

18. Angelou, *The Heart of a Woman*, 185.

19. White, *Genet: A Biography*, 440.

20. Jones and Niven, *James Earl Jones*, 115–123; Angelou, *The Heart of a Woman*, 171.

21. Angelou, *The Heart of a Woman*, 175. Roscoe Lee Brown discusses *The Blacks* in *Jean Genet's The Blacks: A Panel Discussion.*

22. According to Nemiroff, it was through seeing *The Blacks* that for Hansberry "the elements [of *Les Blancs*] began to move into focus and the play [began] to find its final shape and title." Nemiroff, "A Critical Background," 32.

23. Hansberry, "The Negro Writer and His Roots," 6.

24. On the relationship between U.S. policy toward Africa and domestic policy, see Borstelmann, *The Cold War and the Color Line*.

25. Lorraine Hansberry's FBI file, February 5, 1959.

26. Nemiroff, "A Critical Background," 33.

27. Hansberry, "Genet, Mailer, and the New Paternalism," 10, Hansberry's italics.

28. Mailer, "The White Negro," 341.

29. Baldwin, "The Black Boy Looks at the White Boy," 217.

30. Hansberry, "Genet, Mailer, and the New Paternalism," 14. Mailer's comments on the black bourgeoisie in his review of *The Blacks* are an example of his romantic racism: "They cannot know because they have not seen themselves from outside (as we have seen them), that there is a genius in their race—it is possible that Africa is closer to the root of whatever life is left than any other land of earth"; Mailer, "Theatre: The Blacks,"14. Hansberry satirized existentialist primitivism in *The Sign in Sidney*

Brustein's Window: "Ah, *'Pain!'* 'Pain' in recognizing those dark tunnels which lead back to our primate souls, groveling about . . . in caves of sloth. The savage soul of man from whence sprang, in the first place, the Lord of the Flies, Beelzebub himself! (*Rather shouting*) Man, dark gutted creature of ancestral . . . cannibalism and mysterious all-consuming eeevil!"; Hansberry, *A Raisin in the Sun and The Sign in Sidney Brustein's Window,* 263.

31. Genet, *The Blacks,* 12.

32. Hansberry, "Simone de Beauvoir and *The Second Sex,*" 133, 129, Hansberry's italics. Hansberry was not uncritical of aspects of de Beauvoir's existentialism. She called for a writer "with superior theories" (i.e., historical materialism) to "attack and demolish the forlorn and difficult roots of some of the existentialist thought of Mlle. Beauvoir, where it needs attack and demolition" (ibid., 133).

33. Ibid., 130.

34. Kruks, *Retrieving Experience,* 36.

35. Nemiroff quoted in Carter, *Hansberry's Drama,* 6.

36. Rich, "The Problem with Lorraine Hansberry," 247–255.

37. On homosexuality and the Cold War, see D'Emilio, *Sexual Politics*; Edelman, "Tearooms and Sympathy"; and Johnson, *The Lavender Scare.*

38. Both plays have autobiographical elements; Hansberry had studied at the University of Wisconsin, Madison, upon which the setting for "Flowers for the General" is modeled, from 1948 to 1950, and after leaving for New York, she roomed with three other girls in a Lower East Side apartment, similar to Julie's situation in "The Apples of Autumn."

39. Hansberry, "Author's Notes on Characterization, Structure and Content," 4. Cf. de Beauvoir: "The myth is so various, so contradictory, that at first its unity is not discerned: Delilah and Judith, Aspasia and Lucretia, Pandora and Athena—woman is at once Eve and the Virgin Mary. She is an idol, a servant, the source of life, a power of darkness; she is the elemental silence of truth, she is artifice, gossip, and falsehood; she is healing presence and sorceress; she is man's prey, his downfall, she is everything that he is not and that he longs for, his negation and his *raison d'être*"; de Beauvoir, *The Second Sex,* 143.

40. De Beauvoir, *The Second Sex,* 417.

41. Ibid., 424.

42. Hansberry, "Author's Notes on Characterization, Structure and Content," 2.

43. Ibid., 5, 2.

44. Also unlike "The Apples of Autumn," "Flowers for the General" skewers popular narratives of tragic lesbians: when Marcia tries to commit suicide, she survives and even laughs about it with Maxine, who in her astonishment at their resilience says, "My word—people never laugh about this in those grim novels do they?" To which Marcia replies, "God, no! They just have revelations and go off and commit suicide! (*They both explode in laughter at that*)"; Hansberry, "Flowers for the General," 34. The extent to which "The Apples of Autumn" and "Flowers for the General"

differ is further indicated by the fact that while Hansberry consistently used her own name as the author of the more conservative "Apples," she initially used the pseudonym "Emily Jones" with "Flowers for the General." "Emily Jones" was also Hansberry's nom de plume for the first draft of her imaginative recreation of Sappho in her play, "Andromeda the Thief," begun in 1958 (a 1961 draft does not cite an author on its cover page, but a note about the play on the following page is initialed "L.H.") Another connection between "Andromeda the Thief" and "Flowers for the General" is that the latter alludes to both Sappho and Andromeda, who is called a thief; Hansberry, "Flowers for the General," 28, 38.

45. Hansberry, "The Apples of Autumn," 12.

46. Hansberry, "Flowers for the General," 35, 37. Hansberry later amplified the doubts that Marcia expressed: "I am suggesting here that perhaps it is pat and even unfair to suggest that all that remains for the married lesbian, already nursing her frustrations and confusions, is somehow to get rid of her 'self-pity' and 'self-excuses' and make a 'happy marriage without in anyway denying her nature.' I am afraid that homosexuality, whatever its origins, is far more real than that, far more profound in the demands it makes"; Hansberry, "Letter to *The Ladder*," 28–29.

47. Hansberry, "Flowers for the General," 41.

48. Hansberry, "Simone de Beauvoir and *The Second Sex*," 125, Hansberry's italics.

49. Ibid., 134, Hansberry's italics.

50. Sartre, *Being and Nothingness*, 364.

51. Here I draw on Mary Louise Pratt's idea of contact zones and especially a "contact perspective" that illuminates "how subjects are constituted in and by their relations to each other. It treats the relations among colonizers and colonized, or travelers and 'travelees,' not in terms of separateness or apartheid, but in terms of copresence, interaction, interlocking understandings and practices, often within radically asymmetrical relations of power"; Pratt, *Imperial Eyes*, 7.

52. De Beauvoir, *The Second Sex*, xxiii, de Beauvoir's italics.

53. Ibid., 140.

54. Sartre, *Being and Nothingness*, 340.

55. De Beauvoir, *The Second Sex*, 422, de Beauvoir's italics.

56. Ibid., 416.

57. See Hansberry, "'Illegal' Conference Shows Peace Is Key to Freedom," 3.

58. Hansberry, cover page for *The Sign in Sidney Brustein's Window*, Box 19, Lorraine Hansberry Papers, Schomburg Center for Research in Black Culture. The referenced scene from *Who's Afraid of Virginia Woolf?* involves an increasingly drunken conversation between Nick and George at the beginning of Act 2, in which George, having met with an "Up yours!" from Nick after trying to advise him, ruminates, "You take the trouble to construct a civilization . . . to . . . to build a society, based on the principles of . . . of principle . . . you endeavor to make communicable sense out of natural order, morality out of the unnatural disorder of man's mind . . . you make government and art, and realize that they are, must be, both the same . . . you bring

things to the saddest of all points . . . to the point where there *is* something to lose . . . then all at once, through all the music, through all the sensible sounds of men building, attempting, comes the *Dies Irae.* And what is it? What does the trumpet sound? Up yours"; Albee, *Who's Afraid of Virginia Woolf?* 117.

59. I am grateful to Michael Anderson for this insight.

60. Hansberry, *A Raisin in the Sun and The Sign in Sidney Brustein's Window,* 328.

61. Ibid., 328, 330–331. The dancing scene in Act 2 of *Who's Afraid of Virginia Woolf?* develops the debauched viciousness between Martha and George, as Martha dances closely with Nick while taunting her husband verbally. George then tries to strangle Martha.

62. Robert Gilman of *Newsweek* wrote in a review of *The Sign in Sidney Brustein's Window* titled "Borrowed Bitchery" that "[Hansberry] hates homosexuals, liberals, abstract artists, nonrealistic playwrights, [and] white people unwilling to commit suicide"; quoted in Nemiroff, "The 101 'Final' Performances of *Sidney Brustein,*" 171.

63. Hansberry does not specifically mention homosexuals in her catalog of "the damned" whom the new paternalists celebrate—perhaps because of Mailer's homophobia, which pervades "The White Negro" as well as his review of *The Blacks.* However, *Sidney Brustein* makes it clear that she saw homosexuality as similarly subjected to romanticization.

64. Hansberry, *A Raisin in the Sun and The Sign in Sidney Brustein's Window,* 323.

65. Ibid., 269.

66. Genet, *The Blacks,* 126. Esslin writes, "The Negroes in *The Blacks,* acted by Negroes, are not really Negroes. . . . The Negroes in the play are an image of all outcasts of society; they stand, above all, for Genet himself"; Esslin, *The Theatre of the Absurd,* 191.

67. Genet, *The Blacks,* 12.

68. Nemiroff, Memo to Lorraine Hansberry, March 3, 1964.

69. Fanon's *The Wretched of the Earth* was translated into English in 1963; it is likely that Hansberry had read it.

70. Hansberry's excerpt of Douglass' speech concludes, "If we ever get free from the oppressions and wrongs heaped upon us, we must pay for their removal. We must do that by labor, by suffering, by sacrifice, and if needs by, by our lives and the lives of others"; quoted in Hansberry, *Les Blancs,* 38. Unless otherwise indicated, citations to *Les Blancs* are to the published version of the play.

71. De Beauvoir, *The Second Sex,* xxiii, de Beauvoir's italics.

72. Hansberry, "Author's Notes on Characterization, Structure and Content," 5.

73. Ferguson, *Aberrations in Black,* 10.

74. Hansberry, *Les Blancs,* 60. Hansberry had drafted this speech almost exactly as it appears in the published version. Nemiroff only switched "Camus" for "the French." Nemiroff cites Camus rather than Sartre as the problematic existentialist, perhaps due to Sartre's strident support of Algerian independence, in contrast to Camus's acceptance of French colonial rule.

75. Ibid., 103.
76. Ibid., 70–71.
77. As Siobhan Somerville puts it, queerness shows that "to disrupt naturalized constructions of racial difference involves simultaneously unsettling one's relationship to normative constructions of gender and sexuality as well"; Somerville, *Queering the Color Line,* 137.
78. Hansberry, *Les Blancs,* 125.
79. Ibid., 88.
80. Ibid., 108.
81. Ibid., 108.
82. Carter, *Hansberry's Drama,* 118.
83. Nemiroff, Memo to Lorraine Hansberry, 6.
84. Hansberry, *Les Blancs,* 116.
85. Ibid., Hansberry's italics.
86. Hansberry, *Les Blancs* First Final Adaptation by R. N.—"L.," 23–24. Nemiroff's completion of *Les Blancs* after Hansberry's premature death itself instantiates mutual recognition between the Black lesbian playwright and the straight white man who remained her collaborator and comrade after their divorce and whom she appointed as her literary executor. Nemiroff has been criticized by Adrienne Rich for silencing and filtering Hansberry's feminism. Rich's charges have merit; for example, Hansberry's lesbianism is excluded from *To Be Young, Gifted and Black,* which Nemiroff assembled from Hansberry's plays, essays, letters, and other documents. Yet Nemiroff was not entirely unwilling to honor Hansberry's feminism. With *Les Blancs,* Nemiroff maintained the critiques of heteropatriarchy and gender norms that were present in Hansberry's drafts, as we see in his version of Willy's monologue on the awakening of African independence. And Nemiroff's depiction of Eric is even more radical than Hansberry's. Of the possible endings written by Hansberry or himself, he published one emphasizing Eric's militancy. Hansberry had indicated Eric's plans to join the anticolonial insurgency, but left it unclear as to whether he was successful. The published conclusion Nemiroff wrote, however, presents a character that can be read as a gay Black revolutionary. Nemiroff's completion of *Les Blancs,* then, is in keeping with his acknowledgement of the importance of Hansberry's homosexuality to "the sensitivity and complexity of her view of human beings and of the world"; Nemiroff quoted in Carter, *Hansberry's Drama,* 6.
87. Carter, *Hansberry's Drama,* 118. Hansberry wrote below a list of the characters in "Andromeda the Thief," "This play was written with no dependency whatsoever on popular Sapphic lore or responsible history. It draws its characters loosely from mythology and more loosely from history; most of all it draws them from the imagination of the author" (Hansberry, "Andromeda the Thief," n.p.).
88. Hansberry, *Les Blancs,* 53. These prologue notes were written by Nemiroff; the Woman's other appearances are largely as Hansberry wrote them.
89. See Effiong, "History, Myth, and Revolt."

90. Hansberry, *Les Blancs,* 105, 54. As Margaret Wilkerson asserts, the Woman is "both man and woman. . . . Visually, she exhibits the movement and voluptuousness attributed to women while, at the same time, she carries a spear and calls Tshembe to the warrior role most associated with men"; Wilkerson, "Political Radicalism and Artistic Innovation in the Works of Lorraine Hansberry," 52.

91. Hansberry, *Les Blancs,* 105.

92. Cixous, "The Laugh of the Medusa," 341.

93. Hansberry, *Les Blancs,* 105.

94. Ibid., 106, 159.

95. Parker, Russo, Sommer, and Yaeger, "Introduction," 6.

96. Wright, *Becoming Black,* 142, Wright's italics.

97. Lazarus, *Nationalism and Cultural Practice in the Postcolonial World,* 61.

Chapter 3. Rosalind on the Black Star Line

1. Childress, "For a Negro Theatre," 62–63.

2. Maguire, "Alice Childress."

3. Hansberry, "CNA Presents Exciting New Dramatic Revue," 7.

4. Jones, "'Gold Through Trees' Has Beauty and Power."

5. Childress's papers contain two flyers for benefits for the South African resistance movement, one of which advertises *Gold Through Trees* and the other of which does not mention the play but strongly implies its performance, given that its actors are listed and that it was performed on April 23, 1953 (the play premiered earlier that month). Box 8, folder 4, Alice Childress Papers, Schomburg Center for Research in Black Culture.

6. *Amos 'n' Andy*'s creators, Freeman Gosden and Charles Correll, who also performed the eponymous roles during the earlier incarnation of the series as an immensely popular radio show, drew on their experience directing and performing in minstrel and blackface vaudeville shows (the pair would black up again for the 1930 *Amos 'n' Andy* movie, *Check and Double Check*). The radio show had already stirred up opposition among many African Americans for whom "'Amos 'n' Andy' had become a generic term for shuck-and-jive black buffoons who were holding the race back"; Ely, *The Adventures of Amos 'n' Andy,* 202. Although the era of blackface was coming to an end when *Amos 'n' Andy* made its move to the small screen (the show's producers considered blacking up Alvin Childress, who was light skinned, but heeded his protests), the show's enormous popularity ensured that minstrel humor, banter, and caricatures would maintain their hold on the popular national imagination well through the mid-1960s.

The show was produced for only two seasons, from 1951 to 1953, but it ran in syndication from 1954 to 1966. According to Ely, "By late 1954, the series was appearing on more than a hundred local stations—twice as many . . . as it had reached over [CBS]"; Ely, *The Adventures of Amos 'n' Andy,* 239. Furthermore, the reruns were often broadcast during the day, making it especially accessible to children during vacations. Ely points out that the images of Blacks these children saw were ones produced "before the Brown decision, the Montgomery boycott, the sit-ins, and the freedom rides—pictures from a bygone era, preserved intact and disseminated year in and year out among the youth of a new age" (240). *Amos 'n' Andy* was also the first TV show selected by the Department of Defense to be shown to servicemen overseas; Jones, "TV's Amos 'n' Andy," 60.

7. Quoted in Jones, "TV's Amos 'n' Andy," 61.

8. Hansberry, "Negroes Cast in Same Old Roles in TV Shows," 7.

9. *Trouble in Mind* depicts the conflicts that arise around the production of an antilynching play that, despite its racial liberalism, stereotypically depicts Black sharecroppers. All of the Black actors save for Wiletta Mayer agree to the script because they need the work. Wiletta loses her job but maintains her dignity and principles. In her entry on Childress for the *Dictionary of Literary Biography,* Roberta Maguire reads the play in light of the *Amos 'n' Andy* controversy; Maguire, "Alice Childress."

10. In a 1973 interview. Childress said that her marriage to Alvin Childress "just was something that shouldn't have been"; Childress, "Interview with Ann Allen Shockley," 43. Childress became romantically involved with the musician Nathan Woodward, her second husband, in the mid-1950s.

11. Ely, *The Adventures of Amos 'n' Andy,* 8.

12. Childress, "Brief History of the Minstrel Show and It's [*sic*] Form," 1–2. Childress's italics.

13. Ibid., 4, Childress's ellipses.

14. Ibid., 6, Childress's ellipses.

15. Hansberry and Childress, "Negro History Festival."

16. Chude-Sokei, *The Last "Darky,"* 12, 9.

17. Childress, "A Candle in a Gale Wind," 114, Childress's italics.

18. Childress herself clarified the intertextual relationship of her novel and play in the course of pursuing a copyright infringement lawsuit against the actress Clarice Taylor. Taylor, who had held leading roles in several Childress plays, including *Gold Through the Trees,* had commissioned Childress to write *Moms* and then had commissioned a second play about Mabley by playwright Ben Caldwell, whose script contained substantial similarities to Childress's. As evidence that the play contained original material by her, Childress underlined sections from the minstrel show chapter of *A Short Walk* to argue that it was a source for *Moms.* Childress won her lawsuit. See Box 23, Folder 15, Alice Childress Papers, Schomburg Center for Research in Black Culture.

19. Childress, "A Candle in a Gale Wind," 114.

20. Hill, "Making Noise," 184.

21. Stephens, *Black Empire,* 98–100.

22. Chude-Sokei, *The Last "Darky,"* 86. The rhetoric of minstrelsy continued to haunt Garveyism in the 1970s, although Marcus Garvey Jr. tried to turn it back onto

Garvey's critics: "[Critical] commentary on Marcus Garvey has usually taken the form of a Black and white minstrel show built around the general theme [of a] crazy, egotistic and noisy Black who thought up a scatterbrained scheme to remove the Black people from their American paradise to the African jungle"; Garvey, "Garveyism," 375.

23. Clarke, *Marcus Garvey and the Vision of Africa,* 372.

24. Childress told Ann Allen Shockley that she had lived for a time with a family whose father had introduced Marcus Garvey in New York; Childress, "Interview with Ann Allen Shockley," 32. After arriving in the United States from Trinidad, Rosa Guy similarly went to live with a family who belonged to the UNIA. They took her to meetings, and Guy "attributes the activism of her later years . . . and her passion for language to the Garveyite influences of her girlhood"; Norris, *Presenting Rosa Guy,* 7. Paule Marshall writes that in the Brooklyn community of Bajan immigrants and their descendants, with whom she grew up, Garvey's "name was constantly being invoked, for he had been their leader in the early twenties, the revolutionary who had said the end to white domination, the deliverer who had urged the black and poor like themselves to rise up"; Marshall, "Shaping the World of My Art," 103. Consequently, Marshall says, Garvey "became a living legend for me, so that although, when I was a little girl, he had been stripped of his power and was an old man living out his last days in obscurity in England, he was still an impressive figure, a Black radical and freedom fighter whose life and example had more than a little to do with moving me toward what I see as an essentially political perspective in my life" (ibid.).

25. Childress, "For a Negro Theatre," 64. For several pages of Act 1 of *Song of the Storm,* along with some handwritten notes, see Box 38, Folder 13, Alice Childress Papers, Schomburg Center for Research in Black Culture.

26. In her otherwise ambivalent review of the novel for *Ms.*, Walker describes the Garvey section as "the first fictional treatment of that movement I have read. And it is utterly engrossing"; Walker, "A Walk Through 20th-Century Black America," 46. In his essay on Childress, Killens's appreciative discussion of *A Short Walk* is almost entirely devoted to praising its vivid depiction of the Garvey movement; Killens, "The Literary Genius of Alice Childress".

27. Garvey, "Garveyism," 379, 378, 383.

28. Singh, *Black Is a Country,* 43.

29. Moore, "The Critics and Opponents of Marcus Garvey," 231–232. My italics.

30. Childress, *A Short Walk,* 163.

31. Williams, *The Humor of Jackie Moms Mabley,* 70.

32. Brooks, *Bodies in Dissent,* 5.

33. Childress wrote her "Conversation from Life" columns for *Freedom* without recompense from October 1951 until the paper's demise in 1955. The column then appeared in the *Baltimore Afro-American.* In 1956, Childress collected an edited version of the columns in a book, *Like One of the Family.* For a discussion of the column's anticolonial working-class feminism, see chapter 1.

34. Watkins, *On the Real Side,* 305, Watkins's italics.

35. *Copra* takes place on a West Indian island that is "a composite of all the islands, French, British, American and Independent" between "nineteen twenty to the present time"; Childress, *Copra,* n.p. Although the play is undated, correspondence suggests that it was written in the early 1950s; see James D. Proctor to Childress, October 15, 1954, Box 7, Folder 1, Alice Childress Papers, Schomburg Center for Research in Black Culture.

36. Memos from Childress's FBI file claim that she was a member of the CP from 1950 until about 1953. From 1950 through at least 1956, the Leftist organizations with which she worked in various capacities included the Civil Rights Congress; the Committee for the Negro in the Arts; *Freedom* newspaper; the Sojourners for Truth and Justice; the Harlem Committee to Repeal the Smith Act; New Playwrights; the National Council of the Arts, Sciences and Professions; the Harlem Writers Guild; the Jefferson School of Social Science; the Frederick Douglass School; the Emma Lazarus Foundation of Jewish Women's Clubs; the Teachers Union; and Camp Unity.

37. National Council of the Arts, Sciences and Professions, quoted in FBI File on Alice Childress, report filed July 31, 1957, page 3.

38. T. G. Santillan to Childress, July 3, 1967; Childress FBI File.

39. Childress to George Murphy, 1971, page 2; Childress interview by Slava Tynes.

40. Childress, "For a Negro Theatre," 63.

41. Childress, "A Proposal to Set Up a Dialogue Concerning the Production of an Afro-American Film in the U.S.S.R.," 1.

42. Childress, *A Short Walk,* 25, 28, 40.

43. Ibid., 41, 36, 33. Mandy-the-cook's grotesquery is amplified in a final draft of the novel: "[Mandy-the-cook] is big all over but her bosom and backside are huge, billowing balls of fat bursting through the seams of a red and white checkered dress. Sturdy arms peppered with warts and pimples, she too [like Bones] is in black-face and white mouth. She carries a flaming red slice of watermelon in one hand and a broom, aimed at Mr. Bones, in the other"; Childress, "A Short Walk" final manuscript, 36–37.

44. Childress, *A Short Walk,* 36.

45. Ibid., 40.

46. Bordman quoted in Forbes, *Introducing Bert Williams,* 100. Given Childress's historical knowledge of Black minstrelsy and her appreciation of Bert Williams, it is quite likely that she was familiar with *In Dahomey.* She referred to one of its well-known songs, "My Castle on the Nile," in *A Short Walk*; Forbes, *Introducing Bert Williams,* 149. Even the dates of *In Dahomey*'s performances align with Childress's narrative; Cora attends the minstrel show in 1905, when *In Dahomey* toured extensively throughout the United States. While the composers and performers of *In Dahomey* strove to break with minstrelsy, the show included crucial elements of it (e.g., a medicine show featured in its opening).

This minstrel genre exploiting African primitivism carried over into film, including the slapstick comedy *Rastus in Zululand,* the second in a series about the eponymous character that appeared from 1910 to 1911. Donald Bogle's summary of the film's plot shows the conventions it shared with *In Dahomey* and strikingly parallels Childress's "Chief Boo-Roo of Kookalanki," which features a main character called Rastus: "[Rastus] dreams of going to Zululand in the heart of Africa. There he wins the affections of the chief's daughter . . . but when asked to marry her, in true unreliable, no-account nigger fashion, he refuses, expressing a wish for death rather than matrimony. The savage chief (from the beginning, all Africans are savages) nearly grants that wish, too"; Bogle, *Brown Sugar,* 8.

47. Brooks, *Bodies in Dissent,* 226.

48. Chude-Sokei, *The Last "Darky,"* 8.

49. Childress, *A Short Walk,* 40–42.

50. Ibid., 43.

51. Ibid., 85, 88, 79.

52. Garvey, "Why the Black Star Line Failed," 139.

53. On Garvey's mastery of the image, see Hill, "Making Noise"; and Stephens, *Black Empire,* 97–100.

54. Stephens, *Black Empire,* 99.

55. Chude-Sokei, *The Last "Darky,"* 10.

56. Childress, *A Short Walk,* 182.

57. Ibid., 206.

58. Stephens presents a genealogy of the mobile, free, black masculine subjectivity that Garvey promoted; Stephens, *Black Empire,* 103–108.

59. Childress, *A Short Walk,* 181, 192.

60. Ibid., 178–179.

61. Ibid., 180.

62. Ibid., 193, 214–215.

63. Ibid., 310–312, Childress's italics. Childress even suggests that Cora is a truer nationalist than Cecil, who takes a white female lover while rebuilding the Black nationalist movement after Garvey is arrested and deported.

64. Watkins, *On the Real Side,* 367.

65. Childress, *A Short Walk,* 229, 240–241, 250.

66. Ibid., 270, Childress's italics. On Ethel Waters and Bessie Smith, see Watkins, *On the Real Side,* 366.

67. Childress, *A Short Walk,* 284.

68. Jennings, "Afterword: The Black Woman's Life as a Minstrel Show," 335–359.

69. Williams, *The Humor of Jackie Moms Mabley,* 99.

70. Bogle, *Brown Sugar,* 161; Williams, *The Humor of Jackie Moms Mabley,* 50. Mabley was the first woman to appear solo at the Apollo, where from the 1930s through the 1960s she paved the way for the likes of Dick Gregory and Richard Pryor.

71. According to Watkins, the mammy guise "provided the buffer or intermediary

necessary to quell resistance to a woman doing a single comic routine"; Watkins, *On the Real Side,* 391.

72. Watkins, *On the Real Side,* 372. Watkins writes that the few Black comedians who did stand-up on the TOBA circuit of the first three decades of the twentieth century were popular with Black audiences but were "shunned by white bookers and generally unknown outside black cabarets and theatres" (373). According to Elsie Williams, "The mother identification created bonding particularly with the black audience, and worked equally when playing to white audiences, other entertainers with whom Mabley performed also discovered. For example, Ford Lee Buck Washington and John Bubbles described how they slipped out of their stereotyped personae as crap shooters and gin drinkers to evoke 'Mammy'"; Williams, *The Humor of Jackie Moms Mabley,* 49.

73. Sotiropoulos, *Staging Race,* 19–20.

74. Rogin, *Blackface, White Noise,* 39, 176–177.

75. Watkins, *On the Real Side,* 393.

76. Garber, *Vested Interests,* 16. On "Moms" as the strong and wise Black grandmother, see Williams, *The Humor of Jackie Moms Mabley,* 74–75; on her "gritty ethnic quality," see Bogle, *Brown Sugar,* 161.

77. Aiken, oral history interview, 5, 19; Williams, *The Humor of Jackie Moms Mabley,* 48.

78. Aiken, oral history interview, 2.

79. Childress's copy of Aiken's transcribed oral history contains underlining of the sections discussing Mabley's cross-dressing, including the section quoted above.

80. Childress, *Moms,* 43, 27, 30.

81. Ibid., 50, 27.

82. Garber, *Vested Interests,* 17, Garber's italics.

83. Childress, *Moms,* 24.

84. Childress refers to Williams's anti-war militancy in precisely those terms in Childress to Janet (no surname), October 23, 1981. In this letter she speaks of Howard Augusta, a member of the American Negro Theater to which Childress also belonged in the 1940s and 1950s, who "gave accurate and beautiful interpretations of Bert Williams . . . white gloves, that funny little coat and top hat and *no blackface.* . . . because Bert hated it and used it as the only way to break through the white wall barrier to commercial appearances" (3). Childress refers here specifically to "I'm Gone Before I Go" as "anti war" (4) and quotes some of the lyrics.

85. Childress, *Moms,* 60–61, 44. In her letter to Janet, Childress lamented that Williams's political side continued to be cut out of the scholarship on him.

86. Chude-Sokei, *The Last "Darky,"* 35.

87. Horne, *Black and Brown,* 4–5. Horne points out that Villa was savvy about manipulating his image in order to appeal to African Americans; 146–147.

88. Ibid., 146.

89. Brooks and Spottswood, *Lost Sounds,* 132.

90. I rely here on the recording of "I'm Gone Before I Go" in *Bert Williams: The Middle Years, 1910–1918,* Archeophone Records, 2002.

91. Williams's sensitivity to the taboo of interracial romance, especially between a Black man and white woman, is evident in the stipulation in his contract with the Ziegfeld Follies—a stipulation that he himself requested—"that at no time would he be on stage with any of the female members of the company." This was likely a measure of self-protection against racial animosity; Chude-Sokei, *The Last "Darky,"* 40.

92. Johnson quoted in Horne, *Black and Brown,* 2.

93. Horne, *Black and Brown,* 25–37.

94. The 1987 version of the play also omits the lyrics mentioning Booker T. Washington and Jack Johnson discussed above. (These lyrics are included in a 1986 script.)

95. Childress, *Moms,* 74.

96. Forbes, *Introducing Bert Williams,* 273.

97. Childress, *A Short Walk,* 314–315, 41.

98. Ibid., 309.

99. Ibid., 316.

100. Ibid.; Gilkes, "The Roles of Church and Community Mothers," 368.

101. Childress to Anne (no surname), September 9, 1980.

102. Childress, *A Short Walk,* 317.

103. Ibid., 316, 292.

104. Ibid., 290–291.

105. Moore, "The Critics and Opponents of Marcus Garvey," 234.

106. Childress, *A Short Walk,* 159.

107. Ibid., 191–192.

108. Ibid., 315.

109. Ibid., 316.

110. Singh, *Black Is a Country,* 16. Cora's and Marion's reclaiming of America is taken up by Cora's daughter, Delta, who insists that "this country belongs to me as much as it does to anyone else"; Childress, *A Short Walk,* 325. Consequently, she enlists with the Navy WAVEs, thereby realizing the thwarted dreams of her father (Cecil) and her mother to win their civil rights and racial autonomy through transatlantic movement. Although Delta's plans suggest a teleological view of American progress, insofar as avenues for Black freedom closed to her parents are now open to their daughter through fighting for the United States, Childress affirms the importance of Black nationalism in conjunction with reclaiming America. Even as she exposes the sexism of Cecil's anti-imperialist nationalism, she shows that it prompts Delta to question "the soothing vision of the future which she finds in white movie stars," the vision of "a perfect life filled with unlimited chance for careers, wealth, homes, and first-class travel"; ibid., 322.

111. Hansberry and Childress, "Negro History Festival," 16.

112. Ibid., 20.

113. Childress, *A Short Walk,* 332, 33, 333.

114. Ibid.

115. Childress, "The Depression . . . The New York Hard Winter," 4.

116. Stephens, *Black Empire,* 101.

Chapter 4. Rosa Guy, Haiti, and the Hemispheric Woman

1. Belinda Edmondson, for example, lists McMillan along with Alice Walker and Toni Cade Bambara as part of a "powerfully influential group of African American feminist writers"; Edmondson, *Making Men*, 101.

2. Davies, *Black Women, Writing and Identity*, 26.

3. "Bestselling Author Terry McMillan Confronts Her Gay Ex-Husband," 1.

4. After gaining independence from Britain in 1962, Jamaica continued to struggle under neocolonialism. Its major industries were under foreign control, as were many of its public utilities and financial institutions; furthermore, Jamaica was heavily dependent on imports of goods and services, especially from the United States. According to political scientist Euclid Rose, Prime Minister Michael Manley's 1974 declaration that Jamaica was a democratic socialist state led to the "sustained effort [of the United States] to destabilize Jamaica's economy" through "a combination of economic and political pressures by the U.S. government, multinational corporations, the IMF-World Bank group, the local capitalist class, negative press reports, principally in Jamaica and in North America and, in all probability, covert funding of the JLP [Jamaica Labour Party]"; Rose, *Dependency and Socialism*, 363. The United States successfully pushed Manley to negotiate with the IMF. To its increasing detriment, Jamaica has continued on the course of neoliberal reform since then. Tourism "accounts for nearly half of Jamaica's gross, non-remittance foreign exchange flows. However, local elites and foreign interests dominate the profits, while most jobs are low-paid and low-skilled. Exuberant growth projections regularly ignore the social costs of the prevailing model and the level of market saturation, and downplay its vulnerability to the negative publicity associated with Jamaica's growing reputation for violence and to shocks in the international system"; Weis, "A Precarious Balance," 128.

5. Guy, *The Sun, the Sea, a Touch of the Wind*, 115–116.

6. Young, *Soul Power*, 5.

7. Guy, *The Sun, the Sea, a Touch of the Wind*, 35.

8. Ibid., 18.

9. Ibid., 205.

10. Ibid., 279.

11. Guy quoted in Norris, *Presenting Rosa Guy*, 11. Guy reaffirmed her nationalist internationalism in a 1990 interview: "I am aware of the world issues and the things that are affecting most peoples in the world. I, I don't feel that one always has to be autobiographical and the events that affect everyone in the world have to be important. The most important thing is the lives of people at that time[;] for instance, I think right now, the lives of people in Africa, the freedom struggle affects us all and I, I try to see what I can do in my work to point out the fact that if, that, that we all have a responsibility to seeing that this liberation movement in Africa comes to fruition. How we do it, these things I have to think out"; "Interview with Rosa Guy."

12. Guy, "A Conversation between Rosa Guy and Maya Angelou," 224.

13. James, "Preface to the Vintage Edition," n.p.

14. Guy, "Haiti: The Enigma," 417, Guy's italics.

15. Guy, *The Sun, the Sea, a Touch of the Wind,* 304, 130.

16. Benjamin, "Theses on the Philosophy of History," 261.

17. Ibid., 262–263.

18. Guy, *The Sun, the Sea, a Touch of the Wind,* 176.

19. Scott, *Conscripts of Modernity,* 1.

20. See Gaspar and Trouillot, "Afterword: History, Fiction, and the Slave Experience"; and Renda, *Taking Haiti.*

21. Jean-Jacques Dessalines is another figure who replaces L'Ouverture in the novel's representation of revolutionary Haiti, as exemplified in Maxie's characterization of "the island where Dessalines kicked the shit out of the French, established the first independent Black state in the hemisphere, and where Charlemagne fought the U.S. Marines to a standstill"; Guy, *The Sun, the Sea, a Touch of the Wind,* 96. The novel's characters are invested in those military and political leaders who (eventually) fought white imperialist designs, more so than those such as Toussaint who saw the need to work with Europeans in order to modernize and develop Haiti.

22. Guy, *The Sun, the Sea, a Touch of the Wind,* 279.

23. Carby, *Race Men,* 113. Of *The Black Jacobins,* Edmondson writes that James's "emphasis on one central, masterful personality in an otherwise Marxist account of revolution makes sense only if we understand it to be a particularly West Indian, particularly middle-class and male version of revolutionary discourse"; Edmondson, *Making Men,* 106. James laid the groundwork for further literary and historical work on Haiti, including Eric Williams's *Capitalism and Slavery* (1944), Jacques Roumaine's *Masters of the Dew* (1944), Alejo Carpentier's *Kingdom of This World* (1949), and George Lamming's *The Pleasures of Exile* (1960). An earlier Black radical novel that represents revolutionary nationalist consciousness through the legacy of the Haitian Revolution is Claude McKay's *Home to Harlem* (1928). In the mid-twentieth century, Black radicals such as Richard B. Moore and Paul Robeson invoked Toussaint L'Ouverture, calling for not only West Indian but also Afro-Asian solidarity (the latter expressed in Robeson's declaration, "Ho Chi Minh is the Toussaint l'Ouverture of Indo-China"); see Moore, "Caribbean Unity and Freedom"; and Robeson, "Selected Speeches and Writings on Peace, No. 1, 1971," 147.

The Sun, the Sea, a Touch of the Wind should also be read as a response to the radical poetics of Graham Greene's novel *The Comedians* (1966), which internationally publicized the atrocities committed by François Duvalier's regime and his Tonton Macoutes. From the outset, *The Sun, the Sea, a Touch of the Wind* seems to speak to the relative absence of black women in *The Comedians* by revisiting the well-known scene in Greene's novel where his British protagonist, Mr. Brown, discovers the corpse of a Haitian official in the swimming pool of the hotel he has inherited from his mother. Greene's fictional Hotel Trianon is based on Port-au-Prince's Hotel Oloffson, which became world renowned as a result of *The Comedians.* Guy's novel is largely set in her version of the Oloffson, the Old Hotel, the proprietors of which are based on the real-life American couple who ran the Oloffson in the 1970s, when the novel takes place—about ten years later than Greene's. The swimming pool of the Old Hotel is where Guy's protagonist, Jonnie Dash, an African American woman, finds herself soon after blacking out at the beginning of the novel. She is discovered by a handsome British man reminiscent of Greene's Mr. Brown, who thinks she is drowning or trying to kill herself, much to her indignation. Through "reviving" Greene's black corpse in the swimming pool and transforming it into her heroine, Guy presents a Black feminist analysis of Haiti that complicates as well as complements Greene's critique of neocolonialism and U.S. "innocence."

Guy would likely have been familiar with *The Comedians,* which was published the same year as her first novel, *Bird at My Window.* Guy would have been in Haiti around the same time that Graham Greene was staying at the Oloffson and writing *The Comedians.* Guy left for the island in 1962; Greene arrived in mid-August of 1963. Both Greene's and Guy's novels were reviewed favorably in *Freedomways* by Keith Baird, who even concluded his review of *The Comedians* by quoting from Guy's *Freedomways* essay on Haiti—"The people of Haiti are waiting and they will be free"; Baird, "Gripping Novel That's Saying Something," 277. After commenting that "Mr. Greene has made an interesting and edifying display of the dirty linen of the 'black Republic' of Haiti," Baird also wrote, "It is to be hoped that some further masterly exhibitions of this kind will soon be forthcoming" (277). Nearly thirty years later, Guy answered this call with *The Sun, the Sea, a Touch of the Wind.*

24. Moses, *Black Messiahs and Uncle Toms,* 4, 1.

25. Clarke, "The New Afro-American Nationalism," 286. For other examples of messianic rhetoric with respect to Lumumba, see Meriwether, *Proudly We Can Be Africans,* 232–233.

26. Carby, *Race Men,* 129.

27. Edmondson, *Making Men,* 106.

28. Bambara, "On the Issue of Roles," 126.

29. Guy, *The Sun, the Sea, a Touch of the Wind,* 4.

30. Ibid., 42, 67.

31. Ibid., 130. On Péralte, see Nicholls, *From Dessalines to Duvalier,* 148–149.

32. Guy, *The Sun, the Sea, a Touch of the Wind,* 176, 215, 72.

33. Ibid., 73. By contrast, Guy gestures towards the role of Haiti's young intelligentsia in rebuilding their country. In the act of preparing to leave Haiti, Jonnie finds her luggage salesclerk (significantly, a woman) to be one such intellectual: "My country, it is poor. But we cannot all leave. Some must stay—and see if we can help in what happens next" (251).

34. Ibid., 74.

35. Ibid., 106–107.

36. Ibid., 108, 238–239.

37. Guy, "Haiti: The Enigma," 425.

38. Young, *Soul Power*, 5.

39. Guy, *The Sun, the Sea, a Touch of the Wind*, 90. The novel's ironic portrayal of the Black Madonna figure is reprised when Maxie, the fisherman and self-styled revolutionary, comes on to Jonnie: "Who the hell do you think you are lying there wanting me like a goddamn bitch in heat, pretending that you're holier than the Virgin daughter of the Virgin Mary" (175). *Christ in Concrete* is Pietro di Donato's proletarian novel about Italian immigrants in New York City.

40. Cleage, *The Black Messiah*, 24.

41. Ibid., 31.

42. Guy, *The Sun, the Sea, a Touch of the Wind*, 4, 92.

43. See Moynihan, *The Negro Family*, 5, 29.

44. For an example of nationalist rhetoric about the Black matriarch, see Larry Neal's 1968 essay, "The Black Arts Movement." For feminist critiques of the Moynihan Report, see hooks, *Ain't I A Woman*, 71–82, 103–104; Dubey, *Black Women Novelists*, 17–18; and Ferguson, *Aberrations in Black*, 119–123.

45. Guy, *Bird at My Window*, 49, 168, 173, 187, 198.

46. Guy, *The Sun, the Sea, a Touch of the Wind*, 180, 177. Maxie is reminiscent of the transgendered Afro-Jamaican revolutionary Harry/Harriet in Michelle Cliff's *No Telephone to Heaven*. Like Harry/Harriet, Maxie complements the Black female protagonist's efforts to revise traditional gender/sex roles in the process of understanding her role in the freedom struggle of her people.

47. Ibid., 177–178.

48. Ibid., 177.

49. Ibid., 180, 175, 179–180, 286, 295.

50. Carby, *Race Men*, 129. On the appropriation of reproduction by Black male nationalist subjects, see also Wright, *Becoming Black*, 12.

51. Edmondson, *Making Men*, 120. On the gender and race politics of *Waters with Berries*, see ibid., 117–122.

52. One key difference between Guy's novel and Lamming's and Marshall's is that in *The Sun, the Sea, a Touch of the Wind* the relationship is between a white British woman and an African American rather than an Afro-Caribbean. Yet Jonnie's relationship to Jessica is by no means easy, even if Jessica, as an allegory for British empire, is not a "direct" master over Jonnie. Guy had explored the intertwining of women's same-sex desire and political development in her young adult novel *Ruby* (1976), "the first modern lesbian novel for teenagers," according to one reviewer; Dunbar, "The Odd Couple."

Unlike female homosexuality, male homosexuality in *The Sun, the Sea, a Touch of the Wind* appears to signal corruption and imperialistic power through the U.S. attaché McCellan's efforts to obtain Lucknair as his sex slave. However, in *Bird at My Window*, Guy portrays the protagonist Wade's homoerotic attachment to his friend Rocky as a rare instance of true intimacy.

53. Guy, *The Sun, the Sea, a Touch of the Wind*, 130.

54. Ibid., 131, 134, 304.

55. Ibid., 305.

56. Clifford, "Traveling Cultures," 36.

57. Guy, *The Sun, the Sea, a Touch of the Wind,* 304.

58. Gilroy, *The Black Atlantic,* 19.

59. Guy, *The Sun, the Sea, a Touch of the Wind,* 304, my italics.

60. Ibid., 239.

61. Guy, "Haiti: The Enigma," 419.

62. Ibid., 13, my italics.

63. I borrow this phrase from Saidiya Hartman's *Lose Your Mother.*

64. Guy, *The Sun, the Sea, a Touch of the Wind,* 178.

65. Ibid., 136.

66. McAvoy, "A Woman and a Nation Struggle for Identity."

67. Discussing the parallels between Jonnie's struggle and Haiti's history, McAvoy writes, "From the first nation in which black slaves earned their independence, she learns of true strength. . . . Like the slaves before her, Jonnie breaks free of white and male dominance and enjoys a freedom that even fear and poverty cannot steal"; McAvoy, "A Woman and a Nation Struggle for Identity."

68. Moore, "An Allegorical Hodgepodge of Haiti"; Adell, "Foreword," xvii.

69. McAvoy, "A Woman and a Nation Struggle for Identity"; Moore, "An Allegorical Hodgepodge of Haiti."

70. McMillan, *How Stella Got Her Groove Back,* 365.

71. McMillan, Transcript of Declaration, *McMillan vs. Plummer.*

72. McMillan interview with Tavis Smiley, July 12, 2005.

73. These associations are evident in McMillan's "100 Questions I Meant to Ask Him."

74. McMillan, Transcript of Declaration, *McMillan vs. Plummer,* accessed via The Smoking Gun website, which features material "obtained from government and law enforcement sources, via Freedom of Information requests, and from court files nationwide." See http://www.thesmokinggun.com/about.html.

75. McMillan's denial of the salience of sexuality to her animosity toward Plummer parallels liberal denials of the salience of race to economic, cultural, and juridical matters—i.e., the selective privileging of the individual over the group, as in McMillan's assertion, "I'm not a homophobe. I'm a Jon-o-phobe"; McMillan, Interview with Tavis Smiley. With respect to race, McMillan walks a fine line between inscribing and erasing Blackness in her mass market fiction. While she has been lauded for capturing "authentic" Black life, she has claimed that contemporary African American writers "are not as race oriented, and they are not as protest oriented"; McMillan quoted in Davis, "Don't Worry, Be Buppie," 26.

76. McMillan, Transcript of Declaration, *McMillan vs. Plummer.*

77. Quoted in Waldron, "Terry McMillan and Husband Jonathan Plummer Tell Why Their Storybook Marriage Is Ending," 17.

78. As Kaplan asserts, "The American Empire has long followed a double impetus

to construct boundaries and patrol all movement across them and to break down those borders through the desire for unfettered expansion"; Kaplan, *The Anarchy of Empire in the Making of U.S. Culture,* 15.

Chapter 5. Audre Lorde Revisited

1. Fanon, "On National Culture," 179.

2. Grewal, "Autobiographic Subjects and Diasporic Locations," 234. For further examples of postnationalist feminism, see Mohanty, "Cartographies of Struggle"; and Kaplan, Alarcón, and Moallem, *Between Woman and Nation.*

3. See Michelle Wright, *Becoming Black,* 136–182; McGill, "Sister-Outsider," 117–160; Ferguson, *Aberrations in Black*; Dhairyam, "'Artifacts for Survival.'" In a 1993 review for *The Nation* of Lorde's collection of poems *Undersong,* Jan Clausen posited that among feminists "Lorde is best known . . . for her eloquent advocacy of a flexible, non-essentialist identity politics: the 'house of difference'"; quoted in Burr, *Of Women, Poetry, and Power,* 154.

4. McGill, *Constructing Black Selves,* 199.

5. McGill's work illustrates this tendency. While she contextualizes 1960s and 1970s pan-Africanism, its relevance to Lorde is articulated in terms of her "locating and affirming lesbian and women-centered consciousnesses through the historicity of African cultural practices and formations"; McGill, *Constructing Black Selves,* 133. McGill does not note Lorde's later focus on African national liberation; instead, she pays attention to her feminist cultural nationalism whereby "tropes of Africa provided a particular site of liberation, standing as signposts for the necessity of working through racisms and sexisms" (ibid., 147). She mentions strong African nations only briefly and negatively.

Other studies of Lorde place her in an entirely U.S. literary and political context and do not consider Third World national struggles. See for example Obourn, "Audre Lorde"; and Norman, *The American Protest Essay,* 117–121.

6. See Carlston, "*Zami* and the Politics of Plural Identity"; Alexander, "'Coming Out Blackened and Whole'"; Walk, "Audre Lorde's Life Writing"; and Kemp, "Writing Power." See also De Veaux's discussion of *Zami* in *Warrior Poet,* 311–314. Critics have observed that scholarship on Lorde's prose work, especially *Zami,* outweighs that on her poetry.

7. Lorde, *Zami,* 255.

8. Davies, *Black Women, Writing and Identity,* 121.

9. Ibid., 12.

10. Stephens, *Black Empire,* 278, 280.

11. San Juan, *Racism and Cultural Studies,* 350–352.

12. Ibid., 350.

13. Stephens, *Black Empire,* 280.

14. Davies, *Black Women, Writing and Identity,* 122.

15. The marginalization of *A Burst of Light* is especially striking when it comes to studies of Lorde's writings on cancer, which almost exclusively focus on her earlier *Cancer Journals* (1980). This narrow focus unfortunately reproduces the conceptualizations of illness and women's bodies that Lorde is at pains to contest as she brings her anti-imperialism to bear on her struggle with cancer in *A Burst of Light.* Lorde's writing on St. Croix and Hurricane Hugo also interweaves her battles with cancer and with colonialism; see her poem, "Restoration: A Memorial—9/18/91"; and her epigraph to "Of Generators and Survival—Hugo Letter 12/89," which reads, "Driving into town is like looking into a mirror while recuperating from an almost fatal disease. You are so glad to be alive, yet you can't help but mourn the devastation" (201).

16. Although Lorde herself did not use the term "cultural nationalism" and probably would have objected to it given its associations with the masculinist projects of Ron Karenga and others, I use this term to distinguish Lorde's concerns with African spirituality and tradition and with identity politics, separate from concerns with national liberation. We might say that Lorde's work after the invasion of Grenada, which recovers West African traditions to develop a revolutionary aesthetics and analysis, is more reflective of political pan-Africanism. As Nikhil Pal Singh explains it, political pan-Africanism "suggests that the new interest in Africa among U.S. blacks in the 1960s did not simply derive from a psychic quest for positive self-images or genealogical lineages—that is, from racial imputations of shared biological essences—but that such psychic and cultural assertions (when they were made) followed from claims about ethical commonality, global relatedness, and political responsibility"; Singh, *Black Is a Country*, 188.

17. The inattention to the significance of nationalism in Lorde's work might also have at least some roots in terminology: Lorde tended not to use "nation" or "nationalism," preferring instead "community" or "country," perhaps because she associated "black nationalism" with separatism, heteropatriarchy, and specific organizations such as the Nation of Islam. See Lorde, "Learning from the 60s."

18. For examples of these claims that Black feminism opposed nationalism, see Dubey, *Black Women Novelists and the Nationalist Aesthetic*; Ferguson, *Aberrations in Black;* and Michelle Wright, *Becoming Black.*

19. Lorde, "An Interview: Audre Lorde and Adrienne Rich," 91.

20. Lorde to Mayfield, quoted in Welch, "Black Art and Activism,"195.

21. The SEEK (Search for Education, Elevation and Knowledge) provides qualified students with academic and financial support.

22. Lorde discussed with Adrienne Rich her "very uneasy dialogue between me and the Harlem Writers' Guild where I felt I was tolerated but never really accepted—that I was both crazy and queer but would grow out of it"; "An Interview: Audre Lorde and Adrienne Rich," 91.

23. De Veaux, *Warrior Poet*, 280.

24. Lorde devotes considerable space to her time with the Zamani Soweto Sisters in "A Burst of Light: Living with Cancer," 101–106.

25. As Mary DeShazer observes, the struggle against apartheid became a subject of the work of many radical U.S. women of color writers. See DeShazer, *A Poetics of Resistance,* 5.

26. See Fleras, "Politicising Indigeneity."

27. Boldt, *Surviving as Indians,* 47.

28. Lorde, "Learning from the 60s," 134–135, 138.

29. Ibid., 140.

30. Ibid., 144.

31. Lorde, "Grenada Revisited," 184.

32. Davidson, quoted in Lazarus, *Nationalism and Cultural Practice in the Postcolonial World,* 107.

33. Lorde, "Grenada Revisited," 177–178.

34. Ibid., 181.

35. Ibid., 187. Lorde would have been attuned to this superexploitation of Third World women because of her own experience with assembly line work. She processed quartz crystals for radio and radar machinery—probably in service of the Korean War—at Keystone Electronics in Stamford, Connecticut, in the early 1950s, before such work was outsourced to cheaper Third World labor. In *Zami,* Lorde wrote about obtaining this job after being turned down for white-collar positions because of her race. She found that, due to the extremely dirty and dangerous nature of the work, all of the unskilled positions were occupied by blacks and Puerto Ricans recruited in New York City, since "most local [white] people would not work under such conditions"; Lorde, *Zami,* 126.

36. Lorde, "Grenada Revisited," 189, Lorde's italics.

37. Davies, *Black Women, Writing and Identity,* 12.

38. See McGill, *Constructing Black Selves,* 157, for a version of this argument.

39. Lorde, *Zami,* 14, Lorde's italics.

40. Davies, *Black Women, Writing and Identity,* 116. Grewal presents another definition of postnationalist diasporic subjects: "There can be syncretic, 'immigrant,' cross-cultural, and plural subjectivities, which can enable a politics through positions that are coalitions, intransigent, in process, and contradictory. Such identities are enabling because they provide a mobility in solidarity that leads to a transnational participation in understanding and opposing multiple and global oppressions operating upon them; that is, these subjects enable oppositions in multiple locations"; Grewal, "Autobiographic Subjects and Diasporic Locations," 214.

41. Lorde, "Grenada Revisited," 185.

42. Davies, *Black Women, Writing and Identity,* 116; Lorde, "Grenada Revisited," 189.

43. Stephens, *Black Empire,* 277, Stephens's italics.

44. DeShazer writes that "a rigorous self-examination, a struggle for accountability as U.S. citizens" is a distinct strategy of U.S. women's poetry of resistance; DeShazer, *A Poetics of Resistance,* 235.

45. Lorde, "A Burst of Light: Living With Cancer," 53.

46. Lorde makes an analogous point with respect to gender in another journal entry four months later: "Feminism must be on the cutting edge of real social change if it is to survive as a movement in any particular country. *Whatever the core problems are for the people of that country must also be the core problems addressed by women, for we do not exist in a vacuum.* We are anchored in our own place and time, looking out and beyond to the future we are creating, and we are part of communities that interact"; ibid., 64, my italics.

47. Lorde missed Awatere in New Zealand, but she did meet other Maori women activists and writers, many of whom were lesbians familiar with *Zami* or *Sister Outsider.* Lorde worked to introduce their literature to U.S. audiences; De Veaux, *Warrior Poet,* 350–351. In 1985, she wrote about the need to analyze the intersections between African American and indigenous struggles; Lorde, *A Burst of Light,* 74.

48. Lorde, "A Burst of Light: Living With Cancer," 66.

49. Ibid., 70–71.

50. Ibid., 74.

51. Ibid.

52. Lorde, "Turning the Beat Around," 46, 42, 41.

53. Lorde, "The Evening News," in *The Collected Poems of Audre Lorde,* 337.

54. Lorde, "Turning the Beat Around," 46.

55. Ibid. The Anglo-American Corporation of South Africa was a major recipient of U.S. investment; it took advantage of South Africa's financial crisis in the wake of the 1960 Sharpeville Massacre to consolidate its hold on the mining sector and profit from the needs of the state, especially with regard to defense. See Culverson, *Contesting Apartheid,* 39–40.

56. Lorde, "Turning the Beat Around," 39–40.

57. Lorde, "Learning from the 60s," 135, 138.

58. Lorde, "Turning the Beat Around," 46–47, 140. For examples of feminist scholarship on Lorde that warn against hierarchizing identities and oppressions, see Alexander, "'Coming Out Blackened and Whole,'" 218; and McGill, *Constructing Black Selves,* 144.

59. Lorde, "Apartheid U.S.A.," 35, 37, 28.

60. Lorde, "Turning the Beat Around," 42. The impact of the national struggles in South Africa and Grenada on Lorde's work in the 1980s can also be appreciated by comparing "Turning the Beat Around: Lesbian Parenting 1986" with Lorde's earlier essay on lesbian parenting, "Man Child: A Black Lesbian Feminist's Response," originally published in 1979. Both essays make points about raising children to be survivors and warriors equipped with the knowledge they need to choose their battles and about dealing with anger productively rather than taking it out on family members who are closest to you and most vulnerable. But the 1986 essay explicitly ties these issues to Third World anti-imperialist and national struggles, which do not inform the earlier essay.

61. Lorde quoted in Kraft, "The Creative Use," 149.

62. Lorde quoted in Pache and Dackweiler, "Interview," 168.

63. Lorde, "Turning the Beat Around," 46.

64. African political liberation informs Lorde's poems that predate the invasion—perhaps most notably "The Evening News" in *Chosen Poems: Old and New*—but I would argue that national liberation more consistently features in and shapes Lorde's poems written and/or published after the invasion of Grenada, including her last collection of poetry, *The Marvelous Arithmetics of Distance.*

65. Audre Lorde, "Beams," in *The Collected Poems of Audre Lorde,* 415.

66. Audre Lorde, "Sisters in Arms," in *The Collected Poems of Audre Lorde,* 357. Drawing on Lorde's journals, De Veaux writes that "Lorde felt 'Sisters' was the work around which the other poems, as a book, coalesced"; De Veaux, *Warrior Poet,* 348–349.

67. In addition to serving as a symbol of contemporary U.S. investments in South Africa, the American Express Company had aided the historical development of South African tourism; see Culverson, *Contesting Apartheid,* 59.

68. Obourn, "Audre Lorde: Trauma Theory and Liberal Multiculturalism," 229.

69. I locate limitations in Obourn's reading of Lorde's poetry in the study's postmodern skepticism toward representation (in this regard, see also Dhairyam, who further limits revolution to redefining identity; Dhairyam, "'Artifacts for Survival'"). To foreclose questions of the real would leave definitions of reality up to official discourses such as those perpetuated by the *New York Times,* which mystified apartheid state violence by singling out the white victim of Black violence instead of exposing the systemic racial violence against Blacks. As Lorde writes in "On My Way Out I Passed Over You and the Verrazano Bridge," "where is true history written / except in the poems?" (*The Collected Poems of Audre Lorde,* 405).

70. Audre Lorde, "Call," in *The Collected Poems of Audre Lorde,* 417–419.

71. According to John Henrik Clarke, "Yaa Asantewa's War was the last major war led by an African woman"; Clarke, "African Warrior Queens," 133. However, Cheryl Townsend Gilkes contends that "African women . . . developed their own legacy of political leadership which included military campaigns against European colonialism as late as the early twentieth century"; Gilkes, "The Roles of Church and Community Mothers," 372.

72. Rowell, "Above the Wind," 188.

73. See Moore, "The Battering of St. Croix," 34–37.

74. Rowell, "Above the Wind," 185, 186. "Catalytic cracker" refers to one of the major units of oil refineries, the fluid catalytic cracking unit.

75. See Moore, "The Battering of St. Croix," 35. Moore's discussion of FEMA illuminates its neocolonial origins and functions: "For some, the first awareness of FEMA came from Iran/Contra revelations. FEMA officials, coordinating with Colonel Oliver North . . . drew up 'emergency' plans to handle widespread uprisings in U.S. urban ghettos or widespread civil protest against a U.S. invasion of, for example, Nicaragua. Their contingency plans included suspending the constitution, declaring martial law, and establishing detention camps to hold up to 22 million African Americans"; ibid., 37.

76. Rowell, "Above the Wind," 186.

77. Ibid., 188.

78. Lorde, "Restoration: A Memorial—9/18/91," in *The Collected Poems of Audre Lorde*, 456–457.

79. Rowell, "Above the Wind," 185.

80. Lorde, "Grenada Revisited," 189.

81. Lorde, "Of Generators and Survival," 206, 208–209.

82. Rowell, "Above the Wind," 187, 186.

83. Young, *Soul Power*, 14. See also Omi and Winant's critique of the internal colony argument in *Racial Formation*, 47–51.

84. Young, *Soul Power*, 14.

85. Rowell, "Above the Wind," 186.

86. Lorde, "Of Generators and Survival," 211.

87. Ibid., 215.

88. Lorde, "Bicentennial Poem #21,000,000," in *The Collected Poems of Audre Lorde*, 456–457.

89. For an example of this postnationalist view, see Inderpal Grewal's critique of Nancy Hartsock in "Autobiographic Subjects and Diasporic Locations."

90. Lorde, "A Burst of Light: Living With Cancer," 119.

91. Jones, "On the Right to Self-Determination," 69, Jones's italics.

92. Jones, "An End to the Neglect of the Problems of the Negro Woman!" 120.

Chapter 6. Reading Maya Angelou, Reading Black Internationalist Feminism Today

1. Angelou's six autobiographies are *I Know Why the Caged Bird Sings* (1970), *Gather Together in My Name* (1974), *Singin' and Swingin' and Gettin' Merry Like Christmas* (1976), *The Heart of a Woman* (1981), *All God's Children Need Traveling Shoes* (1986), and *A Song Flung Up to Heaven* (2002).

2. I invoke Raymond Williams's concept of the residual to account for "certain experiences, meanings, and values which cannot be expressed or substantially verified in terms of the dominant culture" but that "are nevertheless lived and practiced on the basis of the residue—cultural as well as social—of some previous social and cultural institution or formation"; Williams, "Base and Superstructure in Marxist Cultural Theory," 137.

3. Farr, *Reading Oprah*, 23.

4. "*The Heart of a Woman*: About the Book"; Farr, *Reading Oprah*, 27. Liberal feminism emphasizes individual rights at the expense of understanding the political economy and systemic racism as sources of women's oppression. Within this framework, psychological models for explaining social phenomena tend to preclude structural analysis, a tendency Oprah exemplifies.

5. Canada's *National Post* observes that Angelou has been called "'an elder wise woman,' (*The Washington Post*), 'a cultural diva' (*The New York Times*), 'a self-styled

sister-friend and wise-woman elder of the human tribe' (*The Atlanta Journal-Constitution*) and 'the nearest thing America has to a sacred institution, a high priestess of culture and love' (Salon.com)." Good, "Inspiration for Hire."

6. *I Know Why the Caged Bird Sings* instantly changed Angelou's career, making her one of America's best-known writers. It garnered positive reviews from the mainstream press and remained a bestseller for decades. Although banned by a number of U.S. schools due to its depictions of rape, racism, and out-of-wedlock teen pregnancy, the book has been widely taught and studied and has generated most of the criticism on Angelou's work. Appearing in February 1970—the same year that saw the publication of Toni Morrison's *The Bluest Eye,* Alice Walker's *The Third Life of Grange Copeland,* Louise Meriwether's *Daddy Was a Numbers Runner,* and Michele Wallace's *Black Macho and the Myth of the Superwoman—I Know Why the Caged Bird Sings* heralded and paved the way for the rise of African-American women's literature in the late twentieth century.

7. Moallem and Boal, "Multicultural Nationalism and the Poetics of Inauguration," 247; Braxton, "Symbolic Geography and Psychic Landscapes," 5.

8. For example, Dolly McPherson writes, "In *Caged Bird,* Maya Angelou undergoes the archetypal American journey of initiation and discovery"; McPherson, "Initiation and Self-Discovery and Self-Discovery," 44. Angelou herself emphasizes in later volumes of her autobiography that her sojourn in Africa did not strip her of her liberal Americanism: first in commenting on her temporary unemployment ("When I was young, poor and destitute I had resisted welfare in the U.S. I certainly wasn't about to ask for assistance in a country which was having trouble feeding its own nationals" [*The Heart of a Woman,* 830]) and then in describing the African American expatriate community in Ghana ("we were still American individualists, bred in a climate which lauded the independent character in legend and lore" [*All God's Children,* 948]).

9. See Cruz, "From Farce to Tragedy."

10. See Moallem and Boal, "Multicultural Nationalism and the Poetics of Inauguration." Angelou's reflections on the symbolism of her role as inaugural poet speaks to multiculturalism's impulses to transform and co-opt: "It is probably fitting that a black woman try to speak to the alienation, the abandonment and to the hope of healing those inflictions which have befallen all Americans, that accounts for white Americans feeling so estranged. Somehow a black woman knows all about that"; quoted in Trescott, "Poet to Read," A1. Angelou's representativity challenges the naturalization of white male norms and interests that underwrite U.S. citizenship while enabling her individual success to mystify the systemic racism that would continue to grow under Clinton.

11. The exception to this erasure of the postwar Black Left is Gaines, *African Americans in Ghana.*

12. See Perkins, *Autobiography as Activism.*

13. On Black Power studies, see Joseph, "An Emerging Mosaic." James Campbell's

discussion of Angelou's activism reveals the need to rethink overly rigid paradigms of civil rights and Black Power struggles. He writes somewhat dismissively that "her politics, by her own account, were driven more by enthusiasm than ideological consistency"; Campbell, *Middle Passages,* 344. Campbell assigns Angelou's politics to personal idiosyncrasy, but the postwar Black internationalist Left in fact spanned groups and ideologies that are often placed in discrete categories.

14. Schueller, *Locating Race,* 5.

15. Cudjoe, "Maya Angelou: The Autobiographical Statement Updated"; Lupton, *Maya Angelou: A Critical Companion.*

16. Angelou, *The Heart of a Woman,* 713.

17. The Black feminism of the autobiographical volumes preceding *The Heart of a Woman* is summed up by Angelou's assertion towards the end of *I Know Why the Caged Bird Sings* that the Black woman

> is caught in the tripartite crossfire of masculine prejudice, white illogic hate and Black lack of power.
>
> The fact that the adult American Negro female emerges a formidable character is often met with amazement, distaste and even belligerence. It is seldom accepted as an inevitable outcome of the struggle won by survivors and deserves respect if not enthusiastic acceptance. (209)

18. Johnson, "The Heart of a Woman," 971.

19. Angelou, *The Heart of a Woman,* 623.

20. Ibid., 651.

21. Ibid., 651–652.

22. Ibid., 652.

23. Ibid., 642, 645, 647, 808.

24. Ibid., 664.

25. Ibid., 711–712.

26. Ibid., 712.

27. Ibid.

28. Ibid., 754.

29. Ibid., 748–751.

30. Ibid., 757, 759.

31. In "A Conversation between Rosa Guy and Maya Angelou," the two writers reflect on Malcolm's growth as a result of efforts such as the CAWAH demonstration (229), and *All God's Children* depicts the Malcolm whom Angelou encounters in Ghana as a more introspective, thoughtful, and dialogic leader.

32. Angelou, *The Heart of a Woman,* 810, 809, 823, 825.

33. Ibid., 843.

34. Ibid., 867.

35. On the African American expatriate community in Ghana, see Gaines, *African Americans in Ghana;* and Campbell, *Middle Passages.*

36. Angelou, *All God's Children,* 903.

37. Angelou, *The Heart of a Woman,* 879.

38. See Lupton, *Maya Angelou: A Critical Companion,* 119, for an example of this reading.

39. It is possible to go to the other extreme of privileging the political narrative at the expense of the personal, as Selwyn Cudjoe does. Cudjoe completely assimilates Angelou's reclamation of Black female selfhood into the narrative of the Black social self, evacuating the content and significance of her experience as a mother, which simply becomes an allegory of the racial struggle for self-determination: "The entrance of Guy into the University of Ghana and his attempt to wrest control of his life from his mother (that is, the mother country, the dominant power, and so on) point to a new social self. The movement of Africa suggests that inherent in the formulation of the Afro-American self is the related African dimension that cannot be ignored as Afro-Americans try to determine who they are and where they belong"; Cudjoe, "Maya Angelou: The Autobiographical Statement Updated," 300.

40. Angelou, *All God's Children,* 949.

41. Ibid., 987.

42. Ibid.

43. Ibid., 990.

44. Ibid., 996. On the OAAU see Sales, *From Civil Rights to Black Liberation.*

45. Angelou, *All God's Children,* 903.

46. Ibid., 1050.

47. Ibid., 918. In a scene involving a Black American couple, Angelou depicts an example of the "unceasing parade of naïve travelers who thought that an airline ticket to Africa would erase the past and open wide the gates to a perfect future"; Angelou, *All God's Children,* 919. Angelou and the other women expatriates lambaste the sexist desire to "come to Mother Africa to suckle from her breasts" (ibid., 917), and point out that in the wake of colonialism, "what the continent needs is about five hundred artesian well diggers and about five hundred agronomists" (ibid., 918). However, Angelou later observes that "possibly we saw our now seldom expressed hopes" (ibid., 919) in the desire to be welcomed into Africa, and she arguably fulfills this desire through her vignettes of homecoming. Lupton has criticized the conclusion's romanticization of Africa; see Lupton, *Maya Angelou: A Critical Companion,* 144.

48. Angelou, *A Song Flung Up to Heaven,* 1062.

49. Ibid., 1093.

50. Ibid., 1096.

51. Campbell, *Middle Passages,* 360.

52. Ibid., 359.

53. Williams, "Base and Superstructure in Marxist Cultural Theory," 138.

54. On Childress's *Those Other People*, see Washington, "Alice Childress," 198.

55. Alice Childress also wrote *A Hero Ain't Nothin' But a Sandwich* (1973); *Rainbow*

Jordan (1981); *Many Closets* (1987); and *Those Other People* (1989). Rosa Guy's other novels include her young adult trilogy, *The Friends* (1973), *Ruby* (1976), and *Edith Jackson* (1978); and *The Disappearance* (1979); *Mirror of Her Own* (1983); *New Guys around the Block* (1983); *Paris, Peewee, and Big Dog* (1984); *A Measure of Time* (1983); *My Love, My Love, or, The Peasant Girl* (1985); and *And I Heard a Bird Sing* (1987).

56. See for example Riley, Mohanty, and Pratt, *Feminism and War*; Puar, *Terrorist Assemblages*; Muñoz, *Cruising Utopia*; and Eng, *The Feeling of Kinship*.

57. "Homonormativity," a term coined by Lisa Duggan, and "queer liberalism" refer to lesbian and gay politics that strive for inclusion into rather than contestation of the heteronormative, neoliberal socioeconomic order; see Duggan, "The New Homonormativity: The Sexual Politics of Neoliberalism." On "queer liberalism," see Eng, Halberstam, and Muñoz, "What's Queer about Queer Studies Now?" "U.S. sexual exceptionalism" is Puar's term for celebrations of the exceptional democracy of the U.S. nation-state through its supposed sexual freedoms and incorporation of homosexuals into its citizenry in contrast to Orientalist constructions of repressive, homophobic Muslim masculinism; see Puar, *Terrorist Assemblages*.

58. Collins, *From Black Power to Hip Hop*, 153.

59. Ibid., 155.

60. Ibid., 152.

Bibliography

Adell, Sandra. "Foreword." In Rosa Guy, *Bird at My Window,* ix–xix. Minneapolis: Coffee House Press, 2001.

Ahmad, Aijaz. *In Theory: Classes, Nations, Literatures.* London: Verso, 1992.

Aiken, Charles. Oral history interview. Box 22, Folder 17, Alice Childress Papers. Schomburg Center for Research in Black Culture, New York Public Library.

Alarcón, Norma, Caren Kaplan, and Minoo Moallem. "Introduction: Between Woman and Nation." In *Between Woman and Nation: Nationalisms, Transnational Feminisms, and the State,* ed. Caren Kaplan, Norma Alarcón, and Minoo Moallem, 1–18. Durham, N.C.: Duke University Press, 1999.

Albee, Edward. *Who's Afraid of Virginia Woolf?* New York: Atheneum, n.d.

Alexander, Elizabeth. "'Coming Out Blackened and Whole': Fragmentation and Reintegration in Audre Lorde's *Zami* and *The Cancer Journals.*" In *Skin Deep, Spirit Strong: The Black Female Body in American Culture,* ed. Kimberly Wallace-Sanders, 218–236. Ann Arbor: University of Michigan Press, 2002.

Allen, James S. "The Scottsboro Struggle." In *American Communism and Black Americans: A Documentary History, 1930–1934,* ed. Philip S. Foner and Herbert Shapiro, 307–318. Philadelphia, Pa.: Temple University Press, 1991.

Angelou, Maya. *All God's Children Need Traveling Shoes* (1986). In *The Collected Autobiographies of Maya Angelou.* New York: The Modern Library, 2004.

———. *The Heart of a Woman* (1981). In *The Collected Autobiographies of Maya Angelou.* New York: The Modern Library, 2004.

———. *I Know Why the Caged Bird Sings* (1969). In *The Collected Autobiographies of Maya Angelou.* New York: The Modern Library, 2004.

———. *On the Pulse of the Morning.* New York: Random House, 1993.

———. *A Song Flung Up to Heaven* (2002). In *The Collected Autobiographies of Maya Angelou.* New York: The Modern Library, 2004.

Baird, Keith E. "Gripping Novel That's Saying Something." *Freedomways* 6, no. 3 (1966): 276–277.

Bakhtin, M. M. *The Dialogic Imagination*. Ed. Michael Holquist. Trans. Caryl Emerson and Michael Holquist. Austin: University of Texas Press, 1981.

Baldwin, James. "The Black Boy Looks at the White Boy." In Baldwin, *Nobody Knows My Name: More Notes of a Native Son*, 216–241. New York: Dial Press, 1961.

Baldwin, Kate. *Beyond the Color Line and the Iron Curtain: Reading Encounters between Black and Red*. Durham, N.C.: Duke University Press, 2002.

Bambara, Toni Cade, ed. *The Black Woman: An Anthology*. New York: Washington Square Press, 2005.

———. "On the Issue of Roles." In Bambara, *The Black Woman: An Anthology*, 123–135. New York: Washington Square Press, 2005.

Bartolovich, Crystal. "Global Capital and Transnationalism." In *A Companion to Postcolonial Studies*, ed. Henry Schwarz and Sangeeta Ray, 126–161. Malden, Mass.: Blackwell, 2000.

Beal, Frances. "Double Jeopardy: To Be Black and Female." In Toni Cade Bambara, *The Black Woman: An Anthology*, 109–122. New York: Washington Square Press, 2005.

———. Interview by Loretta J. Ross, March 18, 2005. In Voices of Feminism Oral History Project. Sophia Smith Collection, Smith College, Northampton, Massachusetts.

Beauvoir, Simone de. *The Second Sex*. New York: Vintage Books, 1989.

Benjamin, Walter. "Theses on the Philosophy of History." In Benjamin, *Illuminations*, 253–264. New York: Schocken Books, 1969.

"Bestselling Author Terry McMillan Confronts Her Gay Ex-Husband." Transcript for *The Oprah Winfrey Show*, November 9, 2005. Livingston, N.Y.: Burrelle's Information Services.

Biondi, Martha. *To Stand and Fight: The Struggle for Civil Rights in Postwar New York City*. Cambridge, Mass.: Harvard University Press, 2003.

Black, Cheryl. "'New Negro' Performance in Art and Life: Fredi Washington and the Theatrical Columns of *The People's Voice*, 1943–1947." *Theatre History Studies* 24 (June 2004): 57–72.

"Black Women: Internationalizing the Struggle." *Freedomways* 15, no. 1 (1975): 5–6.

Bogle, Donald. *Brown Sugar: Over One Hundred Years of America's Black Female Superstars*. New York: Continuum, 2007.

Boldt, Menno. *Surviving as Indians: The Challenge of Self-Government*. Toronto: University of Toronto Press, 1993.

Bond, Jean Carey. "For Colored Girls Who Have Considered Suicide." *Freedomways* 16, no. 3 (1976): 187–191.

———, and Carole E. Gregory. "Two Views of *Black Macho and the Myth of the Superwoman*." *Freedomways* 19, no. 1 (1979): 13–26.

———, and Patricia Peery. "Is the Black Male Castrated?" In *The Black Woman: An Anthology*, ed. Toni Cade Bambara, 141–148. New York: Washington Square Press, 2005.

Borstelmann, Thomas. *The Cold War and the Color Line: American Race Relations in the Global Arena.* Cambridge, Mass.: Harvard University Press, 2001.

Braxton, Joanne M. "Symbolic Geography and Psychic Landscapes: A Conversation with Maya Angelou." In *Maya Angelou's I Know Why the Caged Bird Sings: A Casebook,* ed. Joanne M. Braxton, 3–20. New York: Oxford University Press, 1999.

Brennan, Timothy. *At Home in the World: Cosmopolitanism Now.* Cambridge: Harvard University Press, 1997.

Brooks, Daphne A. *Bodies in Dissent: Spectacular Performance of Race and Freedom, 1850–1910.* Durham, N.C.: Duke University Press, 2006.

Brooks, Tim, and Richard Keith Spottswood. *Lost Sounds: Blacks and the Birth of the Recording Industry, 1890–1919.* Urbana: University of Illinois Press, 2004.

Brown, Lloyd L. "Which Way for the Negro Writer?" *Masses and Mainstream* 4 (March 1951): 53–63, and 4 (April 1951): 50–59.

Burr, Zofia. *Of Women, Poetry, and Power: Strategies of Address in Dickinson, Miles, Brooks, Lorde, and Angelou.* Urbana: University of Illinois Press, 2002.

Campbell, James. *Middle Passages: African American Journeys to Africa, 1787–2005.* New York: Penguin Press, 2006.

Campbell, Jennifer. "'It's a Time in the Land': Gendering Black Power and Sarah E. Wright's Place in the Tradition of Black Women's Writing." *African American Review* (1997): 211–222.

Carby, Hazel. *Race Men.* Cambridge: Harvard University Press, 1998.

———. *Reconstructing Womanhood: The Emergence of the Afro-American Woman Novelist.* New York: Oxford University Press, 1987.

———. "White Woman Listen! Black Feminism and the Boundaries of Sisterhood." In *The Empire Strikes Back: Race and Racism in 70s Britain,* ed. The Centre for Contemporary Cultural Studies, 212–235. London: Hutchinson, 1982.

Carlston, Erin G. "*Zami* and the Politics of Plural Identity." In *Sexual Practice, Textual Theory: Lesbian Cultural Criticism,* ed. Susan J. Wolfe and Julia Penelope, 226–236. Cambridge, Mass.: Blackwell, 1993.

Carter, Dan T. *Scottsboro: A Tragedy of the American South.* London: Oxford University Press, 1975.

Carter, Steven. *Hansberry's Drama.* New York: Meridian, 1993.

Cheney, Anne. *Lorraine Hansberry.* Boston: Twayne Publishers, 1984.

Childress, Alice. "Brief History of the Minstrel Show and It's [*sic*] Form." N.d. Box 45, Folder 16, Alice Childress Papers, MG 649, Manuscripts, Archives, and Rare Book Division, Schomburg Center for Research in Black Culture, New York Public Library, Astor, Lenox and Tilden Foundations.

———. "A Candle in a Gale Wind." In *Black Women Writers (1950–1980),* ed. Mari Evans, 111–116. Garden City, N.Y.: Anchor Press/Doubleday, 1984.

———. "Copra: A West Indian Drama." Typescript, n.d. Box 20, Folders 1–5, Alice Childress Papers, Schomburg Center for Research in Black Culture, New York Public Library, Astor, Lenox and Tilden Foundations.

———. "The Depression . . . The New York Hard Winter." Box 18, Folder 10, Alice Childress Papers, Schomburg Center for Research in Black Culture, New York Public Library.

———. FBI File on Alice Childress. Box 1, Folder 8, Alice Childress Papers, Schomburg Center for Research in Black Culture, New York Public Library.

———. "For a Negro Theatre." *Masses and Mainstream* 4 (February 1951): 61–64.

———. Interview by Ann Allen Shockley. Box 1, Folder 6, Alice Childress Papers, MG 649, Schomburg Center for Research in Black Culture, New York Public Library, Astor, Lenox and Tilden Foundations. The original archival location for this interview is Special Collections and Archives, John Hope and Aurelia Elizabeth Franklin Library, Fisk University, Nashville, Tennessee.

———. Interview by Slava Tynes. In "Black Delegation Visits the U.S.S.R." *New World Review* 39, no. 3 (n.d. [ca. 1971]): 9–11.

———. Letter from T. G. Santillan, July 3, 1967. Box 3, Folder 1, Alice Childress Papers, Schomburg Center for Research in Black Culture, New York Public Library.

———. Letter to Anne (no surname), September 9, 1980. Box 7, Folder 6, Alice Childress Papers, Schomburg Center for Research in Black Culture, New York Public Library.

———. Letter to George B. Murphy Jr., n.d. (ca. 1971). Box 4, Folder 4, Alice Childress Papers, Schomburg Center for Research in Black Culture, New York Public Library.

———. Letter to George B. Murphy Jr., n.d. (ca. 1971). Box 4, Folder 7, Alice Childress Papers, Schomburg Center for Research in Black Culture, New York Public Library.

———. Letter to Janet (no surname), October 23, 1981. Box 7, Folder 1, Alice Childress Papers, Schomburg Center for Research in Black Culture, New York Public Library.

———. *Like One of the Family: Conversations from a Domestic's Life.* Boston: Beacon Press, 2001.

———. *Moms: A Praise Play for a Black Comedienne.* Alice Childress Papers, Manuscripts, Archives and Rare Books Division, Schomburg Center for Research in Black Culture, The New York Public Library, Astor, Lenox and Tilden Foundations.

———. "A Proposal to Set Up a Dialogue Concerning the Production of an Afro-American Film in the U.S.S.R." Box 4, Folder 7, Alice Childress Papers, Schomburg Center for Research in Black Culture, New York Public Library.

———. "Report on the Gold Coast." N.d. Box 46, Folder 4, Alice Childress Papers, Schomburg Center for Research in Black Culture, New York Public Library.

———. *A Short Walk.* New York: Feminist Press, 2006.

———. "A Short Walk" final manuscript. Box 18, Folder 1, Alice Childress Papers, Schomburg Center for Research in Black Culture, New York Public Library.

———. "A South African Scene from *Gold Through the Trees.*" 1952. Box 20, Folder 10, Alice Childress Papers, Schomburg Center for Research in Black Culture, New York Public Library.

———, Paule Marshall, and Sarah Wright. "The Negro Woman in American Literature." In *Freedomways Reader: Prophets in Their Own Country*, ed. Esther Cooper Jackson and Constance Pohl, 291–298. Boulder, Colo.: Westview Press, 2000.

Chude-Sokei, Louis. *The Last "Darky": Bert Williams, Black-on-Black Minstrelsy, and the African Diaspora*. Durham, N.C.: Duke University Press, 2006.

Cixous, Hélène. "The Laugh of the Medusa." In *Feminisms: An Anthology of Literary Theory and Criticism*, ed. Robyn R. Warhol and Diane Price Herndl, 334–349. New Brunswick, N.J.: Rutgers University Press, 1991.

Clarke, John Henrik. "African Warrior Queens." In *Black Women in Antiquity*, ed. Ivan Van Sertima, 123–134. New Brunswick, N.J.: Transaction Publishers, 1988.

———. "The New Afro-American Nationalism." *Freedomways* 1, no. 4 (1961): 285–295.

———, ed. *Marcus Garvey and the Vision of Africa*. New York: Random House, 1974.

Cleage, Albert B., Jr. *Black Christian Nationalism: New Directions for the Black Church*. New York: William Morrow & Company, 1972.

———. *The Black Messiah*. New York: Sheed and Ward, 1969.

Clifford, James. "Traveling Cultures." In Clifford, *Routes: Travel and Translation in the Late Twentieth Century*. Cambridge, Mass.: Harvard University Press, 1997.

Collins, Patricia Hill. *From Black Power to Hip Hop: Racism, Nationalism, and Feminism*. Philadelphia, Pa.: Temple University Press, 2006.

Combahee River Collective. "A Black Feminist Statement." In *This Bridge Called My Back: Writings by Radical Women of Color*, ed. Cherríe Moraga and Gloria Anzaldúa, 210–218. New York: Kitchen Table: Women of Color Press, 1983.

Cruse, Harold. *The Crisis of the Negro Intellectual: A Historical Analysis of the Failure of Black Leadership*. New York: Quill, 1984.

Cruz, Jon. "From Farce to Tragedy: Reflections on the Reification of Race at Century's End." In *Mapping Multiculturalism*, ed. Avery F. Gordon and Christopher Newfield, 19–39. Minneapolis: University of Minnesota Press, 1996.

Cudjoe, Selwyn. "Maya Angelou: The Autobiographical Statement Updated." In *Reading Black, Reading Feminist: A Critical Anthology*, ed. Henry Louis Gates Jr., 272–306. New York: Penguin, 1990.

Culverson, Donald R. *Contesting Apartheid: U.S. Activism, 1960–1987*. Boulder, Colo.: Westview Press, 1999.

Curiel, Barbara Brinson, David Kazanjian, Katherine Kinney, Steven Mailloux, Jay Mechling, John Carlos Rowe, George Sánchez, Shelley Streeby, and Henry Yu. "Introduction." In *Post-Nationalist American Studies*, ed. John Carlos Rowe, 1–21. Berkeley: University of California Press, 2000.

Currie, Kathleen. Interview with Marvel Cooke, Washington Press Club Foundation. Transcript at http://www.wpcf.org/oralhistory/cook5.html. Accessed 5 October 2010.

Cuthbert, Marion. *Democracy and the Negro*. New York: Pilgrim Press, 1936.

Dale, Thelma. "Reconversion and the Negro People." *Political Affairs* (October 1945): 894–901.

Davies, Carole Boyce. *Black Women, Writing and Identity: Migrations of the Subject.* London: Routledge, 1994.

———. *Left of Karl Marx: The Political Life of Black Communist Claudia Jones.* Durham, N.C.: Duke University Press, 2008.

Davis, Benjamin. "Introduction." In Harry Raymond, *The Ingrams Shall Not Die! Story of Georgia's New Terror.* New York: Daily Worker, 1948.

Davis, Thulani. "Don't Worry, Be Buppie: Black Novelists Head for the Mainstream." *Village Voice Literary Supplement,* May 8, 1990, 26–29.

Dawahare, Anthony. *Nationalism, Marxism, and African American Literature between the Wars: A New Pandora's Box.* Jackson: University Press of Mississippi, 2003.

D'Emilio, John. *Sexual Politics, Sexual Communities.* Chicago: University of Chicago Press, 1983.

De Veaux, Alexis. *Warrior Poet: A Biography of Audre Lorde.* New York: W. W. Norton and Company, 2004.

Denning, Michael. *The Cultural Front: The Laboring of American Culture in the Twentieth Century.* London: Verso, 1997.

DeShazer, Mary. *A Poetics of Resistance: Women Writing in El Salvador, South Africa, and the United States.* Ann Arbor: University of Michigan Press, 1994.

Dhairyam, Sagri. "'Artifacts for Survival': Remapping the Contours of Poetry with Audre Lorde." *Feminist Studies* 18, no. 2 (Summer 1992): 229–256.

Dixler, Elsa Jane. "The Woman Question: Women and the American Communist Party." Ph.D. diss., Yale University, 1974.

Dubey, Madhu. *Black Women Novelists and the Nationalist Aesthetic.* Bloomington: Indiana University Press, 1994.

Duggan, Lisa. "The New Homonormativity: The Sexual Politics of Neoliberalism." In *Materializing Democracy: Toward a Revitalized Cultural Politics,* ed. Russ Castronovo and Dana Nelson, 175–194. Durham: Duke University Press, 2002.

Dunbar, Robert. "The Odd Couple." *The Irish Times,* October 27, 2004, 12.

Edelman, Lee. "Tearooms and Sympathy, or, The Epistemology of the Water Closet." In *The Lesbian and Gay Studies Reader,* ed. Henry Abelove, Michèle Aina Barale, and David M. Halperin, 553–574. New York: Routledge, 1993.

Edmondson, Belinda. *Making Men: Gender, Literary Authority, and Women's Writing in Caribbean Narrative.* Durham, N.C.: Duke University Press, 1999.

Effiong, Philip Uko. "History, Myth, and Revolt in Lorraine Hansberry's *Les Blancs.*" *African American Review* 32 (1998): 273–283.

Elbaum, Max. *Revolution in the Air: Sixties Radicals Turn to Lenin, Mao and Che.* London: Verso, 2002.

Ely, Melvin Patrick. *The Adventures of Amos 'n' Andy: A Social History of an American Phenomenon.* New York: Free Press, 1991.

Eng, David. *The Feeling of Kinship: Queer Liberalism and the Racialization of Intimacy.* Durham, N.C.: Duke University Press, 2010.

———, Judith Halberstam, and Jose Esteban Muñoz, "What's Queer about Queer Studies Now?" *Social Text* 23, nos. 3–4 (Fall–Winter 2005): 1–17.

Esslin, Martin. *The Theatre of the Absurd.* Woodstock, N.Y.: Overlook Press, 1973.

Fanon, Frantz. "On National Culture." In *The Wretched of the Earth,* trans. Richard Philcox, 145–180. New York: Grove Press, 2004.

Farr, Cecilia Conchar. *Reading Oprah. How Oprah's Book Club Changed the Way America Reads.* Albany: State University of New York Press, 2005.

Ferguson, Roderick. *Aberrations in Black: Toward a Queer of Color Critique.* Minneapolis: University of Minnesota Press, 2004.

Fleras, Augie. "Politicising Indigeneity: Ethno-Politics in White Settler Dominions." In *Indigenous Peoples' Rights in Australia, Canada, and New Zealand,* ed. Paul Havemann, 187–234. Auckland: Oxford University Press, 1999.

Flynn, Elizabeth Gurley. *Woman's Place in the Fight for a Better World.* New York: International Publishers, 1947.

Foley, Barbara. *Radical Representations: Politics and Form in U.S. Proletarian Fiction, 1929–1941.* Durham, N.C.: Duke University Press, 1993.

Forbes, Camille F. *Introducing Bert Williams: Burnt Cork, Broadway, and the Story of America's First Black Star.* New York: Basic Books, 2008.

Gaines, Kevin. *African Americans in Ghana: Black Expatriates and the Civil Rights Era.* Chapel Hill: University of North Carolina Press, 2006.

———. "From Center to Margin: Internationalism and the Origins of Black Feminism." In *Materializing Democracy: Toward a Revitalized Cultural Politics,* ed. Russ Castronovo and Dana D. Nelson, 294–313. Durham, N.C.: Duke University Press, 2002.

Garber, Marjorie. *Vested Interests: Cross-Dressing and Cultural Anxiety.* New York: Routledge, 1997.

Garvey, Marcus. "Why the Black Star Line Failed." In *Marcus Garvey and the Vision of Africa,* ed. John Henrik Clarke, 139–149. New York: Random House, 1974.

Garvey, Marcus, Jr. "Garveyism: Some Reflections on Its Significance for Today." In *Marcus Garvey and the Vision of Africa,* ed. John Henrik Clarke, 375–387. New York: Random House, 1974.

Gaspar, David Barry, and Michel-Rolph Trouillot. "Afterword History, Fiction, and the Slave Experience." In Guy Endore, *Babouk,* 183–199. New York: Monthly Review Press, 1991.

Genet, Jean. *The Blacks: A Clown Show.* New York: Grove Press, 1988.

Gilkes, Cheryl Townsend. "The Roles of Church and Community Mothers: Ambivalent American Sexism or Fragmented African Familyhood?" In *African-American Religion: Interpretive Essays in History and Culture,* ed. Timothy F. Fulop and Albert J. Raboteau, 367–388. New York: Routledge, 1997.

Gilroy, Paul. *The Black Atlantic: Modernity and Double Consciousness.* Cambridge, Mass.: Harvard University Press 1993.

Gomez, Jewelle. "Lorraine Hansberry: Uncommon Warrior." In *Reading Black, Reading Feminist: A Critical Anthology,* ed. Henry Louis Gates Jr., 301–317. New York: Meridian, 1990.

Good, Marcie. "Inspiration for Hire: Hallmark has Hired Poet Maya Angelou." *Saturday Post,* 20 July 2002, SP1.

Gore, Dayo F., Jeanne Theoharis, and Komozi Woodard, ed. *Want to Start a Revolution? Radical Women in the Black Freedom Struggle.* New York: New York University Press, 2009.

Grewal, Inderpal. "Autobiographic Subjects and Diasporic Locations: *Meatless Days* and *Borderlands.*" In *Scattered Hegemonies: Postmodernity and Transnational Feminist Practices,* ed. Inderpal Grewal and Caren Kaplan, 231–254. Minneapolis: University of Minnesota Press, 1994.

Grewal, Inderpal, and Caren Kaplan, eds. *Scattered Hegemonies: Postmodernity and Transnational Feminist Practices.* Minneapolis: University of Minnesota Press, 1994.

———. "Introduction: Transnational Feminism Practices and Questions of Postmodernity." In *Scattered Hegemonies: Postmodernity and Transnational Feminist Practices,* ed. Inderpal Grewal and Caren Kaplan, 1–33. Minneapolis: University of Minnesota Press, 1994.

Griffin, Farah Jasmine. "Conflict and Chorus: Reconsidering Toni Cade's *The Black Woman: An Anthology.*" In *Is It Nation Time? Contemporary Essays on Black Power and Black Nationalism,* ed. Eddie S. Glaude Jr., 113–129. Chicago: University of Chicago Press, 2002.

Guy, Rosa. *Bird at My Window.* Minneapolis: Coffee House Press, 2001.

———. "A Conversation between Rosa Guy and Maya Angelou." In *Conversations with Maya Angelou,* ed. Jeffrey M. Elliot, 218–240. Jackson: University Press of Mississippi, 1989.

———. "Haiti: The Enigma of the Caribbean." *Freedomways* 4 (Summer 1964): 413–423.

———. *The Sun, the Sea, a Touch of the Wind.* New York: Plume, 1996.

Hairston, Loyle. "Black Writers' Views of America." *Freedomways* 19, no. 3 (1979): 151–162.

Hall, James C. *Mercy, Mercy Me: African-American Culture and the American Sixties.* Oxford: Oxford University Press, 2001.

Hamilton, Charles V. *Adam Clayton Powell, Jr.: The Political Biography of an American Dilemma.* New York: Atheneum, 1991.

Hansberry, Lorraine. "Andromeda the Thief." Box 50, Folder 2, Lorraine Hansberry Papers, Manuscripts, Archives and Rare Books Division, Schomburg Center for Research in Black Culture, New York Public Library, Astor, Lenox and Tilden Foundations. Lorraine Hansberry Properties Trust, Joi Gresham and Matthew Lyons, Trustees.

———. "The Apples of Autumn." Box 50, Folder 4, Lorraine Hansberry Papers, Schomburg Center for Research in Black Culture, New York Public Library.

———. "Author's Notes on Characterization, Structure and Content." Box 50, Folder

4, Lorraine Hansberry Papers, Schomburg Center for Research in Black Culture, New York Public Library.

———. "CNA Presents Exciting New Dramatic Revue." *Freedom* 2 (May 1952): 7.

———. "Egyptian People Fight for Freedom." *Freedom* 2 (March 1952): 3.

———. "Flowers for the General." Box 50, Folder 4, Lorraine Hansberry Papers, Schomburg Center for Research in Black Culture, New York Public Library.

———. "Genet, Mailer, and The New Paternalism." *The Village Voice* 1 (June 1961): 10.

———. "'Gold Coast's' Rulers Go, Ghana Moves to Freedom." *Freedom* 1 (December 1951): 2.

———. "'Illegal' Conference Shows Peace Is Key to Freedom." *Freedom* 2 (April 1952): 3.

———. "*Les Blancs* First Final Adaptation by R. N.—'L.'" 1966. Box 33, Folder 2, Lorraine Hansberry Papers. Schomburg Center for Research in Black Culture, New York Public Library.

———. *Les Blancs: The Collected Last Plays.* New York: Vintage Books, 1994.

———. "Letter to *The Ladder.*" *The Ladder* 1 (August 1957): 28–29.

———. "The Negro Writer and His Roots: Toward a New Romanticism." *Black Scholar* 12 (March–April 1981): 2–12.

———. "Negroes Cast in Same Old Roles in TV Shows." *Freedom* 1 (June 1951): 7.

———. "On Arthur Miller, Marilyn Monroe, and 'Guilt.'" In *Women in Theatre: Compassion and Hope,* ed. Karen Malpede, 173–176. New York: Drama Book Publishers, 1983.

———. "The Outsider." *Freedom* 3 (April 1953): 7.

———. Play Scripts *Les Blancs,* Konrad Matthei Production—Artistic Script Revisions with Nemiroff's Annotations 1960s. Box 33, Folder 4, Lorraine Hansberry Papers, Schomburg Center for Research in Black Culture, New York Public Library.

———. *The Sign in Sidney Brustein's Window.* In Hansberry, *A Raisin in the Sun and The Sign in Sidney Brustein's Window.* New York: Vintage Books, 1995.

———. "Simone de Beauvoir and *The Second Sex*: An American Commentary." In *Words of Fire: An Anthology of African-American Feminist Thought,* ed. Beverly Guy-Sheftall, 128–142. New York: The New Press, 1995.

———. *To Be Young, Gifted and Black: Lorraine Hansberry in Her Own Words.* Adapted by Robert Nemiroff. New York: Vintage Books, 1995.

———, and Alice Childress. "Negro History Festival." Box 45, Folder 25, Alice Childress Papers, Schomburg Center for Research in Black Culture, New York Public Library.

Hartman, Saidiya. *Lose Your Mother: A Journey along the Atlantic Slave Route.* New York: Farrar, Straus, and Giroux, 2007.

Hathaway, Heather. *Caribbean Waves: Relocating Claude McKay and Paule Marshall.* Bloomington: Indiana University Press, 1999.

Haywood, Harry. *Black Bolshevik: Autobiography of an Afro-American Communist.* Chicago: Liberator Press, 1978.

———. "The Scottsboro Decision." In *American Communism and Black Americans: A Documentary History, 1930–1934*, ed. Philip S. Foner and Herbert Shapiro, 294–305. Philadelphia, Pa.: Temple University Press, 1991.

Hernton, Calvin. "The Sexual Mountain and Black Women Writers." *Black American Literature Forum* 18, no. 4 (1984): 139–145.

Hill, Rebecca. "Fosterites and Feminists, or 1950s Ultra-Leftists and the Invention of AMeriKKKA." *New Left Review* 228 (March/April 1998): 67–90.

Hill, Robert A. "Making Noise: Marcus Garvey *Dada*, August 1922." In *Picturing Us: African American Identity in Photography*, ed. Deborah Willis, 180–205. New York: New Press, 1994.

Hong, Grace Kyungwon. *The Ruptures of American Capital: Women of Color Feminism and the Culture of Immigrant Labor.* Minneapolis: University of Minnesota Press, 2006.

hooks, bell. *Ain't I a Woman: Black Women and Feminism.* Boston: South End Press, 1999.

Horne, Gerald. *Black and Brown: African Americans and the Mexican Revolution, 1910–1920.* New York: New York University Press, 2005.

———. *Communist Front? The Civil Rights Congress, 1946–1956.* London: Associated University Press, 1988.

———. *Race Woman: The Lives of Shirley Graham Du Bois.* New York: New York University Press, 2000.

Hughes, Langston, and Milton Meltzer. *Black Magic: A Pictorial History of the African-American in the Performing Arts.* New York: Da Capo Press, 1990.

Hull, Gloria T., Patricia Bell Scott, and Barbara Smith, eds. *All the Women Are White, All the Blacks Are Men, but Some of Us Are Brave.* New York: The Feminist Press, 1982.

Hutchinson, Earl Ofari. *Blacks and Reds: Race and Class in Conflict, 1919–1990,* East Lansing: Michigan State University Press, 1995.

Inman, Mary. *In Woman's Defense.* Los Angeles: Committee to Organize the Advancement of Women, 1940.

"Interview with Rosa Guy." At 2nd International Conference of Caribbean Women Writers, Trinidad & Tobago, April 27, 1990. At http://www.pancaribbean.com/banyan/rosaguy.htm. Accessed February 15, 2011.

Jackson, Esther Cooper. "Introduction." In *Freedomways Reader: Prophets in Their Own Country*, ed. Esther Cooper Jackson and Constance Pohl, xix–xxx. Boulder, Colo.: Westview Press, 2000.

James, C. L. R. "Preface to the Vintage Edition." In James, *The Black Jacobins: Toussaint L'Ouverture and the San Domingo Revolution.* 2nd ed., rev. New York: Vintage Books, 1989.

James, Joy. *Shadowboxing: Representations of Black Feminist Politics.* New York: St. Martin's Press, 1999.

Jean Genet's The Blacks: A Panel Discussion. Dir. James Brigs Murray. New York Public Library for the Performing Arts, Theatre on Film and Tape Archive. 2003.

Jennings, La Vinia Delois. *Alice Childress.* New York: Twayne Publishers, 1995.

———. "Afterword: The Black Woman's Life as a Minstrel Show." In Alice Childress, *A Short Walk,* 335–359. New York: Feminist Press, 2006.

Johnson, David K. *The Lavender Scare: The Cold War Persecution of Gays and Lesbians in the Federal Government.* Chicago: University of Chicago Press, 2004.

Johnson, Georgia Douglas. "The Heart of a Woman." In *The Norton Anthology of African American Literature,* 2nd. ed., ed. Henry Louis Gates Jr. and Nellie Y. McKay. New York: W. W. Norton and Company, 1997.

Jones, Claudia. "Dear Comrade Foster, The Following is the Autobiographical (Personal, Political, Medical) History that I Promised . . . Comradely, Claudia Jones (December 6, 1955)." *American Communist History* 4, no. 1 (2005): 85–93.

———. "Discussion Article." *Political Affairs* 25 (August 1945): 717–720.

———. "An End to the Neglect of the Problems of the Negro Woman!" In *Words of Fire: An Anthology of African-American Feminist Thought,* ed. Beverly Guy-Sheftall, 108–123. New York: The New Press, 1995.

———. "For the Unity of Women in the Cause of Peace!" *Political Affairs* 30 (February 1951): 151–168.

———. "International Women's Day and the Struggle for Peace." *Political Affairs* 29 (March 1950): 33–34.

———. "Negro Women Launch New Movement for Peace and Freedom." *The Worker.* 25 November 1951, 8.

———. "On the Right to Self-Determination for the Negro People in the Black Belt." *Political Affairs* (January 1946): 67–77.

Jones, James Earl, and Penelope Niven. *James Earl Jones: Voices and Silences.* New York: Charles Scribner's Sons, 1993.

Jones, John Hudson. "'Gold Through Trees' Has Beauty and Power." *Daily Worker,* April 10, 1953, 10.

———. "TV's Amos 'n' Andy." *Masses and Mainstream* 4 (September 1951): 59–61.

Joseph, Gloria I., and Hortense M. Rowe, eds. *Hell under God's Orders: Hurricane Hugo in St. Croix—Disaster and Survival.* St. Croix: Winds of Change Press, 1990.

Joseph, Peniel E. "An Emerging Mosaic: Rewriting Postwar African-American History." In *A Companion to African-American Studies,* ed. Lewis R. Gordon and Jane Anna Gordon, 400–416. Malden, Mass.: Blackwell Publishing, 2006.

Kaplan, Amy. *The Anarchy of Empire in the Making of U.S. Culture.* Cambridge, Mass.: Harvard University Press, 2002.

———, and Donald Pease, eds. *Cultures of United States Imperialism.* Durham, N.C.: Duke University Press, 1993.

Kaplan, Caren, Norma Alarcón, and Minoo Moallem, eds. *Between Woman and Nation: Nationalisms, Transnational Feminisms, and the State.* Durham, N.C.: Duke University Press, 1999.

Katz, Maude White. "Learning from History—The Ingram Case of the 1940s." *Freedomways* 19, no. 2 (1979): 82–86.

Kelley, Robin D. G. *Freedom Dreams: The Black Radical Imagination.* Boston: Beacon Press, 2002.

———. *Race Rebels: Culture, Politics, and the Black Working Class.* New York: The Free Press, 1994.

———. "Stormy Weather: Reconstructing Black (Inter)Nationalism in the Cold War Era." In *Is It Nation Time? Contemporary Essays on Black Power and Black Nationalism,* ed. Eddie S. Glaude Jr., 67–90. Chicago: University of Chicago Press, 2002.

———, and Betsy Esch. "Black Like Mao: Red China and Black Revolution." In *Afro Asia: Revolutionary Political and Cultural Connections between African Americans and Asian Americans,* ed. Fred Ho and Bill V. Mullen, 97–154. Durham, N.C.: Duke University Press, 2008.

Kemp, Yakini B. "Writing Power: Identity Complexities and the Exotic Erotic in Audre Lorde's Writing." *Studies in the Literary Imagination* 37, no. 2 (Fall 2004): 21–36.

Killens, John O. "Black Man in the New China." *Black World* 25, no. 1 (November 1975): 28–42.

———. "Black Man's Burden." In Killens, *Black Man's Burden,* 147–176. New York: Simon and Schuster, 1965.

———. "The Black Writer Vis-à-Vis His Country." In Killens, *Black Man's Burden,* 23–54. New York: Simon and Schuster, 1965.

———. "The Literary Genius of Alice Childress." In *Black Women Writers (1950–1980),* ed. Mari Evans, 129–133. Garden City, N.Y.: Anchor Press/Doubleday, 1984.

———. "The Myth of Non-Violence versus The Right of Self-Defense." In Killens, *Black Man's Burden,* 99–123. New York: Simon and Schuster, 1965.

———, Ossie Davis, Owen Dodson, and James Baldwin. "The Negro Writer in America: A Symposium." *Negro Digest* (June 1963): 54–65.

Kraft, Marion. "The Creative Use of Difference." In *Conversations with Audre Lorde,* ed. Joan Wylie Hall, 146–153. Jackson: University Press of Mississippi, 2004.

Kruks, Sonia. *Retrieving Experience: Subjectivity and Recognition in Feminist Politics.* Ithaca, N.Y.: Cornell University Press, 2001.

Larsen, Neil. "Imperialism, Colonialism, Postcolonialism." In *A Companion to Postcolonial Studies,* ed. Henry Schwarz and Sangeeta Ray, 23–51. Malden, Mass.: Blackwell, 2000.

Lazarus, Neil. *Nationalism and Cultural Practice in the Postcolonial World.* Cambridge: Cambridge University Press, 1999.

Lewis, David Levering. *W. E. B. Du Bois: The Fight for Equality and the American Century, 1919–1963.* New York: Henry Holt and Company, 2001.

Lipari, Lisbeth. "The Rhetoric of Intersectionality: Lorraine Hansberry's 1957 Letters to the *Ladder.*" In *Queering Public Address: Sexualities in American Historical Discourse,* ed. Charles E. Morris III, 220–248. Columbia: University of South Carolina Press, 2007.

Lorde, Audre. "Apartheid U.S.A." In Lorde, *A Burst of Light,* 27–38. Ithaca, N.Y.: Firebrand Books, 1988.

———. *A Burst of Light.* Ithaca, N.Y.: Firebrand Books, 1988.

———. "A Burst of Light: Living with Cancer." In Lorde, *A Burst of Light,* 49–134. Ithaca, N.Y.: Firebrand Books, 1988.

———. *The Collected Poems of Audre Lorde.* New York: W. W. Norton and Company, 2000.

———. "Of Generators and Survival—Hugo Letter 12/89." In *Hell under God's Orders: Hurricane Hugo in St. Croix—Disaster and Survival,* ed. Gloria I. Joseph and Hortense M. Rowe, 202–215. St. Croix: Winds of Change Press, 1990.

———. "Grenada Revisited." In Lorde, *Zami, Sister Outsider, Undersong,* 176–190. New York: Quality Paperback Book Club, 1993.

———. "An Interview: Audre Lorde and Adrienne Rich." In Lorde, *Zami, Sister Outsider, Undersong,* 81–109. New York: Quality Paperback Book Club, 1993.

———. "Learning from the 60s." In Lorde, *Zami, Sister Outsider, Undersong,* 134–144. New York: Quality Paperback Book Club, 1993.

———. "Man Child: A Black Lesbian Feminist's Response." In Lorde, *Zami, Sister Outsider, Undersong,* 72–80. New York: Quality Paperback Book Club, 1993.

———. *The Marvelous Arithmetics of Distance: Poems 1987–1992.* New York: Norton, 1993.

———. "The Master's Tools Will Never Dismantle the Master's House." In Lorde, *Zami, Sister Outsider, Undersong,* 110–113. New York: Quality Paperback Book Club, 1993.

———. "Restoration: A Memorial—9/18/91." In Lorde, *The Collected Poems of Audre Lorde,* 456–457. New York: W. W. Norton and Company, 2000.

———. *Zami, Sister Outsider, Undersong.* New York: Quality Paperback Book Club, 1993.

———. "Turning the Beat Around: Lesbian Parenting 1986." In Lorde, *A Burst of Light,* 39–48. Ithaca, N.Y.: Firebrand Books, 1988.

———. *Zami: A Biomythography.* Berkeley, Calif.: Crossing Press, 1982.

Lupton, Mary Jane. *Maya Angelou: A Critical Companion.* Westport, Conn.: Greenwood Press, 1998.

Maguire, Roberta S. "Alice Childress." In *Dictionary of Literary Biography: Twentieth-Century American Dramatists,* ed. Christopher Wheatley, 30–39. Detroit: Gale, 2002.

Mailer, Norman. "Mailer to Hansberry." *The Village Voice,* June 8, 1961, 13.

———. "Theatre: The Blacks." *The Village Voice,* May 11, 1961, 14.

———. "The White Negro: Superficial Reflections on the Hipster." In Mailer, *Advertisements for Myself,* 337–358. New York: G.P. Putnam's Sons, 1959.

Marshall, Paule. *Brown Girl, Brownstones.* New York: Dover Publications, 2009.

———. "Shaping the World of My Art." *New Letters* 40 (Autumn 1973): 97–112.

Maxwell, William. *New Negro, Old Left: African-American Writing and Communism Between the Wars.* New York: Columbia University Press, 1999.

Mayfield, Julian. "A Challenge to a Bestseller: Crisis or Cruse." *Negro Digest* (June 1968): 13.

———. "Into the Mainstream and Oblivion." In *The American Writer and His Roots: Selected Papers from the First Conference of Negro Writers,* ed. AMSAC, 29–34. New York: AMSAC, 1960.

McAvoy, Eugene. "A Woman and a Nation Struggle for Identity." *The Virginian-Pilot* (Norfolk, Va.), October 29, 1995, J2.

McDuffie, Erik S. "The March of Young Southern Black Women: Esther Cooper Jackson, Black Left Feminism, and the Personal and Political Costs of Cold War Repression." In *Anti-Communism and the African American Freedom Movement,* ed. Robbie Lieberman and Clarence Lang, 83–114. New York: Palgrave Macmillan, 2009.

McGill, Lisa D. *Constructing Black Selves: Caribbean American Narratives and the Second Generation.* New York: New York University Press, 2005.

———. "Sister-Outsider: African God(desse)s, Black Feminist Politics, and Audre Lorde's Liberation." In McGill, *Constructing Black Selves,* 117–160.

McKay, Claude. *The Negroes in America.* Ed. Alan L. McLeod. Trans. Robert J. Winter. Port Washington, N.Y.: Kennikat, 1979.

McMillan, Terry. *How Stella Got Her Groove Back.* New York: Viking Press, 1996.

———. Interview with Tavis Smiley. *Tavis Smiley: Late Night on PBS,* aired July 12, 2005. Transcript at http://www.pbs.org/kcet/tavissmiley/archive/200507/20050712_mcmillan.html. Accessed October 30, 2010.

———. "100 Questions I Meant to Ask Him." In *The Honeymoon's Over: True Stories of Love, Marriage, and Divorce,* ed. Andrea Chapin and Sally Wofford-Girand, 89–101. New York: Warner Books, 2007.

———. Transcript of Declaration, *McMillan vs. Plummer,* case no. D05–00513, September 22, 2006. Available at "Terry McMillan Sues Her 'Little Fag' Ex." *The Smoking Gun,* March 22, 2007. Accessed August 4, 2007.

McPherson, Dolly. "Initiation and Self-Discovery." In *Maya Angelou's I Know Why the Caged Bird Sings: A Casebook,* ed. Joanne M. Braxton, 21–47. New York: Oxford University Press, 1999.

Mekas, Jonas. "Movie Journal." *The Village Voice,* June 15, 1961, 13.

Meriwether, James. *Proudly We Can Be Africans: Black Americans and Africa, 1935–1961.* Chapel Hill: University of North Carolina Press, 2002.

Moallem, Minoo, and Iaian A. Boal. "Multicultural Nationalism and the Poetics of Inauguration." In *Between Woman and Nation: Nationalisms, Transnational Feminisms, and the State,* ed. Caren Kaplan, Norma Alarcón, and Minoo Moallem, 243–263. Durham, N.C.: Duke University Press, 1999.

Mohanty, Chandra. "Cartographies of Struggle, Third World Women and the Politics of Feminism." In *Third World Women and the Politics of Feminism,* ed. Chandra Talpade Mohanty, Ann Russo, and Lourdes Torres, 1–47. Bloomington: Indiana University Press, 1991.

Moore, Opal. "An Allegorical Hodgepodge of Haiti." *The Washington Post,* October 9, 1995, C10 (final ed.).

Moore, Richard B. "The Battering of St. Croix: Hugo, FEMA, and the White Media." In *Hell Under God's Orders: Hurricane Hugo in St. Croix—Disaster and Survival,* ed. Gloria I. Joseph and Hortense M. Rowe, 34–37. St. Croix: Winds of Change Press, 1990.

———. "Caribbean Unity and Freedom." *Freedomways* 4, no. 3 (1964): 295–311.

———. "The Critics and Opponents of Marcus Garvey." In *Marcus Garvey and the Vision of Africa,* ed. John Henrik Clarke, 210–235. New York: Random House, 1974.

Moraga, Cherríe, and Gloria Anzaldúa, ed. *This Bridge Called My Back: Writings by Radical Women of Color.* New York: Kitchen Table: Women of Color Press, 1983.

Moses, Wilson Jeremiah. *Black Messiahs and Uncle Toms: Social and Literary Manipulations of a Religious Myth.* Rev. ed. University Park, Pa.: Pennsylvania State University Press, 1993.

Moynihan, Daniel Patrick. *The Negro Family: The Case for National Action.* Washington, D.C.: U.S. Government Printing Office, 1965.

Mullen, Bill. *Popular Fronts: Chicago and African-American Cultural Politics, 1935–46.* Urbana: University of Illinois Press, 1999.

Muñoz, Jose Esteban. *Cruising Utopia: The Then and There of Queer Futurity.* New York: New York University Press, 2009.

Murphy, George B., Jr. "Black Delegation Visits the USSR." Ontario: Northern Book House, n.d. [ca. 1971].

Naison, Mark. *Communists in Harlem during the Depression.* New York: Grove Press, 1983.

"National Negro Congress Meets in Chicago." *The Crisis* 43 (April 1936): 110.

Neal, Larry. "The Black Arts Movement" (1968). In *Within the Circle: An Anthology of African American Literary Criticism from the Harlem Renaissance to the Present,* ed. Angelyn Mitchell, 184–198. Durham: Duke University Press, 1994.

Nemiroff, Robert. "A Critical Background." In Lorraine Hansberry, *Les Blancs: The Collected Last Plays,* 27–35. New York: Vintage Books, 1994.

———. Memo to Lorraine Hansberry, March 3, 1964. Box 30 Lorraine Hansberry Papers, Schomburg Center for Research in Black Culture.

———. "The 101 'Final' Performances of *Sidney Brustein.*" In Lorraine Hansberry, *A Raisin in the Sun and The Sign in Sidney Brustein's Window,* 159–203. New York: Vintage Books, 1995.

Nicholls, David. *From Dessalines to Duvalier: Race, Colour and National Independence in Haiti.* Cambridge: Cambridge University Press, 1979.

Norman, Brian. *The American Protest Essay and National Belonging: Addressing Division.* Albany: State University of New York Press, 2007.

Norris, Jerrie. *Presenting Rosa Guy.* Boston: Twayne Publishers, 1988.

Obourn, Megan. "Audre Lorde: Trauma Theory and Liberal Multiculturalism." *MELUS* 30, no. 3 (Fall 2005): 219–245.

Omi, Michael, and Howard Winant. *Racial Formation in the United States from the 1960s to the 1980s.* New York: Routledge, 1986.

Oprah's Book Club. "*The Heart of a Woman*: About the Book." May 9, 1997. At http://www.oprah.com/oprahsbookclub/About-The-Heart-of-a-Woman-By-Maya-Angelou. Accessed June 7, 2010.

Pache, Ilona, and Regina-Maria Dackweiler. "An Interview with Audre Lorde." In *Conversations with Audre Lorde,* ed. Joan Wylie Hall, 164–170. Jackson: University Press of Mississippi, 2004.

Palumbo-Liu, David. "Hybridities and Histories: Imaging the Rim." In *Postborder City: Cultural Spaces of Bajalta California,* ed. Michael Dear and Gustavo Leclerc, 249–275. New York: Routledge, 2003.

Parker, Andrew, Mary Russo, Doris Sommer, and Patricia Yaeger. "Introduction." In *Nationalisms and Sexualities,* ed. Andrew Parker, Mary Russo, Doris Sommer, and Patricia Yaeger, 1–18. New York: Routledge, 1992.

Parker, Pat. "Revolution: It's Not Neat or Pretty or Quick." In *This Bridge Called My Back: Writings by Radical Women of Color,* ed. Cherríe Moraga and Gloria Anzaldúa, 238–242. New York: Kitchen Table: Women of Color Press, 1983.

Parry, Benita. *Postcolonial Studies: A Materialist Critique.* London: Routledge, 2004.

Peery, Nelson, and the Communist League of America. *The Negro National Colonial Question.* Chicago: Workers Press, 1972.

Perkins, Margo V. *Autobiography as Activism: Three Black Women of the Sixties.* Jackson: University Press of Mississippi, 2000.

Peterson, Rachel. "The People's Voice: Anticommunism and the Progressive African American." Paper presented at the American Studies Association Annual Meeting, October 2008.

Petry, Ann. "Harlem Urged to Attend First Meeting of Women, Inc." *People's Voice,* May 2, 1942, 17.

Plummer, Brenda. "Castro in Harlem: A Cold War Watershed." In *Rethinking the Cold War,* ed. Alan Hunter, 133–153. Philadelphia, Pa.: Temple University Press, 1998.

———. *Rising Wind: Black Americans and U.S. Foreign Affairs, 1935–1960.* Chapel Hill: University of North Carolina Press, 1996.

Pratt, Mary Louise. *Imperial Eyes: Travel Writing and Transculturation.* London: Routledge, 1992.

Preface to "Women of Nigeria Meet in a Historic National Conference." *Freedom* 3, no. 9 (September 1953): 6.

Puar, Jasbir. *Terrorist Assemblages: Homonationalism in Queer Times.* Durham, N.C.: Duke University Press, 2007.

Raymond, Harry. *The Ingrams Shall Not Die! Story of Georgia's New Terror.* New York: Daily Worker, 1948.

Renda, Mary. *Taking Haiti: Military Occupation and the Culture of U.S. Imperialism, 1915–1940.* Chapel Hill: University of North Carolina Press, 2001.

Rich, Adrienne. "The Problem with Lorraine Hansberry." *Freedomways* 19, no. 4 (1979): 247–255.

Riley, Robin L., Chandra Talpade Mohanty, and Minnie Bruce Pratt, eds. *Feminism and War: Confronting U.S. Imperialism*. London: Zed Books, 2008.

Robeson, Paul. "Ho Chi Minh is the Toussaint l'Ouverture of Indo-China" (March 1954). In *Freedomways Reader: Prophets in Their Own Country*, ed. Esther Cooper Jackson and Constance Pohl, 147–149. Boulder, Colo.: Westview Press, 2000.

———. "A Message from the Chairman to Members and Friends of the Council on African Affairs." In *Paul Robeson Speaks*, ed. Philip S. Foner, 223–224. New York: Citadel Press Books, 2002.

———. "Selected Speeches and Writings on Peace, No. 1, 1971." In *Freedomways Reader: Prophets in Their Own Country*, ed. Esther Cooper Jackson and Constance Pohl, 145–147. Boulder, Colo.: Westview Press, 2000.

Rocksborough-Smith, Ian. "'Filling the Gap': Intergenerational Black Radicalism and the Popular Front Ideals of *Freedomways* Magazine's Early Years (1961–1965)." *Afro-Americans in New York Life and History* 31, no. 1 (January 2007): 7–42.

Rogin, Michael. *Blackface, White Noise: Jewish Immigrants in the Hollywood Melting Pot*. Berkeley: University of California Press, 1998.

Rose, Euclid A. *Dependency and Socialism in the Modern Caribbean: Superpower Intervention in Guyana, Jamaica, and Grenada, 1970–1985*. Lanham, Md.: Lexington Books, 2002.

Roth, Benita. "Race, Class and the Emergence of Black Feminism in the 1960s and 1970s." *Womanist Theory and Research* 3, no. 1 (Fall 1999): 3–9.

———. *Separate Roads to Feminism: Black, Chicana, and White Feminist Movements in America's Second Wave*. Cambridge: Cambridge University Press 2004.

Rowe, John Carlos, ed. *Post-Nationalist American Studies*. Berkeley: University of California Press, 2000.

Rowell, Charles H. "Above the Wind: An Interview with Audre Lorde." In *Conversations with Audre Lorde*, ed. Joan Wylie Hall, 184–199. Jackson: University Press of Mississippi, 2004.

Sales, William W., Jr. *From Civil Rights to Black Liberation: Malcolm X and the Organization of Afro-American Unity*. Boston: South End Press, 1994.

San Juan, E. *Racism and Cultural Studies: Critiques of Multiculturalist Ideology and the Politics of Difference*. Durham, N.C.: Duke University Press, 2002.

Sandoval, Chela. *Methodology of the Oppressed*. Minneapolis: University of Minnesota Press, 2000.

Sartre, Jean-Paul. *Being and Nothingness*. Trans. Hazel E. Barnes. New York: Gramercy Books, 1994.

Schueller, Malini Johar. *Locating Race: Global Sites of Post-Colonial Citizenship*. Albany: State University of New York Press, 2009.

Scott, David. *Conscripts of Modernity: The Tragedy of Colonial Enlightenment*. Durham, N.C.: Duke University Press, 2004.

Shaffer, Robert. "Women and the Communist Party, USA, 1930–1940." *Socialist Review* 45 (May 1979): 73–118.

Singh, Nikhil Pal. *Black Is a Country: Race and the Unfinished Struggle for Democracy.* Cambridge: Harvard University Press, 2004.

Smethurst, James Edward. *The Black Arts Movement: Literary Nationalism in the 1960s and 1970s.* Chapel Hill: University of North Carolina Press, 2005.

———. *The New Red Negro: The Literary Left and African American Poetry, 1930–1946.* New York: Oxford University Press, 1999.

Smith, Barbara, ed. *Home Girls: A Black Feminist Anthology.* New York: Kitchen Table: Women of Color Press, 1983.

Smith, Judith. *Visions of Belonging: Family Stories, Popular Culture, and Postwar Democracy.* New York: Columbia University Press, 2006.

Solomon, Mark. *The Cry Was Unity: Communists and African Americans, 1917–1936.* Jackson: University Press of Mississippi, 1998.

———. "Rediscovering a Lost Legacy: Black Women Radicals Maude White and Louise Thompson Patterson." *Abafazi* (Fall–Winter 1995): 6–13.

Somerville, Siobhan B. *Queering the Color Line: Race and the Invention of Homosexuality in American Culture.* Durham, N.C.: Duke University Press, 2000.

Sotiropoulos, Karen. *Staging Race: Black Performers in Turn of the Century America.* Cambridge, Mass.: Harvard University Press, 2006.

Springer, Kimberly. *Living for the Revolution: Black Feminist Organizations, 1968–1980.* Durham, N.C.: Duke University Press, 2005.

Stephens, Michelle A. *Black Empire: The Masculine Global Imaginary of Caribbean Intellectuals in the United States, 1914–1962.* Durham, N.C.: Duke University Press, 2005.

———. "Black Transnationalism and the Politics of National Identity: West Indian Intellectuals in Harlem in the Age of War and Revolution." *American Quarterly* 50 (September 1998): 592–608.

Thompson, Louise. "And So We Marched." *Working Woman,* June 1933, 6.

———. "Negro Women in Our Party." *Party Organizer,* August 1937, 25–27.

———. "With Langston Hughes in the U.S.S.R." *Freedomways* 8 (Spring 1968): 152–158.

Trescott, Jacqueline. "Poet to Read at Swearing-In: Maya Angelou Asked to Write New Work." *Washington Post,* December 3, 1992, A1.

Tyson, Timothy B. *Radio Free Dixie: Robert F. Williams and the Roots of Black Power.* Chapel Hill: University of North Carolina Press, 1999.

Valk, Anne M. *Radical Sisters: Second-Wave Feminism and Black Liberation in Washington, D.C.* Urbana: University of Illinois Press, 2008.

Vials, Chris. *Realism for the Masses: Aesthetics, Popular Front Pluralism, and U.S. Culture, 1935–1947.* Jackson: University Press of Mississippi, 2009.

Von Eschen, Penny M. *Race against Empire: Black Americans and Anticolonialism, 1937–1957.* Ithaca: Cornell University Press, 1997.

Wald, Alan. *Trinity of Passion: The Literary Left and the Antifascist Crusade.* Chapel Hill: University of North Carolina Press, 2007.

———. *Writing from the Left: New Essays on Radical Culture and Politics.* London: Verso, 1994.

Waldron, Clarence. "Terry McMillan and Husband Jonathan Plummer Tell Why Their Storybook Marriage Is Ending." *Jet* 108, no. 7 (15 August 2005): 16–18, 59–60.

Walk, Lori L. "Audre Lorde's Life Writing: The Politics of Location." *Women's Studies* 32 (2003): 815–834.

Walker, Alice. "A Walk through 20th-Century Black America." *Ms.*, December 1979, 46–47.

Warrick, John. "*The Blacks* and Its Impact on African American Theatre in the United States." In *Jean Genet: Performance and Politics*, ed. Claire Finburgh, Carl Lavery, and Maria Shevtsova, 131–141. New York: Palgrave Macmillan, 2006.

Washington, Mary Helen. "Alice Childress, Lorraine Hansberry, and Claudia Jones: Black Women Write the Popular Front." In *Left of the Color Line: Race, Radicalism, and Twentieth-Century Literature of the United States*, ed. Bill V. Mullen and James Smethurst, 183–204. Chapel Hill: University of North Carolina Press, 2003.

Watkins, Mel. *On the Real Side: Laughing, Lying, and Signifying—the Underground Tradition of African-American Humor that Transformed American Culture, from Slavery to Richard Pryor.* New York: Simon & Schuster, 1994.

Weigand, Kate. *Red Feminism: American Communism and the Making of Women's Liberation.* Baltimore, Md.: Johns Hopkins University Press, 2001.

Weis, Tony. "A Precarious Balance: Neoliberalism, Crisis Management, and the Social Implosion in Jamaica." *Capital & Class* 85 (Spring 2005): 115–147.

Welch, Rebeccah E. "Black Art and Activism in Postwar New York, 1950–1965." Ph.D. diss., New York University, 2002.

———. "Gender and Power in the Black Diaspora: Radical Women of Color and the Cold War." *Souls* 5, no. 3 (2003): 71–82.

West, Michael O., and William G. Martin. "Contours of the Black International: From Toussaint to Tupac." In *From Toussaint to Tupac: The Black International since the Age of Revolution*, ed. Michael O. West, William G. Martin, and Fanon Che Wilkins, 1–44. Chapel Hill: University of North Carolina Press, 2009.

White, Edmund. *Genet: A Biography.* New York: Knopf, 1993.

Wilkerson, Margaret B. "The Dark Vision of Lorraine Hansberry: Excerpts from a Literary Biography." In *Massachusetts Review* 28, no. 4 (Winter 1987): 642–650.

———. "Lorraine Hansberry: The Complete Feminist." *Freedomways* 19, no. 4 (1979): 235–255.

———. "Political Radicalism and Artistic Innovation in the Works of Lorraine Hansberry." In *African American Performance and Theater History: A Critical Reader*, ed. Harry Elam Jr. and David Krasner, 40–55. Oxford: Oxford University Press, 2001.

Wilkins, Fanon Che. "Beyond Bandung: The Critical Nationalism of Lorraine Hansberry, 1950–1965." *Radical History Review* 95 (Spring 2006): 191–210.

Williams, Elsie A. *The Humor of Jackie Moms Mabley: An African American Comedic Tradition.* New York: Garland Publishing, Inc. 1995.

Williams, Raymond. "Base and Superstructure in Marxist Cultural Theory." In *Media and Cultural Studies: Keyworks,* ed. Meenakshi Gigi Durham and Douglas M. Kellner, 130–143. Oxford: Blackwell, 2006.

Wright, Michelle M. *Becoming Black: Creating Identity in the African Diaspora.* Durham, N.C.: Duke University Press, 2004.

Wright, Sarah. "The Lower East Side: A Rebirth of World Vision." *African American Review* 27, no. 4 (1993): 593–596.

———. "The Responsibility of the Writer as Participant in the World Community." *The Zora Neale Hurston Forum* 3, no. 1 (Fall 1988): 35–39.

———. *This Child's Gonna Live.* New York: The Feminist Press, 2002.

Young, Cynthia. *Soul Power: Culture, Radicalism, and the Making of a U.S. Third World Left.* Durham, N.C.: Duke University Press, 2006.

Index

Aboriginal indigenous activism (Australia), 139, 144–145, 146
absurdism, 60–62, 72–78, 194n10
African American popular front organizations, 39–40, 189–90n32
African Black Brotherhood (ABB), 32, 88
African spirituality, 148–152
Afro-alienation, 89
Afro-American (newspaper chain), 1
Afro-American nationalism, 54–55
Ahmad, Aijaz, 9
Aikens, Charles, 100
Alabama Sharecroppers' Union, 33
Albee, Edward, 72
"Allegorical Hodgepodge of Haiti, An" (Moore), 129
Allen, James S., 18
All God's Children Need Travelling Shoes (Angelou), 160–162, 168–70. *See also* Angelou, Maya
American Women for Peace, 47
Amos 'n' Andy (television show), 83–85, 200–201n6
"Andromeda the Thief" (Hansberry), 78–79, 199n87
And Then We Heard the Thunder (Killens), 53
Angelou, Maya: Americanism, 161; autobiographies overview, 158, 219n17; biographical information, 159; Black female selfhood, 220n39; Black internationalist feminism, 162; Black Power activism, 219n13; on *The Blacks*, 61–62; on CAWAH, 54–55; Harlem Writers Guild, 53; homeland reclamation, 169, 220n47; intersectionality, 162; mass appeal, 158–159, 162, 171–172, 217n3, 218n10; multiculturalism, 159–60; nationalist alliances, 17; overviews, 26, 28; radicalism, 161–162
anti-apartheid struggles, 139, 146, 147–148, 150, 215n51, 216n65
anticolonialist nationalism, 7–9, 24
anti-lynching campaign, 33, 37–38
"Apartheid U.S.A." (Lorde), 138, 147–148
"Apples of Autumn, The" (Hansberry), 67–68, 196–97n44, 196n38
Aptheker, Herbert, 45
Awatere, Donna, 144

Babouk (Endore), 117
Bambara, Toni Cade: anticolonialist nationalism, 10; as bridge between movements, 13–14, 182n48, 182n50; Harlem Writers Guild, 53; heteropatriarchy challenge, 119; Lorde influence, 138
Baraka, Amiri, 61
Beal, Frances, 11, 13–14, 181–82n39, 182n43
Beauvoir, Simone de, 26, 64–65, 66–70, 75, 81
"Bicentennial Poem #21,000,000" (Lorde), 155–156
Big White Fog (Ward), 87

Bird at My Window (Guy), 53, 123–124
Black Arts Movement, 17, 48, 52, 82, 138–139
Black Atlantic, 80–81, 127
Black Atlantic, The (Gilroy), 80–81
Black Belt Nation Thesis, 35; analyses, 187–88n8; Black Left, 2; Communist Party (CPUSA), 33, 42, 43; explained, 20–21, 33; influence, 178n4; internationalism, 23–24; masculinism v. women's liberation, 35
Black Christian Nationalism (Cleage), 122
blackface minstrelsy, 83–87, 92–93, 98–110
Black internationalist feminism: breadth and depth, 173–74; enervation, 171–72; global perspective, 127–129, 173–74; implications for other political and social movements, 6; institutions, 48–54; intersectionality, 156, 173–74; links with second-wave Black feminism, 10–17; Marxist cultural theory, 217n2; nationalism v., 7–8; roots, 1–5; theoretization, 16, 20–24; Third World involvement, 10
Black Jacobins, The (James), 115–116, 208n23
Black Left: anti-Sovietism, 17; Black Arts/Black Power movement, 17, 183n63; Childress role, 90–91; civil rights movement, 17, 183n63; Cold War anticommunist impact, 41–42; delegation to Soviet Union, 1; feminist critique, 2–3, 23, 25; Harlem, 17–18; internationalism, 1, 19, 23–24; Maoism, 17, 183n63; political goals, 1; West Indies origins, 32; women's roles, 16, 54–55; women writers overview, 3–4. *See also* Communist Left
Black lesbian feminism, 26, 148–152, 212n5. *See also* Black internationalist feminism; gender and sexuality
Black Macho and the Myth of the Superwoman (Wallace), 11–12, 15–16
Black Madonna, 118–119, 122, 210n39
Black Man's Burden (Killens), 25, 195n16
Black Messiah, The (Cleage), 122
Black Messiahs and Uncle Toms (Moses), 118
Black nationalism, 7, 10–16, 20–22, 25, 31–38, 75–77, 87–88, 94–96, 122, 138–139, 146–147, 173–74. *See also* Black Left; Black Power movement; cultural nationalism
Black Power movement, 2, 4, 6, 10–11, 15–16, 17, 25, 54, 87–88, 110, 130, 139, 156, 159, 160, 171, 179n16, 183n63
Blacks, The (Genet), 60–63, 64, 73–75
"Blacks—Women—Men—Children, in American Film, The" (Childress), 90–91
Black Scholar, The (journal), 15
Black Star Line, the, 87, 94–95
Black Thunder (Bontemps), 117
Black transnational mobility, 88–89
Black Unicorn, The (Lorde), 135, 137, 148–149
Black universalism, 107–110
Black Woman, The (Bambara), 13–14
"Black Women" (*Freedomways*), 14
Black Women's Alliance (BWA), 11
Blancs, Les (Hansberry): de Beauvoir influence, 65–66; Black internationalist feminism, 26; cultural importance, 61–63; major themes, 75–80, 198n70, 199n86; overview, 4–5
"Blueprint for Negro Writing" (Wright), 35, 48
Boggs, Grace Lee, 13
Boldt, Menno, 140
Bond, Jean Carey, 10, 13, 15–17, 167, 182n53
Bontemps, Arna, 117
"Brief History of the Minstrel Show and It's [*sic*] Form, A" (Childress), 84
Briggs, Cyril, 32
Broadside Press, 138
Brooks, Daphne, 89
Browder, Earl, 21, 42
Brown, Lloyd, 18, 30, 48
Brown, Roscoe Lee, 62
Brown v. the Board of Education, 83
Burgie, Irving, 87
Burnham, Dorothy, 49, 52
Burnham, Louis, 40, 48, 52
"Burst of Light, A" (Lorde), 137, 144–145, 213n15

"Call" (Lorde), 151–152
"Call to Negro Woman, A" (Sojourners for Truth and Justice), 109
Camus, Albert, 198n74
Carby, Hazel, 118
Carter, Dan T., 37
Castro, Fidel, 19–20, 102, 165
CAWAH, 26, 27, 54, 115, 166
Childress, Alice: anticolonialist nationalism, 9; Bambara anthology contribution, 13; as Black Arts movement precursor, 47–48; Black Power–African redemption link, 110–11; essayist, 82; *Freedom* contributions,

49, 50–52, 89–90, 193n79, 193n80; gender and sexuality, 89, 97–105, 110; Harlem Writers Guild, 53; internationalist vision, 82–85; intersectionality, 90, 178n8; lesbian and gay rights, 178n8; materialist feminist analysis, 3–4; nationalist internationalism, 47–48; overviews, 2, 4, 26; radical activism, 90, 203n36; as researcher and historian, 90–91; South African resistance movement, 200n5
Childress, Alvin, 84
Chosen Place, the Timeless People, The (Marshall), 125
Chude-Sokei, Louis, 86, 93, 94
Civil Rights Congress, 19–20, 45
civil rights movement, 4, 6, 17, 24, 51, 55, 62, 84, 151–152, 159–160, 162, 183n63
Clarke, John Henrik, 17, 25, 26, 53, 87, 138
Cleage, Albert, Jr., 118–119, 122
Cliff, Michelle, 26, 173
Clifford, James, 127
Collins, Patricia Hill, 173–174
Combahee River Collective (CRC), 10, 179n16, 181n36
Committee for the Negro in the Arts (CNA), 13, 51, 53, 90
Communist Left: Black nationalism v. Communism, 32; radical studies, 183n61; terminology, 177–78n3. *See also* Black Left
Communist Party USA (CPUSA), 17–25, 31–37; Black Belt Nation Thesis, 18–19, 20–21, 33, 34, 43, 190–91n46; capitulation to imperialist powers, 43; internal complexity and variation, 17–19; masculinism v. women's liberation, 34–35; pre–World War II issues and activities, 32–40; separation from mainstream civil rights movement, 24; Soviet Union influence, 32–33
Communist University of the Toilers of the East (KUTV), 36
Congolese UN delegation, 115
Congress of American Women (CAW), 42, 47, 191n48
"Conversation from Life" (Childress), 50–51, 89–90, 202n33
Cook, Will Marion, 105–106
Cooke, Marvel, 41
Copra (Childress), 90, 203n35
Council on African Affairs (CAA), 40–41, 62
CPUSA. *See* Communist Party USA (CPUSA)
Cudjoe, Selwyn, 161, 220n39
Cultural Association for Women of African Heritage (CAWAH), 26, 27, 54, 115, 166
cultural nationalism, 137, 148–149, 213n16. *See also* Black nationalism
Cuthbert, Marion, 39–40

Daddy Was a Number Runner (Meriwether), 53
Daily Worker, The, 18, 45, 82, 83
Dale, Thelma, 20, 42, 44, 48, 49, 178n7
Davies, Carole Boyce, 22, 135–136
Davis, Angela, 2, 16
Davis, Benjamin, 45, 182n53
Davis, Ossie, 53, 61
Davis, Sallye, 40
Dee, Ruby, 49
Democracy and the Negro (Cuthbert), 39–40
Dennis, Peggy, 47
Domestic Workers' Union, 47
Domingo, W.A., 32
"Double Jeopardy" (Beal), 11–12
Double V Campaign, 43
drag ball, 97–98
Drums at Dusk (Bontemps), 117
Du Bois, Shirley Graham, 17, 19, 20, 29, 40, 49, 52, 167, 183n63
Du Bois, W. E. B., 1, 19, 40–41, 49, 57, 62, 83, 85, 167, 183n63, 192n64
Dunayevskaya, Raya, 13

Elder, Lonnie, 53
Endore, Guy, 117
"End to the Neglect of the Problems of the Negro Woman!, An" (Jones), 20, 22–24, 39, 44–47
eroticism, 150
Ethiopia (Abyssinia), 34, 43
"Evening News, The" (Lorde), 146
existentialism, 63–78, 195n14, 195–96n30, 196n32

Fair Play for Cuba (committee), 54, 115, 133, 187n101
Fanon, Frantz, 75, 134, 139, 177n2
Federal Theater Project, 29
Feldman, Eugene, 47
"Flowers for the General" (Hansberry), 67–68, 196–97n44, 196n38, 197n46

Flynn, Elizabeth Gurley, 42, 47
"For a Negro Theatre" (Childress), 47–48, 82, 85, 91
for colored girls who have considered suicide (Shange), 15
Foster, William Z., 42, 43
Freedom (newspaper): contributing writers and content, 48–52; contributors of early 1950s, 57, 202n33; editors, 40; Guy and Black Left grounding, 115; Hansberry internationalist writing, 57–58; overviews, 2, 18; Robeson legacy, 109
Freedomways (newspaper): Black women's issues, 14–17; contributing writers and content, 52–53; editors, 40; Guy and Black Left grounding, 115, 133; overviews, 2
Friends of the Soviet Union, 37
From a Land Where Other People Live (Lorde), 138

Gaines, Kevin, 3, 24–25
Garvey, Marcus, 27, 86–88, 94–95
Garvey, Marcus, Jr., 87–88
Garveyism, 86–89, 106–108, 110–111, 202n24
"Garveyism" (Garvey Jr.), 87
Garvin, Vicki, 20, 47, 49
Gayle, Addison, 139
gender and sexuality, 135–138, 146–147, 150, 178n8, 178n13, 214n42. *See also entries for specific writers and works*
Genet, Jean, 60–62, 63, 72–73, 195n16, 198n66
Ghana Television, 29
Gilroy, Paul, 59, 80, 81 180n29
Giovanni, Nikki, 14
Give Me a Child (Wright), 29
Gold Through the Trees (Childress), 51–52, 82–85, 90, 201n18
Gomez, Jewelle, 26
Graham, Shirley. *See* Du Bois, Shirley Graham
"Grenada Revisited" (Lorde), 135–137, 140–144, 153
Grewal, Inderpal, 8, 134
Guy, Rosa: anticolonialist nationalism, 9; on CAWAH, 54–55; Fair Play for Cuba, 115, 133; Harlem Writers Guild, 53; hemispheric consciousness, 115–18; heteropatriarchy challenge, 119–29; lesbian and gay rights, 178n8; nationalist alliances, 17; nationalist internationalism, 207n11; overviews, 4, 27–28; Trinidad, 19. *See also entries for specific works*

Haiti, 27–28, 115–130, 208–209n23, 208n21
"Haiti" (Guy), 116, 122
"Half the World" (Jones), 47
Hansberry, Leo, 62
Hansberry, Lorraine: absurdism, 60–62, 65, 72–78; on America, 7; on *Amos 'n' Andy*, 83; anticolonialism, 4–5; anticolonialist nationalism, 9; de Beauvoir influence, 64–71, 196n32; on Childress, 51, 82–83; diasporic dialogism, 80–81; education and background, 49–50; existentialism, 58–60, 63–66, 72–78, 198n74; feminism and nationalism, 81; feminist plays, 66–71; *Freedom* reviews, 49, 51; gender and sexuality, 59, 65, 75–80; internationalism, 57–58; intersectionality, 59, 70–71, 72, 178n8; lesbian and gay rights, 178n8; lesbian intersubjectivity, 70–71; multiculturalism, 172; overviews, 4, 26; review of *The Outsider* (Wright), 58–59
Harlem, 17–18, 19–20, 184n64
Harlem Unemployed Council, 33–34
Harlem Writers Guild: Black Left relationship, 2, 13, 53–54; Guy and Black Left grounding, 115, 133; Guy role, 27; Lorde relationship, 138, 213n22; workshops, 193n90; writers and works, 53
Harlem Writers Quarterly (journal), 138
Haywood, Harry, 1, 18, 37, 43–44
Heart of a Woman, The (Angelou), 162–68; anti-colonial and anti-imperialist critique, 164–67; anti-patriarchial Black Power, 166; free movement v. captivity, 162–63; nationalist struggle, 167–68; overview, 158–59; Pan-African feminist solidarity, 165–66; political turmoil v. personal evolution, 162–64; social and political movement confluence, 168
"Hell Under God's Orders" (Lorde), 153–155
hemispheric consciousness, 115–118, 129–130
Hendricks, Arthur, 32
heteronormativity, 112–113, 130–133
Hill, Robert, 86
homeland reclamation, 108–109, 153–155, 169–170, 220n47
homonormativity, 173, 221n57
Hotel and Restaurant Workers Union, 47

How Stella Got Her Groove Back (McMillan), 28, 112–113, 130–133
Hughes, Langston, 1, 54, 138
Huiswood, Otto, 32
Hunton, William Alphaeus, 40, 52, 83, 167

I Know Why the Caged Bird Sings (Angelou), 53, 159–160, 218n6, 218n8
"I'm Gone Before I Go" (Williams), 102–105
In Dahomey (musical), 93, 105, 203–204n46
Ingram, Rosa Lee, 23, 42, 44–45, 191–92n62, 192n64
Inman, Mary, 39
International Brigades, 34
International Committee on African Affairs (ICAA), 40. *See also* Council on African Affairs (CAA)
International Congress of Women (1945), 42
International Labor Defense, 38
International Women's Year (1975), 14
intersectionality: Angelou, Maya, 162; Black internationalist feminism, 173–175, 178n8; Bond, 16; Childress, 90, 178n8; Civil Rights Movement, 183n63; Cliff, Michelle, 173; Combahee River Collective (CRC), 10, 181n36; Guy, Rosa, 178n8; Hansberry, Lorraine, 59, 72; imperialism, 90, 179n25; Ingram, Mary, 45; Jones, Claudia, 20, 22–23, 31; Jordan, June, 173; Lorde, Audre, 13, 133, 146, 156, 173, 178n8; Marxism, 16, 183n61; national liberation movements, 133, 146; patriarchy, 90; theory, 25; Third World Women's Alliance (TWWA), 12
In Woman's Defense (Inman), 39

Jackson, Esther Cooper, 14, 20, 39, 40, 52–53, 184n64, 193n87
James, C. L. R., 13, 115–117, 133, 208n23
Johnson, Georgia Douglas, 162
Jones, Claudia: analyses of Black women's economic and social status, 45–47; attack on CPUSA capitulation to imperialist powers, 43–44; and Beal, 11–12; Black internationalist feminism, 20–24; communism and self-determination, 18; CPUSA involvement, 33; *Freedomways*, 14–15; Harlem anti-imperialist work, 43; intersectionality, 22–24; and Lorde, 156; on organizing minority women, 192n70; overviews, 26, 48; race, gender, and class analysis, 22–24; on Sojourners for Truth and Justice, 52; on super-exploitation of women, 45–46, 192n65; Trinidad, 19; Women's Commission (CPUSA), 42; Young Communist League, 43
Jones, James Earl, 61, 62
Jordan, June, 53, 138–139, 156, 173
Joseph, Gloria, 139, 152, 153

Kaplan, Caren, 8
Kelley, Robin, 32, 34–35
Killens, John O., 6–7, 17, 25, 49, 52, 53, 54, 61, 87, 183n63, 184n64, 195n16, 202n26
Kitchen Table: Women of Color Press, 147, 151
KUTV (University of the Toilers of the East), 36
Kuzwayo, Ellen, 139, 148

Ladder, The (journal), 59, 68, 197n46
Lamming, George, 125, 208n23
"Language of Difference, The" (Lorde), 145
Lazarus, Neil, 8–9, 81
League of Struggle for Negro Rights, 34
"Learning from the 60s" (Lorde), 140, 146–147
"Left," 177–78n3
Les Blancs (Hansberry). See *Blancs, Les* (Hansberry)
Lincoln, Abbey, 13, 54, 61, 163, 165
Lorde, Audre: anticolonialist nationalism, 9; Black feminist lesbian subjectivity, 135; as bridge between movements, 10, 182n48; Grenada, 19; Harlem Writers Guild, 53; intersectionality, 12–13, 146–147, 156, 173; mentors and influences, 138–39; nationalist internationalism, 13, 137–138, 143–45; overviews, 4–5, 28, 133, 173; poetic realism, 216n65; St. Croix residence and influence, 152–155, 216n71; terminology, 13,137- 138, 213n17; thematic overview, 156
Lumumba, Patrice, 25, 54–55, 115, 118, 124, 166

Mabley, Jack, 102, 105
Mabley, Jackie "Moms," 85–86, 98–102, 106, 107, 204n69
Mailer, Norman, 60–61, 64, 73, 195n30, 198n63
Make, Vusumzi, 62, 166–167
Malcolm X, 19, 54–55, 124, 140, 160, 166, 169, 219n31

mammy role, 89–90, 92, 96–97, 98–101, 109–110, 205n71
Maori indigenous activism, 139, 144–145
Maori Sovereignty (Awatere), 144
Marcus Garvey and the Vision of Africa (Clarke), 27, 87
Marshall, Paule, 13, 26, 90, 125, 156, 173; Barbados, 19; Garvey, 27, 87, 202n24; Harlem Writers Guild, 53; overview, 185–86n94
Masses and Mainstream (journal), 18, 47, 82
Maxwell, William, 35, 38
Mayfield, Julian, 7, 18, 52, 53, 54, 138, 167, 168, 186–87n101
McDuffie, Erik, 52
McKay, Claude, 1, 32, 35, 187n5
McMillan, Terry, 28, 53, 112–113, 130–133, 211n75
Mekas, Jonas, 60–61
Meriwether, Louise, 53
Millard, Betty, 44
minstrel drag, 89, 98–101, 106–110
minstrelsy, 83–87, 92–93
Moms (Childress), 85–86, 88–89, 98–105, 201n18. *See also* Mabley, Jackie "Moms"
Moore, Audley, 41
Moore, Richard, 17, 32, 44, 53, 88, 107
Morgan, Robin, 14
Moses, Wilson Jeremiah, 118
mother-warrior connection, 148–152
Moynihan, Daniel Patrick, 118–119, 123
Moynihan Report, 118–119, 123
multiculturalism, 159–161, 171–172, 218n10
Murphy, George B., Jr., 1, 2, 3, 48, 52, 91

National Association for the Advancement of Colored People (NAACP), 20, 83
National Association of Negro Women, 46
National Committee for the Defense of Political Prisoners, 37
National Council of Negro Women, 42, 46
National Federation of Women's Clubs, 46
nationalism, 4–9, 81, 134–135, 173–175, 180–81n31
nationalist internationalism, 1–2, 10–16, 18–19, 36, 47–48, 137, 177n2, 207n11
National Negro Congress (NNC), 20, 39–40, 42
National Negro Labor Council, 47
National Trade Union Conference for Negro Rights, 47
Needle Trades Workers Industrial Union, 34, 36–37, 39
Negroes in America, The (McKay), 35
Negro Family, The (Moynihan), 118, 123
"Negro Woman in American Literature, The" (conference panel), 53, 90, 185–86n94
Negro Women, Inc., 41
"Negro Women in Our Party" (Thompson), 38–39
Nemiroff, Robert, 63, 65, 68, 75, 77–78, 195n22, 198n74, 199n86
New Masses (journal), 44
New Negro Renaissance, 17
New School for Social Research, 53
New World Review (newspaper), 1
New York Head Shop and Museum (Lorde), 139
Nkrumah, Kwame, 57, 64, 90, 167–168
Nyerere, Julius, 52

Obourn, Megan, 149
"Of Generators and Survival—Hugo Letter 12/89" (Lorde), 153–155
Old Left, 26, 31–40
On Guard for Freedom (activist group), 54, 186–87n101
"On the Pulse of Morning" (Angelou), 159, 160
"On the Right to Self-Determination for the Negro People in the Black Belt" (Jones), 20–21, 44
Organization of Afro-American Unity, 169, 170, 183n63
Other, the, 69, 70
"Our Common Enemy, Our Common Cause" (Woo), 147
Our Dead Behind Us (Lorde), 137, 149–152

Padmore, George, 44
pan-Africanism, 40, 62–63, 83, 86–89, 93, 166, 213n16
Parker, Pat, 10
Peery, Patricia, 16
People's Voice (newspaper), 41
Petry, Ann, 41
Political Affairs (journal), 18, 44
popular romance fiction, 112–113
"Post-Colonial citizenship," 7, 158, 161, 179–80n25
post-Marxism, 174

postnationalist feminism, 7–8, 134–135, 180n29
postnationalist theory, 4–5, 8, 134–136, 173–174, 214n36
Powell, Adam Clayton, Jr., 41
"Proclamation of Southern Negro Youth" (Southern Negro Youth Congress), 40

queer liberalism, 173, 221n57. *See also* gender and sexuality

Raisin in the Sun, A (Hansberry), 61, 62–63, 172
Randall, Dudley, 138
"red feminism," 25
"Report on the Gold Coast" (Childress), 90
"Revolution" (Parker), 10
Roach, Max, 62
Robeson, Eslanda Goode, 49, 52
Robeson, Paul, 1, 2, 40–41, 57, 109, 208n23
Rogers, Norma, 2
Roth, Benita, 11
Rowe, Hortense, 153

Sanchez, Sonia, 52, 139, 183n63
Sandoval, Chela, 8
Sartre, Jean Paul, 65, 69–70, 198n74
Savage, Augusta, 37
Schueller, Malini Johan, 7, 161, 179–80n25
Scottsboro campaign, 33, 37–38, 45, 189n28
"Scratching the Surface" (Lorde), 137
Second Sex, The (de Beauvoir), 26, 64–71, 196n39
second-wave Black feminism, 10–17, 179n16
Selassie, Haile, 34
Senghor, Leopold, 52
sexual and gender rights. *See* gender and sexuality
Shange, Ntozake, 15
Short Walk, A (Childress), 27, 86–89, 91–98, 105–110, 172, 206n110
Sign in Sidney Brustein's Window, The (Hansberry), 63, 65, 72–74, 195–96n30, 197–98n58, 198n62
"Simone de Beauvoir and *The Second Sex*" (Hansberry), 68–72
Sisterhood in Support of Sisters in South Africa (SISA), 139
Sister Outsider (Lorde), 135, 137, 138, 146–147
"Sisters in Arms" (Lorde), 148–151
Smethurst, James, 35, 49
Smith, Barbara, 26
Sojourners for Truth and Justice (activist group), 20, 29, 47, 52, 57, 90, 109
Song Flung Up to Heaven, A (Angelou), 160, 162, 170–171
Song of the Storm (Childress), 87
Soul Power (Young), 5
Southern Negro Youth Congress (SNYC), 39–40, 42, 43
Spanish Civil War, 34
Stalin, Joseph, 20, 35, 189–90n32
Stephens, Michelle, 110, 135–136, 142–143, 180n25
Strong, Augusta, 52
Sun, the Sea, a Touch of the Wind, The (Guy), 113–30; anti-colonial and anti-imperialist critique, 129–30; black feminism and interrelationships, 113–14; Black internationalist feminism, 27–28, 133; Christian symbolism, 119–120, 122–23; *The Comedians*, 208–209n23; gender and sexuality, 124–26; Haitian struggle for independence, 115–118, 128–29; heteropatriarchy challenge, 119–29; masculinism, 118–22; overview, 172–73; reviews, 129–30; sexual and gender rights intersecting with political freedom, 210n52, 211n67; temporality, 116–18; Third World national unity by Black women, 128–29; U.S. imperialism, 113–133
super-exploitation, 14, 45–46, 182n51, 214n31

Tambo, Oliver, 52
Taylor, Recy, 40
temporality, 116–117
Theatre Owners Booking Association (TOBA), 97–98
"Theses on the Negro Question," 33
Third World, 9, 10, 24, 128–129, 140–141, 154–156. *See also entries for specific countries, regions, and works*
Third World Women's Alliance (TWWA), 12
This Bridge Called My Back (CRC), 10
This Child's Gonna Live (Wright), 29–30, 53
Thompson, Louise, 20, 26, 37–39, 48
Those Other People (Childress), 172
Tom-Tom (Du Bois), 29
Trial by Lynching (McKay), 35
Trouble in Mind (Childress), 83–84, 201n9
"Turning the Beat Around" (Lorde), 137, 146–147, 148–149, 215n56

Uncle Tom's Children (Wright), 35
United Nations, 19–20
Universal Negro Improvement Association (UNIA), 87, 96, 106
University of the Toilers of the East (KUTV), 36
"Uses of the Erotic, The" (Lorde), 135
U.S. exceptionalism, 6, 113, 130–133, 161, 221n57
U.S. imperialism, 71–72, 152–55. *See also entries for specific countries, writers*

Vanguard, the, 37
vaudeville, 83–86, 97–98
Village Voice (newspaper), 60–61, 63–64

Walker, Alice, 5, 14, 53, 87, 139, 202n26, 207n1, 218n6
Walker, George, 85–86, 93–94
Wallace, Michele, 11, 15–16
Ward, Theodore, 87
Washington, Fredi, 41
Washington, Mary Helen, 50
Water with Berries (Lammings), 125
Weekly Review (newspaper), 43
Weekly Worker, The (newspaper), 18
Welch, Rebecca, 29
What Use Are Flowers? (Hansberry), 63
"Which Way for the Negro Writer?" (Brown), 48
White, Maude, 1, 13, 26, 36–37, 39, 47, 48, 52
White-Haired Girl, The (Childress), 91
"White Negro, The" (Mailer), 64
Who's Afraid of Virginia Woolf? (Albee), 72–73, 197–98n58, 198n61
Wilkins, Fanon Che, 59
Williams, Bert, 84–86, 93–94, 102–105, 205n84, 206n91
Williams, Robert F., 7, 19, 54, 163, 167
Williams, Sherley, 14
Winfrey, Oprah, 112, 158–159, 161–162, 171, 217n3
"Woman against Myth" (Millard), 44
Woman Today (journal), 42
"Women of Nigeria Meet in a Historic National Conference" (*Freedom*), 49
Women's International Democratic Federation (WIDF), 18, 24, 42
Woo, Merle, 147
Working Woman (journal), 38, 42
World Youth Conference, 18
Wright, Michelle, 80–81
Wright, Richard, 35, 44, 48, 58–59, 60, 80
Wright, Sarah Elizabeth, 29–30, 52, 53, 54, 90, 184n64, 186n94, 186n97, 186–87n101, 193n90

Yergan, Max, 40, 41
Young, Cynthia, 5–6
Youngblood (Killens), 53
Young Communist League, 43

Zamani Soweto Sisters, 139
Zami (Lorde), 135, 137, 143, 148–149, 212n6, 214n31, 214n43
Zulu Heart (Du Bois), 29

CHERYL HIGASHIDA is an assistant professor of English at the University of Colorado at Boulder.

The University of Illinois Press
is a founding member of the
Association of American University Presses.

University of Illinois Press
1325 South Oak Street
Champaign, IL 61820-6903
www.press.uillinois.edu